Adapting Cities to Climate Change
Understanding and Addressing the Development Challenges

Edited by Jane Bicknell, David Dodman and David Satterthwaite

publishing for a sustainable future
London • Sterling, VA

First published by Earthscan in the UK and USA in 2009

Copyright © International Institute for Environment and Development, 2009

ISBN: 978-1-84407-745-8

Typeset by Domex e-data Pvt Ltd
Cover design by Susanne Harris

For a full list of publications please contact:

Earthscan
Dunstan House
14a St Cross St
London, EC1N 8XA, UK
Tel: +44 (0)20 7841 1930
Fax: +44 (0)20 7242 1474
Email: earthinfo@earthscan.co.uk
Web: **www.earthscan.co.uk**

22883 Quicksilver Drive, Sterling, VA 20166-2012, USA

Earthscan publishes in association with the International Institute
for Environment and Development

A catalogue record for this book is available from the British Library

Library of Congress Cataloging-in-Publication Data

Making the most of the water we have : the soft path approach to water management /
edited by David B. Brooks, Oliver M. Brandes, and Stephen Gurman.
    p. cm.
  Includes bibliographical references and index.
  ISBN 978-1-84407-754-0 (hardback)
  1. Water resources development–Environmental aspects. 2. Water-supply–
Management–Environmental aspects. I. Brooks, David B., 1934- II. Brandes, Oliver M.,
1972- III. Gurman, Stephen.
  TD195.W3M35 2009
  363.6'1–dc22

                                        2009005726

At Earthscan we strive to minimize our environmental impacts and carbon footprint
through reducing waste, recycling and offsetting our CO_2 emissions, including those
created through publication of this book. For more details of our environmental policy,
see www.earthscan.co.uk.

This book was printed in the UK by
Cromwell Press Group.
The paper used is FSC certified and the inks
are vegetable based.

Mixed Sources
Product group from well-managed
forests and other controlled sources
www.fsc.org Cert no. TT-COC-2082
© 1996 Forest Stewardship Council

Adapting Cities to Climate Change

Contents

PART 1 INTRODUCTION

PART 2 RISK AND VULNERABILITY FOR CITIES

PART 3 CASE STUDIES ON ADAPTATION

PART 4 MOVING FORWARD

List of Figures, Tables and Boxes

FIGURES

TABLES

BOXES

About the Contributors

EDITORS

Jane Bicknell works with the Human Settlements Group at the International Institute for Environment and Development (IIED) and is managing editor of the international journal *Environment and Urbanization.* jane.bicknell@iied.org

David Dodman is a researcher in the Human Settlements and Climate Change Group at IIED. He is co-editor (with Duncan McGregor and David Barker) of *Global Change and Caribbean Vulnerability: Environment, Economy and Society at Risk* (UWI Press, 2009). david.dodman@iied.org

David Satterthwaite is a senior fellow at IIED and is editor of the journal *Environment and Urbanization.* He has written and edited various books published by Earthscan, including *Squatter Citizen* (1989, with Jorge E. Hardoy), *The Earthscan Reader on Sustainable Cities* (1999) and *Environmental Problems in an Urbanizing World* (2001, with Jorge E. Hardoy and Diana Mitlin). He contributed to the Third and Fourth Assessments of the Intergovernmental Panel on Climate Change; in 2004, he was awarded the Volvo Environment Prize. david.satterthwaite@iied.org

CONTRIBUTORS

Andrew Ochieng Adwera works as a researcher at the ACTS Science and Technology Institute and in the Energy and Water Security Programme. He recently completed an MSc in Science, Society and Development at the University of Sussex. African Centre for Technology Studies, PO Box 45917-00100, Nairobi, Kenya; a.adwera@acts.or.ke

Rais Akhtar is a national fellow at the Centre for the Study of Regional Development, Jawaharlal Nehru University, New Delhi. Centre for the Study of Regional Development, Jawaharlal Nehru University, New Delhi-110067, India; raisakhtar@hotmail.com

Kurshid Alam is a consultant in disaster reduction, livelihoods and governance, based in Bangladesh. alam@khurshidalam.org

Mozaharul Alam is a research fellow at the Bangladesh Centre for Advanced Studies (BCAS) and works on global environmental change and development integration with special adaptation to climate change. He is involved in several national and international activities and also in capacity-building of civil society organizations in the least developed countries to address climate change. Bangladesh Centre for Advanced Studies (BCAS), House 10, Road 16A, Gulshan-1, Dhaka, Bangladesh; mozaharul.alam@bcas.net

Bridget Anderson is an analyst at the Bureau of Waste Prevention, Reuse and Recycling, City of New York, US. banderson@dsny.nyc.gov

Cynthia Brenda Awuor is based in Nairobi, Kenya, where she works as a research associate on climate change for the Stockholm Environment Institute. Her work focuses on climate change impacts, vulnerability and community-based adaptation in Africa. She formerly worked as a research fellow on climate change at the African Centre for Technology Studies, Nairobi, Kenya. cawuor@gmail.com

Jessica Ayers is a PhD candidate at the Development Studies Institute, London School of Economics, UK, working on the governance of climate change adaptation. She is also a contract researcher for the Climate Change Group at IIED. J.M.Ayers@lse.ac.uk

Deborah Balk is associate director of the Institute for Demographic Research at the City University of New York (CUNY) and associate professor at Baruch College (CUNY), New York, US. deborah_balk@baruch.cuny.edu

Sheridan Bartlett is a research associate at the Children's Environments Research Group at the Graduate Center, City University of New York, US, and an associate fellow in the Human Settlements Group at IIED, London, UK. She works primarily in Asia on issues pertaining to children and their environments, providing support to various organizations that currently include Save the Children, Society for the Promotion of Area Resource Centres (SPARC) and the Aga Khan Foundation. sheridan.bartlett@gmail.com

Jack Campbell is disaster risk reduction adviser in the Conflict, Humanitarian and Security Affairs Department at the UK Department for International Development (DFID). DFID, 1 Palace Street, London SW1E 5HE, UK; j-campbell@dfid.gov.uk

Krystel M. R. Dossou holds an MSc in agronomic engineering and is an agricultural socio-economist. He is coordinator of the Energy and Environment Programme at the Organisation des Femmes pour la Gestion de l'Energie, de l'Environnement et la Promotion du Développement Intégré (OFEDI). He is also a CLACC Fellow (Capacity Strengthening of Least Developed Countries for

Adaptation to Climate Change) in Benin. krystod7@yahoo.fr and krystod@gmail.com

Ian Douglas is emeritus professor of physical geography at the School of Environment and Development, University of Manchester, UK. School of Environment and Development, University of Manchester, M13 9PL, UK; ian.douglas@manchester.ac.uk

Bernadette Gléhouenou-Dossou holds a DPhil in forestry and an MSc in rural development. She is a lecturer and researcher at the Faculty of Agronomic Sciences (University of Abomey-Calavi) and president of Organisation des Femmes pour la Gestian de l'Energie, de l'Environment et de la Promotion du Dévelopment Intégré (OFEDI). bebe_dossou@yahoo.fr

Jorgelina Hardoy is a researcher at IIED–América Latina whose main areas of interest are local development, environmental improvement of low-income neighbourhoods and social vulnerability to risks. IIED–América Latina, Avenue General Paz 1180, (1429) Buenos Aires, Argentina; jhardoy@iied-al.org.ar

Saleemul Huq is a senior fellow at IIED. He specializes in links between climate change and sustainable development, with a particular focus on the perspectives of low- and middle-income nations. He is currently working on issues relating to vulnerability and adaptation to climate change in the least-developed countries. Dr Huq was a coordinating lead author of the chapter on 'Adaptation and mitigation' in the Intergovernmental Panel on Climate Change's (IPCC's) *Fourth Assessment Report.* Prior to his role at IIED, he was executive director of the Bangladesh Centre for Advanced Studies. saleemul.huq@iied.org

Sari Kovats is an environmental epidemiologist who works on the impact of climate and weather on human health and is a lead author for the IPCC Working Group II. Centre on Global Change and Health, Department of Public Health and Policy, London School of Hygiene and Tropical Medicine, London, UK; sari.kovats@lshtm.ac.uk

MaryAnne Maghenda is a professor of geography in Kenya. wughangamwalu @yahoo.com

Yasmin McDonnell is ActionAid's emergency policy analyst. ActionAid International, Hamlyn House, MacDonald Road, Archway, London N19 5PG, UK; Yasmin.Mcdonnell@actionaid.org

Gordon McGranahan is director of the Human Settlements Group at IIED in London, UK. Trained as an economist, he spent the 1990s at the Stockholm Environment Institute, where he directed their Urban Environment Programme.

He has published widely on urban environmental issues, with an emphasis on poverty and environmental problems in and around the home, and how the critical scale of urban environmental burdens changes as cities become wealthier. Recent publications include a chapter entitled 'Urban transitions and the spatial displacement of environmental burdens' in a book co-edited with Peter Marcotullio on *Scaling Urban Environmental Challenges: From the Local to the Global and Back* (Earthscan, 2007) and a chapter co-authored with David Satterthwaite on 'Providing clean water and sanitation' in *State of the World 2007* (Earthscan and Worldwatch, 2007). gordon.mcgranahan@iied.org

Louise McLean is ActionAid's emergencies, communications and initiatives manager. ActionAid International, Hamlyn House, MacDonald Road, Archway, London N19 5PG, UK; Louise.McLean@actionaid.org

Pierre Mukheibir is a senior planning and development engineer with Wannon Water, a water utility in Victoria, Australia. He has recently been awarded a doctorate by the University of Cape Town for his thesis entitled *Water, Climate Change and Small Towns.* Wannon Water, 99 Fairy Street, Warrnambool, Victoria 3280, Australia; pierre.mukheibir@wannonwater.com.au

Mike Muller is a civil engineer by training and at present is visiting adjunct professor at the Graduate School of Public and Development Management at the University of Witwatersrand, South Africa. He was director general of the South African Department of Water Affairs and Forestry from 1997 to 2005 and worked for the Mozambican government from 1979 to 1988. He was a member of the United Nations Millennium Project Task Force 7 (Water and Sanitation) and has been a member of the Global Water Partnership's Technical Advisory Committee since 2005. Graduate School of Public and Development Management, University of Witwatersrand, South Africa; mikemuller1949@gmail.com

Victor Ayo Orindi works as a research officer in the Climate Change Adaptation in Africa (CCAA) Programme at the International Development Research Centre, Nairobi, Kenya. His work focuses on participatory action research on climate change adaptation. International Development Research Centre – Eastern and Southern Africa Regional Office, Liaison House, State House Avenue, PO Box 62084-00200, Nairobi, Kenya; vorindi@idrc.or.ke

Gustavo Pandiella trained as a sociologist and is a researcher at IIED-América Latina. IIED–América Latina, Avenue General Paz 1180, (1429) Buenos Aires, Argentina; gpandiella@iied-al.org.ar

Mark Pelling is reader in human geography, King's College London. His research focuses on natural disaster risk and climate change adaptation with a particular interest in urban societies. He is author of *The Vulnerability of Cities: Natural*

Disaster and Social Resilience (Earthscan, 2003) and *Natural Disasters and Development in a Globalising World* (Routledge, 2003). Dr Pelling was also lead author for four chapters on disaster risk for UN-Habitat's *Global Report on Human Settlements 2007: Enhancing Urban Safety and Security.* He is chair of the Climate Change Research Group of the Royal Geographical Society. mark.pelling@kcl.ac.uk

Alex Pulsipher is a PhD candidate in geography at Clark University, Worcester, MA, US. All correspondence to Alex de Sherbinin, CIESIN, Columbia University, PO Box 1000, Palisades, NY 10964, US; adesherbinin@ciesin.columbia.edu

MD Golam Rabbani is a senior research officer at the Bangladesh Centre for Advanced Studies (BCAS) and has an academic background in environment and risk assessment. He has been working on environment and climate change issues at national and regional level for more than six years, mainly in the areas of risk assessment, risk management, and policy and institutional arrangement. Bangladesh Centre for Advanced Studies (BCAS), House 10, Road 16A, Gulshan-1, Dhaka, Bangladesh; golam.rabbani@bcas.net

Hannah Reid is a senior associate with the Climate Change Group at IIED. She works on links between climate change and sustainable development, especially from the perspective of low- and middle-income countries. Dr Reid is particularly interested in links between climate change and both biodiversity and urban areas. hannah.reid@iied.org

Aromar Revi is managing director of the Indian Institute for Human Settlements (IIHS), the first interdisciplinary knowledge and education institution of sub-continental scale to be established in South Asia. He has worked for more than two decades on long-range national and international strategy, risk and social, economic and environmental change. He is one of South Asia's leading disaster mitigation and management experts and has led emergency teams in assessing, planning and executing recovery and rehabilitation programmes for ten major earthquake, cyclone, surge and flood events affecting more than 5 million people. He was awarded the Ashoka Fellowship in 1990 and has contributed to the design of India's national public housing programme and to housing and urban development sectoral plans for many of India's states. He is a fellow of the India China Institute at the New School, New York. aromar.revi@gmail.com.

Debra Roberts heads the Environmental Management Department of eThekwini Municipality (Durban, South Africa). Her key responsibilities include overseeing the planning and protection of the city's natural resource base; ensuring that environmental considerations influence all aspects of planning and development in the city; and directing and developing the Municipal Climate Protection Programme. Prior to joining the municipality in January 1994,

Dr Roberts lectured for ten years at the (then) University of Natal in the departments of biology and geographical and environmental sciences. Dr Roberts has written widely in the fields of open space design and environmental management and has received numerous awards for her work. Environmental Management Department, eThekwini Municipality, PO Box 680, Durban 4000, South Africa; robertsd@durban.gov.za

Patricia Romero Lankao is a social scientist at the Institute for the Study of Society and Environment (ISSE) National Centre for Atmospheric Research (NCAR). She is interested in the interface of the human dimensions of urban atmospheric emissions, and her work analyses how population density and size, lifestyles, governance and other societal factors affect cities' current and future emissions, as well as the ability of urban populations, transportation systems, water systems and industries to cope with (i.e. adapt to) climate change impacts. She has also contributed to a number of international networks of interdisciplinary research projects, and is a member of the scientific committee of the Global Carbon Project and a member of IPCC's *Fourth Assessment Report*. She is also a fellow of the Aldo Leopold Programme and of the International Programme Leadership for Environment and Development (LEAD). prlankao@ucar.edu

Andrew Schiller has a PhD from the Graduate School of Geography, Clark University, Worcester, MA, US, and is president of NeighborhoodScout, Inc. adesherbinin@ciesin.columbia.edu.

Alex de Sherbinin is a senior staff associate for research at the Centre for International Earth Science Information Network (CIESIN), The Earth Institute, Columbia University, New York, US. adesherbinin@ciesin.columbia.edu.

Gina Ziervogel is a lecturer at the Department of Environmental and Geographical Science, University of Cape Town, South Africa. Her research focuses on vulnerability to climate variability and change in a development context where adaptation to climate change needs to be understood in relation to other stresses such as water, health, food security, poverty and governance. Department of Environmental and Geographical Science, University of Cape Town, Private Bag, Rondebosch 7700, South Africa; gina@csag.uct.ac.za

Preface

This book brings together chapters that discuss the possibilities for and constraints to adapting to climate change in urban areas in low- and middle-income nations. With the exception of the introductory chapter and the conclusion, all of the chapters have been published as papers in the journal *Environment and Urbanization* between 2007 and 2009. However, they are scattered throughout five separate issues of the journal and we thought it was worth bringing them together in a single volume; some of the chapters have also been updated by their authors.

Perhaps surprisingly, there is not a lot of published literature on climate change adaptation in urban areas in low- and middle-income nations, although there is some recent (if limited) evidence of increasing support. Although there is a growing body of work on climate change adaptation, very little of it is on urban areas or even considers urban areas. And within this limited literature, most is on urban areas in high-income nations, even though most of the world's urban population is in low- and middle-income nations; these nations also have most of the world's urban population most at risk from climate change. There is more international support for work on greenhouse gas emissions reduction (mitigation) in urban areas in low- and middle-income nations, even though most urban centres in these nations have much lower levels of emissions per person than those in high-income nations and addressing adaptation issues is more pressing.

The editors of *Environment and Urbanization* took a decision in 2006 to encourage and support papers on climate change and cities in low- and middle-income nations, particularly ones that focus on adaptation. By the April 2009 issue, 17 papers had been published on this topic. All but three of these are published as chapters in this volume; the three that are not included did not focus on adaptation, but on mitigation.[1] The chapters in this volume are also intended as a contribution to the Fifth Assessment of the Intergovernmental Panel on Climate Change (IPCC): one of the main difficulties facing the authors of the chapter in the IPCC's Fourth Assessment on adaptation for 'Industry, settlement and society' was the lack of published literature on this topic.

We are very grateful to Sage Publications for allowing us to republish the papers drawn from *Environment and Urbanization* – and also for the many ways in which they have helped to increase the circulation and impact of the journal. Special thanks are due to the Swedish International Development Cooperation

Agency (Sida) and the Royal Danish Ministry of Foreign Affairs (DANIDA) for their support of our work. Special thanks are also due to Saleemul Huq and Hannah Reid within the International Institute for Environment and Development's (IIED's) Climate Change Group for their encouragement and support, without which most of the chapters in this book would never have been written. We are also grateful to our friends and partners within the CLACC programme (Capacity Strengthening of Least Developed Countries for Adaptation to Climate Change), out of which came the chapters in this book on Dhaka, Mombasa and Cotonou. Our thanks also go to Tom Wilbanks, Patricia Romero Lankao and other friends from the IPCC with whom we worked on the chapters on human settlements in the Third and Fourth Assessments. And, as always, special thanks are due to Earthscan for their help in getting this book out. On our count, this is the 17th book that they have published from our research group within the IIED, and without these our effectiveness would have been much diminished. But Earthscan have also built up a large and enviable backlist of other books on human settlement issues in Africa, Asia and Latin America. Through this, they have done much to draw attention to issues that have received far less attention from governments and international agencies than they deserve.

Jane Bicknell
David Dodman
David Satterthwaite
International Institute for Environment and Development (IIED)
May 2009

NOTE

1. Romero Lankao, P. (2007) 'Are we missing the point? Particularities of urbanization, sustainability and carbon emissions in Latin American cities', *Environment and Urbanization*, vol 19, no 1, pp157–175; also Dodman, D. (2009) 'Blaming cities for climate change? An analysis of urban greenhouse gas emissions inventories', *Environment and Urbanization*, vol 21, no 1, pp185–201; and Satterthwaite, D. (2008) 'Cities' contribution to global warming: Notes on the allocation of greenhouse gas emissions', *Environment and Urbanization*, vol 20, no 2, pp539–550.

List of Acronyms and Abbreviations

AAU	assigned amounts units
ADV	Asociación de Damnificados de Viacha
AF	Kyoto Protocol Adaptation Fund
ANC	African National Congress
BCAS	Bangladesh Centre for Advanced Studies
BPDB	Bangladesh Power Development Board
BRAC	Bangladesh Rural Advancement Committee
BWDB	Bangladesh Water Development Board
CATHALAC	Centro del Agua del Trópico Húmedo para América Latina y el Caribe
CBA	cost-benefit analysis
CBO	community-based organization
CCAA	Climate Change Adaptation in Africa
CCP	Cities for Climate Protection
CDM	Clean Development Mechanism
CEPREDENAC	Centro de Coordinación para la Prevención de los Desastres en America Latina
CFA	Communauté Financière Africaine
CIESIN	Centre for International Earth Science Information Network
CIF	World Bank Climate Investment Fund
CLACC	Capacity Strengthening of Least Developed Countries for Adaptation to Climate Change
cm	centimetre
CMC	Cape Metropolitan Council
CNG	compressed natural gas
CO_2	carbon dioxide
CODEL	Comité de Emergencia Local
CODEM	Comité de Emergencia Municipal
CODHES	Consultoría para los Derechos Humanos y el Desplazamiento Forzado
COP	Conference of the Parties to the UNFCCC
COPECO	Comisión Permanente de Contigencias
CRED	Centre for Research on the Epidemiology of Disasters
CUNY	City University of New York

DANIDA	Royal Danish Ministry of Foreign Affairs
DCC	Dhaka City Corporation
DEAT	Department of Environmental Affairs and Tourism
Defra	UK Department for Environment, Food and Rural Affairs
DESA	Dhaka Electric Supply Authority
DESCO	Dhaka Electric Supply Company
DFID	UK Department for International Development
DIT	Dhaka Improvement Trust
DMP	Disaster Management Plan
DWAF	Department of Water Affairs and Forestry
ENSO	El Niño–Southern Oscillation
FEEMA	Fundação Estadual de Engenharia do Meio Ambiente (Brazil's State Environmental Engineering Foundation)
FM–RANET	frequency modulation–radio and internet
GCM	General Circulation Model
GDP	gross domestic product
GEF	Global Environment Facility
GIEC	Groupe Intergouvernemental d'Experts sur le Climat
GIS	geographic information system
GISS	Goddard Institute for Space Studies
GLOSS	Global Sea-Level Observing System
GRUMP	Global Rural–Urban Mapping Project
ha	hectare
IATAL	International Air Travel Adaptation Levy
ICLEI	International Council for Local Environmental Initiatives
IDP	integrated development plan
IDRC	International Development Research Centre
IEG	Independent Evaluation Group (World Bank)
IGAD	Intergovernmental Authority on Development
IIED	International Institute for Environment and Development
IIHS	Indian Institute for Human Settlements
IMERS	International Maritime Emissions Reduction Scheme
IMO	International Maritime Organization
INA	Instituto Nacional del Agua
IPCC	Intergovernmental Panel on Climate Change
ISSE	Institute for the Study of Society and Environment
IT	information technology
IWRM	integrated water resources management
JNNURM	Jawaharlal Nehru National Urban Renewal Mission
km	kilometre
km²	square kilometre
KMD	Kenya Meteorological Department

LA RED	Red de Estudios Sociales en Prevención de Desastres en América Latina (Network of Social Studies in the Prevention of Disasters in Latin America)
LDC	least developed country
LDCF	Least Developed Countries Fund
LEAD	International Programme Leadership for Environment and Development
LECZ	low-elevation coastal zone
m	metre
m^2	square metre
MA	Millennium Ecosystem Assessment
MA	moderately affected
MAGICC	Model for the Assessment of Greenhouse Gas-Induced Climate Change
MAMUCA	Mancomunidad de los Municipios del Centro de Atlántida
MAP	Municipal Adaptation Plan
MCA	multi-criteria analysis
MCPP	Municipal Climate Protection Programme
MDG	Millennium Development Goal
MDTF	Bangladesh Multi-Donor Trust Fund
MGD	million gallons per day
MMR	Mumbai Metropolitan Region
MSA	most severely affected
NAPA	National Adaptation Programme of Action
NDMA	National Disaster Management Authority
NGO	non-governmental organization
NOAA	National Oceanic and Atmospheric Administration
NO$_x$	nitrogen oxides
NSDF	National Slum Dwellers Federation
O$_3$	ozone
O&M	operation and maintenance
ODA	official development assistance
OECD	Organisation for Economic Co-operation and Development
OFEDI	Organisation des Femmes pour la Gestion de l'Energie, de l'Environnement et la Promotion du Développement Intégré
PPCR	Pilot Programme on Climate Resilience
PVA	participatory vulnerability analysis
RIOCC	Red Iberoamericana de Oficinas de Cambio Climático (Ibero-American Network for Climate Change Offices)
SA	severely affected
SAM	social accounting matrix
SCCF	Special Climate Change Fund

Sida	Swedish International Development Cooperation Agency
SIS	small island state
SLR	sea-level rise
SNPMAD	Sistema Nacional para la Prevención, Mitigación y Atención de Desastres
SO_2	sulphur dioxide
SPA	Strategic Priority 'Piloting an Operational Approach to Adaptation'
SPARC	Society for the Promotion of Area Resource Centres
SRTM	Shuttle Radar Topography Mission
SSNAPP	SouthSouthNorth Adaptation Project Protocol
TERI	Tata Energy Research Institute
UK	United Kingdom
UN	United Nations
UNDP	United Nations Development Programme
UNEP	United Nations Environment Programme
UNFCCC	United Nations Framework Convention on Climate Change
UNICEF	United Nations Children's Fund
US	United States
USAID	United States Agency for International Development
WASA	Dhaka Water and Sewerage Authority
WMA	Water Management Area

1

INTRODUCTION

1

Adapting to Climate Change in Urban Areas: The Possibilities and Constraints in Low- and Middle-Income Nations[1]

David Satterthwaite, Saleemul Huq, Hannah Reid, Mark Pelling and Patricia Romero Lankao

Introduction

The lives and livelihoods of hundreds of millions of people will be affected by what is done (or not done) in urban centres with regard to climate change over the next five to ten years. Urban centres are key players both in the generation of greenhouse gases and in strategies to reduce this generation, especially in reducing dependence upon carbon-based fuels.[2] They also concentrate a large proportion of those most at risk from the effects of climate change – and the enterprises that generate most of the gross world product (GWP). While the need for city and municipal governments and civil society groups to act to reduce greenhouse gas emissions is well established – with many city governments in Europe and North America and some in other regions already acting on this – the need to act to reduce urban residents' vulnerability to the many direct and indirect impacts of climate change is not. In addition, most of the urban centres (and nations) that face the highest risks from the negative effects of climate change are those with small contributions to the greenhouse gases in the atmosphere; most also have serious constraints on their capacity to adapt to these effects.

This introductory chapter seeks to provide a brief overview of the key issues that are addressed in more depth and detail in Chapters 2 to 15. It also provides some background on the scale and nature of urban change in low- and middle-income nations, and considers why more attention needs to be paid both to understanding urban contexts and to urban governance frameworks for effective adaptation.

The potential for adaptation

As the Fourth Assessment of the Intergovernmental Panel on Climate Change (IPCC) notes, urban centres and the infrastructure they concentrate – and the industries that are a key part of many such centres' economic bases – are often capable of considerable adaptation in order to reduce risks from the direct and indirect impacts of climate change.[3] All large urban centres have had to make very large 'adaptations' to environmental conditions, site characteristics, natural resources availability and environmental hazards to be able to function – for instance, creating stable sites for buildings, putting in place the infrastructure that all cities require, and ensuring provision for water and for managing wastewater and storm and surface runoff. Successful and healthy cities are proof of the adaptation capacities of their governments, citizens and enterprises. In any well-governed city, there is already a great range of measures in place to ensure that buildings and infrastructure can withstand extreme weather events and that water supply systems can cope with variations in freshwater supplies. Good environmental and public health services should also be able to cope with any increase in other likely climate change-related health risks in the next few decades – whether this is from heat waves or reduced freshwater availability or greater risks from certain communicable diseases.

Thus, it is easy to envisage a process through which urban planning and management ensures planned adaptation – with developments and investments in and around each urban area reducing the risks for inhabitants, enterprises and infrastructure from climate change-related impacts. So, over time, this adapts the building stock, the industrial base, the infrastructure and the spread of urban development to the risks that these changes bring. The tools and methods required to do this are well known and their effectiveness has been demonstrated in many locations – for instance, adjustments to building codes, land subdivision regulations and infrastructure standards, combined with land-use planning that restricts buildings in high-risk areas and makes special provision for extreme events, including the use of insurance to spread risk and emergency services able to act swiftly when needed. An inventory of industries and other activities with the potential to cause serious secondary problems (such as fire or chemical contamination) when a disaster happens is also necessary. There is a well-established literature on the importance of integrating disaster preparedness within urban and peri-urban development, and this disaster preparedness also needs integrating within adaptation. For large well-established cities, there are often particular problems with adjusting existing buildings, infrastructure and land-use patterns to the new or heightened risks that climate change will or may bring; but these can generally be addressed by long-term policies that make these affordable by spreading the cost over long periods and by making use of potential synergies between reducing climate change risks and reducing other environmental risks. Most of the risks from climate change in the next few decades heighten other risks that are already present.

In addition, all low-income and most middle-income nations have what might be considered an advantage in that much of their 'urbanization' is to come in the next few decades and, since it has not yet taken place, it can be planned and managed in ways that accommodate the increased risks that climate change is likely to bring. This can include measures to channel new urban growth away from high-risk sites – for instance, from cities or city sites at high risk of moderate sea-level rise and storm surges. There are some particular worries with regard to the impact of the needed measures on housing and basic services for low-income groups: higher building and infrastructure standards and land-use restrictions (including avoiding new constructions on floodplains) could mean rising land and housing prices and much reduced supplies of cheap accommodation; but special measures can be taken to ensure sufficient supplies of well-located serviced land for new housing. It is also easy to envisage this process addressing disasters and other environmental hazards unrelated to climate change – for instance, improved drainage and provision for coping with occasional heavy concentrated rainfall that has long been a risk (and often produces serious flooding). It is also easy to envisage this process incorporating measures that reduce greenhouse gas emissions. There is evidence from some cities in low- and middle-income nations of the kinds of discussions within their governments on what local adaptations may be needed that can underpin good long-term planning for, and investment in, adaptation – as shown by Debra Roberts's discussion of Durban's adaptation plans in Chapter 11.

Thus, when problems concerning urban areas' adaptation to climate change are considered, independent of current conditions and government structures, it is easy to conceive of a long-term process of support and funding for adaptation. At least in the next 50 years or so, assuming that none of the uncertain but potentially catastrophic climate change impacts take place,[4] it seems that this might produce the necessary adaptations in most locations without high costs. Certain cities, smaller urban centres and rural districts face far more serious risks than others; but it is possible to envisage an international funding system that gives special attention to helping them adapt. It is also possible to envisage national adaptation strategies that encourage and support urban development away from the areas most at risk from climate change-related impacts. Most governments and many international agencies have officially endorsed recommendations to move in this direction – as in, for instance, the Hyogo Framework for Action.[5]

The constraints on implementation

It would be a mistake to assume that the above – a logical, justifiable, fundable process driven by good science – provides a viable roadmap for action. The examples of evolving good practice for adaptation in this book represent exceptions and it is important to understand why this is so. It is easy for national governments to sign declarations at international conferences that recommend all the needed measures – and then ignore them.

The best indication of the constraints on implementing adaptation comes from the last 50 to 60 years of 'development'. During the 1950s, it was easy to envisage a process by which international funding for 'productive activities' and the required infrastructure allied to 'technical assistance' would rapidly reduce poverty and 'underdevelopment' in Africa, Asia and Latin America and the Caribbean. Yet, more than five decades later, the number of people suffering extreme poverty is much larger than it was in the 1950s. Indeed, there was a need to launch the Millennium Development Goals in 2000 precisely to focus attention on the vast scale of unmet needs, despite four 'development decades'. During the 1970s, many international agencies committed themselves to a new focus on 'meeting basic needs', with detailed costings of what additional funding this would require; four decades later, the number of people lacking access to the most 'basic needs' is higher than it was in the 1970s. Today, there are more urban dwellers living in very poor quality, overcrowded housing lacking basic infrastructure and services in low- and middle-income nations than their entire urban populations in 1975.[6]

Much of the physical growth and economic expansion in most cities in low- and middle-income nations takes place outside any official plan and outside official rules and regulations. This is also the case for most new housing that is being built. In part, this is because large sections of the population could never afford a house that met official standards (and often the standards are unrealistic and their implementation cumbersome and costly). In part, it is because of a very large mismatch between the growth of urban centres' economic bases and populations and the competence, capacity and accountability of local government structures. There are important exceptions and these can be held up as examples of 'good practice'; but the political and economic circumstances that underpinned their good practice are rarely transferable.

In urban centres in Africa, Asia and Latin America and the Caribbean, hundreds of millions of people live in accommodation that is of poor quality, with particular problems in relation to overcrowding, unsafe structures, insecure tenure and inadequate provision for infrastructure, including that needed for water, sanitation and drainage.[7] Another indication of the scale of urban problems is the number of people living in illegal settlements because they cannot afford to buy, build or rent legal accommodation. In urban areas, it has now become the norm rather than the exception for high proportions of urban dwellers to live in informal settlements; it is common for cities to have 30 to 50 per cent of their entire population living in settlements that developed illegally.[8] With regard to infrastructure, estimates for 2000 suggested that more than 680 million urban dwellers lacked adequate provision for water and 850 million or more lacked adequate provision for sanitation.[9] There are no estimates on deficiencies in drainage infrastructure; but the lack of provision for sewers gives some indication of deficiencies here. Most urban centres in low-income nations have no sewers at all or sewers that only serve a small proportion of the population.[10] Statistics on infant and child mortality rates for urban populations show that these are often 5 to 20 times what they should be if families had adequate incomes, reasonable quality housing and good healthcare.[11] There are also many case studies focusing on low-income urban populations that show very large health burdens from diseases that should be easily prevented or cured – for instance, diarrhoeal diseases, intestinal parasites, tuberculosis, malaria, dengue fever and acute respiratory infections.[12]

In addition, we cannot consider the 'adaptation' that cities must make with regard to climate change independent of the often very large deficits or deficiencies in basic infrastructure (including storm and surface drains). It makes no sense to discuss the vulnerability of urban populations to climate change and responses to it separately from their current and often long-established vulnerability to climate variability, including extreme weather events. There is a long history of cities being seriously affected by climate variability that has nothing to do with human-induced climate change. In addition, the Asian tsunami of 2004 demonstrated the vulnerability of so many coastal settlements (urban and rural), or specific populations within them, to the risk of flooding and storm surges, even if an earthquake did cause them. The key here is to understand how the processes that shape urbanization create or exacerbate risk – to climate variability, to the direct and less direct impacts of climate change and to other hazards unrelated to climate change or variability. At an international level, there may be a desire to separate out the additional risks created by climate change from those related to climate variability, earthquakes, tsunamis, etc. in measures to assign responsibilities for meeting adaptation costs in low- and middle-income nations to the nations with the largest historic and current contributions to greenhouse gas emissions. But within each locality, what is needed is a coherent, integrated response to all environmental hazards and risks.

There is not much point in discussing how city or municipal governments can adapt to protect the populations within their jurisdiction from risks arising from climate change when they have shown so little inclination or ability to protect them from other environmental hazards. There are really two separate issues here, although they often act together. The first issue is *the incapacity of urban governments* in terms of their powers and the resources at their disposal, and this in turn relates to the refusal of higher levels of governments to allow them the powers and resources they require to address local needs and to the long-established disinterest among most international agencies in supporting urban development and urban governance reforms.[13] The second issue is *the antagonistic relationship between urban governments and most low-income groups*; this also relates to urban governments' lack of accountability to their urban populations, but it goes beyond this. It is strongly reinforced by urban elites' visions of what they see as a modern city and by real estate interests wanting access to land currently occupied by informal settlements. The urban poor are not seen as critical parts of the city economy but as holding back the city's success. Official urban policies often increase poor people's vulnerability to environmental hazards and climate shocks rather than reduce them[14] – and so they are best conceived as maladaptation.

There is also not much point in discussing how to adapt urban planning and its regulatory framework to reduce people's vulnerability to climate change when planning and regulation enforcement will only serve those with power and will be used to evict and dispossess poorer groups whenever it serves those in power to do so. Tens of millions of urban dwellers are forcibly evicted from their homes each year – mostly without compensation or with inadequate or inappropriate compensation.[15]

Many factors have contributed to this – for instance, in most urban centres, the unrealistic minimum standards demanded for housing and plot sizes. Many standards in sub-Saharan Africa, the Caribbean and Asia are still based on regulations created under colonial rule. These were usually based on standards in force in the colonial power, with no adjustment for extreme weather events common in the colonies. Most were also originally instituted for use only within areas of the colonial city that were inhabited by 'non-natives', and under colonial rule these were never seen as measures to be implemented for entire city populations. However, the issue is not that these regulations are inappropriate, but, rather, that they are still used because they serve the interests of those in power. The mechanisms for their enforcement are also often open to corrupt practices, underpinned by the very large increases in land value that usually come with permission to transfer use from agricultural to residential or commercial use.[16] Ironically, poverty may be lower in cities where regulations are not enforced than where inappropriate regulations are enforced. For any growing city, what is worse than expanding 'squatter settlements' is government authorities preventing squatter settlements – which will mean poor families doubling and tripling up within the existing housing stock.

Land-use planning could plan climate-related hazards out of urban expansion by avoiding the sites most at risk and by ensuring that plot layouts and infrastructure standards for new developments can cope with extreme weather. But land-use planning and the regulations it incorporates can act to reduce or increase the price and availability of legal housing because of their influence on the price and availability of land with infrastructure and services. Thus, how land-use planning measures respond to climate change risks has very large implications for the possibilities of low- and middle-income households to buy, build or rent good quality legal accommodation with infrastructure in areas that are not at risk from floods or landslides. Where governments have the competence and capacity to support locally appropriate land-for-housing development and subdivision regulations, this improves housing conditions and greatly widens housing possibilities for low-income households.[17]

Box 1.1 Some definitions of terms

Adaptation to (human-induced) climate change: actions to reduce the vulnerability of a system (e.g. a city), population group (e.g. a vulnerable population in a city) or an individual or household to the adverse impacts of anticipated climate change due to the emission of greenhouse gases. Adaptation to climate variability consists of actions to reduce vulnerability to short-term climate shocks (with or without climate change). Often, adaptation to climate change will also result in adaptation to climate variability (as a co-benefit). However, individual adaptation can undermine collective resilience or compromise collective adaptive capacity (see Chapter 10).

Adaptive capacity: inherent capacity of a system (e.g. a city government), population (e.g. low-income community in a city) or individual/household to undertake actions that can help to avoid loss and can speed recovery from any impact of climate change. Elements of adaptive capacity include knowledge, institutional capacity, and financial and technological resources. Low-income populations in a city will tend to have lower adaptive capacity than high-income populations because of their reduced capacity to afford good-quality housing on safe sites and avoid dangerous livelihoods. There is also a wide range among city and national governments in their adaptive capacities, relating to the resources available to them, the information base to guide action, the infrastructure in place, and the quality of their institutions and governance systems.

Adaptation deficit: lack of adaptive capacity to deal with the problems of climate variability and climate change. In many cities and most small urban centres, the main problem is the lack of provision for infrastructure (such as all-weather roads, piped water supplies, sewers, drains and electricity) and the lack of capacity to address this. This is one of the central issues with regard to adaptation because most discussions on this issue focus on adjustments to infrastructure – but you cannot climate-proof infrastructure that is not there. In addition, funding for climate change adaptation has little value if there is no local capacity to design, implement and maintain the necessary adaptation measures.

Adaptation and mitigation linkages: mitigation (the reduction of greenhouse gas emissions and other measures to reduce global warming) results in avoiding the adverse impacts of climate change in the long run (at least the incremental impacts due to the greenhouse gases not emitted), while adaptation can reduce the unavoidable impacts in the near term (but cannot reduce them to zero). Failure to mitigate will lead eventually to failure of adaptation; hence, adaptation and mitigation are not alternative strategies but complementary ones that need to be pursued together. But most of the people and places at greatest risk from climate change are not those with large historic or current contributions to greenhouse gases. Failure to mitigate sufficiently in high-income nations will create ever more adaptation failures, mostly in low- and middle-income nations, including many nations with insignificant historic and current contributions to climate change.

Adaptation in situ: actions that enable vulnerable populations to adapt successfully to climate change (and climate variability) in the places where they currently live, including adaptations made or supported by local governments. In most instances, vulnerable urban populations would prioritize *in situ* adaptation because their current home and location were chosen for their access to income-earning opportunities.

Autonomous adaptation: in the climate change literature, a distinction is drawn between planned adaptation (the result of a deliberate policy decision) and autonomous adaptation (or spontaneous adaptation) that is not. Autonomous adaptation is also used to refer to adaptations undertaken by households or enterprises, independent of government.

Climate change and climate variability: in this book, the term climate change is used to refer to changes in climate attributed to human activity; climate variability includes variations that are not related to human-induced climate change.

Climate change risk: additional risks to people and their livelihoods/investments (e.g. buildings, infrastructure) due to the potential impacts of climate change. These risks can be direct, as in larger and/or more frequent floods or more intense and/or frequent storms, or heat waves; or less direct, as climate change negatively affects livelihoods or food supplies (and prices), or access to water needed for domestic consumption or livelihoods. Certain groups may face increased risks from measures taken in response to climate change – including adaptation measures (e.g. measures to protect particular areas of a city from flooding that increase flood risks 'downstream') and mitigation measures (e.g. emphasis on new hydropower schemes that displace large numbers of people).

Limits to adaptation: adaptation can reduce the adverse impacts of climate change considerably but cannot reduce them to zero. Thus, there are limits to adaptation. Also, certain places become permanently beyond adaptation (e.g. coastal zones inundated by sea-level rise), and the number of these places (and the populations at risk) obviously rises without successful mitigation.

Maladaptation: actions or investments that increase rather than reduce vulnerability to impacts of climate change. This can include the shifting of vulnerability from one social group or place to another; it also includes shifting risk to future generations and/or to ecosystems and ecosystem services. Many investments being made in cities are, in fact, maladaptive rather than adaptive, as they decrease resilience to climate change. Removing maladaptations is often the first task to be addressed even before new adaptations.

Planned adaptation: adaptations that are planned in anticipation of potential climate change. Generally, government agencies have a key role in providing the information about current and likely future risks and in providing frameworks that support individual, household, community and private-sector adaptation. However, governments often do not fulfil this role, and community-based organizations and other civil society organizations may be the initiators and supporters of planned adaptation.

> *Resilience*: resilience is a product of governments, enterprises, populations and individuals with strong adaptive capacity. It indicates a capacity to maintain core functions in the face of hazardous threats and impacts, especially for vulnerable populations. It usually requires a capacity to anticipate climate change and to plan needed adaptations. The resilience of any population group to climate change interacts with its resilience to other dynamic pressures, including economic change, conflict and violence.

The urban context

The scale of urbanization in low- and middle-income nations[18]

Urban areas in low- and middle-income nations house more than one third of the world's total population, nearly three-quarters of its urban population and most of its large cities. They contain most of the economic activities in these nations and most of the new jobs created over the last few decades. They are also likely to house most of the world's growth in population in the next 10 to 20 years.[19] With regard to climate change, they already house a large proportion of the population and the economic activities most at risk from extreme weather events and sea-level rise – and this proportion is increasing (see Chapter 2).

Half of the world's current population of around 6.4 billion people live in urban centres,[20] compared to less than 15 per cent in 1900.[21] Many aspects of urban change in recent decades are unprecedented, including not only the world's level of urbanization and the size of its urban population, but also the number of countries becoming more urbanized and the size and number of very large cities. The populations of dozens of major cities have grown more than tenfold in the last 50 years, and many have grown more than 20-fold.[22] There are also the large demographic changes apparent in all nations over the last 50 years that influence urban change, including rapid population growth rates in much of Latin America, Asia and Africa after World War II (although, in most cases, these have declined significantly), and changes in the size and composition of households and in age structures.[23]

Table 1.1 shows the scale of urban population growth since 1950. Asia now has close to half the world's urban population, and Africa has a larger urban population than Northern America or Western Europe, even though it is often perceived as overwhelmingly rural. In 1950, Europe and Northern America had more than half the world's urban population; by 2000, they had little more than one quarter.

Two aspects of the rapid growth in the world's urban population since 1950 are the increase in the number of large cities and the historically unprecedented size of the largest cities. Just two centuries ago, only two cities had more than 1 million inhabitants – London and Beijing (then called Peking). By 1950, there

Table 1.1 *The distribution of the world's urban population by region, 1950–2010*

Region or country	1950	1970	1990	2000	Projected for 2010	Projected for 2020
Urban populations (millions of inhabitants)						
World	737	1332	2275	2854	3495	4210
High-income nations	427	652	818	873	925	972
Low- and middle-income nations	310	680	1456	1981	2570	3237
'Least developed countries'	15	41	110	169	254	376
Africa	33	86	204	295	412	566
Asia	237	485	1015	1373	1770	2212
Europe	281	412	509	520	530	540
Latin America and the Caribbean	69	164	314	394	471	543
Northern America	110	171	214	250	286	321
Oceania	8	14	19	22	25	28
Urbanization level (percentage of population living in urban areas)						
World	29.1	36.0	43.0	46.6	50.6	54.9
High-income nations	52.5	64.6	71.2	73.1	75.0	77.5
Low- and middle-income nations	18.0	25.3	35.1	40.2	45.3	50.5
'Least developed countries'	7.3	13.1	21.0	24.8	29.4	35.0
Africa	14.5	23.6	32.0	35.9	39.9	44.6
Asia	16.8	22.7	31.9	37.1	42.5	48.1
Europe	51.2	62.8	70.5	71.4	72.6	74.8
Latin America and the Caribbean	41.4	57.0	70.6	75.3	79.4	82.3
Northern America	63.9	73.8	75.4	79.1	82.1	84.6
Oceania	62.0	70.8	70.6	70.4	70.6	71.4

Region or Country	1950	1970	1990	2000	2010	Projected for 2020
Percentage of the world's urban population living in:						
World	100.0	100.0	100.0	100.0	100.0	100.0
High-income nations	58.0	49.0	36.0	30.6	26.5	23.1
Low- and middle-income nations	42.0	51.0	64.0	69.4	73.5	76.9
'Least developed countries'	2.0	3.1	4.9	5.9	7.3	8.9
Africa	4.4	6.5	9.0	10.3	11.8	13.5
Asia	32.1	36.4	44.6	48.1	50.6	52.5
Europe	38.1	30.9	22.4	18.2	15.2	12.8
Latin America and the Caribbean	9.4	12.3	13.8	13.8	13.5	12.9
Northern America	14.9	12.9	9.4	8.8	8.2	7.6
Oceania	1.1	1.0	0.8	0.8	0.7	0.7
Nations with largest urban populations in 2000						
China	9.8	10.9	13.8	15.9	17.4	18.0
India	8.6	8.2	9.7	10.1	10.5	11.2
US	13.7	11.6	8.5	7.9	7.4	6.9
Brazil	2.6	4.0	4.9	5.0	4.9	4.7
Russian Federation	6.2	6.1	4.8	3.8	2.9	2.3

Source: derived from statistics in United Nations, Department of Economic and Social Affairs, Population Division (2008) *World Urbanization Prospects: The 2007 Revision*, CD-ROM edition, data in digital form (POP/DB/WUP/Rev.2007), United Nations, New York

were 77 'million cities'; and by 2000 there were 378, mostly in low- and middle-income nations. The size of the world's largest cities has also increased dramatically. In 2000, the average size of the world's 100 largest cities was around 6.2 million inhabitants, compared to 2.1 million inhabitants in 1950 and 0.7 million in 1900. While there are examples over the last two millennia of cities that had populations of 1 million or more inhabitants, the city or metropolitan area with several million is a relatively new phenomenon – London being the first to reach this size in the second half of the 19th century.[24] By 2000, there were 44 cities with more than 5 million inhabitants.

Table 1.2 *The distribution of the world's largest cities by region over time*

Region	1800	1900	1950	2000
Number of 'million cities'				
World	2	16	77	378
Africa	0	0	2	37
Asia	1	3	28	192
China	1	1	11	86
India	0	1	5	33
Europe	1	9	23	53
Russian Federation	0	2	2	13
Latin America and the Caribbean	0	0[a]	8	49
Brazil	0	0	2	15
Northern America	0	4	14	41
US	0	4	12	37
Oceania	0	0	2	6
Regional distribution of the world's largest 100 cities				
World	100	100	100	100
Africa	5	2	3	9
Asia	64	21	41	48
China	23	12	17	17
India	19	4	6	8
Europe	28	54	27	10
Russian Federation	2	2	2	2
Latin America and the Caribbean	3	5	8	16
Brazil	1	1	2	8
Northern America	0	16	19	15
US	0	15	17	13
Oceania	0	2	2	2
Average size of the world's 100 largest cities (population)	184,270	722,760	2.1 million	6.2 million

Note: [a] Some estimates suggest that Rio de Janeiro had reached 1 million inhabitants by 1900, while other sources suggest it had just under 1 million.
For 1950 and 2000, only data from the United Nations Population Division is used. Combining data on city populations from different sources can create problems because these sources often use different criteria. For instance, for Germany, there are different interpretations of where major

city and metropolitan area boundaries should be drawn, which greatly influences the number of German cities in any 'large' or 'million' city list. In this table, cities that have changed their country classifications and nations that have changed regions are considered to be in the country or region that they are currently in for this whole period. For instance, Hong Kong is counted as being in China for all the above years, while the Russian Federation is considered part of Europe.

Source: Satterthwaite, D. (2007) *The Transition to a Predominantly Urban World and Its Underpinnings*, Human Settlements Urban Change Discussion Series 4, IIED, London, 90pp; updated drawing data for 1950 and 2000 from United Nations, Department of Economic and Social Affairs, Population Division (2008) *World Urbanization Prospects: The 2007 Revision*, CD-ROM edition, data in digital form (POP/DB/WUP/Rev.2007), United Nations, New York. For 1900 and 1800, data came from an IIED database with census data and estimates for city populations drawn from a great range of sources, including Chandler, T. and Fox, G. (1974) *3000 Years of Urban Growth*, Academic Press, New York and London; also Chandler, T. (1987) *Four Thousand Years of Urban Growth: An Historical Census*, Edwin Mellen Press, Lampeter, UK, 656pp; and Showers, V. (1979) *World Facts and Figures*, John Wiley and Sons, Chichester, 757pp. For Latin America, it also drew on a review of 194 published censuses.

Drivers of urban change

Three drivers of increased vulnerability to climate variability and change in urban areas need consideration: the drivers of urbanization and other aspects of urban change; the weaknesses and incapacities of governments; and the development and expansion of cities in high-risk sites. The interest here is to understand how the processes that drive or shape urban change create risk from a range of hazards, including those that climate change is likely to create or exacerbate. This section focuses on the drivers of urban change, with subsequent sections examining the other two.

Understanding what causes and influences urban change within any nation is complicated. Consideration has to be given to changes in the scale and nature of the nation's economy and its connections with neighbouring nations and the wider world economy – also to decisions made by national governments, national and local investors and the 30,000 or so global corporations that control such a significant share of the world's economy. Urban change within all nations is also influenced by the structure of government (especially the division of power and resources between different levels of government), and the extent and spatial distribution of transport and communications investments. The population of each urban centre and its rate of change are also influenced not only by such international and national factors, but also by local factors related to each very particular local context – including the site, the location and natural resource endowment; the population's demographic structure; the existing economy and infrastructure (the legacy of past decisions and investments); and the quality and capacity of public institutions.

The immediate cause of urbanization[25] is the net movement of people from rural to urban areas. The main underlying cause is the concentration of new investment and economic opportunities in particular urban areas. Virtually all the nations that have urbanized most over the last 50 to 60 years have had long periods of rapid economic expansion and large shifts in employment patterns from agricultural/pastoral activities to industrial, service and information activities. In low- and middle-income nations, urbanization is overwhelmingly the result of people moving in response to better economic opportunities in the urban areas, or to the lack of prospects in their home farms or villages. The scale and direction of people's movements accord well with changes in the spatial location of economic opportunities. In general, it is cities, small towns or rural areas with expanding economies that attract most migration.[26] By 2004, 97 per cent of the world's GDP was generated by industry and services, most of which comes from urban-based enterprises, and around 65 per cent of the world's economically active population were working in industry and services. Most of the world's largest cities are in the world's largest economies.[27] Political changes have had considerable importance in increasing levels of urbanization in many nations over the past 50 to 60 years, especially the achievement of political independence (which often also meant the dismantling of apartheid-like colonial controls on the rights of inhabitants to live or work in urban areas in many nations) and the building of government structures. These had particular importance for much of Asia and Africa but had much less effect in most nations from the 1980s onwards.

Do climate change and disaster specialists understand what drives and shapes urban change? With a few honourable exceptions, the literature suggests that they have a simplistic, often stereotyped 'urban population explosion' or 'rural-push/urban-pull' view of urban change. This often fails to consider why urbanization is taking place, what drives people to concentrate in specific urban locations, and what particular processes make the population of each urban centre (or particular groups within it) vulnerable to environmental hazards. There is often an assumption that all nations are urbanizing (which is not true) and that all urban centres face rapid population increases (which is also not true, as an analysis of urban change in any nation between two censuses shows). There are many large cities, small cities and small towns in Africa, Asia and Latin America that do not have rapidly growing populations. Among the very large cities, Mexico City, São Paulo, Rio de Janeiro, Buenos Aires, Kolkata (formerly Calcutta) and Seoul had more people moving out than moving in during their most recent inter-census period.[28]

Aggregate urban statistics are often interpreted as implying comparable urban trends across the world or for particular continents. But they obscure the diversity between nations and hide the particular local and national factors that influence these trends. Recent censuses show that the world today is actually less urbanized and less dominated by large cities than had been anticipated. Analyses of urban change within any nation over time show the rising and falling importance of different urban centres, the spatial influence of changes in governments' economic policies (e.g. from supporting import substitution to supporting export promotion) and of international trade regimes, the growing complexity of multi-nuclear urban systems in and around many major cities – and the complex and ever-shifting patterns of migration from rural to urban areas, from urban to urban areas and from urban to rural areas. International immigration and emigration have strong impacts upon the population size of particular cities in most nations. But it is not only changing patterns of prosperity or decline that underpin these flows – many cities have been affected by war, civil conflict or disaster, or by the arrival of people fleeing these events.

If our concern is to understand better what makes urban centres and populations at risk from climate change, we need to understand why urban populations (or subgroups within a population) often concentrate in high-risk areas and why urban processes can greatly magnify the size of the risk and of the population at risk. It is common to see urbanization listed as a 'driver' of vulnerability but this is questionable for two reasons: first, in some locations urbanization is associated with much-reduced vulnerability to extreme weather events and other environmental hazards; and, second, urbanization is not so much a driver as a result of other drivers. Unlike other areas of climate change research (e.g. agricultural vulnerability), no systemic methodologies and studies have been developed to understand urban vulnerability in the context of multiple stressors, to address the determinants of vulnerability and poverty in urban areas, and to explore the constraints and windows of opportunity (e.g. innovative approaches) in order to increase the adaptive capacity or resilience of the urban poor.[29]

Although rapid urban growth is often seen as 'a problem', it is generally the nations with the best economic performance that have urbanized most in the last 50 years.[30] In addition, there is often an association between rapid urban change and better standards of living. Not only is most urbanization associated with stronger economies; but, generally, the more urbanized a nation, the higher the average life expectancy and literacy rate and the stronger the democracy, especially at the local level. Many of the largest cities may appear chaotic and out of control; but most have life expectancies and provision for piped water, sanitation, schools and healthcare that are well above their national average – even if the aggregate statistics for each large city can hide a significant proportion of their population living in very poor conditions. Some of world's fastest-growing cities over the last 50 years also have among the best standards of living within their nations.[31] A concern for development and for reducing urban populations' vulnerability to hazards (including those associated with climate change) should include a focus not only on large or fast-growing cities, but also on smaller urban centres and urban centres that are not growing rapidly since these contain a high proportion of the urban population.[32]

There is often an assumption that agriculture should be considered as separate from or even in opposition to urban development, and that 'rural' development is needed to help reduce rural–urban migration. But successful rural development often increases rural–urban migration as higher-value crops and higher incomes among rural populations increase demand for goods and services in urban centres.[33] Many major cities first developed as markets and service centres for farmers and rural households and later developed into important centres of industry and/or services.[34] Many such cities and a high proportion of smaller urban centres still have significant sections of their economy and employment structure related to forward and backward linkages with agriculture.[35] All urban centres rely on rural ecosystem services (see, in particular, Chapter 14). However, rapid urbanization can mean rapid industrial, commercial and residential developments on land sites that should remain undeveloped (see Box 1.2).

Box 1.2 Economic development and ecosystem change in the Gulf of Mexico

The coastal states around the Gulf of Mexico are home to more than 55 million people – and have many critical ecosystems such as wetlands, seagrass beds, mangroves, barrier islands, sand dunes, coral reefs and marine forests. These are obviously influenced by the heavy concentration of economic activities – petroleum production, fisheries, agriculture, forestry and tourism. The Gulf concentrates a high proportion of US offshore oil production and of Mexico's total oil production, and the oil and gas industry supports an enormous complement of land-based companies and facilities, including chemical production, oil field equipment dealers, cement suppliers, caterers, divers, platform fabrication yards and shipyards. The Gulf coastal fisheries are almost entirely dependent upon estuarine wetlands – and wetlands are an important natural buffer for storm surges while also having many important ecological functions, including those related to fisheries and water quality. Almost 1 million hectares of coastal mangroves were destroyed on the Mexican Gulf coast between the 1970s and the early 1990s.[a] The main drivers for wetland conversion in Mexico are large-scale tourism development, urbanization and agriculture. In addition, wetlands are extremely sensitive to sea-level rise; adaptation should mean maintaining their functions and productivity. For some, adaptation is only possible if there is room for them to migrate inland – or space for the creation of new wetlands to compensate for those that cannot migrate inland due to topographical or other natural constraints.

[a]Yanez-Arancibia, A. and Day, J. W. (2004) 'The Gulf of Mexico: Towards an integration of coastal management with large marine ecosystem management', *Ocean and Coastal Management*, vol 47, pp537–563
Source: Levina, E., Jacob, J. S., Ramos, L. E. and Ortiz, I. (2007) 'Policy frameworks for adaptation to climate change in coastal zones: The case of the Gulf of Mexico', Paper prepared for the OECD and International Energy Agency, Paris, 68pp

The other urban issue that needs highlighting is that many of the regions with the most rapid urban growth (and the largest in-migration flows) are coastal areas at risk from sea-level rise and the likely increase in intensity and frequency of extreme weather events (see Chapters 2 and 14). The dynamics behind this will be very difficult to change – and there is also a high potential for government policies aiming to do so to cause serious damage to the economic prospects of low-income nations and the livelihood opportunities for low-income populations. In virtually all nations, it is where private investments and enterprises choose to concentrate that drives most urbanization.[36]

Vulnerability

Vulnerability to climate change is understood to mean the potential of people to be killed, injured or otherwise harmed by the direct or indirect impacts of climate change. This is most obvious with regard to risk from extreme events (such as storms or floods); but it includes risk from less direct impacts – for instance, declining freshwater availability or livelihoods dependent upon climate-sensitive resources.

Do urban specialists concern themselves with urban populations' vulnerability to extreme weather events? Again, with a few honourable exceptions, the literature suggests that they do not – although this is part of a wider failure among urban specialists to give much consideration to the life- or health-threatening risks to which urban populations (or particular groups within urban populations) are exposed in their homes, neighbourhoods and workplaces (see, in particular, Chapters 7, 8 and 10). Why have metropolitan, city and municipal government structures not developed in step with rapid urban growth? This is more easily explained in the many cities and smaller urban centres that lack a prosperous economic base. But a large proportion of the urban population most at risk from climate change lives in urban centres that have had very rapid economic growth.

Aromar Revi's discussion of climate change risk in India (see Chapter 14) includes the comment that 'Overall risk in Indian cities is typically associated more with vulnerability than with hazard exposure'. This is worth considering more generally in that so much of the human cost of extreme weather events in urban centres in low- and middle-income nations comes not from the 'hazard' or the 'disaster event', but from the inadequate provision of protection for urban populations (or particular sections of the population) from these. For instance, in many urban centres, the lack of provision for drainage (and for maintaining existing drains) means that relatively minor rainstorms cause serious flooding (see Chapters 4, 9 and 10).

For extreme events, adaptation has to address pre-disaster and post-disaster vulnerabilities – as noted in many chapters and dealt with in detail in Chapters 8 and 10. For instance, it should focus on reducing the hazard where this is possible (e.g. better drainage that stops a heavy rainstorm creating floods), or reducing people's exposure to it (e.g. working with those who live in areas at risk of flooding to improve their housing or to move to safer locations). Here, the intention is to avoid the event causing a disaster. It should also focus on reducing the impact of the hazard – for instance, by responding rapidly to flooding, both to get the floodwaters away from the flooded settlements and to respond to the flood's impacts upon people's health, living conditions, assets and livelihoods. And, finally, in the post-disaster response, it should not only help people to rebuild their homes and livelihoods, but also encourage and support measures that reduce risks from likely future hazards. But there are two difficulties in adapting to future risks. The first is that the scale and nature of the hazards climate change brings will change (and the scale generally increases). The second is the uncertainty in any locality of exactly what changes will happen and when. In the past, without climate change, it was easier, for any location, to establish from historic records the likely range and frequency of extreme weather events for which provision had to be made. And even in cities that have adapted well to extreme weather, a storm or rainfall just a little more intense than the historic record often becomes a disaster.

Among the populations who are particularly vulnerable to climate shocks are those living in particularly dangerous locations (e.g. on floodplains), those living in settlements lacking protective infrastructure and those living in poor-quality housing. Of course, within any vulnerable population there are differentials in how much they are affected by the hazard (influenced by, for instance, age, health status and gender) and differentials in their coping capacities (see, in particular, Chapter 8). Vulnerability is a product of the exposure of people to such changes (which is influenced by the limits they face in being able to reduce this exposure) and limited or no capacity to cope (the immediate responses) and adapt (longer-term responses).

In all instances, people's capacity to avoid the hazard or to cope with it and to adapt (to reduce future risk) is influenced by individual/household resources (e.g. incomes, asset bases and knowledge) and community resources (e.g. for coping, the quality and inclusiveness of community organizations that provide or manage safety nets and other short- and longer-term responses). But in urban areas, it is also greatly influenced by the extent and quality of infrastructure and public services, especially for vulnerable populations. The two factors that contribute to vulnerability – the risk of being killed, injured or otherwise harmed, and the coping and adaptation capacity – are largely determined by the development context[37] since it is the development context that has such a strong influence on households' income, education and access to information, on people's exposure to environmental hazards in their homes and workplaces, and on the quality and extent of provision for infrastructure and services (including post-event services).

Extreme weather events do not produce disasters if there are no vulnerable populations. But it is difficult to assess the vulnerabilities of urban populations to these events (and to the impacts of climate change) because these vulnerabilities are so specific to each location and societal context. They cannot be reliably estimated from the larger-scale aggregate modelling of climate change;[38] neither can they be reliably estimated without a detailed knowledge of local contexts. Yet, it is still common to find generalizations made about the vulnerability of 'developing countries' or their urban centres.

Climate change and disasters

Extreme weather events in urban areas

There was agreement within the IPCC that in many locations, climate change is likely to increase the intensity and/or frequency of extreme weather events that have the potential to cause disasters (see Box 1.3). There is a clear upward trend in the frequency of large disasters arising from natural events between 1950 and 2005, and this upward trend is entirely due to weather-related events; there is also a rapid increase in both economic losses and in insured losses from weather-related disasters for the same period.[39] 2007 is likely to have the largest number of disasters for any year on record – and up to October 2007, most were weather-related (floods, droughts and storms).[40] A large proportion of the disasters recorded were in urban areas or affected urban areas.[41] The rapid growth in the number of disasters is partly explained by the much-increased size of the urban population, including the prevalence of cities in hazard-prone areas.[42]

It is worth noting the scale of the devastation caused by some recent extreme weather events – see, in particular, Chapter 4 on the impacts of floods in Dhaka over the last 20 years, but also Chapter 3 on Mombasa. These are not 'proof of climate change' (which is difficult to ascertain), but rather proof of the vulnerability of cities and smaller settlements to extreme weather events – for instance, the devastation brought by Hurricane Mitch to Central America in 1998 (thousands killed, millions homeless and billions of dollars worth of damage to already fragile economies),[43] or the devastation brought by flooding in and around Caracas in Venezuela in 1999 (hundreds killed and some 600,000 others seriously affected). The IPCC Working Group II chapter on settlements noted some estimates for the impacts of extreme weather events on nations' GDPs, including a 4 to 6 per cent loss for Mozambique as a result of the flooding in 2000,[44] a 3 per cent loss for Central America as a result of El Niño and a 7 per cent loss for Honduras from Hurricane Mitch. Such aggregate figures for nations can obscure the fact that for specific regions or locales, the impact can be greater – ranging from more than 10 per cent of GDP and gross capital formation in larger, more developed and more diversified affected regions to more than 50 per cent in less developed, less diversified, more natural resource-dependent regions.[45]

Box 1.3 What are disasters?

Disasters are defined by events that result in large numbers of people killed or injured, or in large economic losses. The conventional view is that they are caused by exceptional or unusual events, including 'natural' disasters. However, over the last 30 years this has been questioned – as disasters come to be viewed not as unusual or natural events, but as failures of development since they occur because of little or no attention to reducing vulnerability. Storms, floods, droughts and heat waves need not be disasters if vulnerabilities to these have been much reduced.

The Centre for Research on the Epidemiology of Disasters (CRED), which holds the only publicly accessible global disaster database, defines disaster as 'a situation or event, which overwhelms local capacity, necessitating a request to national or international level for external assistance'. To be entered into the EM-DAT database, at least one of the following criteria has to be fulfilled: 10 or more people reported killed; 100 people reported affected; a call for international assistance; and/or declaration of a state of emergency.[a] Other databases use different thresholds for inclusion – for example, Swiss Reinsurance includes only those events with at least 20 deaths, while DesInventar includes any reported event regardless of the scale of loss.[b]

Disasters are usually classified by their triggering event as either natural or technological. Natural disasters include geophysical disasters such as volcanic eruptions and earthquakes, and hydro-meteorological disasters such as avalanches, landslides, droughts, famines, extreme temperatures, floods, fires and windstorms. Technological disasters include industrial and transport accidents.

Many researchers working on disasters have pointed to the inadequacy of this simplistic categorization between 'natural' and technological disasters. Allan Lavell points to the key distinction between natural hazards, socio-natural hazards (natural hazards that are socially induced), anthropogenic pollutant hazards and anthropogenic technological hazards – and the extent to which the scale and nature of most 'natural' disasters have been much influenced by human activities.[c] As noted already, there is no disaster without a vulnerable population.

Source: [a] CRED EM-DAT, see www.em-dat.net/. See also International Federation of Red Cross and Red Crescent Societies (2002) *World Disasters Report: Focus on Reducing Risk,* Oxford University Press, Oxford and New York, 239pp. [b] Pelling, M (2005) 'Disaster data: Building a foundation for disaster risk reduction', in International Federation of the Red Cross and Red Crescent Societies (eds) *World Disasters Report 2005,* pp173–180. [c] Lavell, A. (1999) *Natural and Technological Disasters: Capacity Building and Human Resource Development for Disaster Management,* Mimeo, 32pp.

Most urban research does not engage with disasters.[46] If disasters are understood as unusual events (usually 'natural' events) that require from the state a capacity to respond when they occur, these do not appear to be within the realm of conventional urban research or conventional urban governance. But if disasters are understood to be caused by urban development (or the scale of their impacts and their frequency increased by urban development) and, as Allan Lavell suggests, socially constructed with their impacts conditioned by existing social and spatial segregation, it is more difficult for urban research to ignore them.[47] Indeed, any urban researcher with an interest in poverty and vulnerability needs to integrate within their work an understanding of the current or potential impact of extreme weather events and other potential causes of disasters.

It is possible to envisage a trend in new investments by larger companies and corporations away from cities and city sites most at risk from extreme weather-related disasters and sea-level rise, which will hardly affect their operations. They have long been adept at shifting production to locations where profits are maximized and it is easy for them to factor in risks from climate change. But it is difficult to conceive of how many of the largest successful coastal cities most at risk from storms and sea-level rise will manage. Large sections of cities such as Mumbai and Shanghai (see Chapter 6), Dhaka (Chapter 4), Mombasa (Chapter 3) and Cotonou (Chapter 5) are at risk from sea-level rise. Mumbai, Shanghai and Dhaka are very large (each having well over 10 million inhabitants), have had considerable economic success in the last few decades, are of great importance to their nations' economies and cultures, and concentrate very large investments and economic interests. Most residents and smaller businesses have far fewer possibilities for moving – and face far more serious losses if the value of their properties declines. Meanwhile, the movement of larger companies and corporations out of large cities also threatens the cities' economic bases and the livelihoods of those who worked for these companies or provided goods and services to them or their workforces.

Cities by their very nature concentrate people and their homes, impermeable surfaces, physical capital, industries and wastes. This can make them very dangerous places in which to live and work, and make their populations very vulnerable to extreme weather events or other physical events that have the potential to be disasters. But this is best seen not as inherent to cities, but as the product of inadequate planning and governance. Concentration produces risk through, for instance, the dangerous conjunction of residential and industrial land uses, the lack of space for evacuation and emergency vehicle access, and the potential for the spread of communicable disease. A high proportion of lower-income groups may settle on hazardous sites (e.g. sites at risk from floods or landslides); but they do so because no other (safer) land is available to them – while also lacking access to the means to reduce their vulnerability.

Urban contexts generally increase the risk of what Allan Lavell has termed 'concatenated hazards' – as primary hazard leads to secondary hazard (e.g. floods creating water supply contamination), as well as 'natech' events, where natural hazards trigger technological disasters. On the ground, the impacts of natural and technological hazards, including pollution events, overlap and compound one another – and this is one of the defining challenges of urban disaster risk management.

Reducing the impact of extreme weather

The concentration of people and enterprises in urban areas also means economies of scale or proximity for many of the measures that reduce risks from extreme weather events – for instance, in the per capita cost of measures to lessen the risks (e.g. better watershed management or drainage reducing the scale of floods), reduce the risks when the event occurs (e.g. buildings better able to withstand floods and early warning systems to allow special measures to be taken), and respond rapidly and effectively when a disaster is imminent or happens. There is a greater capacity among a proportion of city dwellers to help pay for such measures if they are made aware of the risks and the measures are shown to be cost effective.

Improved competence, capacity and accountability within city and municipal governments almost by definition increases adaptation capacity and increases the possibilities of it being 'pro-poor'. Examples of this, in practice, include the environmental and social programmes in Porto Alegre and many other Brazilian cities, and the importance within this of participatory budgeting.[48] However, such examples are mainly from middle-income nations and usually nations that have made advances in strengthening local democracies and reducing anti-poor attitudes among those in government.

It has been suggested that after large disasters, a window of opportunity opens for political will to reform urban planning systems and budgets. But there is little evidence to show that disaster preparedness and risk reduction become institutionalized (see, in particular, Chapter 10). All too often, the next development challenge or political agenda replaces disaster risk reduction and the opportunity is lost. After Hurricane Mitch, there was progress in introducing new legislation; but urban concerns were not fully addressed, especially the links between disaster management and urban management, so urban planning was not fulfilling its potential in contributing to risk reduction.[49]

In many cities, civil society may be more receptive than local government to disaster risk reduction. The IPCC's Fourth Assessment noted various examples of where disaster preparedness at community level had helped to reduce death tolls – for instance, through new early warning systems and evacuation procedures (and the identification of safe places for evacuating to); it also noted the unevenness in the effectiveness of such systems in reaching marginal populations.[50] Even where decentralization has strengthened the capacities of local government, it is difficult to get cross-department agendas such as disaster risk reduction working. Specific sectors that are managed at the local level, such as water, housing, transport and education, can be key allies in mainstreaming disaster risk reduction, and, indeed, may already be undertaking actions that could be described as reducing risk.[51] But less is known about the development and application of disaster management plans in smaller urban centres where the capacity of local government and civil society is limited. Evidence from the Indian Ocean tsunami suggests that these smaller settlements are less likely than larger centres to have disaster management plans, and that in reconstruction, citizens and officials will be less prepared and less able to work effectively with external agencies for local benefit.[52]

Of course, the increasing frequency and growing human and economic cost of disasters from (say) storms/floods in urban areas does not give us any precise information about the likely future cost of climate change. But disaster loss data do provide a good starting point for estimating costs and give an idea of the vulnerability of urban populations to certain physical events that are likely to become more common and/or more intense in many places (see Chapter 3). In addition, the change in how urban disasters are understood and acted on, since they are recognized as failures to understand vulnerabilities and to act on these (see Chapter 10), has relevance for understanding how to build urban centres' resilience to climate change.

Cities and high-risk sites

IPCC Working Group II noted that rapid urbanization in most low- and middle-income nations often takes place in relatively high-risk areas, and that this is placing an increasing proportion of those nations' economies and populations at risk.[53] The issue, then, is why so many cities develop on dangerous sites with regard to risks from storms and floods (and other natural hazards including earthquakes). Six reasons can be suggested for this, although for most cities with populations facing high levels of risk, several of these are relevant:

1   *Economic or political reasons outweighed considerations of risk.* Sites that are at risk from storms, floods, earthquakes, etc. were attractive to those who originally founded and developed a city – for instance, because of a good river or sea harbour, a strategic location with regard to trade or territorial control, a ready supply of freshwater or a fertile delta. Most of the world's major cities are on the coast or beside major rivers because they were already important urban centres before railways, new roads and air transport changed transport systems. Most relied on river or sea ports as their main transport and communication link with other places – and, of course, river and ocean transport is still a key part of the global economy.

2   *The original city site may have been safe but the city has outgrown the site and expanded onto land that is at risk* – for instance, onto floodplains or up unstable hills or mountains (see, in particular, Chapters 6 and 10). Many city sites that were safe and well chosen for cities of 50,000 inhabitants (a comparatively large city 200 years ago) are not safe when the city expands to several million inhabitants. There are comparable problems with regards to freshwater supplies in many cities (i.e. where the size of the city and the increased demand for water has gone far beyond local water resources).

3   *City expansion and development can create new risks* – for instance, as urban development takes place without the necessary investments in protective infrastructure such as a fast-growing concentrated impermeable surface, a lack of investment in storm and surface drains, and new urban developments encroaching on or building over important natural drains (see, for instance, Chapters 4 and 9).

4   *Dangerous sites serve low-income households well in that they are the only places where they can find accommodation close to income-earning/livelihood opportunities.* There is a tension inherent in all cities between the need for a labour force willing to work for low wages and the way in which city land markets push up house prices beyond what much of this labour force can afford. This can be resolved or lessened by a range of means that reduce the cost of housing (including measures to increase the supply and reduce the cost of land for housing and high-quality public transport – bus, metro, light rail, suburban rail, etc.) or increase the income or house-purchasing capacity of low-income groups (e.g. housing subsidies for low-income households as used at scale in Chile and South Africa). But where this does not happen, large sections of the low-income population have to find accommodation within informal or illegal settlements, and the only way that the prices for this can be brought down are by distance from economic opportunity (which means long and expensive commutes), poor-quality, overcrowded and often insecure housing (including lack of provision for infrastructure and services), and high levels of risk (e.g. sites at risk of flooding, landslides or earthquakes).[54]

5   *Once a city has developed, it rarely disappears, even if it experiences some disastrous flood or earthquake because there are too many individuals, enterprises and institutions with an interest in that city's economy.* Most of the world's largest cities have been successful cities for hundreds of years; many have experienced catastrophic disasters but were rebuilt rather than being relocated.

6   *In most cities at risk from floods and storms, the wealthier groups and most formal enterprises do not face serious risks.*

The spatial distribution of urban populations in any nation is not the result of any careful plan to guide urban expansion to 'safe' sites. The main driver of city expansion (or stagnation or contraction) is where new or expanding private enterprises choose to concentrate (or avoid). This is also largely true for how each individual urban centre develops – as the localities within and around the urban centre with the most rapidly growing populations are associated with where new or expanding economic activities concentrate – although the physical growth of the urban centre is also influenced by where lower-income groups can (or cannot) get accommodation or land upon which housing can be built.[55]

So, in seeking to understand the links between city development and risk from climate change, one of the key issues is: to what extent are private enterprises influenced in their choice of location by risks related to climate change? Obviously, formal-sector private enterprises will not generally invest in sites that are risky – unless the risk of loss can be reduced by insurance or by the risk not actually threatening their production (it is particular geographic areas and particular population groups – usually low-income groups – that are most at risk). In addition, if risks from climate change are seen as distant threats that may affect city sites 20 or 50 or more years in the future, this will not provide much discouragement to invest, especially in successful cities. Dhaka, Mumbai and Shanghai have attracted much private investment despite their vulnerability to storms and sea-level rise.

More important is the potential impact upon the urban economy (and employment opportunities) and upon the local government's tax base if companies and corporations move when risk levels increase or after some particular extreme weather event. Even if such enterprises are not directly affected by an extreme weather event, the indirect effects – the disruption of electricity and water supplies or climate-sensitive inputs, the delay in deliveries of key inputs or difficulties in shipping goods to customers, and inconvenience to senior staff – may encourage movement elsewhere or the choice of new locations when enterprises expand.

The challenge facing national governments is how to encourage and support patterns of private investment within national boundaries that are less concentrated in high-risk sites – just as all city governments also have to address this within their own local jurisdictions. This is not easily done. It is also best done with the kind of long-term perspective (several decades' long) that all political systems find difficult. This may be done in ways that damage economic prospects – for instance, as the choice of 'safer' city sites favoured with incentives and infrastructure investments is determined by political factors and not by a careful assessment of where these are most needed.[56] Perhaps more worrying is the likely emergence in some nations of government measures to address the effects of this (trying to control population movements to high-risk sites rather than the private investment flows that underpin these movements) – in effect, a system of apartheid-like controls on the rights of people to move within their national boundaries, justified by the need to make urban patterns less vulnerable to climate change. Some evidence for this can already be seen in India with regard to which residential areas are at risk from new coastal zone regulations limiting developments close to the sea. This can also be seen in inappropriate post-disaster government policies, which did not allow low-income households to return to their settlements – and with land use over time transferred to higher-income residential, commercial or industrial use. The result is increased inequality and social tension without a reduction in disaster exposure. One example of this is the coastal buffer zone established in Sri Lanka, post-tsunami, forcing the relocation of villages, disrupting livelihoods and generating social tensions, while at the same time tourist businesses have expanded their operations into 'vacant' land. A comparable large coastal zone where all rebuilding was to be banned was also proposed in parts of Indonesia after the tsunami.[57]

The continuum of risk from everyday hazards to catastrophic disasters

When serious illness, injury or premature death, disruption to livelihoods and loss of property occur, this is always a 'disaster' for some individuals. But an event will be officially classified as a disaster only if it meets certain criteria – for instance, 10 or more people killed or 100 or more seriously affected (see Box 1.3). Disaster managers generally focus only on events officially classified as disasters, so non-disaster events (and small disasters – for example, fewer than ten people killed) are not considered. This means that such managers may not see the links between non-disaster events and disasters and the risk accumulation processes common in urban areas that increase disaster and non-disaster risks. Meanwhile, urban development policy-makers often focus on non-disaster risks (which, in most urban areas in low- and middle-income nations, contribute far more to health burdens and to poverty than disasters); but this means that they miss the potential links between risk reduction for everyday hazards and small and large disasters.

One way to get some idea of the likely costs of climate change-related disasters would be an analysis of the impact upon urban populations of disasters caused by triggers whose intensity or frequency climate change is likely to increase. Unfortunately, records on the impacts of disasters upon urban

Table 1.3 *Comparing disasters, 'small disasters' and everyday risks in low- and middle-income nations*

Nature of event	Disasters	Small disasters	Everyday risks
Frequency	Generally infrequent	Frequent (often seasonal)	Every day
Scale	Large or potential to be large: 10+ killed, 100+ seriously injured	3–9 people killed, 10+ injured	1–2 people killed, 1–9 injured
Impact upon all premature death and serious injury/ illness	Can be catastrophic for specific places and times but low overall	Probably significant and underestimated contribution	Main cause of premature death and serious injury
	Very large impact		Small impact
		Continuum of risk	
	Low	Frequency	Very high

Source: Bull-Kamanga, L., Diagne, K., Lavell, A., Lerise, F., MacGregor, H., Maskrey, A., Meshack, M., Pelling, M., Reid, H., Satterthwaite, D., Songsore, J., Westgate, K. and Yitambe, A. (2003) 'Urban development and the accumulation of disaster risk and other life-threatening risks in Africa', *Environment and Urbanization*, vol 15, no 1, April, pp193–204

populations are very inadequate. Only data by EM-DAT and Munich Reinsurance and Swiss Reinsurance have global coverage. EM-DAT data are not disaggregated to urban areas (and are held only at the national scale), while the Munich Re and Swiss Re datasets do have some spatially fixed data; but their focus is more on insured and economic losses than on human loss. All of these only include large disasters. Geo-referenced data are available from a growing collection of national-level databases following what is known as the DesInventar methodology (including 16 countries in Latin America and the Caribbean, states in the US and India, and some neighbourhoods in Cape Town, South Africa).

All of these datasets are undermined by the lack of an internationally agreed definition of a disaster event (or range of events at different levels of impact) and the lack of systematic data collection mechanisms. For the international datasets, data are drawn from the news media, non-governmental organization reports and declarations of emergency. This means that 'small disasters' are often not recorded as they are not necessarily reported in the media. The DesInventar methodology seeks to include 'small disasters' that EM-DAT does not record, and its application shows very large discrepancies between official lists of 'disasters' and the actual number of disasters. For instance, in Colombia, 87 disasters were recorded by EM-DAT, although there were 2200 further disasters that were not registered but that met official criteria for what constitutes a disaster, as well as 13,000 other smaller disasters.[58] A database in Cape Town that sought to record all events registered more than 12,500 incidents, which contrasts with the 600 identified large events and declared disasters;[59] almost half of these occurred in informal settlements. An analysis of disaster events in Mexico from 1970 to 2001 sought to document all events with at least one mortality; it was found that floods were the most common disaster, and one quarter of all deaths from flooding came from events with fewer than four deaths (i.e. much too small to be included in international disaster datasets).[60]

The above studies in particular cities and nations show the very large scale of injury, death and loss of property caused by extreme weather events or accidental fires that went unregistered as disasters or were excluded by the criteria used to define a 'disaster'. Such detailed local studies are needed in all urban centres, not only to show the health and other costs from extreme weather events (including 'small' disasters whose aggregate impact may be larger than events classified as 'disasters') but also because of the following:

- The number, territorial spread and impact of disasters or small disasters may be increasing rapidly.
- Risk from these may graduate in time to larger events, as populations and their vulnerabilities increase in the areas close to the hazard sources and as hazards grow in size and potential intensity.
- Developing an ability to intervene to prevent 'small' disasters or limit their damaging impacts can also serve to develop a capacity for doing so for larger events.[61]

Small disasters from extreme weather events that are recurrent – for instance, floods that happen every time there is heavy rainfall – can also undermine any community's resilience and its capacity to make the investments and adjustments needed to protect against larger disasters. This may lead to a general acceptance of risk, or a failure to critique the association of poverty and risk. The need for every urban centre to have strong, locally generated data on risks and local analyses of risk and risk accumulation processes is fundamental to facilitating adaptation.

The changes in understanding of what causes disasters, noted above, with disasters recognized as failures of development, have transformed perceptions of how to avoid them or greatly reduce their impact[62] – and this change in thinking has great relevance to reducing the vulnerability of city populations to climate change. This means a shift from focusing on hazard-prone areas and the increasing magnitude of losses (and on engineering and structural solutions) to understanding (and changing) the complex urban processes that increase risks – for instance, the range of 'risk accumulation' processes that are increasing the vulnerability of large sections of their populations to floods or landslides. This also means a shift in who is seen as responsible for addressing disasters. For instance, the armed forces may be given central responsibilities for responses to disasters – but they can do little or nothing to reduce risk from disasters in urban areas. There is recognition of the need to integrate disaster risk reduction within all line departments of government and to support community–government partnerships in identifying and acting to reduce risks. These two issues are also at the core of reducing vulnerability to climate change. But, as yet, only rarely has this change in understanding of what causes disasters meant a change in policies on disaster management. Local, national and international agencies with responsibility for conventional disaster management lack the skills and capacities to make such a change – and often the motivation to change, especially if their budget depends upon disasters to respond to. Addressing the development failures that underpin urban disasters is more difficult, especially for international agencies, and comes up against powerful vested interests. Meanwhile, few powerful urban actors benefit from risk reduction initiatives for those living in informal settlements.

Even attention to 'small disasters' is unlikely to register the impact of slower changes – for instance, changes in precipitation or temperature or freshwater availability that may be having increasingly serious impacts upon livelihoods or access to water for domestic use.

Building on the Intergovernmental Panel on Climate Change's Fourth Assessment Report

The most important documents with regard to getting governments and international agencies to pay attention to why adaptation is important are the reports of Working Group II of the IPCC. The vulnerabilities of urban populations and urban areas to climate change was discussed in some detail in the Third Assessment[63] and then expanded and extended in the Fourth Assessment.[64] The chapter in the Fourth Assessment on 'Industry, settlement and society' contains a valuable summary table of different aspects of climate change, the evidence for current impacts, projected future impacts and vulnerabilities, current and likely future impacts and zones, and people affected (see Table 1.4). It also notes the need to consider the impacts of abrupt climate change, while also observing that its significance is less clearly established.

The Fourth Assessment noted the following, all with high confidence:

> *The most vulnerable industries, settlements and societies are generally those in coastal and river floodplains, those whose economies are closely linked with climate-sensitive resources, and those in areas prone to extreme weather events, especially where rapid urbanization is occurring.*
>
> *Poor communities can be especially vulnerable, in particular those concentrated in high-risk areas. They tend to have more limited adaptive capacities and are more dependent on climate-sensitive resources such as local water and food supplies.*
>
> *Where extreme weather events become more intense and/or more frequent, the economic and social costs of those events will increase and these increases will be substantial in the areas most directly affected. Climate change impacts spread from directly impacted areas and sectors to other areas and sectors through extensive and complex linkages.* [65]

However, coverage in Chapter 7 of the IPCC's Fourth Assessment, from which Table 1.4 is drawn, was limited by the lack of detailed research on risk and vulnerability in urban areas. None of the chapters that are collected in this volume had been published when the IPCC chapter was written. Now that plans are under way for the IPCC's Fifth Assessment, it is hoped that the chapters in this volume will help to support a more comprehensive and detailed coverage of risk and vulnerability in urban areas in low- and middle-income nations. This will need to include an analysis of social and economic capacity and political will to make needed changes for adaptation and mitigation (see Chapter 15). This dual agenda of so-called climate proofing is essential in reducing the possibility of adaptation measures increasing greenhouse gas emissions and, thus, undermining mitigation (such as the relocation of low-income settlements that then require long-distance transport for work), and also to maximize opportunities for building mitigation into adaptation (such as greening cities and the promotion of low-energy solutions, and the use of renewable energy in urban building and planning regulations).[66]

Table 1.4 *Selected examples of current and projected impacts of climate change upon industry, settlement and society and their interaction with other processes*

Climate-driven phenomena	Evidence for current impact/vulnerability	Other processes/stresses	Projected future impact/vulnerability	Zones and groups affected
(a) Changes in extremes				
Tropical cyclones and storm surges	Flood and wind casualties and damages; economic losses; transport, tourism, infrastructure (e.g. energy and transport) and insurance	*Land use/ population density in flood-prone areas; flood defences; institutional capacities*	Increased vulnerability in storm-prone coastal areas; possible effects on settlements, health, tourism, economic and transportation systems, buildings and infrastructure	*Coastal areas, settlements and activities; regions and populations with limited capacities and resources; fixed infrastructure; insurance sector*
Extreme rainfall and riverine floods	Erosion/landslides; land flooding; settlements; transportation systems; infrastructure	*Similar to coastal storms plus drainage infrastructure*	Similar to coastal storms plus drainage infrastructure	*Similar to coastal storms*
Heat or cold waves	Effects on human health; social stability; requirements for energy, water and services (e.g. water or food storage); or food storage); infrastructure (e.g. energy, transport)	*Building design and internal temperature control; social contexts; institutional capacities*	Increased vulnerability in some regions and populations; health effects; changes in energy requirements	*Mid-latitude areas; elderly, very young, and/or very poor populations*
Drought	Water availability, livelihoods, energy generation, migration, and transportation in water bodies	*Water systems; competing water uses; energy demand; water-demand constraints*	Water resource challenges in affected areas; shifts in locations of population and economic activities; additional investments in water supply	*Semi-arid and arid regions; poor areas and populations; areas with human-induced water scarcity*

(b) Changes in means

Temperature	Energy demands and costs; urban air quality; thawing of permafrost soils; tourism and recreation; retail consumption; livelihoods; loss of melt water	Demographic and economic changes; land-use changes; technological innovations; air pollution; institutional capacities	Shifts in energy demand; worsening air quality; impacts upon settlements and livelihoods depending upon melt water; threats to settlements/ infrastructure from thawing permafrost soils in some regions	Very diverse, but greater vulnerability in places and populations with more limited capacities and resources for adaptation
Precipitation	Agricultural livelihoods; saline intrusion; water infrastructure; tourism; energy supplies	*Competition from other regions sectors; water resource allocation*	*Depending upon the region, vulnerability in some areas to effects of precipitation increases (e.g. flooding, but could be positive) and in some areas to decreases (see drought above)*	Poor regions and populations
Saline intrusion	Effects on water infrastructure	Trends in groundwater withdrawal	Increased vulnerability in coastal areas	Low-lying coastal areas, especially those with limited capacities and resources
Sea-level rise	Coastal land uses: flood risk; waterlogging; water infrastructure	*Trends in coastal development, settlement and land uses*	*Long-term increases in vulnerability of low-lying coastal areas*	*Same as above*
(c) Abrupt climate change	Analyses of potential	Demographic, economic and technological changes; institutional developments	Possible significant effects on most places and populations in the world, at least for a limited time	Most zones and groups

Note: Text in italics and bold indicates very significant in some areas and/or sectors; text in bold indicates significant; normal text indicates that significance is less clearly established.

Source: Wilbanks, T. and Romero Lankao, P. with Bao, M., Berkhout, F., Cairncross, S., Ceron, J.-P., Kapshe, M., Muir-Wood, R. and Zapata-Marti, R. (2007) 'Chapter 7: Industry, settlement and society,' in Parry, M., Canziani, O., Palutikof, J., van der Linden, P. and Hanson, C. (ed) *Climate Change 2007: Impacts, Adaptation and Vulnerability*, Contribution of Working Group II to the Fourth Assessment Report of the Intergovernmental Panel on Climate Change, Cambridge University Press, Cambridge and New York, pp357–390

Government roles and responsibilities

Urban contexts pose particular challenges for governments

The IPCC chapter noted above focused on all human settlements, not just urban centres. This focus is important for at least two reasons: first, a high proportion of those most at risk from climate change live in rural settlements; and, second, effective adaptation needs a consideration of rural and urban areas together because of the multiple linkages between them. But it is also important to understand why urban contexts influence the scale of risk and vulnerability and, as noted already, this is not a topic that has been given much attention in discussions of adaptation. Most urban contexts are different from most rural contexts with regard to the spatial concentration of people, hazards and stressors, the number of hazards (e.g. the range of infectious and parasitic diseases that can spread rapidly among concentrated populations, the close proximity of people, industries and industrial wastes) and their potential for exacerbating each other (e.g. floods contaminating water supplies which lead to water-related disease epidemics). Needed adaptation measures in relation to incomes, livelihoods, land-use management and infrastructure are also generally very different between rural and urban areas.

There are also complex relationships between this mix of hazards and the many (inter-related) components of urban poverty that include not only the urban poor's inadequate incomes and limited asset bases, but also very poor-quality housing, lack of basic infrastructure for providing water, sanitation, drainage and waste removal, and lack of voice and provision to ensure that their civil and political rights are respected. This greatly increases the vulnerability of the urban poor to most environmental hazards, including most of those related to climate change.

Certain urban characteristics are relevant to an understanding of risks from extreme weather events, as outlined below:[67]

- concentrated populations as a result of concentrated labour markets/income-earning opportunities for non-agricultural activities (which is what underpins virtually all urban centres);
- land markets unrelated to the land's agricultural potential, with land costs often pricing most or all low-income groups out of 'official' land-for-housing markets – this means that large sections of the urban population acquire land and build housing outside the official system of land-use controls and building standards that are meant to reduce risk, including stopping settlement on land at risk from floods and storms;
- related to the above, large sections of the population living in housing constructed informally, with no attention to needed health and safety standards and no regulatory framework to protect tenants (it is common in cities for large sections of the low-income population to rent accommodation, often whole households living in one room or many adults sharing a single room);

- high-density populations plus concentrations of their solid and liquid wastes (a particular problem if there are no sewers/drains and waste collection services to remove these); many provisions for disaster avoidance (e.g. thicker walls), response (access for emergency vehicles) or for reducing disaster impacts (readily available open spaces not at risk from falling buildings) are not possible in crowded low-income settlements;
- large impermeable surfaces and concentrations of buildings that disrupt natural drainage channels and accelerate runoff;
- areas within the city that become heat islands when temperatures are high and that exacerbate problems of heat stress – these often include areas with high concentrations of low-income groups;
- patterns of urban form and buildings that do not take current and future hazards into account, which generate increased scales and levels of risk from floods, landslides, fires and industrial accidents;
- industrialization, inadequate planning and poor design generating secondary risks from extreme weather (e.g. industrial chemicals or wastes contaminating floodwater);
- changes in the region around cities that cause or exacerbate risks; poor watershed management, often a particular problem for city governments as the watershed usually lies outside their jurisdiction – it is also common for cities to expand and develop in ways that erode natural defences or buffers (e.g. wetlands); and
- city governments and urban economies unable to cope with sudden movements of people into a city in response to crises elsewhere (linked to extreme weather events nearby or to conflict).

Government and the public good

Whether or not the urban characteristics noted above that can increase risk are present is much influenced by the quality and capacity of local governments. There are very large differentials within most urban centres in people's exposure to hazards from extreme weather, and we need to understand the role of the state in this and whether it acts to create or contribute to these differentials or to modify and reduce them. 'Good local governance' is the main means through which such differentials to risks from extreme weather events (and many other environmental hazards) are reduced. This can take place through government demands made and enforced on private enterprises (e.g. concerning construction standards, occupational health and safety, pollution control, waste management, payment for infrastructure and services, and disaster preparedness) and what it provides, supports and encourages for the population – especially those most at risk. *One of the most powerful measures of the quality of urban governance is the extent to which it reduces or removes the differentials in risk from serious injury, illness or premature death between high- and low-income groups with regard to the whole continuum of environmental hazards, including disasters and 'small' disasters.*

Urban governments typically have a large and diverse range of roles and responsibilities with regard to the built environment, infrastructure and services that have relevance for adaptation (see Table 1.5). Urban governments should have a key role as risk reducers for climate change by:

- providing infrastructure and services (perhaps with some of it contracted to private enterprises or non-governmental organizations);
- guiding where development takes place – for instance, influencing where urban settlements develop and where they do not, and what provision there is to avoid floods, fires, etc.;
- regulating building design and construction (including support and training for builders, especially those who are active in building within low-income settlements);
- regulating hazardous activities that can produce disasters (including industries and transport);
- influencing land availability (through land-use regulations, zoning and official procedures for buying or obtaining land and what can be built on it) – the quality of land-use management influences the proportion of poorer groups having to live on hazardous or disaster-prone sites;
- encouraging and supporting household/community action that reduces risk (e.g. better-quality housing, safer sites, good infrastructure and good disaster preparedness), including support for community-based adaptation;
- providing 'law and order', which should also act to protect low-income groups from risk; and
- coordinating and supporting links between protection (disaster avoidance), disaster preparedness and post-disaster response and rebuilding – for instance, ensuring that all the tasks above integrate with agencies responsible for disaster preparedness and response.

Table 1.5 *The role of city/municipal governments in adaptation*

Role of city/ municipal government	Protection (disaster avoidance)	Disaster preparedness	Immediate post-disaster response	Rebuilding
Built environment				
Building codes	High		High[a]	High
Land-use regulations and property registration	High	Some		High
Public building construction and maintenance	High	Some		High
Urban planning (including zoning and development controls)	High		High[a]	High

Table 1.5 *The role of city/municipal governments in adaptation* (Cont'd)

Role of city/municipal government	Protection (disaster avoidance)	Disaster preparedness	Immediate post-disaster response	Rebuilding
Infrastructure				
Piped water including treatment	High	Some	High	High
Sanitation	High	Some	High	High
Drainage	High	High[b]	High	High
Roads, bridges, pavements	High		High	High
Electricity	High	Some?	High	High
Solid waste disposal facilities	High	Some?		High
Wastewater treatment	High			High
Services				
Fire protection	High	Some	High	Some
Public order/police/early warning	Medium	High	High	Some
Solid waste collection	High	High[b]	High	High
Schools	Medium	Medium		
Healthcare/public Health/environmental Health/ambulances	Medium	Medium	High	High
Public transport	Medium	High	High	High
Social welfare (includes provision for child care and old age care)	Medium	High	High	High
Disaster response (over and above those listed above)			High	High

Notes: The actual allocation of responsibility and of access to funding between city/municipal governments and other institutions will obviously differ between countries; the intention of this table is to make clear the many roles that city/municipal governments should have in adaptation. 'High' denotes that they have the sole or main responsibility; 'medium' indicates that they have substantial responsibility; 'some' implies some role or responsibility but with other institutions having the main responsibility.

[a] Obviously it is important that these do not inhibit rapid responses.
[b] Clearing/de-silting drains and ensuring collection of solid wastes has particular importance just prior to extreme rainfall; many cities face serious flooding from expected extreme rainfall (e.g. the monsoon rains), and this is often caused or exacerbated by the failure to keep storm and surface drains in good order.

Source: Satterthwaite, D. (2007) *Integrating Adaptation to Climate Change in Decision-Making at the Urban/Municipal Level in Low- and Middle-Income Countries*, First draft, Prepared for the OECD Development Assistance Committee, Paris, 33pp

Where urban governments fulfil these key roles, levels of risk for their populations and economies are much reduced, and urban development is associated with much lowered risks. But where urban governments only partially fulfil these roles – or fail to fulfil them – levels of risk are substantially increased.

The justification for having city and municipal governments is that only they can act to address certain key issues with regard to the public good – for instance, ensuring provision of infrastructure and services essential for health and economic success, and controlling or regulating the actions and activities of individuals, households or enterprises that are dangerous or that transfer risks or costs to others. This is not to imply that it is city governments (or higher levels of government) that need to provide all infrastructure and services, or even undertake all the needed policing of rules and regulations; but they have to provide and fund the legal and institutional framework that ensures this with accountability to city populations (usually achieved through city governments overseen by elected politicians).

For climate change, locally accountable government institutions acting 'in the public good' have particular importance for five reasons:

1 Many of the needed measures are public goods in the sense that they will benefit populations, including future residents and others who do not contribute to these public goods. Without government action, such goods will be underprovided.
2 The appropriateness of the regulatory framework for land use, infrastructure and buildings and the extent to which it is applied will have a huge influence on the extent of appropriate adaptation to climate change – and within this 'appropriateness' is the need for such measures not to disadvantage lower-income groups and not to draw investment away from other needed tasks (or run up large debt burdens for city governments).
3 There are many no-cost or low-cost measures, which, if taken now, can help to ensure that any rapidly growing city builds greater resilience into its growth process (and physical and infrastructure expansion). Markets and most individual and community initiatives will not act to reduce risks that are far in the future – but appropriate incentives and controls can make them act on these, without high costs. Most urban disasters have 20- to 30-year processes of risk accumulation that can be identified and acted on.
4 There are very large economies of scale and proximity from citywide action for adaptation (and also for mitigation): the total cost of all households and enterprises making provision for themselves would be much higher and much less effective.
5 A reliance on market mechanisms such as insurance or the capacity to purchase safe housing to produce the necessary changes will not serve those unable to access the formal housing market or afford insurance – which in urban centres in low- and middle-income nations means most of the

population and most enterprises. Public–private partnerships have been suggested where 'the public sector sets a rigorous framework to reduce the physical risks, provides cover for high levels of risk or segments with high administration costs, and sets the rules for a private market for other risks, while the private sector provides services and offers coverage for lower levels of risk and segments that are more easily accessible'.[68] But in most urban areas in low- and middle-income nations, governments do not provide the framework for risk reduction for lower-income households. It is difficult to see how insurance companies can offer good coverage at affordable premiums to low-income households who live in particularly dangerous sites to which governments will not provide infrastructure. The potential for public–private partnerships to address other development issues such as improving provision for water and sanitation for low-income households in urban areas has long been greatly overstated,[69] and there is a danger that it will also be overstated for insurance.

An obvious example of the need for government to act 'in the public good' is measures to stop development on a floodplain or areas of key natural defences against floods, or other areas where development would increase the whole urban centre's vulnerability to the impacts of climate change. Those who own the land may want to develop it, and the state may need to step in to represent the public interest. However, if less well-off residents currently occupy the land, there is a danger that compensation will be insufficient, and even that evicting them would not deploy the 'public interest'. The time dimension is important in such examples since developers or early settlers will be thinking short term but are setting in place infrastructure and settlement patterns for the long term.[70]

Whether or not local governments act in the public good obviously depends upon their relations with the inhabitants in their jurisdiction. Community-based adaptation has particular importance here, both for what it can achieve and for how it can greatly increase the effectiveness of local government action – as discussed in detail in Chapter 16.[71] Of course, the possibilities of city governments ensuring 'the public good' also relate to the policies and practices of higher levels of government, and these have rarely provided adequate or appropriate support for the development of local competence and capacity. A review of what national governments in low- and middle-income nations are doing on adaptation[72] produced the following tentative conclusions:

- Many governments are initiating or sponsoring studies of the likely impacts of climate change, but most are undertaken by natural scientists who lack the knowledge, capacity and often the interest to engage with impacts upon urban areas. This is the case even in nations where more than 90 per cent of GDP is generated by urban-based enterprises and most of the people live and work in urban areas.

- Many (or possibly most) of these studies of climate change impacts are funded by international agencies, and perhaps this diminishes national, city and local governments' interest in them.
- There is an urgent need for locally undertaken studies because of the extent to which local context shapes vulnerabilities and the nature of vulnerable groups and adaptation possibilities. The lack of a strong information base on what local impacts climate change is likely to bring is inhibiting this.

Many central governments are beginning to do something about adaptation; but this has yet to engage the interest of the larger, more powerful national ministries or agencies, or city or municipal governments. Debra Roberts's chapter on Durban (Chapter 11) is interesting for showing the importance of a locally generated study of 'impacts' rooted in local contexts and possibilities for getting the attention of city government. It is also interesting to see the difficulties experienced by those in government working on environmental issues in getting the attention of their colleagues; also worth noting is the extent to which recent storms in Durban helped to sensitize local politicians and civil servants.

The possibilities of building the necessary measures for adaptation into urban development are further limited by the reluctance or refusal of many development assistance agencies to engage with urban development and, in their support for 'good governance', to recognize the importance of 'good local governance'.[73] However, it is also necessary to recognize the complexities in changing political and institutional systems fast enough to cope with such rapid change. The development of more competent, capable and accountable metropolitan, city and municipal governance structures that are able to address environmental risks in today's high-income nations was a slow and highly contested process. It was generally underpinned by greater economic prosperity than is evident today in many low-income nations. The political and institutional constraints on national and local governments being able to develop appropriate policies and measures for climate change adaptation are still not recognized in much of the literature on adaptation.

Planning for adaptation faces very large infrastructure deficits. The poor quality of infrastructure and the lack of maintenance characteristic of so many low- and middle-income nations are key determinants of dams failing and public hospitals, schools, bridges and highways collapsing during or after extreme weather events. There are complex issues of quality control and accountability for public works – for instance, the lack of transparency in procurement, which frequently leads to corruption and poor-quality work. Decentralization has often transferred responsibility for infrastructure maintenance to state and local authorities but without the resources and capacities to fulfil this. The collapse or damage to buildings and infrastructure obviously increases the indirect costs of climate disasters by paralysing economic activities and increasing the costs of reconstruction.[74]

While most adaptation in cities needs local knowledge and capacity, higher levels of government have critical roles to play in ensuring that city governments have this knowledge and capacity – and the funding and expertise to draw on if necessary. One area that needs addressing is the information base to encourage and support action. The density of weather watch stations in Africa is eight times lower than the minimum level recommended by the World Meteorological Organization.[75] Many nations are unable even to monitor the climate, let alone forecast changes;[76] the same is also true for most urban centres. As discussed already, there is a similar dearth of systematic collection of data on hazard events and impacts from everyday crises to 'small disasters' to catastrophic events. This is not just a problem in African cities, but also a major constraint on developing appropriate policy to support adaptation worldwide.

In Latin America, there has been progress in developing the necessary information base at national level – for instance, the increasingly reliable seasonal climate forecasts to understand and predict the El Niño and La Niña phenomena.[77] Improvements exist in climate monitoring and remote sensing, which provide better early warnings on complex climate-related hazards.[78] Different regional networks have been established to predict seasonal climate and climate extremes; but this work needs to be extended to support development of local knowledge and capacity within city governments.

Notes

1. This text is drawn from sections in Satterthwaite, D., Huq, S., Pelling, M., Reid, H. and Romero Lankao, P. (2007) *Adapting to Climate Change in Urban Areas: The Possibilities and Constraints in Low- and Middle-Income Countries*, Human Settlements Climate Change and Cities Discussion Series 1, IIED, London, 107pp.

2. Romero Lankao, P. (2007) 'Are we missing the point? Particularities of urbanization, sustainability and carbon emissions in Latin American cities', *Environment and Urbanization* vol 19, no 1, pp157–175; also Dodman, D. (2009) 'Blaming cities for climate change? An analysis of urban greenhouse gas emissions inventories', *Environment and Urbanization*, vol 21, no 1, pp185–201.

3. Wilbanks, T. and Romero Lankao, P. with Bao, M., Berkhout, F., Cairncross, S., Ceron, J.-P., Kapshe, M., Muir-Wood, R. and Zapata-Marti, R. (2007) 'Industry, settlement and society', in Parry, M., Canziani, O., Palutikof, J., van der Linden, P. and Hanson, C. (eds) *Climate Change 2007: Impacts, Adaptation and Vulnerability*, Contribution of Working Group II to the Fourth Assessment Report of the Intergovernmental Panel on Climate Change, Cambridge University Press, Cambridge and New York, pp357–390.

4. There are some large-scale climate events that have the potential to cause very large impacts, but for which there is less certainty as to whether or when they will occur – for instance, the deglaciation of the Greenland ice sheet and the West Antarctic ice sheet. These events are not considered in this chapter.

5. *The Hyogo Framework for Action 2005–2015: Building the Resilience of Nations and Communities to Disasters*: see www.unisdr.org/eng/hfa/hfa.htm.

6. World Bank statistics suggest that the total number of poor urban dwellers in low- and middle-income countries increased between 1993 and 2002, although the proportion of the urban population that was poor fell. See Ravallion, M., Chen, S. and Sangraula, P. (2007) *New Evidence on the Urbanization of Global Poverty*, WPS4199, World Bank, Washington DC, 48pp. But this uses the widely discredited 'US$1 a day' poverty line, which, for large sections of the urban population, is an inappropriate poverty line because US$1 a day will not get close to covering the cost of food and basic non-food necessities (including housing, transport, water, sanitation and keeping children at school). Applying the US$1 a day poverty line suggests that less than 1 per cent of the urban population of China, the Middle East, North Africa, Eastern Europe and Central Asia were poor in 2002. Applying this poverty line to Latin America and the Caribbean means that less than 10 per cent of their urban population are poor. This greatly understates the proportion of the urban population facing serious deprivation. See Satterthwaite, D. (2004) *The Under-Estimation of Urban Poverty in Low- and Middle-Income Nations*, Human Settlements Poverty Reduction in Urban Areas Discussion Series 14, IIED, London, 69pp.

7. UN-Habitat (2003a) *The Challenge of Slums: Global Report on Human Settlements 2003*, Earthscan, London.

8. See reference 7.

9. UN-Habitat (2003) *Water and Sanitation in the World's Cities: Local Action for Global Goals*, Earthscan, London.

10. Hardoy, J. E., Mitlin, D. and Satterthwaite, D. (2001) *Environmental Problems in an Urbanizing World: Finding Solutions for Cities in Africa, Asia and Latin America*, Earthscan, London, 448pp; also see reference 7; see reference 9; and UN-Habitat (2006) *Meeting Development Goals in Small Urban Centres; Water and Sanitation in the World's Cities 2006*, Earthscan, London.

11. For a review of infant and child mortality rates in urban areas, drawing on the demographic and health surveys, see Satterthwaite, D. (2007) 'In pursuit of a healthy urban environment in low- and middle-income nations', in Marcotullio, P. J. and McGranahan, G. (eds) *Scaling Urban Environmental Challenges: From Local to Global and Back*, Earthscan, London, pp69–105.

12. See reference 10, Hardoy et al (2001); also see reference 11.

13. See, for instance, Satterthwaite, D. (2001) 'Reducing urban poverty: Constraints on the effectiveness of aid agencies and development banks and some suggestions for change', *Environment and Urbanization*, vol 13, no 1, April, pp137–157; also Tannerfeldt, G. and Ljung, P. (2006) *More Urban, Less Poor: An Introduction to Urban Development and Management*, Earthscan and Sida, London, 190pp.

14. See reference 10, Hardoy et al (2001); also see Chapter 14.

15. For a summary, see du Plessis, J. (2005) 'The growing problem of forced evictions and the crucial importance of community-based, locally appropriate alternatives', *Environment and Urbanization*, vol 17, no 1, April, pp123–134.

16. See, for instance, Kelly, P. F. (1998) 'The politics of urban–rural relationships: Land conversion in the Philippines', *Environment and Urbanization*, vol 10, no 1, April, pp35–54.

17. See, for instance, López Follegatti, J. L. (1999) 'Ilo: A city in transformation', *Environment and Urbanization* vol 11, no 2, October, pp181–202; also Mitlin, D. and Muller, A. (2004) 'Windhoek, Namibia: Towards progressive urban land policies in Southern Africa', *International Development Planning Review*, vol 26, no 2, pp167–186.

18. The analysis of urban change and its drivers is drawn from Satterthwaite, D. (2007) *The Transition to a Predominantly Urban World and Its Underpinnings*, Human Settlements Urban Change Discussion Series 4, IIED, London, 90pp, but updated by drawing on a new dataset on urban population statistics: see United Nations, Department of Economic and Social Affairs, Population Division (2008) *World Urbanization Prospects: the 2007 Revision*, CD-ROM Edition, data in digital form (POP/DB/WUP/Rev.2007), United Nations, New York.

19. See reference 18, United Nations (2008).

20. According to the most recent United Nations statistics, the transition to when more than half the world's population now lives in urban areas occurred in 2008. However, it may be that the world became more than half urban some years ago. Many cities undercount their populations by excluding those who live in illegal settlements. Many governments deliberately understate their urban populations by classifying most small urban centres as rural. See reference 18, Satterthwaite (2007).

21. Graumann, J. V. (1977) 'Orders of magnitude of the world's urban and rural population in history', *United Nations Population Bulletin*, vol 8, United Nations, New York, pp16–33.

22. See reference 18, Satterthwaite (2007).

23. See Montgomery, M. R., Stren, R., Cohen, B. and Reed, H. E. (eds) (2003) *Cities Transformed: Demographic Change and its Implications in the Developing World*, The National Academy Press (North America)/ Earthscan (Europe), Washington, DC, 518pp.

24. Chandler, T. and Fox, G. (1974) *3000 Years of Urban Growth*, Academic Press, New York and London.

25. Urbanization is understood to be an increase in the proportion of national populations living in urban areas.

26. There are important exceptions, such as migration flows away from wars/conflicts and disasters.

27. See reference 18, Satterthwaite (2007).

28. See reference 18, Satterthwaite (2007).

29. See reference 2.

30. See reference 18, Satterthwaite (2007).

31. Examples are Curitiba and Porto Alegre, both among the most rapidly growing cities in Latin America over the last 50 years, and both with high standards of living. See Menegat, R. (2002) 'Participatory democracy and sustainable development: Integrated urban environmental management in Porto Alegre, Brazil', *Environment and Urbanization*, vol 14, no 2, October, pp181–206; also Rabinovitch, J. (1992) 'Curitiba: Towards sustainable urban development', *Environment and Urbanization*, vol 4, no 2, October, pp62–77.

32. Satterthwaite, D. (2006) *Outside the Large Cities: The Demographic Importance of Small Urban Centres and Large Villages in Africa, Asia and Latin America*, Human Settlements Urban Change Discussion Series 3, IIED, London, 30pp.

33. Satterthwaite, D. and Tacoli, C. (2003) *The Urban Part of Rural Development: The Role of Small and Intermediate Urban Centres in Rural and Regional Development and Poverty Reduction,* Human Settlements Rural–Urban Linkages Discussion Series 9, IIED, London, 64pp. See also a great range of case studies on rural–urban linkages in Tacoli, C. (ed) (2006) *The Earthscan Reader in Rural–Urban Linkages,* Earthscan Publications, London, 329pp.

34. Hardoy, J. E. and Satterthwaite, D. (1989) *Squatter Citizen: Life in the Urban Third World,* Earthscan, London, 388pp; also see reference 33, Satterthwaite and Tacoli (2003).

35. See reference 33, Satterthwaite and Tacoli (2003); also Benjamin, S. (2000) 'Governance, economic settings and poverty in Bangalore', *Environment and Urbanization,* vol 12, no 1, April, pp35–56.

36. This is referring specifically to urbanization, understood to be an increase in the proportion of the population living in urban centres.

37. See reference 3.

38. See reference 3.

39. Hoeppe, P. and Gurenko, E. N. (2007) 'Scientific and economic rationales for innovative climate insurance solutions', in Gurenko, E. N. (ed) *Climate Change and Insurance: Disaster Risk Financing in Developing Countries,* Earthscan Publications, London, pp607–620.

40. Borger, J. (2007) 'Climate change disaster is upon us, warns UN', *The Guardian,* 5 October, p20, reporting on information released by the UN Office for the Coordination of Humanitarian Affairs.

41. United Nations Human Settlements Programme (2007) *Enhancing Urban Safety and Security; Global Report on Human Settlements 2007,* Earthscan Publications, London, 480pp; also Wisner, B. and Pelling, M. (ed) (2008) 'African cities of hope and risk', in Pelling, M. and Wisner, B. (ed) *Disaster Risk Reduction; Cases from Urban Africa,* Earthscan Publications, London, pp19–45.

42. Kakhandiki, A. and Shah, H. (1998) 'Understanding time variation of risk: Crucial implications for megacities worldwide', *Applied Geography,* vol 18, no 1, pp47–53.

43. EM-DAT: the OFDA/CRED International Disaster Database (www.em-dat.net), Université Catholique de Louvain, Brussels, Belgium.

44. Cairncross, S. and Alvarinho, M. (2006) 'The Mozambique floods of 2000; health impacts and response', in Few, R. and Matthies, F. (eds) *Flood Hazards and Health,* Earthscan Publications, London, pp111–127.

45. Zapata-Marti, R. (2004) *The 2004 Hurricanes in the Caribbean and the Tsunami in the Indian Ocean: Lessons and Policy Challenges for Development and Disaster Reduction,* LC/MEX/L.672, Estudios y Perspectivas Series, 35, 62pp.

46. Pelling, M. (2003) *The Vulnerability of Cities,* Earthscan Publications, London; also Pelling, M. and Wisner, B. (eds) (2008) *Disaster Risk Reduction: Cases from Urban Africa,* Earthscan Publications, London; Mitchell, J. K. (1999) *The Crucibles of Hazard: Mega-cities and Disasters in Transition,* UNU Press, Tokyo; and Warmsler, C. (2008) *Managing Urban Disaster Risk,* Lund University Press, Lund.

47. Lavell, A. (2001) *Environmental Degradation, Risk and Urban Disasters: Issues and Concepts – Towards the Definition of a Research Agenda,* Mimeo.

48. See reference 31, Menegat (2002); also Cabannes, Y. (2004) 'Participatory budgeting: A significant contribution to participatory democracy', *Environment and Urbanization*, vol 16, no 1, April, pp27–46.

49. Gavidia, J. and Crivellari, A. (2006) 'Legislation as a vulnerability factor', *Open House International*, vol 31, no 1, pp84–89.

50. See reference 3; also Vale, L. J. and Campanella, T. J. (eds) (2004) *The Resilient City: How Modern Cities Recover from Disaster*, Oxford University Press, Oxford, 392pp.

51. Pelling, M. (2007) *Making Disaster Risk Reduction Work*, ProVention Forum 2007, ProVention Consortium, www.proventionconsortium.org/themes/default/pdfs/Forum_2007_report.pdf.

52. ACHR (Asian Coalition for Housing Rights) (2005) 'Tsunami: How Asia's precarious coastal settlements are coping after the tsunami', *Housing by People in Asia*, vol 16, ACHR, Bangkok, 52pp.

53. See reference 3.

54. See reference 10, Hardoy et al (2001).

55. Torres, H., Alves, H. and Aparecida de Oliveira, M. (2007) 'São Paulo peri-urban dynamics: Some social causes and environmental consequences', *Environment and Urbanization* vol 19, no 1, April, pp207–233.

56. Note the long history of government policies to promote the growth of smaller urban centres or 'undeveloped regions' that have been ineffective and often very expensive.

57. See reference 52; also ACHR (Asian Coalition for Housing Rights) (2006) *Tsunami Update*, ACHR, Bangkok, 16pp.

58. Marulanda, M. C., Cardona, O. D. and Barbat, A. H. (undated) *Revealing the Impact of Small Disasters to Economic And Social Development*, United Nations University, Institute for Environment and Human Security, UNU, Tokyo, 21pp, www.ehs.unu.edu/file.php?id=295.

59. Bull-Kamanga, L., Diagne, K., Lavell, A., Lerise, F., MacGregor, H., Maskrey, A., Meshack, M., Pelling, M., Reid, H., Satterthwaite, D., Songsore, J., Westgate, K. and Yitambe, A. (2003) 'Urban development and the accumulation of disaster risk and other life-threatening risks in Africa', *Environment and Urbanization*, vol 15, no 1, April, pp193–204; also Pharoah, R. (2008) 'Fire risk in informal settlements in Cape Town, South Africa', in Pelling, M. and Wisner, B. (ed) *Disaster Risk Reduction: Cases from Urban Africa*, Earthscan Publications, London, pp109–130.

60. Data source is DesInventar, www.desinventar.org/desinventar.html.

61. Lavell, A. (1999) *Natural and Technological Disasters: Capacity Building and Human Resource Development for Disaster Management*, Mimeo, 32pp.

62. See, for instance, the work of LA RED in Latin America; and the work of Peri-peri and AURAN in Africa described in Bull Kamanga et al (2003), see reference 59; also Pelling, M. (2003) *The Vulnerability of Cities: Natural Disasters and Social Resilience*, Earthscan, London, 212pp.

63. Scott, M., Gupta, S., Jáuregui, E., Nwafor, J., Satterthwaite, D., Wanasinghe, Y. A. D. S., Wilbanks, T. and Yoshino, M. (2001) 'Chapter 7: Human settlements, energy and industry', in McCarthy, J. J., Canziani, O. F., Leary, N. A., Dokken, D. J. and White, K. S. (ed) *Climate Change 2001: Impacts, Adaptation, and Vulnerability*, Contribution of Working Group II to the Third Assessment Report of the

Intergovernmental Panel on Climate Change, Cambridge University Press, Cambridge and New York.

64. See reference 3.
65. Adger, N., Aggarwal, P., Agrawala, S. et al (2007) *Climate Change 2007: Impacts, Adaptation and Vulnerability: Summary for Policy Makers*, Contribution of Working Group II to the Fourth Assessment Report of the Intergovernmental Panel on Climate Change, IPCC Secretariat, WHO and UNEP, Geneva, p7.
66. Pelling, M., Navarrette, D. and Redclift, M. (2008) *Urban Transformations and Social Learning for Climate Proofing in the Mexican Caribbean*, Working Paper 6, Environment, Politics and Development Group, Department of Geography, King's College London, London.
67. Based on list in reference 62.
68. Dlugolecki, A. and Hoekstra, E. (2007) 'The role of the private market in catastrophe insurance', in Gurenko, E. N. (ed) *Climate Change and Insurance: Disaster Risk Financing in Developing Countries*, Earthscan Publications, London, p648.
69. Budds, J. and McGranahan, G. (2003) 'Are the debates on water privatization missing the point? Experiences from Africa, Asia and Latin America', *Environment and Urbanization*, vol 15, no 2, October, pp87–114.
70. There are examples of city governments that have combined watershed protection with measures to improve conditions for those living in informal settlements in these areas. See van Horen, B. (2001) 'Developing community-based watershed management in Greater São Paulo: The case of Santo André', *Environment and Urbanization*, vol 13, no 1, April, pp209–222.
71. For more discussion of community-based adaptation, see reference 1; also Huq, S. and Reid, H. (2007) *Community-Based Adaptation: A Briefing*, IIED, London, 2pp. For a detailed discussion of the role of community organizations in reducing risks from disasters, see Co, R. and Christopher, J. (2009) *Community-Driven Disaster Intervention: The Experience of the Homeless Peoples' Federation, Philippines*, IIED/ACHR working paper, IIED, London.
72. See reference 1; see also Chapter 14.
73. See reference 13, Satterthwaite (2001); also Crespin, J. (2006) 'Aiding local action: The constraints faced by donor agencies in supporting effective, pro-poor initiatives on the ground', *Environment and Urbanization*, vol 18, no 2, October, pp433–450.
74. Charvériat, C. (2000) *Natural Disasters in Latin America and the Caribbean: An Overview of Risk*, Inter-American Development Bank, Washington, DC, p85.
75. Washington, R., Harrison, M. and Conway, D. (2004) *African Climate Report: A Report Commissioned by the UK Government to Review African Climate Science, Policy and Options for Action*, DFID/DEFRA, December.
76. Stern, N. (2007) *The Economics of Climate Change: the Stern Review*, Cambridge University Press, Cambridge, 692pp.
77. Magrin, G., Garcia, G., Cruz Choque, D., Giménez, J. C., Moreno, A. R., Nagy, G. J., Nobre, C. and Villamizar, A. (2007) 'Chapter 13: Latin America' in Parry, M., Canziani, O., Palutikof, J., van der Linden, P. and Hanson, C. (eds) *Climate Change 2007: Impacts, Adaptation and Vulnerability*, Contribution of Working Group II to the Fourth Assessment Report of the Intergovernmental Panel on Climate Change, Cambridge University Press, Cambridge and New York, pp581–615.

78. Adger, W. N., Agrawala, S., Mirza, M., Conde, C., O'Brien, K., Pulhin, J., Pulwarty, R., Smit, B. and Takahashi, K. (2007) 'Chapter 17: 'Assessment of adaptation practices, options, constraints and capacity', in Parry, M., Canziani, O., Palutikof, J., van der Linden, P. and Hanson, C. (eds) *Climate Change 2007: Impacts, Adaptation and Vulnerability*, Contribution of Working Group II to the Fourth Assessment Report of the Intergovernmental Panel on Climate Change, Cambridge University Press, Cambridge and New York, pp717–743.

2

RISK AND VULNERABILITY
FOR CITIES

The Rising Tide: Assessing the Risks of Climate Change and Human Settlements in Low-Elevation Coastal Zones

Gordon McGranahan, Deborah Balk and Bridget Anderson

Introduction

This chapter focuses on human settlements and, in particular, urban settlements in low-elevation coastal zones (LECZs). To the extent that low-elevation coastal populations are at risk from sea-level rise, stronger storms and other seaward hazards induced by climate change, it is important to assess the size of these populations and how they are distributed internationally. Similarly, it is important to gain a better understanding of how coastal settlements are changing, especially in light of the self-reinforcing and cumulative character of urban development and the difficulties inherent in shifting the direction of population movements and adapting to increasing risk. Mitigation may be the best means of avoiding risks related to climate change; but it is too late to rely solely on mitigation. Migration away from lowest elevation coastal zones will be important, but can be costly and difficult to implement without causing severe disruptions. Modification of the prevailing forms of coastal settlement, so as to protect local residents, will also be needed.

In addition to being at risk from seaward hazards, coastal populations can be a burden on coastal ecosystems, many of which are already under stress. As we have shown elsewhere, coastal systems are more densely populated – in both urban and rural areas – than any other zones defined for the Millennium Ecosystem Assessment (MA), except for the urban systems themselves.[1] This is a further reason for monitoring and adapting coastal settlements, particularly since in some circumstances the loss of ecosystem services can make urban settlements more prone to disaster, amplifying the risks of climate change.

Despite the spatial nature of changing human settlements and urban development – and their relation to environmental conditions such as coastal hazards – urbanization is often analysed without any spatially explicit framework.[2] Prior studies with moderate-resolution spatial data have shown that, historically, populations have preferred to live within 100km of coasts and near major rivers.[3] But a systematic global assessment has not been undertaken of urban areas in a narrower coastal band – that is, those at potential risk from events related to climate change. This chapter fills that gap and begins to examine the implications for vulnerability to climate change.

This study integrates recently constructed, spatially explicit global databases and analyses them to assess the distribution of population and settlement size in the LECZ. The chapter first examines the critical issues involving LECZs and the risks of climate change. It then reviews the methodology for data integration and analysis. The findings are presented for different country groups (e.g. by region and by economic status) and for some of the countries with particularly large populations or population shares in the LECZ. For China and Bangladesh, some of the changes between 1990 and 2000 are presented. The chapter ends with a summary discussion, emphasizing some of the implications of these findings.

Climate change, coastal settlement and urban vulnerabilities

Both urban disasters and environmental hot spots are already located disproportionately in low-lying coastal areas.[4] Climate change will increase the risk of both. In particular, rising sea levels will increase the risk of floods, and stronger tropical storms may further increase the flood risk. Low-income groups living on floodplains are especially vulnerable. Given the long lead times required for climate change mitigation, this will be insufficient to prevent these risks from increasing. Moreover, most other measures, such as encouraging urban development in more environmentally suitable locations, or adapting coastal settlements to reduce their vulnerability, also have long lead times. The scale and nature of the risks need to be better understood in order to motivate and target timely measures. Much of the relevant information is local. However, given the global nature of climate change, it is also important to assess the international dimensions of the coastal risks that it is already beginning to pose.

Human settlement has long been drawn to coastal areas, which provide many resources and trading opportunities but also expose residents to various hazards. Historically, the attraction of coasts has been particularly strong among trading nations and empires. In Indonesia, for example, the Mataram Empire, which relied on tribute from rice farmers, favoured inland cities and monuments, while the Sri Vijaya Empire, which relied on controlling trade, favoured coastal cities. Colonialism and the expansion of international trade during the colonial period contributed to the coastal location of many contemporary cities. The recent expansion of international trade has also contributed to population movements towards the coast. The pre-eminence of ocean shipping has declined, with air freight growing in relative importance.[5] At least in terms of tonne-kilometres shipped, however, ocean shipping still dominates. Shipping now accounts for less than half of the value of US merchandise imports and exports but about three-quarters of the weight. In other countries, the decline in shipping is far less evident – for Japan, the corresponding figures rise to almost three-quarters of the value and over 99 per cent of the weight.[6] China's ongoing economic boom is one of the clearest examples of trade-related coastward movement that the world has ever seen, although one could argue that government economic policies have been as important as market pressures in causing this movement.[7]

The concentration of populations and economic activities on and near the coast has had serious environmental consequences. Urban systems have radically altered the flows of water, energy and materials, transforming the pre-existing ecosystems.[8] The review of coastal systems undertaken for the MA concluded that coastal ecosystems, both onshore and offshore, are among the most productive in the world and also among the most threatened by human settlement.[9] It is estimated that about one third of coastal mangrove forests and one fifth of coral reefs have already been lost.[10] In many parts of the world, coastal fish populations have declined considerably. When scientists recently reviewed conditions in 12 harbours of major Asian cities, all but one had exhibited drastic fishery declines (as well as numerous other environmental problems) in recent decades.[11]

Many coastal populations are at risk from flooding – particularly when high tides combine with storm surges and/or high river flows. Between 1994 and 2004, about one third of the 1562 flood disasters, half of the 120,000 people killed, and 98 per cent of the 2 million people affected by flood disasters were in Asia, where there are large population agglomerations in the floodplains of major rivers (e.g. Ganges–Brahmaputra, Mekong and Yangtze) and in cyclone-prone coastal regions (e.g. Bay of Bengal, South China Sea, Japan and the Philippines).[12]

Some features of urban development increase the risk of flooding. Water drains more rapidly from built-over land, increasing peak flows and flood risks, particularly if the built drainage system is not adapted accordingly. In many parts of the world, developers have drained wetlands, sometimes reducing malaria prevalence or opening up valuable land for urban development, but also removing a buffer against tidal floods. Particularly in delta regions, land compaction, subsidence due to groundwater withdrawal and reductions in the rate of sediment deposition (due to water regulation) can lead, in effect, to sea-level rise, increasing flood risk (as well as creating various other problems).[13]

While economic activity and urban development often increase the environmental pressures that lead to flooding, low-income settlements, and poor groups within all settlements, tend to be the most vulnerable. On the one hand, affluent settlements and groups are in a better position to take protective measures and adapt or escape when flooding does occur (as media coverage and research on Hurricane Katrina and New Orleans amply demonstrated).[14] On the other hand, the poorest residents of the cities of low-income countries are often forced (implicitly or explicitly) to settle in floodplains or other hazard-prone locations as they cannot afford more suitable alternatives.[15]

Climate change will increase the risk of flooding as well as cause other environmental damage in coastal areas.[16] The estimates of global mean sea-level rise in the *Special Report on Emissions Scenarios* of the Intergovernmental Panel on Climate Change (IPCC) range from 22cm to 34cm between 1990 and the 2080s.[17] Far faster sea-level rise (more than 1m per century) could result from accelerated melting of the Greenland ice sheet or the collapse of the West Antarctic ice sheet, although this is not considered likely during the 21st century.[18] It has been estimated that in the absence of any other changes, a sea-level rise of 38cm would increase fivefold the number of people flooded by storm surges.[19]

The risks to human settlements could be reduced if people and enterprises could be encouraged to move away from the coast, or at least from the most risk-prone coastal locations (this would also reduce the pressures human settlements place on coastal ecosystems). As described in more detail below, current population movements are in the opposite direction. Given the character of urban development, and that the factors driving coastward movement are still poorly understood, turning these flows around is likely to be slow, costly or both. In particular, there is the danger that ill-considered or politically short-sighted measures to shift population from the coastal areas will impose unnecessary economic costs on key coastal enterprises and fail to provide the basis for viable alternatives inland or in more appropriate coastal locations. More appropriate measures are sorely needed, and the earlier the better.

Few of the environmental disadvantages of coastal urbanization are reflected in the economic incentives that drive urban development. Moreover, the economic advantages typically ascribed to urban agglomeration are based primarily on the benefits that come from people and enterprises clustering, and only secondarily on the natural features that make some (e.g. coastal) locations more attractive than others.[20] A comparatively small natural advantage – which may soon cease to be an advantage at all[21]– can eventually make the difference between a future megacity and a lightly developed stretch of coast or patch of farmland. Larger urban settlements and more urban regions, generally, tend to stay larger and more urban for very long periods.[22] Most urban infrastructure is immobile and long lasting, making rapid shifts in urban location very costly. Moreover, urban settlements tend to be nodes of growth, attracting more enterprises and people. As a result, urban settlement is highly path dependent, with urban coastal settlement past and present likely to attract more urban coastal settlement in the future.

In order to support efficient and equitable means for moving the most vulnerable urban settlements, a better understanding is needed of why (and, in some cases, whether) urban settlements in coastal areas are growing more rapidly than inland. Avoiding policies that favour coastal development (such as the special economic zones in China, whose rapid population growth is described below) and imposing more effective coastal zone management could make a difference in the longer term. Relatively small shifts in settlement location, out of a coastal plain onto more elevated ground, can make a major difference. However, experience after the Indian Ocean tsunami of 2004, in which more than 200,000 people lost their lives and millions more their homes,[23] has demonstrated the profound difficulties involved in instituting more restrictive coastal settlement policies without further undermining the lives and livelihoods of the most vulnerable residents.

Coastal development can also be encouraged to adapt to the risks of climate change. To date, adaptation motivated by climate change has been minimal. However, measures to reduce exposure to existing weather-related hazards can also serve as means of adapting to climate change.[24] Embedding adaptive measures within the urban infrastructure is again either very costly or very slow. It is likely to be easier if action is taken as new areas are settled rather than after their infrastructure is in place. It has been suggested that development assistance projects could introduce measures to assist in adaptation to climate change.[25] More generally, there are likely to be important areas of overlap between adaptation to climate change, other forms of disaster preparedness and measures to address local environmental health issues (e.g. improved water, sanitation, waste disposal and drainage systems). Particularly for the urban poor, an equitable resolution of the land issues that drive people to settle on land already susceptible to flooding could make a large difference.

Although local and regional information is needed in order to assess the risks of climate change and identify opportunities for adaptation, climate change is a global phenomenon. Assessment of its international dimensions is important not only to target national, regional and local policy efforts, but also to mount international responses.

Estimating population and human settlement patterns in low-elevation coastal zones (LECZs)

This study integrates recently developed spatial databases of finely resolved global population distribution, urban extents and elevation data to produce country-level estimates of urban land area and population in LECZs. The data set is complex, but the basic approach is simple: by overlaying geographic data layers, we calculate the population and land area in each country, in its LECZ, and then summarize by country, region and economic grouping.

Three geographic data sets are required. The first delineates the extent of the LECZ itself. We defined the LECZ as land area contiguous with the coastline up to a 10m rise elevation,[26] based on the measure from the Shuttle Radar Topography Mission (SRTM) elevation data set.[27] In some places, mostly the mouths of major rivers such as the Amazon in Brazil and the Yenisey River in Russia, the LECZ extends well beyond 100km inland, although for most of its extent, the zone is much less than 100km in width.[28]

Sea-level rise is not expected to reach anything like 10m above the current mid-tide elevations, at least in the foreseeable future. Even with storm surges, the 10m elevation leaves a large margin of safety regarding direct flooding. Sea-level rise and storm surges can certainly cause damage to people living well above the high-water level – for example, through saline intrusion into the groundwater. However, the principal reason for choosing this elevation is that estimates based on elevations below 10m could not be considered globally reliable, particularly in some types of coastal areas, such as those characterized by mountainous bays.[29]

The second required data set is one that delineates urban footprints. The only globally consistent urban footprint data set is Columbia University's Centre for International Earth Science Information Network's Global Rural–Urban Mapping Project (GRUMP).[30] GRUMP urban extents are based largely on the National Oceanic and Atmospheric Administration's (NOAA) night-time light 'city lights' 1994/1995 satellite data set coupled with settlement information (e.g. name and population) to verify that the lighted area corresponds to a human settlement (e.g. rather than an industrial location).[31]

While the lights are not a perfect proxy for the footprint of urban areas, the consistency of measurement and global coverage make them the most reliable satellite source available for this purpose. The lights are characterized by an 'over glow' – that is, an overestimation of areal extent due to the intrinsic characteristics of the sensor.[32] In practice, this means that the GRUMP urban footprints largely represent urban agglomerations, including their surrounding suburban and, perhaps, peri-urban areas.[33]

The third data set required for this analysis is a population grid for each country, and associated with each grid cell, the land area. Estimates for population (1990 and 2000) and land area are based on the GRUMP gridded data sets, which are created from a compilation of geo-referenced census data for each country as allocated to urban extents and surrounding rural areas.[34]

All data are expressed at 1km resolution. As with overlays of any geographic data sets, precision and spatial correspondence at coastlines can substantially influence estimates. In this analysis, the GRUMP urban footprints, population and land area grids all share the same coastal boundaries. In most instances, these corresponded very well with the elevation buffer; but small islands were the most likely to display inconsistencies due to imprecision and inaccuracies associated with the geo-coding of small islands. Therefore, the LECZ extends beyond the coastline to include areas with bathymetry down to approximately 4000m to accommodate minor mismatches between the elevation and GRUMP data sets. Calculations of exposed urban and rural persons and land area are made and summarized for each country and continent. Figure 2.1 illustrates, for the central China coast, the data layers with which the calculations were made.

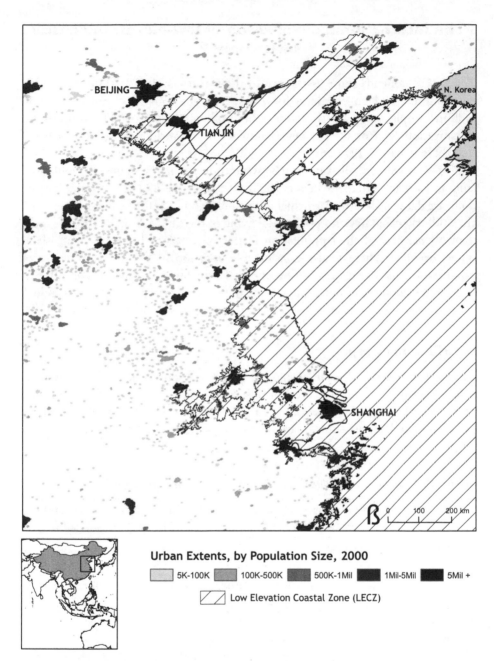

Figure 2.1 Yellow Sea coastal region

The international distribution of low-elevation coastal settlement[35]

The LECZ contains some 2 per cent of the world's land and 10 per cent of its population, based on estimates for 2000.[36] Of the somewhat more than 600 million people living in the zone, 360 million are urban. This implies an urbanization level of 60 per cent compared to a world urbanization level of slightly less than 50 per cent.

There is considerable variation between countries in the shares of population, land and urban settlement in this LECZ. Thus, of the 224 countries for which there are data on all of the principal indicators being presented in this chapter, 41 are landlocked and have no population living in the LECZ,[37] while 21 have more than 50 per cent of their population in this zone (16 of these are small island states, or SISs). There is also considerable variation in the levels and rates of urbanization and in the distribution of population among settlements of different sizes. This variation is not always evident in the paragraphs and tables below, which rely heavily on averages and highly aggregated statistics.

Distribution by region

Table 2.1 provides a selection of statistics by IPCC region.[38] In absolute numbers, Asia accounts for about one third of the world's land in the LECZ; but because of far higher population densities, it accounts for two-thirds of the urban population and almost three-quarters of total population in the zone.

Table 2.1 *Population and land area in the LECZ by region (2000)*

Region	Population and land area in the LECZ				Share of population and land area in the LECZ			
	Population (million)		Land (000 km²)		Population (%)		Land (%)	
	Total	Urban	Total	Urban	Total	Urban	Total	Urban
Africa	56	31	191	15	7	12	1	7
Asia	466	238	881	113	13	18	3	12
Europe	50	40	490	56	7	8	2	7
Latin America	29	23	397	33	6	7	2	7
Australia and New Zealand	3	3	131	6	13	13	2	13
North America	24	21	553	52	8	8	3	6
Small island states	6	4	58	5	13	13	16	13
World	634	360	2700	279	10	13	2	8

The region with the highest share of its total land area in the zone is, not unexpectedly, the SISs, with about 16 per cent – roughly five times the share in Asia.[39] What is more surprising is that the share of the total population of the SISs that are in the zone is, at 13 per cent, only 3 per cent above the world average, while the urban population share, also at 13 per cent, is the same as the world average. On the other hand, Africa, the only region with as little as 1 per cent of its land in the zone and one of the lowest population shares in the zone, has 12 per cent of its urban population there.

Distribution by national income

A country's vulnerability to coastal hazards depends, in part, upon its per capita income. Table 2.2 provides summary statistics for countries grouped according to the World Bank's national income classification (the world totals are slightly less in this table due to missing income data for some countries and territories).

There is no obvious reason to expect a country's income to be systematically related to the share of its population in the coastal zone, and none appears in Table 2.2. The upper middle-income countries, on average, have appreciably lower shares of their population and urban population in the LECZ; but otherwise the shares are similar across the different groups. Overall, there are about 247 million people in low-income countries living in the zone, of which some 102 million are urban.

While there is no statistically significant difference between the high-income and low-income countries in the fraction of the total populations living in the

Table 2.2 *Population and land area in the LECZ by national income (2000)*

Income group	Population and land area in the LECZ				Share of population and land area in the LECZ			
	Population (million)		Land (000 km²)		Population (%)		Land (%)	
	Total	Urban	Total	Urban	Total	Urban	Total	Urban
Low income	247	102	594	35	10	14	2	8
Lower-middle income	227	127	735	70	11	14	2	8
Upper-middle income	37	30	397	42	7	9	2	8
High income	107	93	916	129	12	12	3	9
World	618	352	2642	275	10	13	2	8

Note: Total population estimate for the world does not match that found in Table 2.1 because no income classification was available for several countries.

LECZ, the difference in average urban population shares is significant ($p < 0.05$).
As illustrated in Figure 2.2, the tendency for the LECZ to be more urbanized
than the rest of a country applies to all income levels; but the difference is more
pronounced in the lower-income groups (41 compared to 28 per cent). It is not
only evident that wealthier countries are more urban overall, but their balance
between the fractions of urban dwellers within and outside of the LECZ also
narrows considerably. Thus, while the LECZ urbanization level is about 1.1 times
that of the rest of the land area in high-income countries, this figure rises to
almost 1.5 in low-income countries. One might wonder why the trend does not
reverse (i.e. with greater urban fractions outside the LECZ) among the higher-
income countries. The fact that it does not underscores the strong preference for
vulnerable and dense coastal dwelling, with greater relative vulnerabilities found
in the poorest countries.

There are marked differences in the LECZ population shares of two
politically important income-related groups engaged in climate change
negotiations: the least developed countries (LDCs) – 50 very low-income
countries whose economic status is explicitly recognized as making them
particularly vulnerable; and the Organisation for Economic Co-operation and
Development (OECD) – 30 mostly high-income countries committed to
fostering democratic government and market economy. The LDC group has a
particularly high share of its population and urban population in the LECZ (14
and 21 per cent, respectively) despite a comparatively modest land share (1.2 per
cent). OECD countries, in contrast, only have 10 per cent of their overall
population and 11 per cent of their urban population in the zone, with about 2.8
per cent of the land in the zone.

As indicated above, these averages hide a great deal of variation, with some
countries having far larger shares or quantities of land and population in the zone

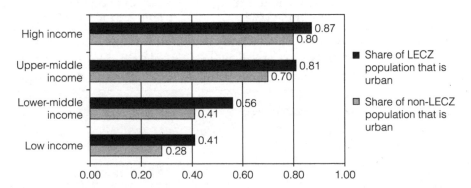

Figure 2.2 Urban population share in the LECZ versus the rest of the
country (2000)

than others in the same group. Thus, for example, the figures for the LDCs are heavily influenced by Bangladesh, which accounts for two-thirds of the group's population in the LECZ.

Country rankings

The distribution of population in the LECZ closely corresponds to the list of the world's most populous countries: China, India, Brazil, the US and Indonesia are all found among the top 20. The top 10 alone account for close to three-quarters of the total population of the zone, and the top 20 account for 85 per cent of the entire zone. Table 2.3 presents the top ten countries, first in terms of the actual number of people living in the zone and then in terms of the share of the country population living in the zone.

The ten countries with the highest numbers of people in the LECZ are not only populous, but can mostly be characterized as large countries in Asia with significant delta regions. Indeed, there are only two non-Asian countries on the list – Egypt and the US. The LECZs of these top 10 countries combine to account for about 463 million people, or about 73 per cent of the people who live in the zone globally. These same countries account for about 241 million urban dwellers, or 67 per cent of the urban population in the zone. Indeed, the top ten countries with the largest population in the zone are also among the top ten ranked by their urban population in the zone, except that The Netherlands, with its highly urban population, replaces the Philippines in tenth place.

The shares of the ten countries with the highest percentages of population in the LECZ range from 38 to 88 per cent, and only one is an SIS – top-ranked Bahamas. However, as indicated in a note to Table 2.3, this ranking would have been dominated by SISs were it not that countries with populations of under 100,000, or areas of less than 1000km^2, were excluded. Looked at in another way, many of the smallest countries in the world are SISs, with a large share of their population living in LECZs. Thus, of the 20 smallest countries (by population) included in this analysis, 16 are SISs and more than half of these have more than 38 per cent of their population in the zone. Even with these small countries eliminated, only three countries are in the top ten in terms of both overall numbers of persons in the LECZ and the share of population in the zone: Bangladesh, Vietnam and Egypt.

A noteworthy aspect of the list of the top ten countries with the highest shares of population in the LECZ is that, with the exception of The Netherlands and the Bahamas, these are all low- or lower middle-income countries. This level of dominance of low- and lower middle-income countries suggests a relationship between a country's income and its likelihood of being on the list. Low- and lower middle-income countries make up only 56 per cent of the countries that could have been on the list and, if there were no relationship, the probability of finding eight or more of the countries on the list from this group would be about one in ten.

Table 2.3 *Ranking of countries with largest population counts and shares in the LECZ (2000)*

| Top ten | Ranked by total population in the LECZ | | | | Ranked by share of population in the LECZ | | | |
| | Country | Overall rank* | Population in the LECZ | | Country** | Overall rank* | Population in the LECZ | |
			Counts (000)	Percentage			Counts (000)	Percentage
1	China	1	143,880	11	Bahamas	174	267	88
2	India	2	63,188	6	Suriname	170	318	76
3	Bangladesh	8	62,524	46	Netherlands	59	11,717	74
4	Vietnam	13	43,051	55	Vietnam	13	43,051	55
5	Indonesia	4	41,610	20	Guyana	157	415	55
6	Japan	9	30,477	24	Bangladesh	8	62,524	46
7	Egypt	16	25,655	38	Djibouti	160	289	41
8	US	3	22,859	8	Belize	179	91	40
9	Thailand	19	16,478	26	Egypt	16	25,695	38
10	Philippines	14	13,329	18	The Gambia	150	494	38

Notes: *Refers to overall rank in total population.

** Countries with a total population of under 100,000 people or smaller than 1000km² were excluded from this list. If all countries were included, seven of the top ten would be places with fewer than 100,000 individuals, the top five having more than 90 per cent of their country in the LECZ (Maldives, Marshall Islands, Tuvalu, Cayman Islands, Turk and Caicos Island).

Figure 2.3 includes the 50 countries with the largest population shares in the LECZ, sorted by share of the population living in the zone and illustrating the shares of rural and urban population in the zone. With some important exceptions – notably Bangladesh and Vietnam – most countries with large population shares in the zone have particularly large shares of their urban populations in the zone.

Turning to the top ten countries with the largest land areas in the LECZ (Table 2.4), Asia is less dominant, with the top three ranking countries being

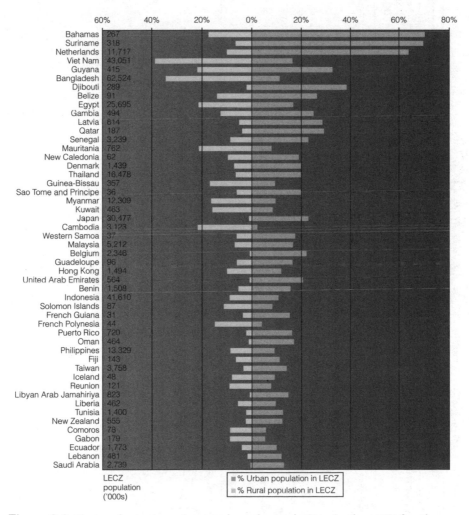

Figure 2.3 Share of country urban and rural populations in the LECZ for the 50 countries with the highest total share of population

Note: Numbers next to country names refer to the total number of people in the country who live in the LECZ.

Table 2.4 *Countries with the largest amount and share of land in the LECZ (2000)*

| Top ten | Ranked by total land area in the LECZ | | | | Ranked by share of their land in the LECZ | | | |
| | Country | Overall rank* | Land area in the LECZ | | Country** | Overall rank* | Land area in the LECZ | |
			(000 km²)	(%)			(000 km²)	%
1	Russia	1	276	2	Bahamas	158	12	93
2	Canada	2	262	3	Netherlands	132	31	75
3	US	4	235	3	Bangladesh	93	54	40
4	China	3	182	2	French Polynesia	171	1	32
5	Indonesia	15	177	9	The Gambia	163	3	26
6	Australia	6	122	2	Denmark	131	11	26
7	Brazil	5	122	1	Qatar	162	3	23
8	Mexico	13	93	5	Cuba	102	23	21
9	India	7	82	3	Vietnam	65	66	20
10	Vietnam	65	66	20	Guinea-Bissau	137	7	19

Notes: * Refers to overall rank in total land area.
** Countries with a total population of under 100,000 people or smaller than 1000km² were excluded from this list.

Russia, Canada and the US. The top ten countries account for about 61 per cent of the overall land in the zone and about 53 per cent of the population. As with population, the ranking in terms of the share of land in the zone is very different, with only Vietnam appearing in both lists. Also, just as India appeared second in the population ranking simply by virtue of its large overall population, Russia and Canada appear in the land area ranking simply by virtue of their large size.

Distribution of settlements of different sizes

Just as the LECZ contains a greater share of the world's urban population than of its rural population, it also contains a greater share of large urban settlements (and their inhabitants) than of small urban settlements. This is not surprising. On the one hand, the higher population densities and concentrations of commerce and industry in coastal areas favour not only urbanization, but also larger urban settlements. On the other hand, one of the roles of urban settlements inland is to link rural populations with the wider polity and economy, and since rural populations are dispersed, their administrative and market centres tend to be comparatively small and dispersed, although many are large enough to be considered urban.[40]

Table 2.5 displays the distribution of urban settlements of different sizes, treating a settlement as being in the zone if any part of it extends into the zone. Overall, while only 13 per cent of urban settlements with populations under 100,000 extend into the LECZ, the share rises steadily to reach 65 per cent of the settlements with populations over 5 million. While there are also regional variations, with the urban settlements of the small islands and of Australia and New Zealand being notably more coastal than those of any other region, the tendency for larger urban settlements to be more likely to overlap the LECZ applies to every region.

Table 2.5 *Share of urban settlements whose footprints intersect the LECZ by urban settlement size (2000)*

Region	<100,000 (%)	100,000– 500,000 (%)	500,000– 1 million (%)	1 million– 5 million (%)	5 million+ (%)
Africa	9	23	39	50	40
Asia	12	24	37	45	70
Europe	17	22	37	41	58
Latin America	11	25	43	38	50
Australia and New Zealand	44	77	100	100	NA
North America	9	19	29	25	80
Small island states	51	61	67	100	NA
World	**13**	**24**	**38**	**44**	**65**

The data in Table 2.5 should not be taken to reflect the degree to which residents of different-sized urban settlements live in the LECZ. On average, only 33 per cent of the population of an urban settlement whose footprint overlaps with the zone actually live in the zone. Moreover, there are differences both regionally and by settlement size class. One would expect smaller coastal settlements to have, on average, a higher share of their population in the zone, if only because they are less likely to extend long distances inland. There is some evidence for this. As illustrated in Figure 2.4, while the overall share of settlements intersecting the LECZ increases steeply with settlement size, the overall share of the population of settlements living in the LECZ increases far less.[41] Thus, only 21 per cent of the population of settlements of over 5 million people are estimated to reside in the LECZ despite almost two-thirds of these settlements having at least some part of their land area in the zone.

Table 2.6 presents the shares of urban population in the LECZ by settlement size and region for all urban settlements, including those that do not overlap with the zone. As already indicated in Figure 2.4, the world average share of the population of cities over 5 million in the zone is a high 21 per cent; but as this table illustrates, this average is highly influenced by the coastal location of large Asian cities, where 32 per cent of the population of cities over 5 million reside in the LECZ.

Africa, although it contributes much less to the statistics on largest cities, has higher shares of its population in cities of 100,000 to 5 million people living in the LECZ than does Asia, Europe or the Americas. This is noteworthy because

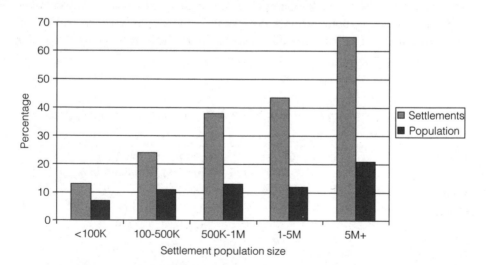

Figure 2.4 The share of population living in the LECZ for settlements intersecting the LECZ, grouped by settlement size and region (2000)

Table 2.6 *Share of population (percentage) in the LECZ for all urban settlements grouped by size (2000)*

Region	<100,000 (%)	100,000– 500,000 (%)	500,000– 1 million (%)	1 million– 5 million (%)	5 million+ (%)
Africa	5	15	20	18	10
Asia	8	13	14	16	32
Europe	6	7	11	6	12
Latin America	6	8	12	7	6
Australia and New Zealand	16	20	26	10	NA
North America	4	7	6	5	13
Small island states	18	11	13	12	NA
World	7	11	13	12	21

Note: NA = not available.

Africa's medium to large cities are growing at much higher rates than cities in these other continents. Given that the African cities tend to be much poorer than cities elsewhere, this raises the question of their potential vulnerability.

Table 2.7 shows the shares of urban land area in the LECZ by settlement size for all urban settlements, including those that do not overlap with the zone. The land shares follow a similar pattern to those of the population, although they are generally lower as coastal settlements tend to be more densely settled. The increasing share associated with larger urban settlements is most evident in Asia and hard to discern in other regions. The pattern is very different in the SISs, where the smallest settlements have both the largest share of population and the

Table 2.7 *Share of land area (percentage) in the LECZ for all urban settlements grouped by size (2000)*

Region	<100,000 (%)	100,000– 500,000 (%)	500,000– 1 million (%)	1 million– 5 million (%)	5 million+ (%)
Africa	4	7	18	13	4
Asia	6	10	10	13	27
Europe	6	6	9	5	13
Latin America	6	9	12	6	6
Australia and New Zealand	12	18	26	9	NA
North America	3	8	6	5	13
Small island states	17	11	4	11	NA
World	5	8	9	9	16

Note: NA = not available.

largest share of land area in the zone. It should be noted, however, that more than
80 per cent of the SIS urban areas have a population of less than 100,000 (and all
but nine urban areas, about 95 per cent, have a population of less than 500,000).

Changes in low-elevation coastal settlement between 1990 and 2000: The examples of China and Bangladesh[42]

As described above, China is the country with the largest population in the LECZ
and Bangladesh the third largest. Moreover, China is one of the more rapidly
urbanizing countries, with particularly rapid urban growth along the coast, while
Bangladesh contains one of the most populous delta regions of the world and
already has almost half (46 per cent) of its population in the LECZ. The
settlement patterns in both of these countries raise serious concerns about the
need for adaptation to climate change to start as soon as possible.[43]

As illustrated in Table 2.8, for both Bangladesh and China, the population in
the LECZ grew at almost twice the national population growth rate between
1990 and 2000. Moreover, in both countries, the urban populations in the LECZ
grew particularly rapidly. Indeed, the urban population growth in China's LECZ
was more than three times the national rate, although GRUMP estimates of
China's urbanization rate for the period are lower than estimates from the United
Nations and the Chinese census estimates.[44]

Thus, even as the seaward risks associated with climate change are increasing,
the areas most at risk are experiencing particularly high population growth. Some
of this may be due to urbanization, although in Bangladesh flooding is already a
major concern, and yet the predominantly rural population of Bangladesh's

Table 2.8 *Urban population counts and growth between 1990 and 2000 for China
and Bangladesh - by total and in the LECZ*

Country	Population (000)		Annual growth rate 1990–2000 (%)
	1990	2000	
China	1,138,676	1,262,334	1.04
Urban China	336,577	423,730	2.33
LECZ China	119,103	143,880	1.91
Urban LECZ China	56,059	78,278	3.39
Bangladesh	110,024	123,612	1.17
Urban Bangladesh	23,097	26,865	1.52
LECZ Bangladesh	50,568	62,524	2.14
Urban LECZ Bangladesh	11,686	15,429	2.82

LECZ is growing at an even faster rate than the country's urban average. The movement towards the coast in China is linked to urbanization; but it is also being driven by the trade-oriented economic strategy and policies that favour urban development along the coast.

China's rapid urbanization and coastward population movements, and the economic liberalization and growth that are driving these demographic trends, date back to the early 1980s.[45] The geographical advantages of coastal development have been enhanced by the creation of special economic zones in coastal locations.[46] It has been estimated that the advantages conferred by geography were about equal to those conferred by preferential policies.[47] By amplifying the advantages of coastal settlement with their special economic zones, China is not only attracting more people to the coast now, but is establishing an urban structure that will continue to attract people to the coast far into the future. Unless something is done, there is the possibility that, as well as the people living in the LECZ, China's economic success will be placed at risk.

Overall, the risks of climate change are clearly far more threatening and intractable for Bangladesh than for China. Only about one fiftieth of China's land area is in the LECZ compared to more than two-fifths of Bangladesh's land. Nevertheless, China, too, faces potentially serious threats, the evolution of which depend upon policy agendas that do not as yet treat climate change as a serious issue.

Conclusions

From an environmental perspective, there is a double disadvantage to excessive (and potentially rapid) coastal settlement. First, uncontrolled coastal development is likely to damage sensitive and important ecosystems and other resources. Second, coastal settlement, particularly in the lowlands, is likely to expose residents to seaward hazards, such as sea-level rise and tropical storms, both of which are likely to become more serious with climate change. Unfortunately, such environmental considerations do not have the influence on settlement patterns that they deserve.

As described above, although the LECZ accounts for only about 2 per cent of the world's land area, about 10 per cent of the world's population and 13 per cent of the world's urban population live in the zone. In terms of regional distribution, Asia stands out as it contains about three-quarters of the population in the zone and two-thirds of the urban population (compared to about 60 per cent of world population and 49 per cent of the world's urban population).

Settlements in the LECZ are likely to be especially vulnerable in lower-income countries with limited resources. Effective adaptation will require a combination of effective and enforceable regulations and economic incentives to redirect new settlement to better-protected locations and to promote investments in appropriate infrastructure, all of which require political will as well as financial and human capital. A tabulation of population and urban population shares in the LECZ for different national income classes does not provide, in itself, evidence of a systematic relationship between national income and settlement in the LECZ. However, the data did show a statistically significant difference between the urban population in the zone for low-income versus high-income countries. Politically notable is the appreciable difference found between the populations of the LDCs and OECD countries living in the zone: 14 and 10 per cent, respectively. This divide is even wider when looking at the urban population percentages in the LECZ: 21 per cent for the LDCs and 11 per cent for OECD countries.

There is considerable variation within regions and income categories, and there are a number of features that can lead a country to have a large share of its urban and rural populations in the LECZ. These include long coastlines (relative to the country's size), wide and heavily populated coastal lowlands and sparsely populated interiors.

Most of the countries with large populations in the LECZ are also among the most populous countries overall, with large Asian countries dominating. The countries with large shares of population (or urban population) in the LECZ are a more varied group and include countries characterized by each of the three factors mentioned in the previous paragraph.

Although SISs do not, in aggregate, have an especially large share of their population in the LECZ, some of them do, and they would dominate the listing if no additional population or land area criteria were used. If very small countries (under 100,000 people or 1000km^2) are excluded, among the SISs only the Bahamas is in the top ten. Vietnam, Bangladesh and Egypt reappear from among the top ten listed in terms of population in the LECZ, and these are all countries with large, heavily populated delta regions, which at least originally attracted people primarily for agriculture. Alternatively, both Suriname and Guyana are countries with sparsely inhabited interiors and populations concentrated on a small coastal strip.

Of particular concern in terms of vulnerability, all but two of the countries with the largest shares of their population in the LECZ (excluding the very small countries) are of low or lower-middle income. This is despite the fact that urban settlements are generally more coastal than rural settlements, while low- and lower middle-income countries are less urban than more affluent countries.

In the world, as a whole, but most notably in Asia, not only are urban populations more likely to be in the LECZ than rural populations, but larger urban settlements are more likely to overlap with the LECZ than are smaller urban settlements. While only 13 per cent of urban settlements with populations under 100,000 overlap with the LECZ, this rises to 65 per cent among cities of 5 million or more. Perhaps even more striking, of the 183 countries with people living in the LECZ, 130 have their largest urban area extending into the zone. When large urban settlements at least overlap with the zone, they tend to have a smaller share of their population in the zone than do smaller settlements. Nevertheless, as one moves up through the size classes of urban settlements, the overall share of population and land in the LECZ does tend to increase – from 7 per cent in urban settlements of under 100,000 to 21 per cent in settlements of over 5 million.

There is a legitimate concern that continued urbanization will draw still greater populations and population shares into the LECZ. During recent decades, this tendency has been especially remarkable in China, where export-driven economic growth has been associated with very rapid coastward migration. Although the GRUMP database upon which the analysis in this chapter is based estimates a considerably lower rate of urbanization between 1990 and 2000 than most other sources, a very high rate of growth is nevertheless evident in the LECZ. Moreover, in Bangladesh, with its lower rates of economic growth and urbanization, a shift towards the LECZ is also evident.

Looking to the future, the responses to the growing risks to coastal settlements brought on by climate change should include mitigation, migration and modification. To avoid severe disruptions, measures for each of these need a long lead time. As the effects of climate change become increasingly clear, the location of the coastal settlements most at risk should also become evident. Unfortunately, by this time, most of the easier options for shifting settlement patterns and modifying them so that they are better adapted to the risks of climate change will have been foreclosed. Large companies may be able to shift the location of their activities relatively quickly, using the same procedures that have allowed them to adapt to economic globalization. Others will not find it so easy. Moreover, it is already evident that settlements in the coastal lowlands, and particularly those in low-income countries and those also at risk from tropical storms, are especially vulnerable.

Particularly as the need for action becomes more urgent, care will be needed to prevent government responses themselves from being inequitable or unnecessarily disruptive economically. Economically successful urbanization is based typically on the decentralized decisions of economic enterprises and families, supported by their governments. When governments try to decide centrally where urban development should occur or where people should migrate, a range of political interests can intrude, favouring economically unviable locations and/or land-use regulations that are particularly burdensome to the urban poor. Adaptation cannot be left to the market; but nor should it be left to arbitrary central planning.

In many cases, there may be measures that can both address current problems while also providing a means of adapting to climate change. These provide an obvious place to start, even if such coincidences of interest are unlikely to be sufficient to provide the basis for all of the adaptive measures needed.

At the national level, measures to support previously unfavoured inland urban settlements, away from the large cities on the coast, could not only reduce risks from climate change, but also support a more balanced and equitable pattern of urban development. In China, for example, giving inland urban settlements the support needed to redress the imbalance caused by the creation of special economic zones along the coast would not only help to reduce coastward migration, but would also reduce the increasingly severe regional inequalities that threaten China's national integrity.

Alternatively, among coastal settlements in low-income countries, those that find more equitable means to resolve the land problems that so often push their poorest urban residents to settle informally on un-serviced and environmentally hazardous land (such as floodplains) will also be in a far better position to adapt to the risks of climate change. More generally, measures that support more efficient and equitable resolution of existing land issues are likely to provide a better basis for addressing the land issues brought on by climate change.

Vulnerable settlements in low-income countries clearly deserve international support in these and other measures to adapt to climate change. If climate change were simply an unfortunate accident of nature, such support could be justified on ethical grounds. In fact, climate change is closely associated with the past and present lifestyles of high-income groups in high-income countries. This makes it doubly important that the governments of these countries contribute to adaptation as well as mitigation. It also implies that this assistance should be viewed as additional to, rather than part of, development assistance. On the other hand, adaptive measures that respond to existing local needs, contribute to other development goals and can be locally driven, are among the most likely to succeed.

Notes

1. McGranahan, G., Marcotullio, P. J., Bai, X. et al (2005) 'Urban systems', in Rashid Hassan, Robert Scholes and Neville Ash (eds) *Ecosystems and Human Well-Being: Current Status and Trends*, Island Press, Washington, DC, pp795–825.
2. Montgomery, M. R., Stren, R., Cohen, B. and Reed, H. E. (eds) (2003) *Cities Transformed: Demographic Change and its Implications in the Developing World*, National Academy Press, Washington, DC.
3. Small, C. and Nicholls, R. J. (2003) 'A global analysis of human settlement in coastal zones', *Journal of Coastal Research*, vol 19, no 3, pp584–599; also Small, C. and Cohen, J. (2004) 'Continental physiography, climate and the global distribution of human population', *Current Anthropology*, vol 45, no 2, pp269–277.
4. See maps in Pelling, M. (2003) *The Vulnerability of Cities: Natural Disasters and Social Resilience*, Earthscan, London; also Dilley, M., Chen, R. S., Deichmann, U., Lerner-Lam, A. L. and Arnold, M. (2005) *Natural Disaster Hotspots: A Global Risk Analysis*, World Bank, Washington, DC.
5. Hummels, D. (1999) *Have International Transportation Costs Declined?*, University of Chicago, Chicago.

6. WTO (World Trade Organization) (2004) *World Trade Report 2004*, WTO, Geneva.
7. Han, S. S. and Yan, Z. X. (1999) 'China's coastal cities: Development, planning and challenges', *Habitat International*, vol 23, no 2, pp217–229; also McGranahan, G. and Tacoli, C. (2006) *Rural–Urban Migration, Urban Poverty and Urban Environmental Pressures in China*, Contribution to the China Council Task Force on Sustainable Urbanization Strategies, International Institute for Environment and Development (IIED), London.
8. Rakodi, C. and Treloar, D. (1997) 'Urban development and coastal zone management: An international review', *Third World Planning Review*, vol 19, no 4, pp401–424; also Timmermann, P. and White, R. (1997) 'Megahydropolis: Coastal cities in the context of global environmental change', *Global Environmental Change*, vol 7, no 3, pp205–234.
9. Agardy, T., Alder, J., Dayton, P. et al (2005) 'Coastal systems', in Hassan, R., Scholes, R. and Ash, N. (eds) *Ecosystems and Human Well-Being: Current Status and Trends*, Island Press, Washington, DC, pp513–549.
10. Alder, J., Arthurton, R., Ash, N. et al (2006) *Marine and Coastal Ecosystems and Human Well-Being*, United Nations Environmental Programme, Nairobi, Kenya.
11. Wolanski, E. (ed) (2006) *The Environment in Asia Pacific Harbours*, Springer, Dordrecht, The Netherlands.
12. Few, R. and Matthies, F. (2006) *Flood Hazards and Health: Responding to Present and Future Risks*, Earthscan, London.
13. Ericson, J. P., Vorosmarty, C. J., Lawrence Dingman, S., Ward, L. G. and Meybeck, M. (2006) 'Effective sea-level rise and deltas: Causes of change and human dimension implications', *Global and Planetary Change*, vol 50, pp63–82
14. Dreier, P. (2006) 'Katrina and power in America', *Urban Affairs Review*, vol 41, no 4, pp528–549.
15. Hardoy, J. E., Mitlin, D. and Satterthwaite, D. (2001) *Environmental Problems in an Urbanizing World*, Earthscan, London.
16. For summaries of the range of different environmental consequences of climate change, see Nicholls, R. J. (2002) 'Rising sea levels: potential impacts and responses', *Issues in Environmental Science and Technology*, vol 17, pp83–107; also Nicholls, R. J., Wong, P. P., Burkett, V. et al (2006) 'Coastal systems and low-lying areas', in *IPCC WGII Fourth Assessment Report – Draft for Government and Expert Review*; and Klein, R. J. T., Nicholls, R. J. and Thomalla, F. (2003) 'Resilience to natural hazards: how useful is this concept?', *Environmental Hazards*, vol 5, pp35–45.
17. Nicholls, R. J. (2004) 'Coastal flooding and wetland loss in the 21st century: Changes under the SRES climate and socioeconomic scenarios', *Global Environmental Change*, vol 14, no 1, pp69–86.
18. See reference 16, Nicholls et al (2006).
19. Nicholls, R. J., Hoozemans, F. M. J. and Marchand, M. (1999) 'Increasing flood risk and wetland losses due to global sea-level rise: Regional and global analyses', *Global Environmental Change*, vol 9, pp69–87.
20. See, for example, Fujita, M., Krugman, P. R. and Venables, A. (1999) *The Spatial Economy: Cities, Regions and International Trade*, MIT Press, Cambridge, MA; also Fujita, M. and Thisse, J.-F. (2002) *Economics of Agglomeration: Cities, Industrial Location and Regional Growth*, Cambridge University Press, Cambridge, UK; and

Henderson, J. V. and Thisse, J.-F. (eds) (2004) *Handbook of Regional and Urban Economics: Volume 4, Cities and Geography*, Elsevier North Holland, Amsterdam.

21. Some argue that the ecological reasons why cities originally located in coastal areas have been reversed. See reference 8, Timmermann and White (1997).

22. United Nations (2004) *World Urbanization Prospects: The 2003 Revision*, United Nations, New York; also Gabaix, X. and Ioanides, Y. M. (2004) 'The evolution of city size distributions', in Henderson and Thisse (eds) see reference 20, pp2341–2378.

23. See reference 12.

24. See reference 16, Klein et al (2003).

25. Bigio, A. G. (2003) 'Cities and climate change', in Alcira K., Arnold, M. and Carlin, A. (eds) *Building Safer Cities: The Future of Disaster Risk*, World Bank, Washington, DC, pp91–99.

26. As a validation to our LECZ zone, we generated summary statistics based on the Millennium Ecosystem Assessment's (MA) coastal boundary, which we also constrained to 10m or less in elevation. Although there were some inconsistencies between the MA boundaries and population/land area datasets used here, the results were quite similar.

27. ISciences (2003) *SRTM30 Enhanced Global Map – Elevation/Slope/Aspect* (release 1.0), ISciences, LLC, Ann Arbor (based on the raw SRTM data from Jet Propulsion Laboratory).

28. Only a small fraction of the buffer includes land areas beyond 100km. In contrast, some prior estimates of coastal population have relied exclusively on buffers of at least 100km. See reference 3.

29. Farr, T. G. and Kobrick, M. (2000) 'Shuttle radar topography mission produces a wealth of data', *Transactions of the American Geophysical Union*, vol 81, pp583–585; also Rabus, B., Eineder, M., Roth, A. and Bamler, R. (2003) 'The shuttle radar topography mission – a new class of digital elevation models acquired by spaceborne radar', *Journal of Photogrammetry & Remote Sensing*, vol 57, pp241–262.

30. Global Rural–Urban Mapping Project, alpha version (GRUMP alpha) Centre for International Earth Science Information Network (CIESIN) Columbia University, International Food Policy Research Institute (IFPRI), World Bank and Centro Internacional de Agricultura Tropical (CIAT) (2004) *Global Rural–Urban Mapping Project (GRUMP) Alpha Version: Urban Extents Grids*, Socioeconomic Data and Applications Centre (SEDAC) Columbia University, Palisades, NY, http://sedac.ciesin.columbia.edu/gpw (February 2006); also Balk, D., Pozzi, F., Yetman, G., Deichmann, U. and Nelson, A. (2005) 'The distribution of people and the dimension of place: methodologies to improve the global estimation of urban extents', in *International Society for Photogrammetry and Remote Sensing: Proceedings of the Urban Remote Sensing Conference*, March 2005, Tempe, AZ.

31. Where lights are insufficient to detect urbanized areas, alternate estimates of urban extent are used. Examples of alternate urban extent data sets include Digital Chart of the World, Tactical Pilotage Charts. Extents are also modelled with regression estimators. See reference 30, Balk et al (2005).

32. Elvidge, C. D., Safran, J., Nelson, I. L., Tuttle, B. T., Hobson, V. R., Baugh, K. E., Dietz, J. B. and Erwin, E. H. (2004) 'Area and position accuracy of DMSP nighttime

lights data', in Lunetta, R. S. and Lyon, J. G. (eds) *Remote Sensing and GIS Accuracy Assessment*, CRC Press, Chapter 20, pp281–292.

33. The lights 'over glow' under all conditions, so that in coastal zones the lights would glow over the ocean where there was no corresponding land. Thus, we have determined the fraction of all lights that appear over water to be 6 per cent globally. For coastal urban areas, the areas over water have been clipped (as have all major water bodies); but for urban extents not intersecting a coastline we have adjusted the estimated land area total of those urban extents by 6 per cent. The urban footprints falling in coastal areas also experience over glow on their non-water edges; but, at this time, no adjustment for those areas has been made.

34. Global Rural–Urban Mapping Project, alpha version (GRUMP alpha), Centre for International Earth Science Information Network (CIESIN) Columbia University, International Food Policy Research Institute (IFPRI), World Bank and Centro Internacional de Agricultura Tropical (CIAT) (2004) *Gridded Population of the World, Version 3, With Urban Reallocation (GPW–UR)*, Socioeconomic Data and Applications Centre (SEDAC) Columbia University, Palisades, NY, http://sedac.ciesin.columbia.edu/gpw (February 2006).

35. This section includes an updated version of major parts of McGranahan, G., Balk, D. and Anderson, B. (2006) 'Low coastal zone settlements', *Tiempo*, no 59, pp23–26. Please note that some of the statistics have changed as a result of some of the data refinements discussed in the previous section.

36. Unless stated otherwise, estimates are for the year 2000.

37. There are 42 landlocked countries in the data set but the LECZ extends into one – Moldova.

38. IPCC regions used here are as defined by the Intergovernmental Panel on Climate Change (IPCC) for Working Group 2. Countries not in the IPCC list were assigned to one of the regions.

39. For the purposes of Table 2.1, this group has 65 members, 32 of which are not listed as small island states in the IPCC regional listing.

40. Satterthwaite, D. and Tacoli, C. (2003) *The Urban Part of Rural Development: The Role of Small and Intermediate Urban Centres in Rural and Regional Development and Poverty Reduction*, Working Paper 9 in the Rural–Urban Interactions Series, IIED, London.

41. Based on the nature of the underlying gridded data sets, in localities where the underlying data inputs were coarse, these estimates assume that the population is distributed evenly within the urban area. This could exaggerate the share in the zone if, for example, people intentionally avoided settling in the floodplains, or could underestimate that share if, for example, the less densely populated urban fringe were located inland and out of the zone.

42. The GRUMP urban extents, which form a basis for this analysis, are based on estimates of urban footprint in 1994/1995. This precludes an analysis of changes in spatial extents or in derived variables such as densities. For this reason, the discussion focuses on the question of whether the rate of population change – particularly in urban areas – is greater in the LECZ than elsewhere.

43. At the time of writing, estimates for 1990 and 2000 were not yet available for all countries. This analysis is thus restricted to the important examples of China and Bangladesh, although future updates will extend the analysis to the rest of the world.

44. The United Nations estimates that China (including Tawain) was 27 and 36 per cent urban, respectively, in 1990 and 2000. See reference 22, United Nations (2004). The 1990 and 2000 census estimates were 26 and 36 per cent, as described in Chan, K. W. and Hu, Y. (2003) 'Urbanization in China in the 1990s: New definition, different series and revised trends', *The China Review*, vol 3, no 2, pp49–71. The GRUMP estimates are 30 and 34 per cent. GRUMP-based estimates differ from UN urban population estimates for several reasons: the UN estimates concentrate on understanding the growth of large cities (especially those with more than 500,000 persons); UN estimates are not spatially derived, whereas GRUMP-based estimates are linked to spatially identified settlements of more than 5000 individuals; and GRUMP and the United Nations estimate growth by somewhat different methods. With respect to China in particular, the UN estimates may rely on country estimates of population for particular cities.

45. See reference 7, McGranahan and Tacoli (2006).

46. As a means of demonstrating the viability of a trade-oriented economic strategy, there is logic to setting up special economic zones in favourable (e.g. coastal) locations and giving them preferential treatment (e.g. less government regulation and lower taxes). This justification disappears, however, once a national strategy of economic liberalization has been adopted. Coastal locations will be favoured by markets and do not need to be given special treatment.

47. Demurger, S., Sachs, J. D., Woo, W. T., Bao, S. M. and Chang, G. (2002) 'The relative contributions of location and preferential policies in China's regional development: Being in the right place and having the right incentives', *China Economic Review*, vol 13, no 4, pp444–465; also Demurger, S., Sachs, J. D., Woo, W. T., Bao, S. and Chang, G. H. (2004) 'Explaining unequal distribution of economic growth among China provinces: Geography or policy?', in Aimin C., Liu, G. G. and Zhang, K. H. (eds) *Urbanization and Social Welfare in China*, Ashgate, Aldershot, pp269–306.

3

Climate Change and Coastal Cities: The Case of Mombasa, Kenya

Cynthia Brenda Awuor, Victor Ayo Orindi and Andrew Ochieng Adwera

Introduction

Climate change has been singled out as a major challenge currently facing the world. It is caused by the emission of greenhouse gases, largely from energy production and consumption, agriculture and other ecological processes. The activities causing most emissions are key drivers of global socio-economic development. High-income countries are responsible for a large percentage of these emissions, with the US and Europe emitting 51 per cent of total greenhouse gases into the atmosphere compared to Africa's 2.5 per cent.[1]

Low- and middle-income countries are considered more vulnerable to the effects of climate change than high-income nations because of high dependence upon natural resources and low capacity to adapt. For Africa, low adaptive capacity results largely from the limited financial, technological and institutional capacity, relatively low levels of economic development, and high levels of poverty widely experienced in the continent. Increased climate change threatens to undo decades of development and poverty reduction efforts so far achieved in most countries.

It is therefore important to strengthen the link between climate change adaptation and development, increase public awareness and understanding of the issues, and pragmatically tackle the challenges posed by the phenomenon.

Many world cities, including those in Africa, are centres of economic, political, cultural, social and commercial activities. Human populations in cities tend to be highly concentrated compared to those in rural areas because of the availability of more employment and business opportunities, as well as the better quality of social services. Due to the high population densities, cities are also associated with high levels of energy, water and food consumption.

The impacts of climate change upon cities threaten to cause very serious damage and loss of resources. The latest report from the Intergovernmental Panel on Climate Change (IPCC) identifies various climate change-related health impacts, including altered distribution of some infectious diseases and disease vectors. According to the report, projected trends in climate change-related exposures will see an increase in malnutrition and consequent disorders; an increase in the number of people suffering disease and injury and dying from heat waves, floods, storms, fires and droughts; and will continue to change the range of some infectious disease vectors. The burden of diarrhoeal diseases will increase, the geographical range of malaria will expand in some nations and contract in others, and transmission seasons will alter.[2]

Vulnerability of Mombasa to climate change

In this chapter, the city of Mombasa is considered to be Mombasa District and consists of four divisions – namely, Mombasa Island, Kisauni, Likoni and Changamwe. Situated within Kenya's coast province in the south-east of the country, Mombasa is Kenya's second largest city. It is situated about 4.1° south of the Equator and 39.7° east of Greenwich meantime.

According to the Mombasa District Statistics Office, the district had a population of 856,209 individuals in 2007.[3] Mombasa residents derive their livelihoods from a variety of economic activities, ranging from formal employment in different sectors, such as industry and hospitality, to small-scale agriculture, livestock production and fishing, especially in the peri-urban space. Some of the major industries in Mombasa include cement manufacturing from the abundant limestone, salt processing from seawater, and businesses associated with import and export at the city's port. Food security and general economic performance are, however, very low; the latest available figures (from 1997) show that 38.2 per cent of the population face absolute poverty and 38.6 per cent face food poverty.[4]

Mombasa is the largest seaport in East Africa and has two harbours – Kilindini and Old Port. It plays an important role in both the country's and the region's economy because the commercial imports and exports of land-locked countries such as Uganda, Rwanda, Burundi, Congo and even parts of Tanzania transit through Mombasa. Anything affecting the port and, by extension, the city's operations, is therefore likely to be felt beyond the coastal and national boundaries. The city is also a popular tourist destination due to the presence of various terrestrial and marine-based ecological attractions, including warm weather, sandy beaches and historical and cultural monuments. Tourism remains an important foreign exchange earner for Kenya. In 2007, the sector earned the country about 65.4 billion Kenya shillings (equivalent to US$934,285,714) and contributed more than 12 per cent of the gross domestic product (GDP) in 2007, and continues to grow.[5]

Three factors contribute to Mombasa's high level of vulnerability to climate change: low altitude, and high temperatures and humidity levels. Regarding the first of these, Mombasa is on the coastal plain, which is 4km to 6km wide and lies between sea level and about 45m above sea level. Parts of the city and its surroundings are likely to be submerged with a rise in sea level, and this would consequently disrupt ecosystem functions and balance, disrupt agricultural and industrial activities, cause the destruction of human settlements, and interfere with the water supply.[6] This will impact negatively upon the city's economy and, by extension, upon the national economy due to the many activities and investments found in the area.

According to the IPCC Fourth Assessment Report, it is estimated that during the 20th century, sea level has been rising at a rate of about 2mm per year, with the fastest recorded rates averaged along the global coastline (4mm per year) occurring in the 1990s.[7] It is estimated that about 17 per cent of Mombasa, or 4600ha of land area, will be submerged with a sea-level rise of only 0.3m.[8] At the same time, there will be large areas that may be rendered uninhabitable as a result of flooding or waterlogging, or will be agriculturally unsuitable due to salt stress, especially in the peri-urban space where agriculture is practised. Sandy beaches and other features, including historical and cultural monuments such as Fort Jesus, several beach hotels, industries, the ship-docking ports and human settlements, could be negatively affected by sea-level rise.

Other potential impacts of sea-level rise that could affect Mombasa include increased coastal storm damage and flooding; sea-shore erosion; saltwater intrusion into estuaries and freshwater aquifers and springs; changes in sedimentation patterns; decreased light penetration to benthic organisms leading to loss of food for various marine fauna; and loss of coral reefs, contributing to loss of biodiversity, fisheries and recreational opportunities, among others.

The high average temperatures (26.4°C) and humidity (65 per cent at noon) are already approaching intolerable limits and can be uncomfortable at times.[9] An increase in temperatures and humidity could create health-related problems such as heat stress, both on land and in the ocean, leading to ecosystem disruption, migration and the possible extinction of various species of fauna, flora and microorganisms. In addition, increased temperatures could result in the increased use of energy to power air-conditioners. This increased use of energy for cooling would essentially mean increased use of fossil fuels, as Kenya partly generates her electricity from imported fossil fuel resources.

In addition to the low altitude and high average temperatures and humidity, socio-economic factors, particularly unplanned settlements and structures, are also contributing to the city population's increased level of vulnerability to climate change impacts. The high population densities, together with the large number of unplanned settlements in areas such as Bombolulu, Kisauni, Mlangoni, Mwandoni, Kongowea and Likoni that have encroached into areas demarcated for infrastructure, such as roads, drainage and sewerage lines, not only increase the risk of flooding whenever it rains but also make rescue operations difficult whenever disasters strike. The Mombasa district commissioner, while inspecting the extent of damage caused by floods in April/May 2006, attributed the poor drainage to the mushrooming of slums and land grabbing in Mombasa.[10] The district commissioner also noted that the building of perimeter walls and unplanned structures along waterways interferes with water drainage, leading to flooding in most parts of the city (see Figures 3.1 and 3.2).

Figure 3.1 Flooding in Mombasa – November 2007

Source: © ICPAC and Dr C. Owdhe

Figure 3.2 Settlements close to the ocean shore in Mombasa Old Town – February 2007

Source: © Kenya Meteorological Department

Climate change impacts in Mombasa

The impacts of climate variability and change pose grave threats to the city dwellers' lives and livelihoods, as well as to the country's socio-economic development.

Mombasa is already affected by climate-related disasters, especially floods, droughts and strong winds (see Figure 3.3). These climate-related disasters are projected to increase in frequency and intensity with long-term climate change, and Table 3.1 provides a summary of those that have occurred in Mombasa during the recent past.

Figure 3.3 Cargo containers at the Port of Mombasa partly submerged in water during flooding – February 2008

Source: Adapted from Orindi, V. A. (2006) 'Reducing emissions and vulnerability to a changing climate: The case of Mombasa', presented at the World Urban Forum, Vancouver, Canada, unpublished

Wind storms, cyclones and floods damage productive land, thus causing agricultural losses and increased food insecurity; they also damage transport and telecommunications infrastructure such as roads, bridges and pipelines, as well as electricity and telephone lines. When they occur, they negatively affect economic and commercial activities.

Sea-level rise and frequent flooding may not only cause damage to existing infrastructure in cities such as Mombasa, but may also result in inundation, rendering many areas uninhabitable and unsuitable for commercial activities and food production. This, in turn, can lead to migration in extreme cases and loss of cultural heritage, especially historical and archaeological sites and monuments. It could also cause the spread of climate-sensitive diseases such as cholera, which may affect large numbers of people due to high population densities in cities, and could lead to high loss of life as people are often caught unawares. These impacts also disrupt normal livelihood activities and school attendance.

The 2004 Indian Ocean tsunami and the 2006/2007 flooding experienced on the Kenyan coast exemplify the risks that Mombasa faces. They led to very large economic losses as major infrastructure and fishing vessels were damaged, and one life was reportedly lost in the tsunami. During the flooding in Mombasa in 2006, the Ministry of Health issued a cholera alert and the chief public health officer in the Ministry of Health reported 94 suspected cases of cholera on the coast between 20 October and 11 November 2006. Thirteen cases were found to be positive for cholera and at least two deaths were reported. In addition, water

Table 3.1 *Climate-related disasters typology, trends and impacts that have occurred in Mombasa*

Disaster type	When is/was experienced	Established incidence rate or return period	Impact profile: who/what was affected most and quantity/extent of damage	Remarks
El Niño	1947 1961 1997	Approximately five years	• Houses destroyed • Property lost • Livestock and crops lost • Human lives lost • Increased incidence of disease (cholera and typhoid)	Most affected areas are estates located near the ocean that either lack or have poor drainage structures or systems
Floods	Frequently (almost annually)	Unpredictable	• Houses destroyed • Property lost • Livestock lost (all types) • Human lives lost • Increased incidence of disease (cholera and typhoid)	Most affected areas are estates that either lack or have poor drainage structures or systems
Tsunami	2006	Unpredictable	• Several fishing boats reportedly destroyed	One human life reportedly lost
Drought	2005/2006	Every four to five years	• All agricultural activities are affected • Women spend more time looking for water	As time is spent looking for water, other activities suffer from time allocation; droughts also cause famine

| Hunger/famine | Every year | Every year | • Loss of human lives from starvation (not quantified)
• Gross malnutrition and underfeeding leading to poor economic productivity | Effects are felt across all age groups and gender |

Source: Adapted from Danda, M. (2006) *Vulnerability and Capacity Assessment in Mombasa District*, Survey report for the Kenya Red Cross Society, Mombasa Branch, Mombasa

sources were contaminated, several drainage systems collapsed and water pipes were washed away. The Kenya Red Cross estimated that approximately 60,000 people were affected by the floods in the coastal part of Kenya, a high proportion of whom were in Mombasa (the coast's main population concentration).[11]

Indirect and anticipated impacts of climate change upon Mombasa

Frequent droughts and the attendant reduced water availability in the city's water catchments could lead to more severe water shortages. During droughts, food prices normally increase, exacerbating food insecurity and malnutrition, especially among poor city residents. Among the low-income groups in the city, who either depend upon communal taps or water kiosks, or, in some cases, upon wells, drought often translates into increased amounts of time spent fetching water.

The exacerbated loss of biodiversity is also a threat as several ecosystems, particularly the marine ecosystem, are changing rapidly, and some of the species (especially endemic species such as coral reefs) that inhabit them may be unable to adapt. Anything that has a negative impact upon the marine ecosystem is bound to have a negative affect on the local people who depend upon fishing.

Sea-level rise could also lead to the inundation of land and saltwater intrusion into inland waterways. The fact that some city residents get their water from such sources means that they are likely to experience problems obtaining freshwater. As noted above, migration may be necessary, leading to overcrowding upstream and potentially fuelling social conflict between migrants and other residents. This disrupts activities such as schooling and other livelihood and social activities such as small-scale local industries. Inundation would push many peri-urban farmers into destitution as the source of their livelihoods is destroyed. It could also necessitate major infrastructural investments such as redesign and reconstruction of the city's ports to enable their optimal functioning. Industries such as the cement industry and the oil refinery may also require heavy financial and capital investments to reduce the negative impacts of climate change on their operations. In extreme cases, it may be necessary to relocate such industries further inland – a very costly endeavour, indeed.

The complexity and uncertain nature of various climate change impacts are a major challenge for development given that climate change mainly has negative implications for economic growth, human security and improved social welfare in the region.

In view of the country's relatively limited capacity to adapt, it is important that the issue of climate change is taken seriously and given the necessary attention. It is also important that context-specific measures are put in place to adapt to current impacts and to mitigate anticipated future impacts. It is worth noting that, lately, there has been increased activity from various civil society organizations, development agencies and government ministries geared towards understanding and addressing the challenges posed by climate change. These include the development of various adaptation policies, strategies and programmes.

From the foregoing discussion, key issues that need to be addressed include:

- timely prediction of climate-related disasters and effective early warning;
- disaster preparedness;
- effective coordination of disaster relief and recovery;
- facilitation of climate change adaptation and restoration of communities' livelihoods;
- integration of climate change adaptation within relevant policies, programmes and projects (and effective implementation of these); and
- climate change mitigation, where feasible.

Adaptation to climate change in Mombasa

It is noteworthy that many residents of the city are aware of the changes in climate, especially with respect to extreme weather events and disasters such as floods, windstorms, droughts and famine. However, the link with global climate change is deficient. Government officials, such as those working in the municipal council of Mombasa, are also aware of climate change. However, so far, they have not integrated climate change adaptation within the city's master plan for infrastructure and in the formulation and implementation of various citywide policies and plans.

The Kenya government, through various ministries, departments, the city council and various state corporations and other stakeholders, such as non-governmental organizations (NGOs), private companies, charity foundations and religious institutions, are making efforts to address some of the challenges faced as a result of current climate variability and long-term climate change. Most of these efforts are geared towards disaster management, with a focus on recovery and relief and with little, if anything, being done to prevent some of the effects.

Efforts to adapt to climate change impacts in Mombasa have been promoted since the occurrence of the tsunami and are geared towards dealing with future tsunamis, floods and cyclones. The government, through the local administration and the Kenya Meteorological Department (KMD), has taken a leading role in gathering climate information and sending information to the residents and businesses in the expected impact areas, especially strategic holiday and business areas. The KMD is working towards establishing an operational weather observation network of the western Indian Ocean within Kenya's exclusive economic zone, and has procured and installed various equipment, including three tidal gauges fitted with meteorological sensors, 35 drifting buoys and one marine automatic weather station. This will help in monitoring sea-level rise and in detecting extreme events such as storm surges, coastal flooding, tsunamis and tropical cyclones.[12]

Scientists from the KMD and the University of Nairobi, among others, have undertaken an analysis of Kenya's climate change vulnerability and adaptation and have submitted this to the United Nations Framework Convention on

Climate Change (UNFCCC) in their first national communication. The report identified sectors that are most vulnerable to climate change, as well as gaps in the country's adaptation and mitigation strategies. In addition, the KMD undertook a project aimed at improving the factoring of weather and climate information into the various sectors of the economy between 2001 and 2002.[13] Currently, the country is in the process of preparing the second national communication to the UNFCCC. The government is also increasing its efforts to create public awareness of climate change – and associated communication and dissemination – by installing an automatic message switching system at Moi International Airport in Mombasa. This equipment is capable of receiving early warnings of marine hazards, including tsunamis, on a real-time basis. In addition, a radio frequency modulation–radio and internet (FM–RANET) transmitter station for vulnerable communities is being installed on the coast, in Kwale. All of these are expected to serve not only the coastal urban population, but also the whole coastal region. A number of wind-up radios have also been procured.[14]

Concerted efforts by the government, marine scientists, NGOs and local communities are being undertaken to reforest the degraded coastal areas to ensure a healthy sea wall, among other important benefits. In addition, the government is in the process of formulating an effective and enforceable coastal zone management policy, as required under the Environment Management and Coordination Act of 1999, to regulate developments along the coastline and provide for appropriate management of coastal resources. This policy will also provide for the type of structures to be constructed, depending upon the vulnerability of different areas. It is in this respect that the government has drawn up a National Tsunami Action Plan under a multi-hazard framework, which will be implemented in cooperation with various development partners.

During the floods in 2006, the government sent a team of engineers to the coast to assess requirements for roads and bridges in light of the unusually long and heavy rains. This may be considered as an effort towards ensuring that any roads built can withstand increased rainfall associated with increasing climate variability and long-term change. The Ministry of Health is also establishing emergency health management measures to deal with the sharp rise in cases of diarrhoea when floods occur.[15]

The Intergovernmental Authority on Development (IGAD) Climate Prediction and Applications Centre initiated regional climate outlooks, national user workshops and pilot applications projects. These projects aimed to address problems associated with information-sharing and application among users and vulnerable communities. They have helped to build capacity in many regions, have linked meteorologists and end-users of seasonal forecasts, have stimulated interest in, and recognition of, the impacts of inter-annual climate variability, and have helped to demonstrate the economic value of applying climate information and prediction products in socio-economic development.[16] There is a need for increased activity and a collective campaign to raise public awareness of climate change impacts and adaptation, particularly with regard to cities, which apart from being centres of economic activity also have the highest concentration of populations.

A team comprising the Kenya Red Cross Society, the Kenya Navy, the Kenya Ports Authority and the African Marine and Boat Operators carries out monitoring of the sea for any possible disaster and determines whether there is a need for evacuation in the event of any consequential effects of disasters, such as the tsunami.

The actual extent and efficacy of the activities and initiatives cited above on reducing the vulnerability of Mombasa to climate change have yet to be determined, as the initiatives are still in their early implementation stages. So far, most initiatives have focused on dealing with impacts of extreme events and not on the preparedness aspects that should form part of adaptation.

Reducing Mombasa's vulnerability to a changing climate

A number of activities could be carried out to minimize the city's vulnerability to climate change, both in terms of adaptation and mitigation:

- In order to adapt to climate change, all natural system effects are allowed to occur and human impacts are minimized by adjusting human use of the coastal zone. In Kenya, as in many other low-income countries, adaptation is the immediate priority in response to climate change impacts.
- To mitigate against climate change impacts, natural system effects are controlled by soft or hard engineering, reducing human impacts in the zone that would be affected without protection.

This chapter focuses on measures that could reduce Mombasa's vulnerability to the anticipated climate change impacts, as well as promoting adaptation. These range from immediate actions, such as enforcing the existing legislation, to long-term measures, such as coming up with development plans that take into account future climatic conditions.

There is a need to create greater awareness and sensitization about climate change at the global level and its interaction with local effects. This could be done through awareness campaigns, the print and audio-visual mass media, local performing arts such as drama and music, and the education system at schools, among other. This could play an instrumental role in enhancing understanding of climate change and its impacts and, possibly, motivate the generation of innovative ideas and feasible options for adaptation at local and city levels.

Enforcing the Physical Planning Act and city bylaws to ensure that areas earmarked for basic services such as water and sanitation are not interfered with could help to reduce flooding and the outbreak of water-borne diseases. The district commissioner, as the chair of the District Environmental Committee, should undertake the steps necessary to repossess all public utility land and beach access roads that have been allocated to private developers and have these registered under the Land Perpetual Succession Act, CAP 286 of the Laws of Kenya. In addition, construction, expansion and maintenance of drainage facilities in estates with near-zero gradient and poor water seepage could significantly reduce prolonged flooding and its resultant side effects. Local residents must be made aware of, and sensitized to, the need to improve the management of the areas they inhabit, even more so because of climate variability and its attendant impacts such as increased rainfall and flooding.

The issue of squatters or landlessness is more acute in the coast province, including Mombasa, than in other parts of the country. Much of the land and other property are in the hands of absentee landlords and this contributes to the problem of unplanned settlement, especially in the supra-urban space. There is a need to solve the problem of landownership in order to encourage the construction of planned settlements, which makes it easy to provide basic services and to reduce the risk of flooding. Without addressing the issue of landlessness, it may be difficult to plan settlements, especially in the low-income areas.

It is recommended that the Coast Development Authority develops a strategic plan to guide future development of the coastal city, taking climate change considerations into account. In addition, a code of conduct to guide developers and users of coastal resources should be developed and existing coastal management legislation reviewed.

Planning and construction of new settlements outside Mombasa Island is necessary to avoid further concentration of population and activities in the most vulnerable areas. The city authority and government should encourage settlement in peri-urban space away from the ocean shores. It is now agreed that some impacts of climate change are unavoidable, irrespective of what is done now, as a result of past emissions. Encouraging settlement away from the most vulnerable areas remains one of the least expensive and proactive ways through which future vulnerabilities may be reduced.

Building standards that can accommodate future climatic conditions, such as high temperatures, humidity and flooding, should be promoted. For example, it would be useful to construct buildings with strong, unoccupied open spaces on the ground floor or with foundations; these could avert damage and loss of property and life during floods. In addition, buildings could be designed and constructed in ways that promote natural air circulation and cooling to reduce temperatures and high humidity indoors. It would be important to engage qualified architects to provide guidance in designing such buildings.

The main water pipeline serving Mombasa is old and leaks frequently. This further reduces the daily amount of water reaching the city. There is a need to improve the management and renovation of the city's water and sanitation infrastructure to serve the increasing water demand. The Ministry of Land Reclamation and Regional Development and the Ministry of Water and Irrigation should work together with the city council to promote water reuse and recycling and to implement other effective measures to increase water availability in Mombasa and its environs. This would stem the overexploitation of underground water that is exacerbating saltwater intrusion.

The impacts of sea-level rise could be reduced through properly planned irrigation away from sea shores and through other land management practices that could be used to manage floods and reduce water run-off into the oceans. The government, NGOs and local communities should collaborate to construct water reservoirs and apply appropriate land management practices. In this regard, the measures taken should ensure the proper conservation and management of the coastal environment, including beaches and related ecosystems, taking into account available scientific information and indigenous environmental conservation practices.

The use of renewable energy at both household and industrial level should be promoted. Wind and solar energy are widely available in Mombasa and can be used in a number of areas. Solar energy can be used for water heating at the household level and in salt processing at the industrial level, while wind energy may be used in water pumping from boreholes. It is worth noting that the salt processing plants are already using solar energy for drying. More industries should be encouraged to adopt such environmentally friendly methods. At the household level, one of the factors that has limited the adoption and wider use of solar technology is the high initial cost. Even though the government zero-rated solar panels with regard to taxation, other components were not; hence, it remains an expensive technology for the average household. The government can change this by removing all taxes and supporting local industries to produce the panels and components locally.

It is important that the existing district-level disaster surveillance and management committee becomes proactive and focuses more on disaster preparedness than on 'after the event' relief and impacts management. The formation of similar committees at the sub-location, location and divisional levels, in collaboration with the municipal council, is also highly recommended. These will bear the responsibility of educating communities and enforcing regulations such as those barring the construction of buildings in flood-prone areas and ensuring proper drainage. Stakeholders need to make concerted efforts to track and/or explore predictive mechanisms for various climate-related disasters through networking, further research and information-sharing. Interest- and economic activity-based groups such as boat operators, fishermen, food vendors, farming and other community-based groups need to be brought into the disaster management committees so that they can better understand and make use of early warning information signs, responses and recovery strategies. In addition, training in appropriate disaster preparedness and response should be undertaken.

Existing community-based groups can be used as immediate entry points towards improving livelihoods through the formation of simple/low-capital and focused economic enterprises, such as high-value agriculture (vegetable growing and horticulture), and livestock enterprises (e.g. poultry and dairy goat production).

Strengthening existing enterprises through technical/professional support from relevant ministries and NGOs would also contribute to increased incomes and possibly improve capacities to adapt to climate-related disasters. Diversification of economic activities (e.g. through the promotion of community-based seafood farming) could be encouraged as an adaptation measure in suitable areas.

Conclusions

Implementing many of these changes/recommendations requires support from the various government departments, city hall, civil society organizations (including NGOs) and the public, in general. This will only be achieved if people are made aware of, and understand the need for, such action now rather than continue with business as usual.

Effective and timely early warning systems are needed to deal with climate-related disasters. There is a need for the city council to work with meteorological/maritime departments, relevant government ministries and other stakeholders to facilitate coordinated efforts.

Enforcement of city bylaws to ensure that people only construct buildings in safer and approved areas far from the beaches, and avoid sewage lines and drainage. etc. should be ensured. This will also reduce the risk of flooding and piped water contamination.

The government should resolve problems of landlessness and absentee landlords at the coast by repossessing grabbed public land, purchasing legally acquired land from absentee landlords, and subdividing and allocating this land to the poor equitably. This would enable security of land tenure and encourage people to follow guidelines and build houses according to set standards.

To implement the recommendations above, appropriate capacity, both at the individual and institutional levels, and enforceable regulations and economic incentives are required. These depend upon political will, funding and human capital.

Notes

1. Dow, K. and Downing, T. (2006) *The Atlas of Climate Change*, Earthscan, London.
2. Confalonieri, U., Menne, B., Akhtar, R., Ebi, K. L., Hauengue, M., Kovats, R. S., Revich, B. and Woodward, A. (2007) *Human Health. Climate Change 2007: Impacts, Adaptation and Vulnerability*, Contribution of Working Group II to the Fourth Assessment Report of the Intergovernmental Panel on Climate Change, Cambridge University Press, Cambridge, UK, pp391–431.
3. District Statistical Office, Mombasa (2008) *Population and Housing Statistics: Mombasa*, Report to the Ministry of Planning and National Development, Mombasa.

4. IEA (2002) 'Socioeconomic and political profiles of Kenya's districts', in Danda, M. (2006) *Vulnerability and Capacity Assessment in Mombasa District*, Survey Report for the Kenya Red Cross Society, Mombasa Branch, Mombasa.
5. Government of Kenya (2007) *Statistical Analysis of Tourism Trends Globally and Locally*, Ministry of Tourism and Wildlife, www.tourism.go.ke/ministry.nsf/pages/facts_figures.
6. Government of Kenya (2002b) *Kenya's First National Communication to the Conference of Parties to the United Nations Framework Convention on Climate Change*, Ministry of Environment and Natural Resources, Government Printers, Nairobi; also Government of Kenya (2002a) *Mombasa District Development Plan 2002–2008*, Ministry of Finance and Planning. Nairobi.
7. Bindoff, N. L., Willebrand, J., Artale, V., Cazenave, A., Gregory, J., Gulev, S., Hanawa, K., Le Quere, C., Levitus, S., Nojiri, Y., Shum, C. K., Talley, L. D. and Unnikrishnan, A. (2007) 'Observations: oceanic climate change and sea level', in Solomon, S., Quin, D., Manning, M., Chen, Z., Marquis, M., Averyt, K. B., Tignor, M. M. and Miller, H. I. (eds) *Climate Change 2007: The Physical Science Basis*, Contribution of Working Group I to the Fourth Assessment Report of the Intergovernmental Panel on Climate Change, Cambridge University Press, Cambridge and New York, pp385–432.
8. Mahongo, S. (2006) 'Impacts of sea-level change', Paper presented at the ODINAFRICA/GLOSS Training Workshop on Sea-Level Measurement and Interpretation, 13–24 November, Oostende, Belgium.
9. See reference 6, Government of Kenya (2002a).
10. *The Daily Nation Newspaper* (2007) 'Kenya: Climate change fuelling conflicts', Nairobi, 8 May.
11. OCHA (United Nations Office for the Coordination of Humanitarian Affairs) (2006) *Regional Overview of the Flooding in the Horn of Africa*, no 1, www.reliefweb.int/rw/RWB.NSF/db900SID/KKEE-6VMNPX?/OpenDocument.
12. The Kenya Meteorological Department (2007) *Polar Meteorology: Understanding Global Impacts*, Report for the World Meteorological Day 2007, Nairobi, Kenya.
13. See reference 12.
14. See reference 12.
15. See reference 11.
16. See reference 12.

4

Vulnerabilities and Responses to Climate Change for Dhaka

Mozaharul Alam and MD Golam Rabbani

Introduction

Dhaka, the capital of Bangladesh and one of the world's largest megacities, accommodates more than 13.1 million people within its 1353km² area.[1] According to the most recent United Nations estimate, its population will reach 16.8 million by 2015.[2] This megacity comprises Dhaka City Corporation (DCC) and five adjacent municipal areas – namely, Savar, Narayanganj, Gazipur, Kadamrasul and Tongi.[3] In 2005, the DCC, the heart of the megacity, covered 276km² and had a total population of 8.4 million. The city is surrounded by the Buriganga River to the south, the Balu and Shitalakhya rivers to the east, the Tongi canal to the north and the Turag River to the west.

Dhaka is 2m to 13m above mean sea level, with most of the urbanized areas at elevations of 6m to 8m. It has been reported that about 20km² of land are more than 8m above mean sea level; about 75km² are between 6m and 8m, and 170km² are below 6m.[4] Dhaka has hot, humid summers, short, mild winters and heavy rain during the monsoon season.[5]

Brief history and growth

Human settlement and the development of infrastructure started in the 16th century in the southern part of the present city corporation that is known as 'old Dhaka'. Over the last 400 years, the city has experienced a number of dramatic historic events. Political changes and shifts in power have also brought about changes in demography and structural development.

Over the last few centuries, Dhaka has extended to approximately 40km from north to south and 14km from east to west. In 1951, it covered 85km² and had 0.4 million inhabitants. It experienced a very rapid expansion in area and population after independence in 1971. Since then, the rapid development of human settlements, the growth of national and international business, the opening of new trades and the expansion of private and public establishments, industry and infrastructure have made Dhaka one of the most unplanned urban centres. To meet the rapidly growing demands of different sectors, utility services were established and expanded at different times, but not at the same pace as population growth and demand. This disparity and the unequal development and management of the utility services and improper management of the natural resources and natural hazards (e.g. floods and excessive rainfall) have degraded the overall environment of the city.

Key concerns

The high rate of population growth for Dhaka, much of it the result of rural–urban migration, is not a new or unusual problem. Many cities in low- and middle-income nations have long faced a number of environmental and development problems. But now they will face additional stresses as the global climate continues to warm and as they have fewer of the resources needed to adapt or respond to the impact of climate change. Stresses for the cities related to global warming include higher temperatures, water shortages, increased flooding and rising sea levels, particularly for coastal cities.

Dhaka, as a megacity, is already facing a number of environmental problems and risks related to natural disasters. Most environmental problems are human induced, resulting either from a lack of compliance with national policies, rules and regulations, or from resource constraints to implementing different measures. Flooding is the most common disaster in Dhaka.

Other key environmental concerns for the city include air quality (both indoors and outdoors), surface water contamination, a reduction in groundwater, inadequate solid waste and sewage management, waterlogging, transport congestion and the expansion of slums and squatter settlements. Erratic changes in temperature and rainfall and increased frequency of floods are becoming more evident. There are also particular problems of drainage congestion due to excessive rainfall and flooding rivers. Both are a major concern to city dwellers, posing adverse effects on different sectors including infrastructure (road, rail and housing), industry (large, medium and small), trade and commerce (through, for instance, a disruption of communications), utility services (water supply and sanitation), sewage management, and the supply of electricity and gas. Of course, they also bring very serious problems in relation to human health and livelihoods, especially for the poor.

Key institutions

The government of Bangladesh has divided administrative, regulatory and utility services among different ministries, departments and agencies, with specific mandates and responsibilities. The DCC, Dhaka Water and Sewerage Authority (WASA), Dhaka Electric Supply Authority (DESA), Titas Gas Limited, Bangladesh Telephone and Telegraph Board, Rajdhani Unnyan Kortripakhkha and Dhaka Electric Supply Company (DESCO) are responsible for providing utility services to different sectors, including the domestic, industrial and commercial sectors. The Department of Environment, under the Ministry of Environment and Forests, is primarily responsible for implementing environmental rules and regulations, including those related to climate change issues. The Dhaka Metropolitan Police force is responsible for law and order in daily life and also during natural disasters. Health, education, planning, housing, transportation and other infrastructure-related organizations also exist in the city area, along with non-governmental organizations (NGOs), development partners, corporate business and trade communities, and other related organizations concerned with environmental issues in the city.

Dhaka's contribution to global climate change

Climate and cities have a long relationship that is now becoming more complex. The United Nations forecasts that by 2050, some 65 per cent of the world's population will be living in urban areas – as these increasingly become the world's centres of culture, industry and economy. Many cities have grown to a size that is unprecedented historically. The United Nations Population Division forecasts that by 2015, 35 cities – more than half of them in coastal zones – will have populations exceeding 8 million.[6] While modern cities cannot be considered separately from the larger regional climate systems, they exert profound effects on both regional weather and global climate as they are concentrated islands that absorb heat. Production and consumption that are concentrated within their boundaries are also generators of the heat and carbon dioxide emissions that have been driving global climate change.

Greenhouse gases come from both natural and anthropogenic activities. Anthropogenic activities, mainly the burning of fossil fuels in different sectors, are a key source of greenhouse gases. A national greenhouse gas inventory for Bangladesh revealed that the energy sector contributes more than 60 per cent of the total greenhouse gases of 15,178 gigagrams per year.[7] Energy industries, other industries, transport and the residential sector are key consumers of different types of fossil fuels. Among these sectors, the energy industry contributes more than 35 per cent of the greenhouse gases, while transport (road, rail, navigation and domestic aviation) contributes about 17 per cent, of which 70 per cent comes from the road transport system.

As the country's capital city, and with its multiplicity of sectors, Dhaka is consuming different types of fossil fuels. The commercial, residential and industrial sectors are using mainly electricity, of which more than 85 per cent is generated from natural gas. They also use gasoline and diesel-fuelled generators to meet electricity demand during electricity outages. The transport sector depends mostly upon petroleum products (i.e. diesel and gasoline). Very recently, compressed natural gas (CNG) entered into the energy mix within the transport sector. Residential and some commercial sectors are also using natural gas for cooking, while slum dwellers are using mostly biomass as their primary fuel for cooking.

DESA and DESCO provide electricity in the city. DESA was created in 1990 to improve services to consumers and to enhance revenue collection by reducing high system losses. DESCO was created in 1996 and started its operations in 1998 as part of a process to restructure the power sector and improve the key operational and financial activities in the electricity distribution system.

Bangladesh Power Development Board (BPDB) performance data show that energy imported by DESA and DESCO accounts for almost 50 per cent of the total energy sold by BPDB. However, data for the fiscal year 2006–2007 and 2007–2008 show that imports have declined for Dhaka against total energy sold by BPDB. This may be due to higher demand at the national level against lower generation. Table 4.1 provides figures for net energy generation, energy sold and energy imported by DESA and DESCO from 1991–1992 to 2007–2008.

The registration database for the Bangladesh Road Transport Authority reveals that about 45 per cent of all vehicles in the nation (up to 2005) are registered in Dhaka. National estimates suggest that about 70 per cent of emissions from the transport sector are from road transport. The fact that movements of vehicles do not follow administrative boundaries makes estimates problematic. But considering the

Table 4.1 *Bangladesh Power Development Board performance*

Year	Net energy generation	Total energy sold	Energy imported by DESA and DESCO	Percentage of imported energy against total energy sold
		Gigawatt hours		
1991–1992	8393	6329	3066	48.44
1992–1993	8699	6906	3356	48.60
1993–1994	9221	7447	3696	49.63
1994–1995	10,166	8371	4162	49.72
1995–1996	10,832	8995	4550	50.58
1996–1997	11,242	9446	4961	52.52
1997–1998	12,194	10,176	5418	53.24
1998–1999	13,637	11,352	5946	52.38
1999–2000	14,739	12,468	6504	52.17
2000–2001	16,254	14,002	7241	51.71
2001–2002	17,444	15,243	7845	51.47
2002–2003	18,422	16,331	8320	50.95
2003–2004	20,062	18,023	7070	39.23
2004–2005	21,162	19,195	6977	36.35
2005–2006	22,742	20,962	7350	35.06
2006–2007	22,783	21,181	7433	35.09
2007–2008*	20,091	18,710	6357	33.98

Note: * Up to April 2008.

Source: Bangladesh Power Development Board (2006) www.bpdb.gov.bd/executive.htm

Table 4.2 *Types and number of vehicles registered in Bangladesh and Dhaka up to 2005*

Type of vehicle	Number of vehicles registered in Bangladesh	Number of vehicles registered in Dhaka	Percentage registered in Dhaka
Motor car	128,037	98,233	76.72
Jeep/station wagon/microbus	55,837	37,808	67.71
Taxi	11,987	10,406	86.81
Bus	32,257	4121	12.78
Minibus	34,347	7946	23.13
Truck	56,749	22,883	40.32
Auto-rickshaw/auto-tempo	112,330	39,599	35.25
Human haller	1349	829	61.45
Covered van	581	527	90.71
Motorcycle	389,514	140,050	35.96
Other	29,488	16,175	54.85
Total	**852,476**	**378,577**	**44.41**

Source: Bangladesh Road Transport Authority (2006) www.brta.gov.bd

types of vehicle registered in Dhaka and Bangladesh, and the amounts of different types of fuel consumed, it may be concluded that about 25 to 30 per cent of the emissions from the road transport system come from Dhaka city. Table 4.2 shows the types and numbers of vehicles registered in Bangladesh and Dhaka up to 2005.

Thus, a large proportion of greenhouse gases come from the electricity and transport sectors, although their contribution to total global greenhouse gas emissions is negligible. Given the rate of population growth in Dhaka, electricity consumption and the transport sector, the city's contribution to global greenhouse gases will increase. It must be noted that brick kilns around the city and landfill sites also contribute to global greenhouse gases. They usually operate for about six months a year, and every year in the dry season, they burn nearly 2 million tonnes of coal.[8]

The effects of climate change in Dhaka

Climate change will affect Dhaka primarily in two ways: through floods/drainage congestion and through heat stress. The melting of glaciers and snow in the Himalaya and increasing rainfall will lead to more frequent flooding in Bangladesh. The waterlogging and drainage congestion due to river floods and excessive rainfall during the monsoon are already causing very serious damage. Furthermore, Dhaka may also face 'heat island'[9] problems because temperatures in the city are a few degrees higher than in the surrounding areas. Indeed, vehicle exhaust emissions, industrial activity and increasing use of air conditioning are contributing to heat generation and this will increase in the future. An overview of the major floods that have affected Dhaka is given below.

Major floods in Dhaka

Dhaka has faced a number of severe floods since its early days and its vulnerability to these resulted in the building of the Buriganga River flood embankment in 1864. Severe flooding in Greater Dhaka is mainly the result of spill-over from surrounding rivers that flow to and from the major rivers of the country, as well as internal waterlogging. In recent history, Dhaka has experienced major floods in 1954, 1955, 1970, 1974, 1980, 1987, 1988, 1998, 2004 and 2007 due to overflowing of surrounding rivers. Of these, the 1988, 1998 and 2004 floods were the most damaging.

Flooding due to excessive rainfall is also a severe problem in certain parts of the city, which are inundated for several days mainly due to drainage congestion and inadequate pumping facilities to remove the stagnant water. The water depth in some areas may be as high as 40cm to 60cm, which creates large infrastructure problems for the city, economic losses in production and damage to existing property and goods. The impacts of river flooding are even more severe and disrupt economic activities and the livelihoods of people dependent upon urban activities.

During July and August 2004, devastating floods seriously affected Bangladesh. The north and west-central districts suffered severe flooding, which continued to spread, eventually reaching Dhaka and other central districts. The floods affected about 38 per cent of Bangladesh and caused extensive damage to standing crops, physical and social infrastructure, the environment and the livelihoods of 36 million people. Furthermore, in September 2004, a localized low pressure depression swept over Bangladesh, resulting in excessive rainfall – three times the normal levels. This intense rainfall caused another round of flooding in Dhaka and central and south-western districts.

The main reason for the 1998 flood was excessive rainfall over the catchment area of the Ganges–Brahmaputra–Meghna River Basin. Three different flood waves passed through this river basin and the last one coincided with peak flows in the Ganges and the Brahmaputra. In addition, the impact of the lunar cycle, and the resulting high tide, was responsible for the slow recession of the floodwaters. These factors resulted in prolonged flooding in both the country and the city for two months.

The main causes of flooding inside the protected area were hydraulic leakage, a failure to operate the regulators (sluice gates) and a lack of timely pumping of accumulated water upstream from the Rampura regulator. As 75 per cent of the work for Phase I of the Dhaka Integrated Flood Protection Project had been completed, it was assumed that the Gulshan, Banani, Baridhara and Tejgaon areas would not be flooded. However, four or more drainage pipes measuring about four feet in diameter connect this part of the city with the floodplain on the eastern side, and hydraulic leakage and failure in the operation of the Rampura regulator resulted in flooding in these areas. There was an apparent lack of coordination between the Bangladesh Water Development Board (BWDB) and WASA to prevent the flooding. Although the authority is responsible for ensuring proper drainage, the BWDB is in charge of operating the regulators and gates. In fact, there was neither operating policy nor assigned person to operate the Rampura regulator that controls the drainage of 40 per cent of the protected area under Phase I of the Dhaka Integrated Flood Protection Project.

In the 1998 flood, there was excessive rainfall in Dhaka, causing short duration flooding in the areas of Shantinagar, Nayapaltan, Rajarbag, Dhanmodi, Azimpur and Green Road. The runoff generated by the rainfall could not flow into the surrounding rivers as the river stage was higher than the inside flow.[10] Therefore, the accumulated runoff in low-lying areas remained stagnant until the river stage receded, causing extensive waterlogging in Dhaka West. Figure 4.1 shows the extent of 1998 flooding in Dhaka.

In 1988, one of the most severe floods in recent history hit Dhaka and inundated 85 per cent of the city. It was estimated that floods of this intensity hit the country only once every 70 years. Inundation depths ranged from 0.3m to more than 4.5m and about 60 per cent of the city dwellers were affected.[11] This unprecedented level of flooding disrupted city life and air travel, and communications between Dhaka and the outside world were cut off for about two weeks. Data on the impacts and damage from the 1988 flood were compiled and analysed according to component eight of the flood action plan. All of eastern Dhaka and all of the low-lying areas of western Dhaka were under floodwater. Only parts of Mirpur, Tejgaon, Banani, Sher-e-Banglanagar, Azimpur and the Old Town were not flooded.

Overall rainfall patterns and trends

The Bangladesh Meteorological Department has 35 meteorological stations throughout the country. Rainfall data from the Dhaka station for 1971 to 2005 show that the annual average rainfall in the city is about 2120mm, of which about 50 per cent falls during the months of June, July and August, generally referred to as the monsoon season. Average rainfall during the winter months (December, January and February) is negligible – less than 2 per cent of annual rainfall.

While Dhaka's long-term trend in annual rainfall shows no significant change, the trend in seasonal rainfall appears to be erratic. Two important facts support this finding. First, trend analysis reveals that although there is no

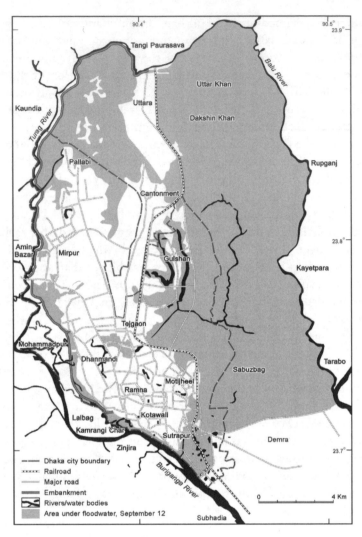

Figure 4.1 Extent of 1998 flooding in Dhaka City

Source: adapted from data from the Geographical Information Systems Division of the Bangladesh Centre for Advanced Studies (BCAS)

significant change in annual average rainfall, the number of 'days without rainfall' is increasing. Second, seasonal rainfall data in both the monsoon (June, July and August) and winter (December, January and February) seasons show a decreasing trend over time. However, it should be noted that the R^2 value (denoting the statistical strength of this trend) is very low. Figure 4.2 shows annual average rainfall and 'days without rainfall'. However, these two facts together indicate that more rainfall is occurring in other months of the year and that rainfall intensity is increasing.

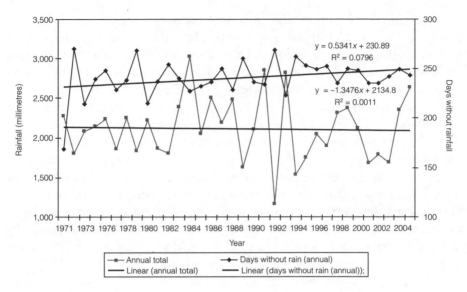

Figure 4.2 Trend for annual rainfall and days without rainfall

Source: Author's analysis of meteorological data

Affected sectors and vulnerabilities

Infrastructure, industry, trade and commerce and utility services are key sectors that are vulnerable to floods and their impacts. The limited performance of these sectors during and after flooding increases the vulnerability of city dwellers, and this vulnerability varies according to economic and social status. Loss of life and livelihoods and impacts upon human health are key vulnerabilities for lower-income groups.

Infrastructure

Extreme events such as floods, drainage congestion and waterlogging due to excessive rainfall cause very serious damage to such infrastructure as roads and railways, formal and informal housing and educational institutions. According to available literature, the eastern part (nearly 119km²) of Dhaka was 100 per cent inundated in the floods that occurred in 1988, 1998 and 2004. In western Dhaka, 117km² (75 per cent) were submerged in 1988; but due to the construction of the flood protection embankment along the Turag and Buriganga rivers, only 36km² (23 per cent) were submerged in the 1998 flood.[12] Waterlogging due to continuous rainfall is a near-regular occurrence in the rainy season in the eastern part of the city. In 1998 and 2004, both inter- and intra-city bus links from eastern Dhaka were shut down because of inundation.

It is estimated that the number of institutions and houses affected by the 1988 flood was 14,000 and 400,000, respectively. The estimated damage was about 4 billion Bangladeshi taka for residential buildings and more than 400 million taka for institutions. The 1998 flood caused damage to more than 262,000 shelter units, or 30 per cent of the 860,552 units in the Dhaka Metropolitan Area, at a cost of 2.3 billion taka.[13] Of these, 32 per cent were permanent and semi-permanent structures belonging to wealthy or well-to-do households not dependent upon help for repairs and rehabilitation. About 36 per cent of shelter units that were temporary or of poor quality (of *katcha*-1 type) and that belonged to lower-middle and poorer classes suffered damage of 283 million taka. Their owners had the ability to cope with repairs but would likely face hardship. In the bottom rung, nearly 32 per cent of shelter units of *katcha*-2 and *jupri* types, belonging to poorer groups (including the poorest – known as hard core poor, who lack the income needed for sufficient food) suffered severe damage of 195 million taka. The owners were too poor to mobilize funds on their own.[14]

It is evident from various studies that damage to infrastructure, including roads, water supply and housing, was severe in 1998. It has been reported that more than 600km of the total 2300km of road were damaged in this flood. All the informal settlements and business enterprises located in eastern Dhaka were affected. All academic institutions (primary schools, high schools and colleges) in the area were also closed during the flood. It was estimated that 384km of paved road were inundated, a large proportion in Gulshan *thana*.[15] There was also severe damage in Sabujbag *thana* and in Demra. The most severe disruption to water supplies from deep tubewells was in the Cantonment *thana*, also in Gulshan and Uttara. Considering the major impacts of the floodwater, it appears that Sabujbag and Gulshan *thanas* were the worst affected, followed by Demra, Uttara and Cantonment *thanas*.[16]

Industry

Most small-, medium- and large-scale industries and factories are affected by floods. This includes garments, textiles, leather, cold storage, timber and furniture, and food and agro-based industries. Most of the affected industries and factories usually discontinue their operations during floods as floodwater often disrupts physical, mechanical and electronic functioning. As a result, garment industries, for example, often fail to meet shipment or delivery deadlines in both the local and international markets. The total loss to large-scale industry in Dhaka in the 1998 flood was equivalent to more than US$30 million, while the loss to small- and medium-sized industry in the city was US$36 million.[17]

Trade and commerce

Any disruption in communications causes a slowdown in the mechanisms of local, national and international trade and commerce. Both flooding and waterlogging due to excessive rainfall cause very serious damage in the trade and commercial sectors (see Box 4.1). The waterlogging especially becomes a burden for the dwellers of Dhaka city as it poses challenges to social functioning, the environment and economic activity.

Box 4.1 Effects of waterlogging

In September 2004, business and economic activities came to a virtual standstill in Dhaka as a result of heavy rainfall. On 12 and 13 September, constant rains inundated most of the business centres, including Motijheel commercial hub, and the Meteorological Department measured a record 315mm rainfall in the city during those 48 hours. The overnight downpour forced the suspension of Dhaka's Stock Exchange and the weather also disrupted production in garment factories. Many workers could not reach the factories because the roads from their houses, mostly located in the city's low-lying areas, were inundated. Sales in shopping malls and activities in other business houses were unusually low – people preferred to stay at home unless there was an emergency. Many airline flights, especially on domestic routes, were delayed by one hour or two hours. A report by WASA indicates that waterlogging during September affected 250 schools and 681 garment factories in Dhaka city, and the garment sector lost 632 billion Bangladeshi taka. Road repairs cost 12.8 billion taka and damage to the telephone sector totalled 175 million taka.

Source: Tawhid, K. G. (2004) *Causes and Effects of Waterlogging in Dhaka City, Bangladesh,* TRITA–LWR MSc thesis, Department of Land and Water Resource Engineering, Royal Institute of Technology, Dhaka

Utility services

Water supply, sanitation, solid waste management, sewage management, electricity and gas supplies, and telecommunications all suffer damage as a result of flooding and waterlogging. For example, water becomes contaminated in the supply pipes as many of these are old and damaged and leak (see Box 4.2). Both DCC and WASA fail to manage the solid waste and sewerage network, and it was estimated that the total cost to repair and rehabilitate the damage to the sewerage system after the 1998 flood was more than US$9 million.[18] Another estimate calculates the total damage to the water, sewerage, electricity, gas and telephone services after the 1998 flood at more than US$20 million.[19] Roadside waste bins and containers are usually submerged during floods, and door-to-door solid waste collection and disposal services are impossible in many parts of the city. In fact, all utility services grind to a halt during flood events.

Box 4.2 Flood-hit Dhaka reels from water crisis

A late July newspaper report during the 2004 flood noted that more than 2 million city residents faced an acute drinking water crisis as supplies had become contaminated. Thirty water pumps operated by the Dhaka Water and Sewerage Authority (WASA) were inundated by rising floodwater. Water pipelines stretching over a few hundred kilometres and many reservoirs were also under water, posing a serious threat to public health. Floods had already affected more than 5 million people, or half the total city population. People in 18 out of 22 thanas were marooned at that point.

Source: The Daily Star, 26 July 2004, Dhaka

During the 1998 flood, 44 deep tubewells were affected by floodwater and water production was suspended in 13 of them, with an estimated loss in production of 45 million litres per day. The remaining tubewells were kept operational by adopting protection measures, including the erection of a protection wall around the pump house and raising housing pipes and electrical appliances above the floodwater levels. Five of the 13 suspended tubewells were badly damaged and required replacement.

Population and health

Estimating the impact of flooding on people and their health is complex due to the many dimensions of the impacts. According to available literature and information, the death toll was about 150 in the 1988 flood, but the affected population was reported as about 2.2 million people.[20] Professor Hye carried out a rapid appraisal on flood-affected people during the 1998 flood, dividing the flood-affected areas into three categories: most severely affected (MSA), severely affected (SA) and moderately affected (MA). It was found that the flood displaced or dislocated 94 per cent of families in the MSA areas, about 52 per cent of families in the SA areas and 50 per cent in the MA areas. The estimate for the total flood-affected population was about 4.55 million.[21]

Floods, waterlogging and extreme temperatures affect human health, local health infrastructure and routine healthcare services. The prevalence of disease during extreme events such as floods increases greatly. These diseases include diarrhoea, dysentery, acute respiratory infection, fever, skin diseases and eye infections (see Box 4.3). One study shows that 191,867 people in Dhaka were admitted to different hospitals for treatment during the 1998 flood.[22] Of these, 284 died. Another study undertaken by the Bangladesh NGO Bangladesh Rural Advancement Committee (BRAC) shows that 10,217 people in 10 out of 22 *thanas* had suffered from

---

Box 4.3 Flooding and the health crisis in Dhaka (2004)

A massive health crisis is looming in Bangladesh as sewage mixes with floodwaters swirling through Dhaka. CNN correspondent Satinder Bindra described the health situation there as 'quite grim'. He said half the city was under water, the sewerage system had broken down and the risk of waterborne disease for Dhaka's population of 10 million was very high. Naseem-Ur Rehman, chief of communications in Bangladesh for the United Nations Children's Fund (UNICEF), said the situation for children in urban areas was 'extremely dangerous ... The water in the cities is filled with filth, and the children who are playing and walking through it are vulnerable. They are easy prey to infectious diseases.' The UN said sludge was gushing out of manholes in many parts of Dhaka, and diseases such as acute respiratory infection, diarrhoea, watery dysentery, jaundice, typhoid and scabies were being reported.

Source: CNN.com (2004) 'Flood health crisis looms in Dhaka', www.cnn.com/2004/ WORLD/asiapcf/07/29/southasia.floods/, 29 July

---

diarrhoea during the 1998 flood.[23] It should be noted that in the same month in a normal year, the figure for those affected by diarrhoea is reported to be half that.

Livelihoods

Floods hit nearly half of the total area of the city. Around 40 per cent of the population live in 'slums' and squatter settlements; they draw their livelihoods from industry (e.g. garments, textiles, leather, etc.), the transport sector, shopping centres, hotels and restaurants, the construction sector and as domestic workers. These people are severely affected by floods, waterlogging and other relevant problems. A field survey conducted during the 1998 flood found that at least 7.2 per cent of people had changed their occupation while 27.4 per cent were unemployed as a result of the flood. In addition, working hours were reduced for many workers. Poorer groups always suffer more from disasters such as floods.

Response measures

The Ministry of Environment and Forests, WASA and the BWDB have undertaken several measures to improve environmental quality and manage floods, including addressing drainage congestion. Policy decisions and different measures have also been taken to reduce greenhouse gas emissions and to improve air quality in Dhaka. Most of these measures can be considered win–win options.

Responses to improve air quality in Dhaka

The government of Bangladesh has undertaken several initiatives to improve the air quality in Dhaka, including the following:

- the introduction of compressed natural gas for transport – recent increases in gasoline prices have pushed this further and more vehicles are being converted to CNG;
- since 2002, the banning of buses more than 20 years' old and trucks more than 25 years' old in Bangladesh;
- since 1 January 2003, the banning of two-stroke engine three-wheeler vehicles in Dhaka;
- a reduction in the number of non-motorized vehicles along with restrictions on their movement within certain areas of the city and during specific periods of the day; this helps to reduce traffic congestion and thus reduces the consumption or burning of fuels;
- updating and installing new traffic signals and the construction of bypasses and flyovers for smoother traffic flows;
- the introduction in 2002 of an environmental clearance certificate, mandatory for the establishment of brick fields; and
- a movement to promote the use of compact fluorescent lamps in Bangladesh; these are used quite extensively at both domestic and commercial levels and consume around one quarter of the electricity of incandescent bulbs.

The Dhaka Transportation Coordination Board is currently preparing a strategic transport plan, which will provide a long-term strategic vision for Dhaka's transport system.

Flood protection measures

The first flood protection embankment along the Buriganga River was constructed in 1864 to protect the riverbank from flooding and erosion and to modernize the riverside. Launched by C. T. Buckland, the commissioner of Dhaka at the time, this scheme (known as the Buckland Bound) was completed in three phases during the 1880s.

Plans for flood protection for Greater Dhaka have been under study and consideration for many years; but the extreme flooding that occurred in 1987 and 1988 brought into focus the urgent need for immediate action. Subsequently, the government of Bangladesh prepared an urgent flood protection and drainage plan, which included enclosing the Greater Dhaka area with flood embankments, reinforced concrete walls and drainage/flood regulation structures such as sluices and pumping stations.

Construction activities started with a 'crash programme' in 1989, and most of the work defined under phase I has been completed. It provides flood protection facilities to the western half of Dhaka city, which includes the most highly urbanized areas comprising about 87 per cent of the population in 1998. Important components of the flood protection measures are:

- approximately 30km of earthen embankment along the Tongi canal and the Turag and Buriganga rivers;
- approximately 37km of raised roads and floodwalls;
- a total of 11 regulators along the embankment at the outfall of *khals* (canals) to the surrounding rivers;
- one regulator and 12 sluice gates on the *khals* at the crossings with the Biswa, Dhaka Improvement Trust (DIT), Pragati Sarani and Mymensingh roads and the railway line at Uttar Khan;
- one pumping station at the outfall of the Kallyanpur *khal* into the Turag River and another at the outfall of the Dholai *khal* to the Buriganga River; these pumping stations are for draining rainwater from parts of Dhaka West; and
- a special 10.53km embankment surrounding the Zia international airport.

A rail/road embankment that will run for 29km along the Balu River is proposed for the eastern part of the city. This will be constructed under phase II of the Dhaka Integrated Flood Protection Project to protect the area between Biswa Road and the Balu River.

These flood control and drainage works have brought major changes in the flood regime of Dhaka West, including major changes in land use.

The embankment/road in the western part of Dhaka helped to protect more than 50 per cent of the city from the floods in 1998 and 2004. It saved people and property from complete inundation, but it causes waterlogging or internal drainage congestion, which becomes severe during heavy rainfall. This may be due to inadequate pumping facilities and lack of proper planning and design of infrastructure. However, the lessons can be utilized in the construction of the eastern bypass, which is under consideration to protect the other half (eastern part) of the city.

Improvement of the drainage system

The surface drainage system is usually not very effective, even without extreme weather events, and is especially ineffective during floods. However, the banning of polythene bags has reduced the regular clogging of the city drainage system. The relevant government agencies have taken the initiative several times to recover the many canals and canal banks that are illegally occupied by influential local people, most of them affiliated with local politics and the power structure. These recovery programmes have not been implemented fully in the past. These canals need to be recovered using any measures to improve the city's natural drainage system. It has been reported that WASA has recovered 15 out of the 26 canals that can still be rescued from encroachment.[24] The report also shows that Dhaka had 43 natural canals in the past, 17 of which no longer exist and can only be traced in history books. Eight of the canals were filled in to construct roads; but the rest of them are still occupied by either government or private-sector buildings that had been built on top of filled-in canals.

The 2008 Bangladesh Climate Change Strategy and Action Plan has recognized the vulnerability of the major cities and the regular problem of waterlogging in Dhaka city as the drainage capacity of the city's sewer system, with its current design, is not able to cope with the load. It has suggested assessing the drainage capacity of major cities, including Dhaka, and investigating structural and non-structural causes of waterlogging within the cities and their immediate surroundings using hydrodynamic models; and based on this study, a design and investment plan for improvements to the drainage capacity of the major cities should be drawn up.

Role of civil society organizations

During extreme events, including floods, NGOs, the business community and community-based organizations become very active with relief, recovery and rehabilitation programmes. During the 2004 flood, many individuals came forward to help flood-affected people and NGOs have provided health and sanitation in many areas, as well as health services for poor pregnant women who normally do not get attention during relief operations.

Conclusions

Cities have always been prone to disruption (such as traffic congestion) from heavy rainfall because of their large populations, high population densities and heavy concentration of businesses and other establishments. Because so many cities are on the coast and/or next to rivers, they are also severely affected by flooding. They also represent large areas of concrete, brick and asphalt, which absorb solar radiation and aggravate heat waves. Air pollution from vehicle exhausts and industrial emissions contributes to heat and can contribute to the increased incidence of respiratory illnesses among city dwellers. Furthermore, industry, motor vehicle traffic, the heating, cooling and lighting of buildings, solid waste sites and brick kilns around the city produce a high proportion of total greenhouse gas emissions.

Dhaka has already undertaken a number of measures to improve ambient air quality. Many have been effective both in improving air quality and in reducing greenhouse gas emissions – for example, the introduction of CNG in the transport sector. But many other sectors that consume electricity have not undertaken any significant measures to improve efficiency on the demand side. There is still untapped potential and opportunity to reduce electricity consumption and, thus, reduce greenhouse gas emissions – for instance, by promoting energy-efficient lighting devices, using more efficient cooling systems at household and industrial levels, making changes in the transport sector and changing behaviour.

Devastating floods can cause extensive damage to the economy. Dhaka has already experienced three major floods in less than 20 years and each has caused very serious damage to infrastructure and significant economic loss. One of the key questions related to this is can Dhaka afford frequent large-scale flood damage and economic losses or should it prepare better to combat floods and reduce impacts and vulnerabilities? Another important issue concerns the adverse impacts of climate change, which will not only affect Dhaka directly but will also have indirect effects in other parts of the country, particularly as a result of floods, riverbank erosion and cyclones. If these destroy or damage people's livelihoods, it is likely that rural–urban migration will increase and that more people will migrate to Dhaka.

To protect Dhaka from river floods, a flood protection embankment has been constructed on the western side and a comparable embankment is under consideration for the eastern side. The south-eastern part of the megacity is protected by the Dhaka–Nayrayangong–Demra flood protection embankment. Recent erratic rainfall brought unusual urban flooding as a result of drainage congestion and inadequate facilities for pumping water from inside the embankment. This raises the question: are the existing flood management measures adequate to address future flooding, which is anticipated to be more frequent and intense? Thus, spatial planning for un-built areas of Dhaka should incorporate aspects of climate change and should include all necessary measures. It is also necessary to make changes to the design of the embankment/road and to allow for adequate pumping systems to drain rainwater from the city – and overall, to adapt so that Dhaka can cope with the changes in intensity and patterns of rainfall under a warmer climate.

Notes

1. BBS (2003) *Bangladesh Population Census 2001, National Report (Provisional)*, vol 1, Dhaka; also UNEP (United Nations Environment Programme) (2005) *Dhaka City State of Environment Report: 2005*, UNEP Dhaka.
2. United Nations (2006) *World Urbanization Prospects: the 2005 Revision*, United Nations Population Division, Department of Economic and Social Affairs, CD-ROM Edition – data in digital form (POP/DB/WUP/Rev.2005), United Nations, New York.
3. Akash, M. M. and Singha, D. (2003) 'Provision of water points in low-income communities in Dhaka, Bangladesh', Paper prepared for the Civil Society Consultation on the 2003 Commonwealth Finance Ministers Meeting, Bandar Seri Begawan; also BBS (1991) *Statistical Year Book of Bangladesh*, Bangladesh Bureau of Statistics, Ministry of Planning, Government of Bangladesh.

4. JICA (Japan International Cooperation Agency) (1987) *Study on Stormwater Drainage System Improvement Project in Dhaka City*, Supporting Report, Local Government Division of Ministry of Local Government, Rural Development and Cooperatives, Dhaka.
5. Siddique, K., Ghosh, A., Bhowmik, K. S., Siddique, S. A., Mitra, M., Kapuria, S., Ranjan, N. and Ahmed, J. (2004) *Megacity Governing in South Asia: A Comparative Study*, University Press Limited, Dhaka.
6. See reference 2.
7. MoEF (Ministry of Environment and Forests) (2002) *Initial National Communication to the United Nations Framework Convention on Climate Change*, Ministry of Environment and Forests, Government of Bangladesh, Dhaka.
8. *The Daily Prothom Alo*, 5 March 2004, Dhaka.
9. A 'heat island' is an area that is significantly warmer than its surroundings. On hot summer days, urban air can be 2° to 6°C hotter than the surrounding countryside. This phenomenon is not to be confused with global warming and scientists call it the 'urban heat island effect'.
10. 'River stage' refers to the river water level and 'inside flow' to the water level of the runoff flow.
11. JICA (Japan International Cooperation Agency) (1991) *Master Plan for Greater Dhaka Flood Protection Project, FAP 8A*, Main Report and Supporting Report I and II, Flood Plan Coordination Organization (currently WARPO), Dhaka; also JICA (1992) *Feasibility Study of Greater Dhaka Flood Protection Project, FAP 8A*, Interim and Main Reports, Flood Plan Coordination Organization (currently WARPO), Dhaka.
12. Nishat, N., Reazuddin, M., Amin, R. and Khan, A. R. (ed) (2000) *An Assessment of Environmental Impacts of the 1998 Flood on Dhaka City*, Department of Environment and International Union for Conservation of Nature, Dhaka.
13. To get some sense of the scale of these figures, US$1 was roughly equivalent to 32 taka in 1988, 48.6 taka in 1998 and 61.5 taka in 2004.
14. Islam, N. and Ali, K. (1999) *Housing Damage Study*, Centre for Urban Studies (CUS), Dhaka.
15. A *thana* is a sub-district.
16. See reference 12.
17. See reference 12.
18. WASA (Dhaka Water and Sewerage Authority) (1998) 'Minutes of the 12th Special Emergency Board Meeting of the Dhaka WASA held on 19 September 1998', WASA, Kawran Bazar, Dhaka.
19. See reference 12.
20. See reference 11.
21. Hye, S. A. (1999) 'Livelihood of flood-affected people: Disruption and rehabilitation', Bangladesh Unnayan Parishad (BUP), Dhaka.
22. Kafiluddin, A. K. M. (2000) *Impact Study on Health*, National Institute of Preventive and Social Medicine (NIPSOM), Dhaka.
23. See reference 12.
24. *The Daily Star*, 25 September 2005, Dhaka.

5

The Vulnerability to Climate Change of Cotonou (Benin): The Rise in Sea Level

Krystel M. R. Dossou and Bernadette Gléhouenou-Dossou

Introduction

Climate change has an impact upon the development of West African cities such as Cotonou, which are located right on the coast. Cotonou's vulnerability to rising sea levels and exposure to coastal erosion currently threaten the city's economy and development, as well as the coastal and lagoon ecosystems. This vulnerability is exacerbated by the socio-economic and political constraints affecting the city, especially rapid demographic growth and inadequate resources for urban development. This chapter examines the potential and actual effects on the city of the rise in sea level and considers what possible adaptations could reduce its vulnerability to the effects of climate change.

Cotonou

Cotonou is the economic capital of Benin and one of the largest cities in West Africa, with a population now in excess of 1 million. The city is located on the coast of Benin, which stretches for 125km between Nigeria to the east and Togo to the west, and extends for 79km² on either side of the Cotonou Lagoon (see Figure 5.1). Lake Nokoué lies to the north, covering 200km² to 300km², the Atlantic Ocean is to the south, Godomey to the west and Agblangandan to the east.

   The coastal strip upon which Cotonou is built is composed of alluvial sand with a maximum depth of 4m. The strip's relief features longitudinal depressions parallel to the coastline and swamps (valley bottoms) fed by rainwater. The channel[1] (or Cotonou Lagoon) links the sea with Lake Nokoué and divides the city into two unequal parts (see Figure 5.1). According to the National Statistics and Economics Institute, in 1992 Cotonou had a population of 536,826 inhabitants; in 1998, it had an estimated 850,000 inhabitants and in 2005, an estimated 963,031 (this included the western and eastern extensions of the city).[2]

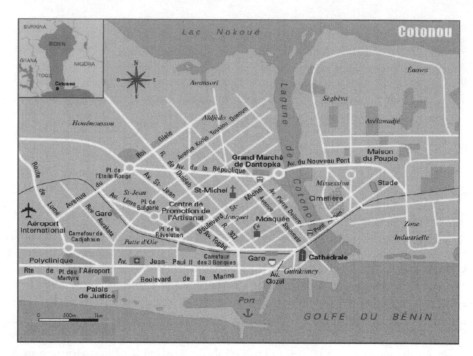

Figure 5.1 The city of Cotonou

Source: scanned from road map

Cotonou has a sub-equatorial climate with two rainy seasons (April to July and September to November) alternating with two dry seasons (December to March, and August). The sea ensures a mild climate, and average temperatures in the city (around 27°C) do not vary very much. There is an average of around seven hours of sunshine per day. Relative humidity is almost constant (around 85 per cent) due to the influence of the sea. The city receives an average annual rainfall of 1309mm (calculated over 40 years, 1945 to 1995). The prevailing coastal winds are southerly, with speeds of around 3m to 7m per second. The tide cycle is approximately 12 hours and the height range generally around 1m.[3]

Benin's economic potential depends to a large extent upon that of Cotonou, which hosts a large number of tertiary-sector activities and trading centres of international importance, as well as supplying financial resources to the country and the municipality. Activities undertaken in the city are essentially non-agricultural (apart from inland fisheries), particularly along the coast and the city's major roads, where activities are primarily commercial and services oriented. This dynamism is facilitated by infrastructure, including the port of Cotonou and Dantokpa international market. Cotonou's self-governing port accounts for 90 per cent of the country's customs receipts, while Dantokpa market has an annual turnover of 350 billion Communauté Financiere Africaine (CFA) francs.[4]

This market is the trading hub of West and Central African countries and Benin. In addition, service and craft production activities in the city, tourism, transport and small trades (artisan services) produce substantial income.[5]

Coastal fishing is also a mainstay of Cotonou's economy, providing a livelihood for more than 15,000 people (those engaged in fishing and also associated jobs such as fish wholesaling and boat repairs). Traditional fishing is undertaken by people of different ethnic origins (Toffin, Xwla, Aïzo, etc.) on Cotonou Lagoon and Lake Nokoué and on inshore waters (up to 5 nautical miles from the coast), as well as in the inter-dune depressions that are temporarily submerged at high tide. Authorized, more sophisticated foreign vessels also undertake industrial fishing on the continental plateau beyond the 5 nautical mile zone.[6]

The city of Cotonou is laid out in a conventional grid pattern and is divided into residential areas, administrative and social facilities, the military camp and industrial/commercial areas. The built-up area accounts for 74 per cent of the total area; 80 per cent of housing is located within the built-up area and constitutes 60 per cent of the city's surface area.[7] The city has developed along an east–west axis because of the natural constraints imposed by Lake Nokoué to the north and the Atlantic Ocean to the south. The bulk of the population (around 75 per cent) is concentrated in the western part of the city. Environmental problems include air pollution, greenhouse gas emissions and water and soil pollution.

Cotonou's vulnerability to sea-level rise

One of the main climate hazards facing Cotonou is the rise in sea level (or the net increase in the level of the ocean in relation to the level of local terrestrial movements). A Groupe Intergouvernemental d'Experts sur le Climat/ Intergovernmental Panel on Climate Change (GIEC/IPCC) report predicts: 'The rising sea level ... will have a detrimental effect on coastal human settlements, especially in the Gulf of Guinea.'[8] This prediction is very relevant to Cotonou, which has some areas that are at, or below, sea level. A rise in sea level could trigger a number of climatic phenomena, such as coastal and riverbank erosion, flooding and saltwater intrusion into Lake Nokoué. Furthermore, there has been decreasing rainfall in Benin, especially in the south,[9] with precipitation decreasing by 9 per cent over 20 years in Cotonou. Each of these hazards undermines human systems (land use, livelihoods and human settlements) and disrupts the functioning of coastal and lagoon ecosystems.

According to climatic simulations based on increased temperature carried out by the Model for the Assessment of Greenhouse Gas-Induced Climate Change (MAGICC),[10] the sea level along the coast of Benin could rise gradually (according to IPCC scenario IS92a) between now and 2050 and 2100. Table 5.1 shows the basic, average and extreme scenarios.

Table 5.1 *Assessment of the rise in sea level along the coast of Benin*

	Sea-level rise (cm)	
Timeframe	Year 2050	Year 2100
Average scenario	20	49
Extreme scenario	39	59
Basic scenario	7	20

Source: Ministère de l'Environnement, de l'Habitat et de l'Urbanisme (MEHU) (2001) *First National Communication of Benin*, UNDP, 76pp (this government paper was submitted to the UNFCCC; it described the inventory of processes emitting greenhouse gases in Benin and characterized the country's vulnerability to climate change)

Table 5.1 shows a predicted rise in sea level in the medium term (2050, 2100). Although these are hypothetical scenarios, the predicted rise in sea level (based on temperature data recordings taken in Benin between 1961 and 1990) could impact quite heavily upon human and natural systems, as noted above, and the figures show that urgent measures are needed with respect to preparedness, prevention and adaptation.

Impact of rising sea level

Rising sea level has many potential effects on natural systems and their operation, as well as on human systems. These related phenomena reflect such climatic stresses as riverbank erosion, flooding, coastal erosion and salting-up of lagoon waters, among others. Figure 5.2 clearly shows the consequences of a rise in sea level for Cotonou and its surrounding area.

These phenomena are already occurring, with serious consequences for the affected communities in Cotonou and its surrounding area, as well as other coastal and lagoon areas.

Coastal erosion in Cotonou and the surrounding area

Definition of the most vulnerable areas and people

In Cotonou, the area most vulnerable to coastal erosion comprises the first and fourth *arrondissements* (districts of Tokplégbé, Finagnon, Donatin, Akpakpa-Dodomey and JAK) (see Figure 5.3). According to the 2002 census, the number of people affected in the threatened area of Cotonou is estimated at 94,425, around one tenth of the city's population.

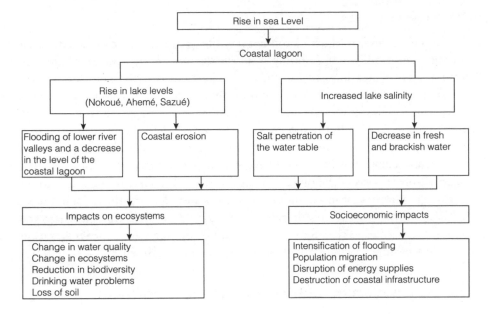

Figure 5.2 Summary table showing the impact of climate change on the coastal lagoons

Source: adapted from Ministère de l'Environnement, de l'Habitat et de l'Urbanisme (MEHU) (2003) *Stratégie Nationale de Mise en Oeuvre au Bénin de la Convention Cadre des Nations Unies sur les Changements Climatiques*, UNDP and UNITAR, 80pp

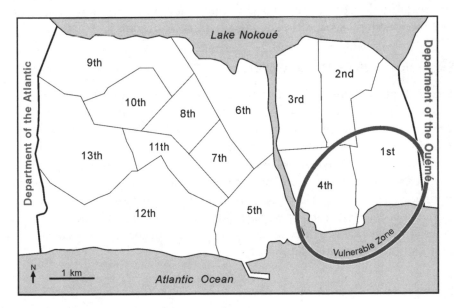

Figure 5.3 The most vulnerable area of Cotonou

Source: adapted from scanned road map

Overview of causes

The coastal erosion to which Cotonou and other places are exposed is a dynamic sub-regional phenomenon resulting from the disruption (by upstream (dams) or shoreline (ports) development) of the coastal currents carrying sand. In fact, the coast is subject to ocean swells of distant origin, with waves measuring 160m to 220m long arriving at intervals of between 10 and 16 seconds. The oblique angle of the swell in relation to the shore varies between 4° and 9°, causing coastal drift (also known as coastal transport) from west to east. This coastal transport carries 1.5 million cubic metres of sand every year from Lomé to Cotonou. The construction of ports in the two cities has diverted sediment upstream (i.e. to the west of the port of Cotonou) and reduced the sandy deposits that should enrich the coast of the first and fourth *arrondissements* and beyond. Until recently, this erosion has been exacerbated by the operation of marine sand quarries along the Cotonou coastline (Jacquot and Tokplégbé beaches, PK10, etc.)

Threats to residential districts and road infrastructure

In the first *arrondissement*, some very smart residential districts (JAK and Tokplégbé) with prestigious buildings are inhabited by expatriates, senior government officials and other eminent individuals. Camps set up by fishermen and homeless people can be found all along this portion of the coast. Population densities are very high in the dormitory suburbs of Donatin and Akpakpa-Dodomey in the fourth *arrondissement*. Here, some former roads and other amenities (drains, pavements and coconut plantations) have now disappeared, swallowed up by the sea as the shoreline retreats (see Figure 5.4).

Exposure of the industrial sector

The bulk of the industrial area of Benin is in Cotonou's fourth *arrondissement*, which is exposed to coastal erosion. Consequently, industrial activities are threatened. So, too, are the livelihoods of around 1500 people working in more than 30 state enterprises (brewery, textiles, gas, agricultural development, cement works and many others), as well as private or small-scale enterprises specializing in various kinds of production and service provision – the sale of drinks, cotton hulling, building and public works, printing, the manufacture of cement, textile production, the timber industry, gas production, painting and pharmaceuticals. Although industrial activities are not very developed, they make a considerable contribution to the national economy.

Threats to the tourism sector

Hotel infrastructure is being undermined and destroyed by the sea (e.g. the Hotel Eldorado has been severely damaged and the Hotel du Lac, PLM Aledjo, Palm

Beach and other establishments have also suffered). The disappearance of these facilities would represent a loss to the tourism-based economy, especially as Benin does not have enough of these kinds of facilities.

Other coastal cities in Benin also have vulnerable infrastructure (whether administrative, health, hotel, industrial or socio-economic), where the coastal erosion exhibits other features and affects different socio-economic groups to varying degrees (e.g. in Sèmé, Grand Popo and Ouidah).

Signs and consequences of rising sea level and coastal erosion

A rise in sea level related to global warming is a factor that will considerably worsen coastal erosion. The shoreline of Benin is a fragile ecosystem exposed to the negative effects of climate change, such as:

*   rising sea and ocean levels;
*   changes in average rainfall patterns;
*   increased atmospheric temperature affecting natural ecosystems, human settlements, water resources and coastal infrastructure; and
*   the marked coastline regression to the east of Cotonou.[11]

Coastline regression is one of the signs of rising sea level and encroachment. In fact, diachronic studies based on remote sensing to assess changes in the shoreline have revealed the vulnerability of the coast of Benin, especially the first and fourth *arrondissements* of Cotonou.

The first of these studies,[12] conducted during an analysis of the kinematics of the coastline using remote sensing, compared a map of Cotonou dating from 1963 with a picture obtained 24 years later.[13] This comparison reveals the impact of the rise in sea level. The area east of the port of Cotonou (first and fourth *arrondissements*) has been undermined by coastal erosion, the shoreline having retreated by 400m at a maximum speed of 16m per year, with a total loss of around 112ha of land.

The second study,[14] highlighting the same phenomenon, is based on computer processing of satellite pictures taken in 1986 and 2000. Figure 5.4 has been prepared by superimposing the satellite images.

Loss of human settlements

In the Gulf of Guinea, the impacts of coastal erosion are often disastrous for the countries concerned,[15] resulting in the disappearance of infrastructure along the coast. Infrastructure to the south of Cotonou that is threatened with disappearance includes:

*   the buildings of people living around Cotonou Lagoon;
*   the self-governing port of Cotonou and its handling facilities;

Figure 5.4 Coastline regression in the east of Cotonou

Source: Ministère de l'Environnement, de l'Habitat et de l'Urbanisme (MEHU) (2003) *Stratégie Nationale de Mise en Oeuvre au Bénin de la Convention Cadre des Nations Unies sur les Changements Climatiques*, UNDP and UNITAR, 80pp

- a number of hotels dependent upon the self-governing port of Cotonou;
- the fishing port;
- the presidential buildings;
- the international conference centre; and
- the international airport.

Infrastructure and urban structures have been lost to the sea, including housing and some roads and earth tracks in the first and fourth *arrondissements* (Tokplégbé and JAK districts). Similarly, the villas (built by Fagace Co) and hotels such as the Aledjo have seen parts of their installations swept away (see Figures 5.5 and 5.6).

Impacts upon human health

Submersion, causing flooding in the inter-dune areas, will have an impact upon people's health. There is a risk of resurgence of endemic tropical diseases as a result of the development of breeding grounds for *anopheles* mosquitoes (which spread malaria[16]) and tsetse fly larvae, which have adapted to saltwater, as well as other threats to health amplified by climatic variability and change. There could be an increase in cardiovascular and cerebral diseases related to high saline levels in the water, which could increase mortality rates, especially among elderly people, pregnant women and children.[17] This situation would exacerbate the

Figure 5.5 Hotel infrastructure (holiday village) being destroyed by coastal erosion

Source: Biagi, R. (2002) 'Erosion littorale à l'est de la lagune de Cotonou. Les choix énergétiques: De l'évaluation des impacts à l'évaluation environnementale stratégique', Colloque de Cotonou du 24 au 27 avril 2001, Agence Intergouvernementale de la Francophonie, Institut de l'Energie et de l'Environnement de la Francophonie, Agence de l'Environnement et la Maîtrise de l'Energie, pp691–694

Figure 5.6 An undermined (lateritic) beaten earth road in Cotonou showing an erosion micro-cliff (about 1m high) at the top of the beach, generated by the rapidly retreating shoreline

Source: Biagi, R. (2002) 'Erosion littorale à l'est de la lagune de Cotonou. Les choix énergétiques: De l'évaluation des impacts à l'évaluation environnementale stratégique', Colloque de Cotonou du 24 au 27 avril 2001, Agence Intergouvernementale de la Francophonie, Institut de l'Energie et de l'Environnement de la Francophonie, Agence de l'Environnement et la Maîtrise de l'Energie, pp691–694

poverty and the precariousness of the living conditions of inhabitants and have serious consequences for the city's economy and, indeed, the entire country, jeopardizing the achievement of development objectives.

Biophysical disruption

Geomorphological changes due to eustatic, neotectonic and sedimentological phenomena are altering the shores of Benin, which have a great variety of ecological zones colonized by very diverse plant formations – for example, mangroves, freshwater marshy forests and hydrophytic and halophytic meadows. A 50cm rise in sea level would cause a systematic reduction in the area colonized by these plant formations (especially mangroves) and a flooding of lowland areas. Currently, various animal species (e.g. crabs and marine turtles) are experiencing disruption to their ecological niche. Those whose livelihoods depend upon fishing have already declared some species of fish to be scarce in both inshore waters and lagoons.

The level of the main lakes and lagoons (Lake Nokoué–Porto Novo Lagoon complex and Lake Ahémé) will rise. Lake Nokoué is likely to double in size and a large part of its high-water bed will be flooded due to the geometry of its basin.

Impacts upon traditional fishing

Fishing is under threat. It represents a major part of the livelihoods of more than 15,000 people in Cotonou, especially those living in districts on the coastal strip of Cotonou, along the lagoon canal and around Lake Nokoué. Many of the homes on the banks have been swept away by the sea. Many families in the fishing hamlets have been obliged to migrate, having no further room to retreat to protect their camps. Those determined to remain on the coast live in makeshift accommodation (from Placodji to PK6) (see Figure 5.7).

Salt intrusion

The hyaline characteristics of freshwater will be changed permanently by salinization, with the concomitant risk of changes to and, indeed, the disappearance of freshwater ichthylogical fauna. The shallow water table in Cotonou and its surrounding area (1m to 3m) could become brackish. This physicochemical change would be accompanied by the spread of many diseases among the local population. In the field of civil engineering (buildings and other structures), an increase in the salt content of the soil would alter the resistance properties of materials, attacking the foundations of masonry structures. An increase in salt content would also destroy some of the flora of the slopes and sides of the plateau, bringing about considerable ecological changes in the coastal zone.[18]

Figure 5.7 Fishermen's camps threatened by sea erosion

Source: K. Dossou

Adapting to the rise in sea level and its consequences

It is a matter of urgency to find ways for people and ecosystems to adapt so that they become less vulnerable. A brief description of the options is given below. It must be pointed out that adaptive measures are not confined to addressing the vulnerability in Cotonou, as the phenomenon is widespread throughout the Gulf of Guinea. An analysis of measures implemented so far shows that adaptation takes two forms: passive and active.[19]

Passive adaptive measures

Passive measures call for the adoption of decisions or attitudes to avoid or alleviate the negative effects of rising sea level and coastal erosion. Such measures were implemented just after the port of Cotonou was built and involved adding sandy sediment to vulnerable areas. For example, sandy sediments may be taken from well-stocked areas to areas that are deficient in sand, and beach rocks may be used to protect the shoreline (see Figure 5.8).

Figure 5.8 Passive adaptation: Using rocks in human settlements on the Benin coast

Source: K. Dossou

Active adaptation

These measures involve building structures either along the coast or out into the sea. There are two types: lengthways structures such as breakwaters, seafront walls and beach defences; and transverse structures, such as groynes that are constructed of different materials (wood, concrete, etc.) and that run perpendicular to the coastline (see Figure 5.9).

In view of the obvious signs and scale of erosion in Cotonou, beach defences cannot work and breakwaters and groynes would appear more appropriate.

A concrete barrier was constructed at the entrance to Cotonou Lagoon to reduce sea encroachment on the lagoon and Lake Nokoué and to protect the first Cotonou bridge. When the lagoon was constructed in 1885, it was just a small canal intended to drain off rainwater following floods; but it is now more than 200m wide due to the force of water runoff.[20] However, the barrier has now been reopened to allow sufficient contact between the lagoon/lake complex and the sea and to avoid the accumulation of sediment from the banks of the lagoon and Lake Nokoué.

Figure 5.9 The concrete barrier on which fishermen stand at the entrance to Cotonou Lagoon

Source: K. Dossou

Technical measures

As part of its strategy to implement the United Nations Framework Convention on Climate Change (UNFCCC), various technical measures are planned by Benin to adapt to the rise in sea level and coastal erosion. These adaptation options are the stabilizing of the coastline by constructing groynes, and moving the communications, transport and hotel infrastructure.

The construction of groynes to stabilize the coastline has the objective of making it possible to remain in the city of Cotonou in the event of a rise in sea level. For example, the Siafato groyne is designed to safeguard the substantial socio-economic, administrative and residential infrastructure established beside the sea. Although effective in alleviating the local problems caused by erosion, the protective system would, according to the environmental impact analysis conducted in 2004, transfer erosion further along the coast to the municipality of Sèmé and then on to Nigeria (to the east). The city's installations would be safeguarded; but the impact study estimated that 195ha of land would be lost from the eastern coast in 20 years' time. The project includes a plan both to resettle or compensate people affected by the transfer of erosion and to conserve the area vulnerable to erosion.[21]

The second option, involving moving infrastructure, has both psychological and financial constraints. Favourable factors are the moves towards decentralization already under way in Benin in response to the policy of administrative decentralization aimed at balanced development of the different regions of the country, especially municipalities with land on both the plateaux and the coast. With regard to Cotonou airport, there are financial constraints; but an enabling factor is an already existing plan to construct a new airport in Glo-Djigbé on the Allada plateau (to the north of Cotonou). Such infrastructure development would have to be followed by a land-use plan and an urban blueprint, registering all property around the airport within a radius of 2km.

All of these measures require the mobilization of substantial financial investment as well as political will, and the communities concerned should participate in the decision-making process.

Adaptation in the health sector

The measures identified in the health sector to adapt to the rise in sea level and flood occurrence include:

*   using impregnated mosquito nets to protect against malaria;
*   developing more widespread vaccination against tsetse fly;
*   developing health insurance and mutual health insurance companies;
*   desalinizing water to use for drinking; and
*   recycling rainwater.

Adaptation in the fisheries industry

Fish farming, as an adaptive measure, would help to reconstitute the ichthylogical fauna and provide catches for those whose livelihoods depend upon fishing. It would also improve the availability of fish and prawns in Cotonou Lagoon and other bodies of water, which are experiencing problems of overfishing and conflicts relating to the lagoon and lake ecosystems[22] and the use of prohibited techniques.[23]

Conclusions

The city of Cotonou is vulnerable to climate change, which will cause a rise in sea level (with its associated impacts) due to global warming. This chapter has analysed its projected effects on human systems (activities, human settlements, health, etc.) and on the coastal and lagoon natural ecosystems.

In its national strategy to implement the UNFCCC, Benin has prepared two scenarios: technological adaptation through the installation of protective groynes to stabilize the coastline; and the relocation of activities, infrastructure and communities. However, the search for funding is delaying implementation of the first option, which will be extremely beneficial for coastal municipalities and towns such as Grand Popo, Ouidah and Abomey-Calavi, and especially the city of Cotonou. The phenomena described in connection with coastline regression and risks of rising sea level demand good planning. In this regard, advantage should be taken of the ongoing preparation of the National Adaptation Programmes of Action (NAPAs) in Benin. The identification of priorities, as expressed by the most vulnerable communities, must be used to transform the selected, approved adaptation options into projects. With the support of national and international financial partners (the World Bank, the Global Environment Facility, the United Nations Development Programme and non-governmental organizations), the proposed adaptive measures must be implemented as soon as possible to reduce communities' vulnerability and suffering.

Moreover, national NGOs must play their advocacy role, drawing politicians' attention to the other climatic hazards that could further impoverish people. They should also raise the awareness of local communities and encourage them to take responsibility with regard to:

- the occupation of land already identified as affected (threatened coastal zone, swamps or valley bottoms, runoff routes); and
- the protection of the environment through the adoption of appropriate behaviour.

The vulnerability of the coastal region, particularly in the case of Cotonou, is real. This is why NGOs, communities, political leaders (local councillors, planners and funders) and scientists (natural resources specialists, climatologists, agronomists, etc.) must combine their efforts to:

- improve documentation of climate change and extreme phenomena at local, national and regional levels (such as the rise in sea level and its consequences); and
- plan and initiate effective, concerted action to adapt to future climatic conditions.

Notes

1. The lagoon (channel) was dug under French colonial rule in September 1885.
2. Institut National de la Statistique et de l'Analyse Economique, Cotonou, database accessible at www.insae-bj.org.
3. MEHU (Ministère de l'Environnement, de l'Habitat et de l'Urbanisme) (1998) Profil de la Zone Côtière du Bénin, MEHU, Cotonou, 109pp.
4. Local currency, equivalent to around US$700 million.
5. LARES (Laboratoire d'Analyse Régionale et d'Expertise Sociale) (2001) *La Problématique de l'Intercommunalité dans le Fonctionnement des Communes Béninoises*, Coopération Suisse, 245pp.

6. FAO (United Nations Food and Agriculture Organization) (2004) *Profil de la Pêche au Bénin*, www.fao.org/fi/fcp/fr/BEN/profile.htm.

7. Voglozin, A. (1999) *Étude des Problèmes Liés à la Circulation Urbaine: Aspects Organisationnels, Institutionnels et Économiques*, Ministère de l'Environnement, de l'Habitat et de l'Urbanisme (MEHU) Cotonou, 30pp.

8. GIEC/IPCC (Groupe Intergouvernemental d'Experts sur le Climat/Intergovernmental Panel on Climate Change) (2001) *Bilan des Changements Climatiques: Rapport de Synthèse*, Cambridge University Press, Cambridge, 205pp.

9. Bokonon-Ganta, E. (1999) *Vulnérabilité et Adaptation du Secteur Santé – Établissements Humains – Littoral au Changement Climatique*, Université Nationale du Bénin/Faculté des Lettres, Arts et Sciences Humaines, 54pp.

10. MAGICC has been the primary model used by the IPCC to produce projections of future global mean temperature and sea-level rise. The climate model in MAGICC is an upwelling–diffusion energy balance model that produces global and hemispheric mean output. IS92a is widely adopted as a standard scenario for use in impact assessments when using MAGICC, although the original IPCC recommendation was that all six IS92 emissions scenarios be used to represent the range of uncertainty in emissions.

11. MEHU (Ministère de l'Environnement, de l'Habitat et de l'Urbanisme) (2001) *First National Communication of Benin*, UNDP, 76pp.

12. CODJIA, C. L., Dubois, J.-M., Donnay, J. P., Ozer, A., Boivin, F. and Lavoie, A. (1997) 'Application de la télédétection à l'étude des changements urbains et des transformations du littoral à Cotonou (Bénin). Télédétection des milieux urbains et périurbains', *AUPELF-UREF*, no 6, Liège, pp299–306.

13. SPOT-1 HRV multi-band image, 22 December 1987; see reference 12.

14. MEHU (Ministère de l'Environnement, de l'Habitat et de l'Urbanisme) (2003) *Stratégie Nationale de Mise en Oeuvre au Bénin de la Convention Cadre des Nations Unies sur les Changements Climatiques*, UNDP and UNITAR, 80pp.

15. See references 3 and 11; also Blivi, A. (2000) 'Vulnérabilité de la côte togolaise à l'élévation du niveau marin: Une analyse de prévision et d'impact', *Patrimoines*, no 10, pp643–660; and Kaki, C. and Oyédé, M. (2000) 'Implications of accelerated sea-level rise (ASLR) for Benin', in de la Vega-Leinert, A. D., Nicholls, R. J., Nasser Hassan, A. and El-Raey, M. (eds) *Proceedings of SURVAS Expert Workshop on African Vulnerability and Adaptation to Impacts of Accelerated Sea-Level Rise (ASLR)*, Alexandria University, Middlesex University, pp31–38.

16. See reference 9; also Bokonon-Ganta, E. (forthcoming) 'Changements climatiques et santé au Bénin: Cas du paludisme à Cotonou', in *Capacity Strengthening in LDCs for Civil Society for Adaptation to Climate Change (CLACC)*

17. See reference 14.

18. See reference 14.

19. See reference 3.

20. Colleuil, B. (1984) *Un Modèle d'Environnement Lagunaire Soumis aux Conditions des Climats Équatoriaux Tempérés: Le Lac Nokoué*, Université de Bordeaux, 135pp.

21. MEHU (Ministère de l'Environnement, de l'Habitat et de l'Urbanisme) (2004) *Projet de la Protection de la Côte à l'Est de l'Épi de Siafato: Étude d'Impact Environnemental*, MEHU, Cotonou, 112pp.

22. Dossou, D. and Dossou, K. (2005) *Guide Gestion Concertée des Écosystèmes Partagés*, Agence Béninoise pour l'Environnement, Cotonou, 57pp.
23. For example, *médokpokonou*, *wan* and *acadja* are traditional technologies that are forbidden in Benin in order to reduce pressure on fisheries development. *Médokpokonou* employs nets with fine, tight stitches, which collect small and immature fish. *Wan* and *acadja* are fish traps.

6

The Vulnerability of Global Cities to Climate Hazards

Alex de Sherbinin, Andrew Schiller and Alex Pulsipher

Introduction

Global cities are engines of economic growth and centres of innovation for the global economy and the hinterlands of their respective nations. The foundations of prosperity and prominence for most global cities lie in their longstanding commercial relationships with the rest of the world. Most global cities are located on or near the coast, which has facilitated trade and contributed to their wealth. They are also often located in low-lying areas near the mouths of major rivers, which served as conduits for commerce between interior agricultural and industrial regions and the rest of the world. As it happens, these locations place global cities at greater risk from current and projected climate hazards such as cyclones, high winds, flooding, coastal erosion and deposition, and sea-level rise.[1]

Global cities are also important centres of population concentration and growth. According to Brockerhoff, just 25 years ago less than 2 per cent of the global population resided in 'megacities' of 10 million or more inhabitants.[2] Today, the proportion exceeds 4 per cent and by 2015 it will top 5 per cent, when megacities will likely house 400 million people. The phenomenal growth rates that most low-income country megacities experienced from the 1960s to the 1980s have now somewhat tapered off; but because lower rates are being applied to higher population bases, the absolute numbers being added to their populations are still high. The fact that so many people reside in megacities near coastlines, and that these cities continue to grow, underscores the importance of assessing the vulnerability of such cities to coastal climate hazards.

Recent incidents have highlighted the vulnerability of urban areas, in general, to climate hazards. Hurricane Katrina in August 2005 effectively obliterated much of the Gulf Coast of Mississippi and flooded large portions of New Orleans, resulting in the evacuation of all residents and more than 1000 deaths. The flooding was greatest in African-American neighbourhoods, and in the aftermath there were widespread accusations that the slow and ineffectual government response reflected a racial bias.[3] In July 2005, Mumbai, India, was struck by a cyclone that dumped 94cm of rain in 24 hours, also leaving more than

1000 dead, mostly in slum settlements. In terms of casualties, an even more devastating set of flash floods and landslides in Caracas and on the north coast of Venezuela in December 1999 killed 30,000 people and affected another 483,000.[4] Each of these events underscores the vulnerability to climate hazards faced by the urban poor, especially those living in substandard housing in the most vulnerable locations.

Researchers at the Centre for Research on the Epidemiology of Disasters (CRED) have tracked an increase in almost all disasters, with the time trends for climate-related disasters, including floods, windstorms and droughts, showing the greatest increase, well above all geological hazards.[5] There are two factors behind this rise in climate-related disasters. One is regional increases in the severity and periodicity of hazard events.[6] For example, in the Atlantic and Pacific cyclone-generating areas, increased sea surface temperatures associated with global warming are responsible for an increase in the intensity and duration of tropical storms (although not necessarily an increase in their frequency).[7] The second factor – as alluded to above – is the large and growing proportion of the world's population that is living in cities and towns near the coast or in drought-prone or low-lying areas and that consequently is exposed to these hazards. Research by McGranahan et al finds that more than 600 million people (or 10 per cent of the global population) reside in coastal zones of less than 10m elevation, and that 13 per cent of them, or 77 million people, reside in megacities.[8] This combination of increased hazards and exposure results in greater numbers of disasters that claim lives and cause major economic losses.

The emphasis of climate change policy has largely been on mitigation. As necessary as these efforts are, it is clear that more attention needs to be given to adaptation to the climatic changes that are already under way and which will be exacerbated by future emissions of greenhouse gases. Rayner and Malone argue:

> ... the record and prospects of achieving emissions reductions suggest it would be prudent to expand the repertoire of climate change policies, if only because our past emissions and the timetable for any plausible reduction programme mean climate change is already upon us.[9]

Among other elements, disaster preparedness and management plans are vital components of an adaptation strategy. But to design these, we need a better understanding of which people and systems are vulnerable to what kind of climate hazards, what makes them vulnerable, and where they are located.

In the following section, we briefly describe the vulnerability framework applied in this chapter. In the section thereafter, we apply the framework to an examination of three cities that are particularly vulnerable to multiple climate-related hazards: Mumbai (formerly Bombay) in India, Rio de Janeiro in Brazil and Shanghai in China (see Figure 6.1). Conclusions from this research are provided in the final section.

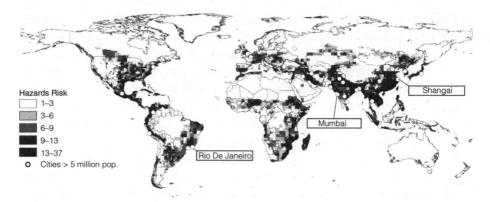

Figure 6.1 Large cities in relation to current climate-related hazards

Note: The cities included in this figure have populations greater than 5 million. Hazard risk represents a cumulative score based on risk of cyclones, flooding, landslides and drought.

Source: for cities: CIESIN (2006) *Global Rural-Urban Mapping Project* (GRUMP), alpha version, data available from http://sedac.ciesin.columbia.edu/gpw/. For hazards: Dilley, M., Chen, R. S., Deichmann, U., Lerner-Lam, A. L. and Arnold, M. (2005) *Natural Disaster Hotspots: A Global Risk Analysis*, World Bank, Washington, DC, 132pp, data available from www.ldeo.columbia.edu/chrr/research/hotspots/coredata.html

Framing vulnerability

Vulnerability is the degree to which a system or unit is likely to experience harm due to exposure to perturbations or stresses. The concept of vulnerability originated in research communities examining risks and hazards, climate impacts and resilience. The vulnerability concept emerged from the recognition by these research communities that a focus on perturbations alone (environmental, socio-economic and technological) was insufficient for understanding the responses of, and impacts on, systems (social groups, ecosystems and places) exposed to such perturbations.[10] With the concept of vulnerability, it became clear that the ability of a system to attenuate stresses or cope with the consequences through various strategies or mechanisms constituted a key determinant of system response and, ultimately, of system impact. A clearer understanding of coping strategies or mechanisms can thus throw light on who and what are at risk from what, and how specific stresses and perturbations evolve into risks and impacts.

Vulnerability in the social sciences is typically identified in terms of three elements: system exposure to crises, stresses and shocks; inadequate system capacity to cope; and consequences and attendant risks of slow (or poor) system recovery. This perspective suggests that the most vulnerable individuals, groups, classes and regions or places are those that experience the most exposure to perturbations or stresses; are the most sensitive to perturbations or stresses (i.e. most likely to suffer from exposure); and have the weakest capacity to respond and ability to recover. In this chapter, we apply a vulnerability framework, described elsewhere,[11] to better understand the vulnerabilities of three megacities to hazards resulting from climate change and variability. The framework addresses the vulnerability of interacting human–environment systems to multiple and synergistic stresses that emanate from within as well as from outside the system.

Within this extended vulnerability framework, there is formal recognition that macro-forces – broad-scale environmental and human systems within which the local system resides – come together to affect the local system and, simultaneously, influence the pressures that act upon it. Different pressures across scales come together in various sequences to create unique 'bundles' of stress that affect local systems. A major hypothesis holds that when stresses or perturbations emanating from the environment coalesce with those arising from society, significant consequences can result. For example, economic depression reduces society's capability to develop or maintain pre-emptive coping measures to reduce the impacts of drought, such that the co-occurrence of drought and economic depression synergistically enlarges the vulnerability of the system. The risks resulting from such vulnerabilities emerge from multiple sources and at different scales. These risks cascade through interacting human and environmental systems to create adverse consequences.

We find that the framework provides new insights into vulnerabilities because it considers multiple, synergistic stresses and perturbations, on one side of the equation, and multiple, synergistic physical and social characteristics of the exposed system, on the other. This enables us to conduct a 'gap analysis' that identifies areas of exposure and vulnerability and points to areas of greatest need for strengthened adaptive capacity and risk management.

The case studies

We examine here three case studies of global coastal cities in light of climate hazards: Mumbai (formerly Bombay) in India, Rio de Janeiro in Brazil and Shanghai in China. Each of these cities has urban agglomerations in excess of 10 million people, the threshold that the United Nations applies to designate a 'megacity', and they each represent important national and regional engines of economic development and innovation.

This chapter addresses current and future vulnerability to climate hazards. The respective sections provide baseline information on climate in each of the cities. To assess future vulnerability, we use standard sets of climate change and sea-level rise scenarios. Figure 6.2 provides projected temperature changes by season for reduced emissions ('sustainable path') and increased emissions ('business as usual') scenarios.[12] Compared to temperature changes, precipitation changes are considered to be more difficult to model accurately and therefore are not included here. Projections of sea-level rise due to melting land-based glaciers and polar ice

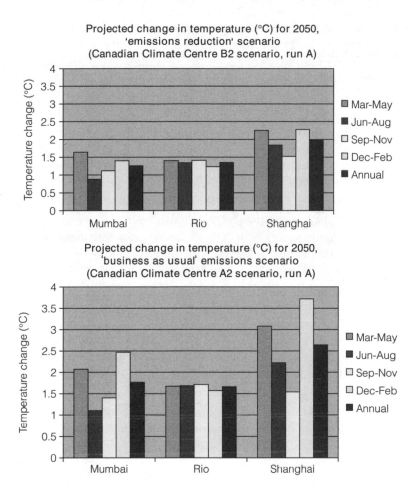

Figure 6.2 Projected changes in temperature for the global cities

Source: pers comm with Richard Goldberg from the Goddard Institute for Space Studies, New York

caps range from 0.2m to 0.9m by 2100,[13] although recent rapid melting in Greenland and Antarctica suggest that these estimates could be superseded.[14] We adopt a common projected sea-level rise of 50cm by 2050, although local variations in land subsidence will affect the relative sea-level rise in each location.[15]

These global cities are located in very different physical environments, which make for interesting comparisons. The climate of Mumbai is tropical moist, Rio is sub-tropical wet and dry, and Shanghai is on the border between sub-tropical and warm-temperate. Shanghai is located at the mouth of a major river (the Yangtze), and all are coastal cities with significant areas just above sea level. Two of the cities, Mumbai and Shanghai, are subject to hurricane (tropical cyclone) landfalls at least once a year.

Table 6.1 *Data collected to test the expanded vulnerability framework*

Stresses/perturbations		System characteristics	
Climate related	Temperature increases	Physical environment	Topography/bathymetry
	Extreme rainfall		Geology
	Drought frequency		Current/ recent climate
	Wind speeds		Wetlands/low-lying areas
	Sea-level rise	Infrastructure	Domestic water needs
Socio-economic	Population growth		Industrial water needs
	Economic downturn		Sanitation/waste disposal
	Globalization	Endowments	Income/poverty rates
			Education
			Healthcare
		Direct-coping abilities	Early warning system
			Evacuation plan
			Disaster management plan
			Appropriate zoning
			Dykes or other armaments
			Building codes
		Indirect coping (social capital)	Percent migrants
			Crime rate
			Single-parent households
			Voter turnout
			Households with secure tenure

(Endowments, Direct-coping abilities, and Indirect coping (social capital) fall under the vertical label "Socio-economic conditions".)

We focused on collecting data in the categories shown in Table 6.1 in order to explore climate hazard vulnerability for these three global cities. Note that data on stresses and perturbations include both climate and social components, some of which arise endogenously to the system. Likewise, system characteristics include elements of physical geography and built infrastructure, coupled with socio-economic conditions that include what we term endowments, and coping abilities (both direct and indirect).

Mumbai

Mumbai is the largest and most economically important city in India. Its 17 million people (1.7 per cent of India's total) contribute roughly 17 per cent of India's income tax and 37 per cent of India's corporate tax annually.[16] Mumbai hosts India's largest stock exchange, its largest high-tech centre, the world's most prolific film industry, the world's largest metro-suburban rail system and Asia's largest squatter community. Across the bay from the old city, Navi Mumbai (New Mumbai) is taking shape as the world's largest totally planned city. Unfortunately, with its downtown located on a flood-prone, poorly drained peninsula composed largely of landfill, Mumbai is highly vulnerable to climate hazards, as demonstrated by the extensive monsoon flooding in July 2005 that killed more than 1000 residents. Among the most vulnerable are the approximately one half of the city's residents who live in squatter communities, many of which are located in low-lying areas without adequate sanitation or water supplies. Finally, these vulnerabilities are compounded by Mumbai's location on several seismic faults, as well as its unsanitary methods for raw sewage and industrial waste disposal into the waters and air surrounding Mumbai.

Physical environment

The Portuguese were first attracted to Mumbai, known then as Bom Bahia ('good bay' in Portuguese), for its excellent harbour and the opportunities for trade with several communities on islands within the harbour. The British gained control of Mumbai (then Bombay) from the Portuguese in 1661 and, as trade and population increased, the need for additional land led to the filling in, between 1784 and 1845, of the shallow waters and tidal mudflats connecting the original seven islands with rock and dirt from the island's own hilltops. Today, most of Mumbai city centre, which includes the stock exchange, the main train stations and train lines and numerous high rises, is located on landfill. The inland suburbs, where most of the population now lives, are located at higher elevations. However, much new settlement (industrial, residential and commercial) has occurred along the coastal areas of Greater Mumbai, which are low-lying and flood prone.[17]

Mumbai's climate is tropical, with temperatures ranging between 16° and 33°C. Temperature and rainfall are strongly affected by the Indian monsoon, which normally starts in June and ends around the middle of September. Approximately 2500mm of Mumbai's 2700mm annual rainfall comes at this time, with flooding common when spells of heavy rainfall coincide with high tides or storm surges. On 26 July 2005, the city received an unprecedented 944mm of rainfall in a 24-hour period, resulting in the most devastating floods in recent history.

Built environment

Mumbai has a diverse built environment with unique combinations of urban problems associated with its drainage system and its squatter communities, including building collapses, likely future water shortages and poor sewage disposal.

Drainage. Most landfill areas (i.e. most of the old city) are prone to flooding during the monsoon, especially when heavy rains combine with high tides or storm surges. Even in wealthy areas, drains are often blocked by trash and debris, and monsoon flooding often shuts down Mumbai's commuter rail lines, which are among the most heavily used in the world.[18] Flooding of this type would likely increase with sea-level rise, necessitating major upgrades in the drainage systems and possibly an elevation of major rail lines. Projects are already under way to upgrade the drains that run alongside the rail lines and to demolish squatter communities also situated alongside rail lines, which contribute to clogged drains. However, this work was not designed with sea-level rise in mind. A national study ranking India's coastal zones according to their vulnerability to sea-level rise found Mumbai to be the most likely to experience damage.[19]

Squatter communities. It is estimated that 55 per cent of Mumbai's population live in squatter communities, locally referred to as slums, roughly half of which are severely dilapidated. Many squatter structures are single storey and built of salvaged materials. Nevertheless, population densities for roughly one half of Mumbai's squatter communities are estimated to be as high as 94,000 people per square kilometre, making it one of the most densely settled districts in the world. Mumbai's squatter communities suffer from inadequate access to potable water and sanitation, with the World Bank estimating that 170 people depend upon each public latrine in these areas and that one third of the 35,000 latrines in Mumbai are out of service.[20] As demonstrated in July 2005, even without sea-level rise, many squatter communities in Mumbai are already frequently flooded as they are often located in low-lying coastal areas and along stream banks. Flooding is common even on the higher ground in Mumbai's squatter communities, as the large amount of refuse and debris in these areas tends to clog storm sewers, causing a backup of water that would otherwise run off or find its way into storm drains.[21] Landslides are another threat to squatter communities that are near or on the few hillsides in the city.

Historically, Mumbai authorities have dealt with the problems caused by squatter communities by demolishing them and forcibly relocating the inhabitants to new areas in the suburban fringe. Increasingly, non-governmental organizations (NGOs) are organizing to meet the needs of squatter dwellers for better access to sanitation and water; but their efforts are still limited in scope and their impact is quite small, especially with regard to some of the squatter communities most vulnerable to sea-level rise and flooding. This is because funding from the Indian government cannot be used in violation of zoning regulations that prohibit residential development in coastal areas.[22] While, in theory, restricting coastal zone settlements reduces settlement in vulnerable areas, in practice, this has not deterred such settlement and has merely stalled efforts to make these areas less susceptible to damage and loss of life.

Drinking water/potable water capacity. Mumbai's water supply consists of several artificial rain-fed lakes located in the suburbs to the north of the old city. Their location on hills makes them less susceptible to impacts from sea-level rise, although their dependence upon local rainfall (as opposed to canal systems or piping from other regions) means that increasing rainfall variability could threaten local supply. The World Bank's Bombay (Mumbai) Water Supply and Sewage Disposal projects, which were implemented between 1975 and 1995, increased the city's water supply from 984 to 2460 million litres per day.[23] Yet, according to the Mumbai Metropolitan Region Development Authority, as of 1995, demand still outstripped supply by 23 per cent, and they have projected that total demand will exceed 7940 million litres per day by 2011.[24] Antiquation, leaking and partially unmetered water delivery are cited by the World Bank as major problems holding back improvement of the city's water system.

Pollution. Both air and water pollution have been identified as major problems in Mumbai. The World Bank describes Mumbai's air pollution as 'severe' and, with regard to Mumbai's water pollution, states: 'about 75 per cent of all sewage is untreated and discharged to local waterways and coastal waters, causing extensive environmental hazard'.[25]

Socio-economic conditions

Endowments. While Mumbai has by far the largest concentration of wealth in India, it is unevenly distributed within the city. Per capita income, adjusted for purchasing power parity, is estimated to be three times the Indian average, or equal to US$6600;[26] yet income distribution in the city is a major problem. In 1989, 62 per cent of households in the Mumbai Metropolitan Region (MMR) earned less than US$ 20 per month, and one quarter of all households in the area were below the US$48 per month poverty line.[27] The unemployment rate is close to 15 per cent.[28] In 2001, the urban agglomeration's population was 16.4 million, and it is now estimated to be 17.7 million. By 2011, these figures are projected to rise to 22.4 million, with 12.9 million in the old city and its immediate suburbs and 9.5 million in the rest of the MMR.

Direct coping. Mumbai is the headquarters for the State of Maharashtra Disaster Management Plan. An emergency operations centre (central control room) in Mumbai is the main hub for a network connected to a variety of sophisticated technologies aimed at emergency planning and disaster management. Multi-hazard response plans, financed by the UK's Department for International Development (DFID), are also in place in Mumbai as well as in six other centres across the state. There are multi-hazard response plans in place for each district, including risk assessment and vulnerability analysis with reference to earthquakes, floods and cyclones, epidemics, road accidents, fires, and chemical and industrial disasters. These systems also contain a multi-hazard response structure, capability analysis, inventory of resources, mitigation strategies, and a directory of personnel and institutions in the districts with their contact addresses, telephone and fax numbers.[29] Revi laments, however, that despite identifying flood risks and pinpointing vulnerable slums, no systematic action has been taken in the five years since the plan's development to mitigate the risk.[30] Moreover, the ongoing landfill projects of various Mumbai development authorities suggest that a prevention-oriented approach to disaster avoidance and reduction is lacking.

Regulations are in place that prohibit the location of new industries in the old central part of the city. This has been done in order to reduce congestion and pollution and to discourage further dense settlement in this old portion of the city that has an antiquated built environment. These regulations have an added and, as yet, unappreciated benefit of decreasing settlement on landfill areas that are susceptible to flooding and potential shifting due to sea-level rise and increased storm frequency. However, some of the new settlements to which industries and people are being relocated are also in low-lying coastal areas that may be similarly susceptible to sea-level rise and storm surges.

Indirect coping. Despite its many chaotic qualities, Mumbai is socially highly organized, a quality that mitigates some of the city's vulnerability to natural hazards. The internationally known squatter organization, the National Slum Dwellers Federation (NSDF), is based in Mumbai. The NSDF received the prestigious Scroll of Honour from the United Nations Human Settlements Programme for its work in the collective design and construction of low-cost houses and toilets, improving environmental sanitation in ways that can help to mitigate the disease impact during and after flooding.[31] The NSDF has more than 90 housing projects that are either built or are under way, providing housing for more than 35,000 households.[32] The NSDF and similar organizations in Mumbai have built strong partnerships between poor communities, NGOs and various levels of government.[33]

Despite the existence of slum federations, Revi decries the 'institutionalization of disparity' in Mumbai, citing a decline in the quality of law enforcement and justice institutions and a rise in organized crime and terror networks. He cites the income disparity, one manifestation of which is the overpriced land market that contributes to the spread of informal settlements, as a significant vulnerability.[34]

Another important aspect of Mumbai's social support system is the city's ability to garner resources from abroad. As the wealthiest and most cosmopolitan city in India, and as the centre of India's film industry (the world's largest in terms of output), Mumbai looms large in the minds of Indians living abroad. This community is recognized throughout India as a key to the country's overall development, and Mumbai's unique ability to broadcast its problems and needs to this community abroad may prove an important factor in reducing the impacts of climate hazards on the city. This may be especially true in the case of dramatic perturbations, such as sea-level rise and associated flooding, which could threaten Mumbai's status as the leading city of India.

Likely future climate hazards and overall vulnerability assessment
The Canadian Climate Centre's A2 (business as usual) and B2 (sustainable path) scenarios predict an average annual temperature increase of 1.75° and 1.25°C, respectively, by 2050 (see Figure 6.2). This increase is similar to that predicted for

Rio, but lower than the increases for New York or Shanghai. Mumbai is predicted to have an average annual decrease in precipitation of 2 per cent for the A2 scenario and an increase of 2 per cent for the B2 scenario. The predicted sea-level rise of 50cm by 2050 could prove seriously damaging for Mumbai.

Potential impacts of precipitation extremes. The A2 (business as usual) scenario may engender water shortages in Mumbai given the city's complete dependence upon locally stored rainfall for its water supply. The fact that both scenarios predict a decrease in rainfall during the first part of the year (January to August) suggests that droughts will become more common in the MMR, although predicted reductions during the monsoon season are less dramatic. Furthermore, both scenarios show an increase in rainfall from September to November, which may mitigate water shortages from reduced monsoons. If droughts do increase in severity, this could trigger migrations from surrounding agricultural areas (a common occurrence during drought years), which could tax the city's resources in the context of multiple climate change impacts.

Coastal/marine issues. A 1996 Tata Energy Research Institute (TERI) study put the cost to Mumbai of a 1m sea-level rise at US$71 billion.[35] The study concluded that US$24 million invested in protection against sea-level rise would reduce the economic impact by about US$33 billion dollars. The predicted rise in sea level of 50cm, together with storm surges, would render uninhabitable the coastal and low-lying areas where many squatter communities are located. Moreover, shifting would likely occur in the subsurface of the landfill areas, resulting in many buildings becoming uninhabitable due to structural instability. Mumbai's landfill areas contain a mixture of high-value commercial properties, such as the Stock Exchange, important public facilities, such as the main train stations and train lines, numerous high-value residential high-rises and a number of squatter communities. The few hills, formerly islands, which were not levelled to create the landfill that the majority of the city was built on, comprise mostly upscale residential areas long-prized for their relative immunity to flooding. These areas lack the commercial potential to take up slack should the landfill areas go into decline. However, provided that sea-level rise occurs gradually, and is recognized early enough, Mumbai might be able to mitigate damage, perhaps by shifting much of the old city to the adjacent suburbs or to Navi Mumbai.

Overall vulnerability. What emerges from using the extended vulnerability framework is the identification of a set of stresses and perturbations that collectively converge to create great 'stress bundles' for Mumbai. An example is the convergence of extreme rainfall and floods. Mumbai's various characteristics of topography (flat), geology (unconsolidated fill material), numerous wetlands and flood-prone areas, the city's building conditions (not meeting building codes, squatter dwellings and previously flood-damaged buildings), poor sanitation and poor waste treatment and removal capabilities together create a particular bundle of stresses that 'collide' with the set of socio-environmental conditions of Mumbai, such that vulnerabilities emerge for the system.

In addition, a stress bundle composed of population (large and growing), projected sea-level rise and economic stresses converges to create some particularly problematic issues for Mumbai. This is because of a set of characteristics for Mumbai that include the lack of dykes and other coastal armaments for dealing with sea-level rise, weak disaster preparedness at the scale of sea-level rise, building conditions (as noted above) and low incomes that do not allow the city to improve building conditions to the level required or to better develop and fund disaster preparedness. Mumbai is thus facing threats that local authorities have very little ability to control, dampen or mitigate. This suggests that a reinforcing spiral could emerge for this set of issues, where increasing population comes together with sea-level rise and a stressed economy to further damage already weak buildings, undermine efforts to improve disaster preparedness and build coastal armaments; and these, in turn, further erode the economy while sea-level rise marches on. Mumbai's informal coping capacities, as a result of notably strong social networks and cooperation, emerge as important parts of Mumbai's resistance and resilience in the face of stresses. These informal coping systems are expected to help reduce vulnerabilities to some degree for both sets of issues that emerge from this preliminary analysis. Yet, by themselves, these informal coping capacities appear quite inadequate to meet the challenges from climate hazards and population size and growth that now face Mumbai.

Mumbai's overall vulnerability appears to be high. While the city is relatively prosperous compared to the rest of India, and it does have an elaborate disaster management plan in place, the challenges posed by climate change, especially flooding and subsurface shifting in landfill areas, are unlikely to be met effectively. In particular, subsurface shifting of the type that Mumbai might face could well overwhelm the adaptive abilities of any city, and particularly one with some of the other critical issues that Mumbai now faces.

Rio de Janeiro

Rio de Janeiro is a city of just over 10 million people located on the south-eastern coast of Brazil and covers an area of 1171km². Guanabara Bay, where Rio is situated, faces almost due south. Rio is the second most populous city in Brazil, after São Paulo, and ranks second only to São Paulo in industrial production. This erstwhile capital of Brazil is known for its beautiful beaches and the granite hills that rise dramatically from sea level to more than 1000m. Yet, Rio faces significant environmental sustainability challenges stemming from unregulated settlement in hazardous areas, sewage disposal and industrial wastes. These will be exacerbated by potential climate changes.

Physical environment
Rio's dramatic topography has made it more prone to certain types of hazard. When the Portuguese discovered Guanabara Bay in 1501, the coastal mountains

were carpeted in thick Atlantic rainforest. As this protective covering has been progressively stripped away to make room for settlements, the thin soils have become prone to landslides and the granite and gneiss bedrock has been left exposed to weathering, making it more prone to decomposition and erosion.

The coastline in this area was characterized by lagoons, estuaries and low-lying coastal marshes, many of which have been filled in. The flat topography of low-lying areas, combined with a lack of drainage, has continued to result in flooding during the summer rainy season (January to March). The few remaining lagoons, mangroves and marshes have been affected by sedimentation, reducing their absorptive capacity during extreme rainfall events. Ninety per cent of mangroves surrounding Guanabara Bay have been removed and intense sedimentation has resulted in the need for dredging to maintain shipping lanes. Rio's beaches, a major tourist asset, are subject to intense erosion during storms (with up to 5m recession), but usually recover quickly through the deposition of sand laterally along the coast.[36] Significant resources are also expended on beach nourishment following intense erosion.

The climate in Rio is moderated by the coastal effect, its southern exposure and the mountain ranges to the north. The mountain ranges block cooler north-easterly winds during the winter months and enhance orographic precipitation during the summer months, when winds are predominantly south-westerly. Rio experiences wet summers (December to March), with an average temperature range of 24° to 26°C, and dry winters (June to September), with an average temperature range of 20° to 22°C (see Figure 6.3). Maximum temperatures rarely exceed 42°C. From year to year, precipitation ranges between 1200mm and 1500mm, and evaporation between 800mm and 1200mm.

Rio has never been affected by tropical cyclones, although this may change. The first recorded South Atlantic hurricane reached land in the state of Santa Catarina in March 2004, suggesting that what was once thought to be a meteorological impossibility is no longer so, with global warming-induced increases in regional sea surface temperatures.[37] The city receives a strong El Niño–Southern Oscillation (ENSO) signal, and during El Niño years the city receives higher then normal precipitation during the summer months. During one recent El Niño year, 1988, the city was affected by severe floods as a result of two intense periods of rainfall in early February that produced a total of 480mm of rain, one third the annual total rainfall.

Built environment

Rio's peculiar geography, and the circumscribed nature of suitable building sites, has spawned two kinds of response. One is the construction of high-rise apartments close to the coastline (e.g. Copacabana, Ipanema and Leblon) and in flood-prone areas further inland; the other is unregulated construction on steep slopes, particularly on the Tijuca Mountain range. The unregulated construction

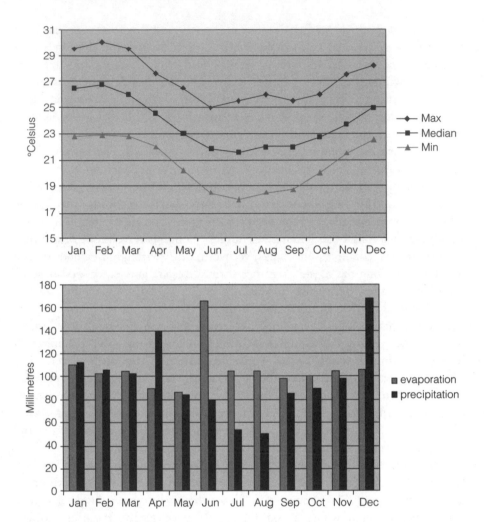

Figure 6.3 Average temperatures (top) and hydrographs (bottom) for Rio de Janeiro (1961–1990)

Note: Temperature does not vary significantly through the year. In contrast, the hydrograph shows that precipitation is greatest in April and December, whereas potential evapotranspiration greatly exceeds rainfall from June through August (the Southern Hemisphere winter months).

Source: Instituto Nacional de Meteorologia (INMET) www.inmet.gov.br/html/clima.php, accessed 26 September 2007

of *favelas* (shanty towns) has a long history and stems from the invasion of both private and public urban lands by poor urban squatters who become *de facto* (and, in some cases, *de jure*) owners of plots of land.[38] Many *favelas* have evolved over time from ramshackle collections of wooden shacks lacking even the most basic amenities to organized communities of largely concrete housing with cemented walkways, electricity, plumbing, sewerage and other services.

Although *favelas* have always suffered during rainy seasons, the paving of walkways has had the effect of increasing runoff to the point where water is often ankle or knee deep between the houses. Runoff from communities on steep hillsides, including Petropolis and *favelas* on the Maciço da Tijuca massif, are channelled down cemented and quasi-natural watercourses to the narrow coastal lowlands where they join canals whose limited flow capacity causes frequent flooding. By contrast, the Baixada Fluminense, a large marshy lowland somewhat removed from the steeper parts of the city, has had reasonably adequate drainage since the 1930s.[39]

In terms of services, the city has a reasonably clean and reliable water supply that is piped in from rivers in the state of Minas Gerais to the north. Over 84 per cent of the population is supplied with water. Eighty-three per cent have their own sanitary installations. Ninety-four per cent of the population has access to electricity supply at home. Electricity is largely generated by Brazil's major hydroelectric facilities, which supply 92 per cent of the country's electricity needs. A drought in 2001 led to electricity shortages throughout the country and consumers in Rio de Janeiro were ordered to cut consumption by 20 to 25 per cent.

Waste disposal is a significant problem. Trash disposal for *favelas* remains haphazard, with some estimates that 5400 tonnes per day or more end up in rivers and drainage channels, blocking channels during peak flow.[40] This compares with 7000 tonnes per day that end up in city dumps, mostly on the margins of Guanabara Bay. Daily discharges into the bay include 465 tonnes of organic matter, 68 tonnes of which receive adequate treatment, and 9.5 tonnes of oil. The Iguacu and Estrela rivers, which drain the bay's watershed, are often anoxic and produce a strong hydrogen sulphide smell.[41]

Guanabara Bay is surrounded by a mix of industrial and residential land uses. As the second largest industrial zone in the country, it has 10,000 industries, 10 oil terminals, 12 shipyards and 2 oil refineries. Petrobras, the Brazilian oil company, has numerous off-shore drilling platforms near Rio and uses Rio as its primary distribution point. A giant causeway crosses the bay, leading to Niteroi, and two airports are located just above sea level on the margins of the bay.

Socio-economic conditions

Endowments. Although Rio's product per capita is roughly double the national average, its income distribution is highly skewed. The existence of pockets of extreme poverty side by side with some of the most affluent neighbourhoods is characteristic of the city. Rocinhas, among the oldest and largest of Rio's *favelas*, clings precariously to the steep slopes of the Tijuca Mountain range just above Gavea, one of the city's wealthiest neighbourhoods. It is estimated that 1.1 million people live in *favelas*, or 20 per cent of the municipality's population.

According to the 2000 census, the population of the Rio metropolitan area is 10.9 million, with 5.8 million residing in the municipality.[42] Population density in the latter is 4640 individuals per square kilometre; but densities in the smaller administrative units of the metro area are between 8000 and 12,000 people per square kilometre, indicating that some parts of the city have significant population concentrations. Although rapid population growth of 3.8 per cent was predicted for the 1990s, the recent census figures suggest that the rate may have been slower. Corrêa do Lago notes that the metro area received 758,000 migrants between 1970 and 1980, but that between 1980 and 1991 the number had decreased by 24 per cent to 573,000.[43] It is possible that continued declines in migration account for the somewhat lower than expected overall population growth. The 2005 estimated population of the municipality was 6.1 million, a 1 per cent growth rate between 2000 and 2005.

Direct coping. The state of Rio de Janeiro has a 15,000-member Civil Defence, which includes the fire department, emergency medical services, sea rescue services and the Community Relief Department. Brazil's State Environmental Engineering Foundation (Fundação Estadual de Engenharia do Meio Ambiente, or FEEMA) is responsible for coastal monitoring and land-use zoning in the state. Baptista de Araújo urges more micro-planning for disaster management such as occurred under the Rio Reconstruction Project, which was implemented in the wake of the 1988 floods.

In terms of zoning, until recently there was little effort to segregate industrial or waste disposal activities from residential areas. This could result in potential vulnerabilities, particularly should flooding lead to the dispersion of pollutants to surrounding areas. New regulations have been put in place that restrict building in hazard-prone areas and, according to Kreimer et al, 'major emphasis has been placed ... on command and control mechanisms to regulate urban growth'.[44] Efforts to 'regularize' *favelas* have also been under way for several years with various government programmes to undertake cadastral surveys, grant deeds to *de facto* owners and provide basic infrastructure. These same plans limit the further expansion of *favelas* in flood-prone or steeply sloped areas.

Indirect coping. There are several issues that weaken Rio's indirect coping capacity. These include official corruption and political tensions between federal, state and municipal governments; and large migrant communities with low security of tenure, decreasing levels of social cohesion and low levels of education.

Geddes and Ribero Neto write of the widespread corruption during the Collor administration.[45] According to them, the weakening of the executive branch's ability to build coalitions and to ensure the loyalty of supporters in Congress created strong incentives to exchange material benefits (in the form of public works projects) for congressional support. Unfortunately, for those jurisdictions (such as Rio de Janeiro) that had leaders in rival political parties, this led to the denial of federal financing for public works projects and even problems in the implementation of disaster relief programmes. Allen[46] describes how political wrangling between federal, state and municipal authorities negatively affected relief and reconstruction efforts after the floods of 1988. She writes:

> ... *political rivalry between state and municipal government, between both of them and the federal government, and even at managerial level within the Caixa Economica Federal, exacerbated problems of project implementation, involving an 18-month delay in starting the reconstruction plan.*

However, clearly, the political landscape has changed significantly since then and recent evidence suggests a more cooperative atmosphere.

Rio has a large migrant population from the poorest parts of Brazil's arid north-east region. The fact that many of them do not have personal experience with mudslides or mass wasting may account for their building practices. Migrants move up hillsides in search of new land, consistently eating away at the vegetation cover on the slopes above the *favelas*, despite government efforts to cordon off such areas to prevent further development. Improved local environmental knowledge and an understanding of slope dynamics might cause *favela* dwellers to reconsider such activities.

Rio de Janeiro has invested more than US$600 million in its Programa Favela Bairro to improve access to basic infrastructure, health and education for half a million of its poorest residents.[47] In terms of social cohesion, the *favelas* do have some rudimentary organization, including neighbourhood watches and self-improvement societies. However, the level of cohesion has apparently declined over time as the levels of drug-related crime and violence have increased. One observer speaks of the prevalence of young predatory gangs, which contrasts with the kinds of gangs that, at one time, had a sense of allegiance to *favela* residents and would even provide protection for their own.[48]

Likely future climate hazards and overall vulnerability assessment

The Canadian Climate Centre's A2 (business as usual) and B2 (sustainable path) scenarios predict roughly equal average annual temperature increases of 1.5°C by 2050 (see Figure 6.2). This increase is about the same as that predicted for Mumbai, but is lower than that for Shanghai. Unlike the other cities, the same approximate 1.5°C increase is predicted across all four seasons. As mentioned earlier, projected precipitation changes are less reliable, although Canadian A2 and B2 scenarios suggest declines of 7 per cent and 2.5 per cent, respectively. Sea-level rise, as mentioned earlier, is predicted to be in the order of 50cm by 2050.

Potential impacts of precipitation extremes. Given the potential decreases in precipitation during winter and/or spring, it is likely that these seasons will suffer from increased drought. Summer months may also experience drought as evapotranspiration increases due to increased temperatures with no offsetting increases in precipitation. Drought conditions could precipitate two kinds of problem. One is water scarcity, particularly if the droughts extend into the

Paraíba River Basin in Minas Gerais, from where Rio obtains the majority of its water. The other is electricity shortages, as were experienced recently throughout the country in 2001.

Although average precipitation during the summer rainy season may decline, increases in sea surface temperature and in the severity of ENSO events could result in periodic flooding of the kind encountered during February 1967 and again in February 1988. The 1967 floods were even more extreme than those in 1988 – 1985mm fell over two days (83 per cent higher than average annual rainfall).[49] Generally, precipitation extremes are expected to increase in severity with climatic change and these will have adverse impacts upon Rio given that the city already experiences extreme flooding on a 15- to 20-year basis. Poor neighbourhoods are particularly vulnerable to this kind of flooding; roughly 300 people died and more than 20,000 people were made homeless during each of the floods in 1967 and 1988.

Coastal/marine issues. Rio does not suffer from subsidence, so this will not exacerbate sea-level rise. However, should sea-level rise be coupled with more extreme coastal storms, there is significant likelihood of increased beach erosion, which will affect nourishment costs and could ultimately affect the tourism sector of the economy.[50] However, Muehe indicates that it is unlikely that high-rise apartment buildings in Copacabana and Ipanema will be directly affected by a rise in sea level of 50cm even in the event of storm surges.[51]

As mentioned above, Guanabara Bay has lost most of its coastal mangroves and significant portions of coastal marshes have been filled in. The potential for mangroves or marshes to retreat inland with rising sea level is impeded by the concentrated development along the coast. This will reduce the capacity of the few remaining wetlands to act as buffers during storm surges.

Rising water temperatures may precipitate algae blooms in Guanabara Bay, especially if no effort is made to treat discharges into the bay.

Overall vulnerability. We find that there are three stress bundles that are particularly troublesome for Rio de Janeiro. Each converges with a particular set of system characteristics to produce vulnerabilities that result from gaps in Rio's socio-ecological system and which do not allow it to withstand, respond to or cope effectively with these predicted stress bundles.

Temperature increases come together with drought to put stress on Rio's drinking water supply. In addition, problems with governance exist that could further hinder the city in developing more robust potable water storage and delivery systems. Extreme and unpredictable rainfall and floods converge with projected sea-level rise to increase stresses that will be difficult for Rio to handle owing to the city's topography (narrow coastal shelf backed by steep mountains subject to mass erosion), poor building conditions, the lack of secure land tenure for a notable portion of the city's population, poverty coupled with large income inequalities, high rates of crime that reduce social trust, and large problems with sanitation systems and sewage disposal.

Lastly, sea-level rise converges with the tourism-based economy of a beach city to create a third stress bundle of great importance to Rio de Janeiro. Because of Rio's characteristically narrow beach, which is backed by steep slopes and mountains, modest increases in sea level will likely magnify sand erosion. In addition, Rio has no dykes or other armaments that could protect the beach from modest sea-level rise or even from great storm surges. This situation illuminates a gap between the stress bundle and Rio's ability to resist or cope with it. Because of Rio's economic dependence upon beach tourism, such damage will likely have reciprocal effects on the economy, thus creating additional stress on the city.

Based on this preliminary assessment, we conclude that Rio suffers from a significant ongoing vulnerability to climate hazards, particularly flooding and landslides. Although civil defence institutions have been set up to cope with natural disasters, underlying structural problems, including political clientelism and spatial segregation based on income, render the city vulnerable to climate hazards. Little in the way of concrete flood protection infrastructure has been set up in the wake of the 1988 floods. It is possible to speak of highly vulnerable sub-populations living in *favelas* and near waterways, and relatively less vulnerable upper classes living in high-rise apartments in locations less susceptible to inundation. At the same time, climatic changes are predicted that will likely increase the severity of intense rainfall events and raise sea level. Although the economy of Rio de Janeiro is relatively robust, significant portions of gross domestic product (GDP) will be required for relief and reconstruction if floods of the magnitude of 1967 and 1988 are repeated. Unless more concerted efforts are made to prepare for climate hazards, the city will remain vulnerable.

Shanghai

Shanghai ('on the sea' in Chinese) is one of the world's largest seaports and a major industrial and commercial centre of the People's Republic of China. It is located at 31°41' latitude north and 121°29' longitude east. Bordering Jiangsu and Zhejiang provinces to the west, Shanghai is washed by the East China Sea to the east and Hangzhou Bay to the south. North of the city, the Yangtze River (or Changjiang) pours into the East China Sea. The municipality covers 6185km², which includes the city itself, surrounding suburbs and an agricultural hinterland. It is also China's most populous urban area, with a 2000 population of more than 16.5 million inhabitants in the municipality and almost 10 million in the city.

Physical environment
With the exception of a few hills in the south-west corner, most of the Shanghai area is flat and is situated on the alluvial plain of the Yangtze River delta. Shanghai's elevation is only 3m to 5m above sea level and averages 4m. There are no high mountains in the surrounding area and the Jiangshuai and Huabei plains

extend northwards. Cold air masses from the north and moist warm air from the south meet and mix above Shanghai, with no topographical hindrance.[52]

Geologically, the Shanghai area lies in the north-east section of the southern Changjiang land mass. Since the beginning of the quaternary era, this area has undergone tectonic subsidence and global marine transgressions and regressions. With the exception of the west, where there are several scattered stripped kops (igneous Mesozoic rocks), most of the area is covered by unconsolidated sediments, including fluvial, lacustrine and littoral facies that range in thickness from 100m to 150m in the west to 350m to 400m in the east.[53]

Being located at the mouth of the Yangtze River, the Shanghai region is very much the product of riverine and marine processes. The evolution of the landscape has been deeply influenced by local hydrodynamics, especially tidal flows and runoff. The Yangtze is a major river, with a yearly discharge of $9.24 \times 10^{11} m^3$, and carries an annual sediment load of 4.86×10^8 tonnes. These sediments feed the delta's continued seaward expansion. The basin drains a humid region, with an average annual precipitation greater than 1000mm, rising to 2000mm in certain localities.[54]

The Shanghai area experiences a sub-tropical monsoon climate. Frequent summer and autumn typhoons bring not only rainstorms that greatly increase surface runoff, but also cause storm surges in coastal areas. Both significantly modify the geomorphic evolution of the coastal area, as illustrated by Typhoon Number 14 that occurred in 1981. This typhoon created high tidal flats while simultaneously strongly scouring middle and low tidal flats along the local coast. Waves produced by strong north-east river mouth winds can also cause significant coastal erosion, which lowers the surface of the tidal flats and promotes shoreline recession.

Built environment

Shanghai utilizes the uniform system of classifying urban land use and codes created by the Construction Ministry to structure different land uses. Typically, the centres of large cities have high population densities. In the central districts of Shanghai, residential land use occupies 30.1 per cent of the area. Good and normal residential quarters (codes R2 and R3) account for 82.4 per cent of this residential land, while high-quality residential quarters (code R1) and poor-quality residential quarters (code R4) represent only 2.7 and 12.6 per cent, respectively.

In the central urban area, there are $13.4 m^2$ of residential land per person, which equates to a housing density of 74,600 individuals per square kilometre. The proportion of land devoted to industrial and warehouse use is 22 per cent.

The Huangpu River is Shanghai's main source of water. There are over 30 waterworks in Shanghai, 11 of which are located in the urban district along the Huangpu River. Five million tonnes of tap water are supplied to the urban district every day. Each suburban county also has one or two waterworks. Water resources are used in three significant ways in Shanghai – namely, industry, agriculture and public water use, in a ratio of 3:6:1. Even in a dry year, such as 1988, consumption was only 12 billion cubic metres – that is, about 19 to 22 per cent of the available water.

One of the serious water resource problems is the overexploitation of groundwater resources in the surrounding agricultural lands, which has caused significant subsidence.[55] Since 1921, groundwater has been exploited on a large scale. Because recharge is slow, the water table has fallen and soil moisture has dropped, leading to compression. During the period of 1921 to 1965, mean subsidence in the city of Shanghai was 1.76m and the highest recorded figure was 2.63m. This process of subsidence has encouraged greater intrusion of seawater into Shanghai's waterways, thus decreasing their quality. Since 1965, the level of groundwater exploitation has been reduced and aquifer-recharging projects have been carried out. As a result, subsidence was reduced to as little as a few millimetres a year; however, since 1984, with the development of new industry in suburban counties, the exploitation of groundwater has increased again with no adequate control.

Socio-economic conditions

Endowments. Shanghai has 9.8 million residents in the city proper and an average residential density of 74,600 individuals per square kilometre. Owing to stringent application of the 'one child' family planning policy, in 1993 Shanghai was the first area in China to report a negative natural growth rate (births minus deaths). In 2000, the city registered a negative population growth rate of –1.9 per 1000, based on a birth rate of 5.3 per 1000 and a mortality rate of 7.2 per 1000. However, rapid rates of in-migration more than make up for declining fertility.

Perhaps the biggest single endowment is the city's burgeoning economy, coupled with its pre-eminent status as China's financial capital. Thus, whatever the threats that may exist in the way of subsidence and sea-level rise, the government of China and the local authorities are likely to make whatever investments are required in order to build coastal defences.

Direct coping. In August 1998, China experienced devastating floods when the Yangtze River overflowed, causing more than 3000 deaths, affecting 223 million people, displacing 16 million people, flooding 25 million hectares of crop land and causing US$36 billion worth of damage.[56] Heavy rainfall in 1999 also caused flooding, although less extensive. This put disaster management institutions to the test.

Shanghai has a Municipal Civil Defence Office, which cooperates with the public security and fire protection agencies. In addition, 284 streets and counties have civil defence organizations, which, in turn, organize communities into volunteer civil defence teams.[57] According to ex-United Nations Secretary-General Kofi Annan:

> In China, where extensive disaster control policies have been
> introduced over the years, the death toll from floods has fallen
> dramatically. Flooding cost more than 3000 lives in China in 1998;
> but similar floods in 1931 and 1954 cost 140,000 and 33,000,
> respectively. Prevention strategies saved tens of thousands of lives.[58]

Among the prevention strategies employed are massive afforestation and
reforestation campaigns in the Yangtze River basin to reduce runoff and prevent
flooding and landslides, as well as dyke construction.

Although such responses have demonstrated a commitment by national,
provincial and municipal authorities to disaster mitigation and preparedness,
there are underlying structural impediments to disaster management that are very
similar to those found in Mumbai and Rio. These include fragmentation of
political authority at central government, provincial and municipal level, and lack
of coordination in the areas of environmental policy.[59]

Indirect coping. Shanghai's population, at close to 17 million, is largely poor
and is composed of an increasing number of migrants from rural hinterlands.
Official statistics do not provide a clear picture of income and wealth distribution
or measures of social cohesion in Shanghai. However, broader trends in China
suggest that disparities are increasing in urban areas, that urban unemployment
is rising and that the *hukou* system of household registration is limiting access to
benefits.[60] While inequalities may be rising and social cohesion may be low in
areas settled predominantly by migrants, official efforts have been made to
involve citizens in disaster response.

Since 1993, Shanghai's natural population growth has reversed from positive
to negative, making it the first provincial region in China to experience this
phenomenon. Low birth rates could engender population ageing, and a growing
elderly population could imply vulnerability to heat stress. High immigration
means that the base of the population pyramid is continuously being replenished.
As of the 2000 census, 3.8 million migrants resided in the city.

Likely future climate hazards and overall vulnerability assessment

Temperature changes for Shanghai suggest that the city will be the most severely
affected of the three cities considered here, with average annual temperature
increases of between 2° and 2.5°C. This will have an impact upon
evapotranspiration and, consequently, upon the moisture balance. Temperature
changes will also likely lead to more severe extra-tropical storms and consequent
flooding. However, the greatest issue of immediate concern for Shanghai is flood
defences in response to subsidence, sea-level rise and the likelihood that future
extreme precipitation will cause flooding from the Yangtze.

Overall vulnerability. As in Mumbai and Rio, recent and severe flooding has
tested Shanghai. Perhaps given the magnitude of the city's losses (3000 dead and

16 million displaced in the Yangtze Basin, against 300 dead in Rio), the government appears to be taking a genuine interest in long-term disaster planning. The municipality has also engaged citizens in 'volunteer' civil defence networks, which presumably means that citizens know what to do in the event of disaster and are prepared to take action.

Nonetheless, several key bundles of stresses converge to create specific vulnerabilities for Shanghai that emerge out of gaps in the city's ability to resist and cope with these stresses. First, sea-level rise along with increasing severity and frequency of heavy rains and floods come together with Shanghai's topography (level and low lying), geology (unconsolidated), land subsidence due to groundwater withdrawal, many wetlands and flood-prone areas, the inability of many buildings to withstand shifting land and water damage due to their poor condition, sanitation and waste disposal systems that are near capacity, and relatively modest income levels. This mix is likely to produce significant vulnerabilities for a large proportion of the city's residents, the city's built infrastructure and the Shanghai region's economy. Second, Shanghai's population is already large and continues to grow rapidly. When this massive trajectory comes together with projected sea-level rise and increasing water use by the city, this exacerbates land subsidence, probably puts greater numbers of people in harm's way from climate hazards and coastal erosion, and places people in greater concentration within areas that are likely increasingly flood prone. This set of circumstances may lead to a diminishing capacity for Shanghai to cope with such stresses because of its burgeoning population on already vulnerable lands and a greater draw-down of groundwater, causing densely populated lands to subside while sea level continues to rise. This could lead to increases in direct mortality, economic downturn and, potentially, large-scale disease outbreaks. On the other hand, as noted above, Shanghai's wealth means that the city has a high adaptive capacity. Resources will likely be invested in technological solutions even if such solutions fail to address root causes of vulnerability.

Conclusions

The foregoing sections provide a snapshot of vulnerabilities to climate-related hazards in three global cities. Our aim here was not to assess definitively the vulnerability of each of these cities but, instead, to apply a selection of data identified by the vulnerability framework in order to better understand multiple synergistic stresses and perturbations on one side of the equation, and multiple interacting physical and social characteristics of the exposed human–environment system on the other. Vulnerabilities that may have been hidden with simple 'summations' of stresses when compared with 'summations' of vulnerabilities were, instead, highlighted with this process.[61] A novelty of this chapter is that we apply a more traditional approach to vulnerability assessment – using scenario-based models to assess likely climate impacts, or a 'top-down' approach – and couple this with more recent advances in vulnerability mapping through 'bottom-up' assessments.[62] The result is something of a hybrid, which facilitates an understanding of likely future climate impacts while assessing the resilience of the current socio-ecological system in the face of bundles of stresses that are partly related to climate impacts and partly related to fragilities in the system itself.

From a policy perspective, there are few easy prescriptions for reducing vulnerability and better preparing for future climate hazards, at least in the case of the low-income country cities we describe above. Among other things, this may be attributed to the following factors:[63]

- Disasters are an unequally distributed public 'bad' that are more likely to affect poorer, more vulnerable sub-populations with the least political influence. Mitigation measures, by contrast, are a public 'good' that require substantial investment and adequately functioning institutions.
- Low tax collection capacity and low incomes constrain the resources available to government to make necessary infrastructural or institutional investments. Government resources themselves may become highly contested through political manoeuvring (as in the case of Brazil).
- The wealthy and more influential classes may simply choose to 'exit' from political decision-making processes rather than voice their concern over the lack of disaster preparedness. 'Exit' means that they opt out of public resources and, instead, choose to invest in their own capability set (e.g. purchasing a well-built home in a safe location, insurance policies, or private education and healthcare).
- Adaptation measures are difficult to implement because they require long time horizons, whereas politicians typically operate on short-term horizons. Incentives need to be intelligently designed so that politicians, officials and the private sector find it in their interests to build less risk-prone equitable cities.[64]
- If vulnerability mitigation/prevention measures are expensive, there may exist a 'moral hazard' on the part of state decision-makers, as they may assume that the international relief community will come to their assistance in the event of a significant natural disaster. Thus, to act means committing scarce public resources to a medium- or even low-probability future event, whereas to 'wait and see' if disaster strikes, and later claim that the disaster could not be foreseen, shifts the financial burden onto international agencies.

The authors do not underestimate in any way the difficulties entailed in preparing adequately for future climate change-related vulnerabilities. Given these political and institutional issues, it is worth considering how communities themselves, through micro-planning or other efforts at collective organization, might develop plans and infrastructure necessary to reduce their vulnerability to natural disasters in contexts where governments either lack the resources or are unwilling to consider investments in preparedness.[65] Many efforts to improve local environments, such as enhanced drainage and improved waste disposal, also reduce vulnerabilities to disasters and their consequences (such as the spread of disease).

Notes

1. Nicholls, R. (1995) 'Coastal megacities and climate change', *GeoJournal*, vol 37, no 3, pp369–379; also Rosenzweig, C. and Solecki, W. D. (2001) 'Climate change and a global city', *Environment*, vol 43, no 3, April, pp8–18.
2. Brockerhoff, M. (2000) 'An urbanizing world', *Population Bulletin*, vol 55, no 3, September, www.prb.org.
3. SEDAC (Socioeconomic Data and Applications Centre) Katrina Hazard Mapping Project, http://sedac.ciesin.columbia.edu/katrina2005.html; also Dyson, M. (2006) *Come Hell or High Water: Hurricane Katrina and the Colour of Disaster*, Basic Civitas, New York.
4. CRED (Centre for Research on the Epidemiology of Disasters) (2006) *EM-DAT: The OFDA/CRED International Disaster Database*, CRED, Université Catholique de Louvain (UCL), Brussels.
5. CRED (Centre for Research on the Epidemiology of Disasters) (2005) 'Are natural disasters increasing?', *CRED CRUNCH*, August, CRED, Université Catholique de Louvain (UCL), Brussels.
6. Easterling, D. R., Evans, J. L., Groisman, P. Y., Karl, T. R., Kunkel, K. E. and Ambenje, P. (2000) 'Observed variability and trends in extreme climate events: A brief review', *Bulletin of the American Meteorological Society*, vol 81, no 3, pp417–425.
7. Santer, B. D., Wigley, T. M. L., Gleckler, P. J., Bonfils, C., Wehner, M. F., AchutaRao, K., Barnett, T. P., Boyle, J. S., Brüggemann, W., Fiorino, M., Gillett, N., Hansen, J. E., Jones, P. D., Klein, S. A., Meehl, G. A., Raper, S. C. B., Reynolds, R. W., Taylor, K. E. and Washington, W. M. (2006) 'Forced and unforced ocean temperature changes in Atlantic and Pacific tropical cyclogenesis regions', *Proceedings of the National Academy of Science*, vol 103, September, pp13905–13910.
8. See Chapter 2; also McGranahan, G., Balk, D. and Anderson, B. (2006) 'Low coastal zone settlements', *Tiempo: A Bulletin on Climate and Development*, no 59. The megacities estimate is based on an analysis of Global Rural–Urban Mapping Project data, which define city boundaries based on night-time lights rather than the contiguously built-up 'urban agglomeration'.
9. Rayner, S. and Malone, E. L. (1997) 'Zen and the art of climate maintenance', *Nature*, vol 390, November, pp332–334.
10. Liverman, D. (1990) 'Vulnerability to global environmental change', in Kasperson, R. E. et al (eds) *Understanding Global Environmental Change: The Contributions of Risk Analysis and Management*, The Earth Transformed Programme, Clark University, Worcester, MA, pp27–44. The vulnerability concept has been applied to cities by several authors, including Mitchell, J. K. (ed) (1999) *Crucibles of Hazard: Megacities and Disasters in Transition*, UN University Press, Tokyo; also Pelling, M. (2003) *The Vulnerability of Cities: Natural Disaster and Social Resilience*, Earthscan,

London; and Sanderson, D. (2000) 'Cities, disasters and livelihoods', *Environment and Urbanization*, vol 12, no 2, October, pp93–102. Multiple definitions and methods for measuring vulnerability have been developed. See, in particular, Wisner, B., Blaikie, P., Cannon, T. and Davis, I. (2004) *At Risk: Natural Disasters, People's Vulnerability and Disasters*, Routledge, London.

11. Turner, B. L., Kasperson, R. E., Matson, P. A., McCarthy, J. J., Corell, R. W., Christensen, L., Eckley, N., Kasperson, J. X., Luers, A., Martello, M. L., Polsky, C., Pulsipher, A. and Schiller, A. (2003) 'A framework for vulnerability analysis in sustainability science', in *Proceedings of the National Academy of Science*, vol 100, no 3, July, pp8074–8079.

12. We utilize Canadian Climate Centre's B2 (emissions reduction) scenario and A2 (business as usual) scenario because these data were readily available from the NASA Goddard Institute for Space Studies, which ran the local temperature change estimates for us. They are generally consistent with B2 and A2 scenarios from the Hadley Centre, Goddard Institute for Space Studies (GISS) and other models.

13. See reference 1, Nicholls (1995).

14. The projected sea-level increase from the melting of land-based glaciers on Greenland alone is 7m; should the West Antarctic ice sheet also melt, this would contribute an additional 8m. See RealClimate (2006) 'How much future sea-level rise? More evidence from models and ice sheet observations', www.realclimate.org/, 26 March 2006.

15. Bird, E. C. F. (1995) 'Present and future sea level: the effects of predicted global changes', in Eisma, D. (ed) *Climate Change Impact on Coastal Habitation*, Lewis Publishers, Boca Raton, FL.

16. *Bombay First* (2006) www.bombayfirst.org/g-statistics.htm, accessed 19 September 2006.

17. Regional Plan for Mumbai Metropolitan Area, 1996–2011, http://theory.tifr.res.in/bombay/amenities/housing/masterplan.html, accessed 19 September 2006.

18. Wikipedia, 'Mumbai suburban railway', http://en.wikipedia.org/wiki/Mumbai_Suburban_Railway, accessed 19 September 2006.

19. TERI (Tata Energy Research Institute) (1996) *The Economic Impact of a One-Metre Sea-Level Rise on the Indian Coastline: Method and Case Studies*, Report submitted to the Ford Foundation.

20. World Bank (2006) 'From rationing to full service: water and sanitation challenge for Bombay', http://wbln0018.worldbank.org/oed/oeddoclib.nsf/View+to+Link+WebPages/-9A7152C54E38F2EE852567F5005D8DD5?OpenDocument, accessed 19 September 2006.

21. Sharma, V. K. (2000) 'Problems of marine ecosystems and sustainability of coastal cities: A focus on Mumbai, India', *Indian Journal of Environmental Health*, vol 42, no 2, pp82–91.

22. See reference 21.

23. See reference 20.

24. *Bombay Pages*, 'Future plans for the water supply', http://theory.tifr.res.in/~sgupta/bombay/amenities/water/future.html, accessed 20 November 2006.

25. See reference 20.

26. CIA (Central Intelligence Agency) (2001) *World Fact Book*, Government Printing Office, Washington, DC.

27. See reference 21.
28. *Asia Week*, www.asiaweek.com/asiaweek/features/asiacities/ac1999/data/bombay.html, accessed 20 September 2006.
29. Maharashtra State Disaster Management Plan, http://mdmu.maharashtra.gov.in/pages/State/statedmpShow.php, accessed 20 September 2006.
30. Revi, A. (2005) 'Lessons from the deluge: Priorities for multi-hazard risk mitigation', *Economic and Political Weekly*, vol 40, no 36, September, pp3911–3916.
31. UNDP (United Nations Development Programme) (2001) Press Release, www.undp.org.in/NEWS/PRESS/press138.htm, 21 September 2006.
32. United Nations Millennium Project (2005) *A Home in the City*, Task Force on Improving the Lives of Slum Dwellers, Earthscan, London.
33. SPARC (Society for the Promotion of Area Resource Centres) (2001) 'SPARC and its work with the National Slum Dwellers Federation', www.sparcindia.org/documents/alliance.html, accessed 23 June 2001.
34. See reference 30.
35. See reference 19.
36. Pers comm with Professor Dietre Muehe, Department of Geography, Federal University of Rio de Janeiro, 22 August 2001.
37. UK Meteorological Office (2006) 'Catarina hits Brazil: South Atlantic hurricane breaks all the rules', www.metoffice.com/sec2/sec2cyclone/catarina.html, 21 September 2006.
38. Fernandes, E. (2000) 'The legalization of *favelas* in Brazil: Problems and prospects', *Third World Planning Review*, vol 22, no 2, pp167–188.
39. Cunha, L. R. and Miller Santos, M. (1993) 'The Rio reconstruction project: the first two years', in *Towards A Sustainable Urban Environment: The Rio de Janeiro Study*, World Bank Discussion Paper 195, World Bank, Washington, DC.
40. Baptista de Araújo, S. (1994) 'Rio de Janeiro and natural disasters', *STOP Disasters*, no 21, September–October, IDNDR Secretariat, Geneva.
41. Kreimer, A., Lobo, T., Menezes, B., Munasinghe, M., Parker, R. and Preece, M. (1993) 'Rio de Janeiro – in search of sustainability', in Cunha and Miller Santos (1993): see reference 39.
42. IBGE (Instituto Brasileiro de Geografia e Estatistica) www.ibge.gov.br, accessed 21 September 2006.
43. Corrêa do Lago, L. (1999) 'Divisão sócio-espacial e mobilidade residencial: Reprodução ou alteração das fronteiras espaciais?', Instituto de Pesquisa e Planejamento Urbano e Regional, Universidade Federale do Rio de Janeiro (IPPUR/UFRJ).
44. See reference 41.
45. Geddes, B. and Neto, A. R. (1992) 'Institutional sources of corruption in Brazil', *Third World Quarterly*, vol 13, no 4, pp641–661.
46. Allen, E. (1994) 'Political responses to flood disaster: the example of Rio de Janeiro', in Varley, A. (ed) *Disasters, Development and Environment*, John Wiley & Sons Ltd, New York.
47. UN-Habitat (2006) *State of the World's Cities*, Earthscan, London.
48. Pers comm with D. Maimon, President, Association for Support and Incentives to Environmental Management (SIGA). 22 August 2001.
49. See reference 40.

50. Schnack, E. J. (1993) 'The vulnerability of the East Coast of South America to sea-level rise and possible adjustment strategies', in Warrick, R. A., Barrow, E. M. and Wigley, T. M. L. (eds) *Climate and Sea-level Change: Observations, Projections and Implications*, Cambridge University Press, UK.

51. See reference 36.

52. Zhang, C. and Wang, Y. (1998) 'The climate of Shanghai', in Foster, H. D., Chuenyan Lai, D. and Zhou, N. (eds) *The Dragon's Head: Shanghai, China's Emerging Megacity*, Canadian Western Geographical Series, vol 34, Western Geographical Press, University of Victoria, Canada, 317pp.

53. Xu, S. and Tao, J. (1998) 'The geomorphology of Shanghai', in Foster et al (1998): see reference 52.

54. Milliman, J. D. and Mei-e, R. (1995) 'River flux to the sea: Impact of human intervention on river systems and adjacent coastal areas', in Eisma (1995): see reference 15.

55. See reference 1: Nicholls (1995); see also reference 54.

56. Abramovitz, J. (1999) 'Natural disasters: at the hand of God or Man?', *Environmental News Network*, 23 June 1999, www.enn.com/enn-features-archive/1999/06/062399/disaster_3932.asp, accessed 29 October 2001; also NOAA/OGP Climate Information Project (1998) US Department of Commerce.

57. *China Fire* (2001) 'New disaster assistance management help residents away from misadventure', http://eng.china-fire.com/news/domestic/New%20Disaster%20Assistance%20Management.htm, accessed 30 October 2001.

58. Annan, K. (1999) 'An increasing vulnerability to natural disasters', *International Herald Tribune*, 10 September 1999, www.un.org/Overview/SG/annan_press.htm, accessed 29 October 2001.

59. Lieberthal, K. (1997) 'China's governing system and its impact on environmental policy implementation', *China Environment Series 1*, autumn, Woodrow Wilson International Centre for Scholars, Washington, DC.

60. A *hukou*, or household registration record, officially identifies a person as a resident of an area and includes identifying information, such as the name of the person, date of birth, the names of parents and name of spouse, if married. See McGranahan, G. and Tacoli, C. (2006) *Rural–Urban Migration in China: Policy Options for Economic Growth, Environmental Sustainability and Equity*, Working Paper no 12, Rural–Urban Interactions and Livelihoods Strategies Series, IIED, London.

61. We found some parts of the extended framework currently beyond our ability to gather appropriate data. This was particularly true when we tried to identify data on informal coping abilities for Shanghai. Informal coping, as we defined it, relies on surrogate measures of social cohesion, cooperation and social safety net. Such data, even though they are surrogate measures for such characteristics, were impossible to collect for Shanghai and difficult to collect for Mumbai and Rio de Janeiro. While the extended framework includes much richness, it simultaneously begs for better data for the framework to be used to its full potential.

62. For an example of the latter, see Adger, N. (1999) 'Social vulnerability to climate change and extremes in coastal Vietnam', *World Development*, vol 27, no 2, pp249–269.

63. Selected elements of this list are derived from Di John, J. (2001) 'An institutionalist political economy perspective of risk and vulnerability', Presentation at a joint World

Bank/Columbia University Workshop on Assessment of High Risk Disaster Hotspots, 6–7 September 2001, Palisades, NY.

64. See reference 30.
65. Goethert, R. and Hamdi, N. (1988) *Making Microplans. A Community-based Process in Design and Development,* Intermediate Technology Publications, London. In some instances, community preparedness is directly supported by the government, as in the case of Cochin in the state of Kerala, India. See Alungal, N. B. (2006) 'Management strategies for urban coastal zones: Integrating DPSIR concepts with GIS tools in people's participatory programmes', Paper presented at the Earth Systems Science Programme Open Conference, 9–12 November 2006, Beijing, China.

7

Climate, Climate Change and Human Health in Asian Cities

Sari Kovats and Rais Akhtar

Introduction

Climate change will affect the health of urban populations. Current attempts to reduce carbon emissions are insufficient to avoid further climate warming, and so the policy and research agendas are moving from mitigation (controlling greenhouse gas emissions) to adaptation (responding to climate change), and from global to local studies of impacts and responses.

Irrespective of global climate change, cities alter their local climate particularly by reducing rainfall and increasing night-time temperatures.[1] The 'urban heat island' effect is caused by day-time heat being retained by the fabric of the buildings and by a reduction in cooling vegetation. In temperate latitudes, this has the effect of raising night-time temperatures by 1° to 5°C. In tropical cities, the mean monthly urban heat island intensities can reach 10°C by the end of the night, especially during the dry season.[2] Urban heat islands are measured as the difference in temperature between inside the city and the surrounding areas. The magnitude of the urban heat island is, in general, proportional to the size of the city.[3] Urban areas also cause considerable intensification of rain, hail and thunderstorms. Due to these factors and to their location by rivers or in coastal zones, cities are particularly prone to floods.

Cities are a significant source of greenhouse gas emissions and have an important role to play in mitigation.[4] In this chapter, however, we shall focus only on the potential impacts of climate change upon the health of urban populations. Currently, populations in cities have to deal with a range of environmental hazards[5] and global climate change is likely to exacerbate many of these problems. We have reviewed the published literature for the health effects of climate and weather (including extreme weather) in urban settlements in Asia. We then discuss these environmental health hazards in the context of future social and environmental changes and regional climate changes, in particular.

Adapting to climate change in cities in low- and middle-income countries is now an additional concern for local governments[6] and we will briefly discuss the public health interventions that can reduce the current impacts upon health of weather and climate. Priority should be given to adaptation measures that provide immediate improvements to the health of urban populations.

Climate change and health

The Fourth Assessment Report of the Intergovernmental Panel on Climate Change (IPCC) was published in 2007. The report confirms that climate change is already taking place[7] and also assesses future changes in climate at the regional scale. Very few city-level projections are available, as confidence in the output of climate models decreases rapidly as one moves from regional to local-scale projections.

With respect to urban populations and human health in Asia, the key results of the IPCC report are:

- regional freshwater resources will be strongly affected by, and vulnerable to, climate change;
- increased rainfall intensity, particularly during the summer monsoon, in temperate and tropical Asia;
- increased risk of weather disasters, particularly flood events; and
- vulnerability of coastal cities due to climate change and sea-level rise.

The greatest concern about the impacts of climate change upon human health regards changes in freshwater resources, food supplies and increases in extreme weather events such as floods and droughts[8] (see Table 7.1). The Indian National Assessment of Vulnerability and Adaptation has addressed the potential impact of climate change upon malaria[9] and other reviews have described the impacts upon the health of heat waves[10] and flood events.[11] However, there is a lack of good scientific information on the assessment of the potential impacts of climate change upon health in Asian populations.

The potential impacts of climate change upon natural disasters have been described in papers in *Environment and Urbanization*,[12] particularly the vulnerability of Asian cities in coastal zones.[13] Table 7.2 describes the range of environmental risks to coastal megacities associated with sea-level rise. Historically, cities in South-East Asia have been most affected by storm surges in terms of numbers of deaths.[14]

Climate, water supplies and sanitation and health

Climate is a key determinant of water availability. Surface water availability depends upon the timing and volume of precipitation. The current burden of disease as a result of inadequate access to improved water and sanitation has long

Table 7.1 *Summary of known effects of weather and climate on urban health*

Health outcome	Known effects of weather
Heat stress	• Deaths in older people and people with chronic disease increase with high and low temperatures • Heat-related illness and death due to heat waves
Air pollution-related mortality and morbidity	• Weather affects air pollutant concentrations • Weather affects distribution, seasonality and production of aeroallergens
Health impacts of weather disasters	• Floods, landslides and windstorms cause direct effects (deaths and injuries) and indirect effects (infectious disease, loss of food supplies, long-term psychological morbidity)
Mosquito-borne diseases, tick-borne diseases (e.g. malaria, dengue)	• Higher temperatures reduce the development time of pathogens in vectors and increase potential transmission to humans • Vector species require specific climatic conditions (temperature, humidity) to be sufficiently abundant to maintain transmission
Water-/food-borne diseases	• Survival of important bacterial pathogens is related to temperature • Extreme rainfall can affect the transport of disease organisms into the water supply; outbreaks of water-borne disease have been associated with contamination caused by heavy rainfall and flooding associated with inadequate sanitation • Increases in drought conditions may affect water availability and water quality (chemical and microbiological load) due to extreme low flows

been recognized, particularly the very high rates of infant mortality in deprived urban areas.[15] There are clear social and economic reasons for the lack of access to improved water at the household level. However, cities in both high- and low-income countries have experienced failures in supply due to extreme drought events. It is also known that access to water within cities is not equally distributed and any reductions in supply are likely to have a greater impact on impoverished populations.

Climate change may affect water supplies to populations in cities through a range of mechanisms. Rivers that are sustained by glacier melt in the summer season – for example, in the Hindu Kush–Himalaya region – are likely to experience increased river flows in the short term as glaciers melt due to higher temperatures. However, the contribution of glacier melt will gradually decrease

Table 7.2 *Major weather-related hazards and the occurrence of subsidence in coastal megacities during the 20th century*

City	Erosion	Storm and wind damage		Flooding		Salinization	Major subsidence
		Hurricane landfall*	Extra-tropical storms	River	Surge		
Tokyo	Y	Y(3)	–	Y	Y	?	Y
Bombay	Y	Y(<1)	–	–	Y	?	–?
Lagos	Y	–	–	–	Y	?	?
Dhaka	–	Y(<1)	–	Y	–	Y	Y?
Karachi	Y	Y(<0.1)	–	–	Y	?	–?
New York	Y	Y(<1)	Y	–	Y	?	–
Jakarta	Y	–	–	Y	–	?	Y
Calcutta	–	Y(<1)	–	Y	–	Y	Y?
Metro Manila	Y	Y(>3)	–	–	Y	?	Y
Shanghai	–	Y(1)	–	Y	Y	Y	Y
Los Angeles	Y	–	Y	–	Y	–	Y**
Buenos Aires	Y	–	Y	Y	Y	?	–?
Cairo	–	–	Y	Y	–	–	–?
Istanbul	Y	–	Y	–	Y	?	–
Rio de Janeiro	Y	–	–	–	Y	–	–
Osaka	Y	Y(3)	–	Y	Y	?	Y
Tianjin	–	Y(<0.1)	Y	Y	Y	Y	Y
Bangkok	Y	Y(<1)	–	Y	Y	?	Y
Seoul	–	Y(1–3)	Y	Y	–	–	–?

Lima	Y	–	–	?	Y	–
Madras	Y	Y(<1)	–	–	Y	?

Notes: Y = yes; – = no; ? = uncertain.

* The relative frequency of hurricane landfall is indicated by the annual occurrence of tropical storms and cyclones (Beaufort force 8 and above).

** Due to oil and gas extraction rather than groundwater withdrawal.

Source: Klein, R. J. T., Nicholls, R. J. and Thomalla, F. (2003) 'The resilience of coastal megacities to weather-related hazards', in Kreimer, A., Arnold, M. and Carlin, A. (ed) *Building Safer Cities: The Future of Disaster Risk*, World Bank, Washington, DC, pp101–120; also Nicholls, R. J. (1995) 'Coastal megacities and climate change', *Geojournal*, vol 37, no 3, pp1–11.

over the next few decades. Current trends in glacial melt suggest that the Ganga, Indus, Brahmaputra and other rivers in the northern Indian plain could become seasonal rivers in the near future.[16] Thus, cities that rely on glacial melt water will eventually lose this source and will have to seek alternatives, such as reservoirs or deep groundwater wells. Demand for groundwater may increase in other areas where the availability of surface water decreases.

For cities that rely on coastal aquifers, sea-level rise and any decrease in groundwater recharge levels will exacerbate saltwater intrusion (see Table 7.2). Inland aquifers are also at risk of saltwater intrusion from neighbouring aquifers, as groundwater recharge decreases. Shallow aquifers in arid and semi-arid regions are at risk of salinization as a result of increased evapotranspiration.

Climate impact assessments are often conducted at the river catchment level and converted to water availability per capita or withdrawal to resource ratio. Such indicators are useful to some extent, but provide no information on the level of access to water, the quality of water or any differences between rural or urban areas. Climate change is likely to cause a decline in environmental water resource availability in certain cities where water resource management is poor or non-existent. This will have a negative impact upon water availability at the household level, particularly in the households of the urban poor.

The impact of climate change upon water availability is likely to be one of the most significant for the health of populations.[17] However, due to the complexity of the factors that determine access to clean water (social, political and environmental), the impacts upon health are not well addressed in the literature on climate impacts. A substantial amount of endemic diarrhoeal disease is transmitted via the faecal-oral route. Although disease rates can be reduced very cost effectively by improvements in hygiene behaviour, such improvements require access to sufficient quantities of water. Esrey et al[18] cite a number of studies where improvements in water quality failed to deliver a significant reduction in diarrhoeal disease in places where water availability was limited.

Heavy rainfall and flooding is also an important issue for environmental health in urban areas[19] as surface water is quickly contaminated during heavy rainfall events. In July 2005, severe flooding occurred in Mumbai, India. The city received 944mm of rainfall in a 24-hour period, compared to an average of 21.7cm of rainfall per year. The consequent flooding affected many households, including those in the more affluent parts of the city. Most metropolitan cities in India, including Mumbai, have poor urban drainage systems, which are easily blocked even during short spells of rain. The flooding in Mumbai was exacerbated by blocked canals and drains.

Urban poor populations often experience increased rates of infectious disease after flood events. Increases in cholera,[20] cryptosporidiosis and typhoid fever have been reported in low- and middle-income countries.[21] Flood-related increases in diarrhoeal disease have been reported in India[22] and Dhaka, Bangladesh.[23]

There are relatively few studies that have investigated the effects of rainfall on morbidity, particularly diarrhoeal disease. A recent study using hospital visit data in Dhaka found that rates of disease increased during both high and low rainfall extremes.[24] The number of non-cholera diarrhoeal cases increased by approximately 5 per cent for every 10mm increase in rainfall above a threshold of 52mm (averaged over eight weeks). In addition, the number of cases increased by around 4 per cent for every 10mm below the same threshold. Diarrhoeal disease morbidity was also shown to increase at higher temperatures, particularly in the more deprived populations.

After the floods of 2000 and 2001 in Mumbai, outbreaks of leptospirosis were reported in children living in informal settlements[25] and the prevalence of leptospirosis increased eightfold following the major flood event in July 2005.[26] Two hospital-based observational studies found that the risk of disease was associated with children either playing in the floodwater or wading through it while going to school and, in some cases, with floodwater inside the house.[27] However, these studies, like many other observational studies of flood impacts, did not use a control group, making it difficult to establish the level of baseline or pre-flood morbidity for comparison.[28]

Flooding may also lead to the contamination of waters with chemicals, heavy metals or other hazardous substances, either from storage or from chemicals already in the environment (e.g. pesticides).[29] There is little published evidence demonstrating a causal effect of chemical contamination on the pattern of morbidity and mortality following flooding events because it is difficult to assess individual exposures.[30] Increases in population densities and industrial development in areas subject to natural disasters increases the potential for mass human exposure to hazardous materials released during disasters. The contamination of floodwaters (and the longer-term contamination of soil) is a particular problem for populations situated near factories and industrial areas.

Inadequate drainage resulting in stagnant water is also a cause of mosquito-borne diseases such as malaria in urban areas. The effects of climate on such disease transmission is well understood from laboratory studies – as temperatures increase, the extrinsic incubation period (i.e. the time the parasites need to mature) decreases; this has been shown to be the case for dengue[31] and malaria.[32] However, rainfall effects that drive the abundance of mosquitoes depend upon the vector's local ecology. For urban vectors of dengue, such as *Aedes*, the effects of rainfall patterns are more complex.[33] Climate warming may increase the risk of outbreaks of dengue in urban areas where temperature is currently a limiting factor in disease transmission.

High temperatures and heat wave events

Heat is an environmental and occupational hazard. The risk of heat-related mortality increases with natural ageing; but people with particular social and/or physical vulnerability are also at risk.[34] There are important differences in vulnerability between populations, depending upon climate, culture, infrastructure (housing) and other factors. Episodes of extreme temperature can have significant impacts upon health and present a challenge for public health and local government services.

Human populations are 'acclimatized' to their local climate in physiological, behavioural and cultural terms; but there are clear limits to the amount of heat exposure that an individual can tolerate. The capacity of populations to adapt to varied climates and environments is considerable; but people do not live comfortably in temperatures outside the range of 17° to 31°C. The tolerance range of an individual is usually much less than this and will narrow with age or disability.

Global climate change is likely to be accompanied by an increase in the frequency and intensity of heat waves and by warmer summers and milder winters. Even small increases in average temperature can result in big shifts in the frequency of extremes. The impact of extreme summer heat upon human health may be exacerbated by increases in humidity.[35] In 2002, a heat wave was reported to have killed 622 people in the southern Indian state of Andhra Pradesh. Information from news reports indicated that daily wage earners such as labourers and rickshaw pullers were at risk as they have no option but to work outdoors under any conditions. National and state governments issued advice during heat waves, such as to stay indoors and drink water.

High temperatures are also an important occupational health hazard. In order to cope with heat, an instinctive adaptive action by a worker is to reduce work intensity or increase the frequency of short breaks. Therefore, one direct effect of a higher number of very hot days is likely to be a 'slowing down' in work and other daily activities.[36] This may result in 'self-pacing' and a reduction in productivity or it will incur risks to the health of workers unless proper occupational health management is implemented.[37]

In general, urban populations experience the highest heat load in cities in the dry tropics.[38] It is not clear how climate change will interact with local climate modifications due to the built environment;[39] but, clearly, the two causes of increased temperature will increase the heat load for urban populations and will also increase the risks to health. A central question in estimating future heat-related mortality is the rate at which populations will adapt to a warmer climate. Populations are likely to acclimatize to warmer climates through a range of behavioural, physiological and technological adaptations. The initial physiological acclimatization to hot environments can take place in a few days; but complete acclimatization may take several years. The rate at which changes in infrastructure will take place is likely to be much slower, however, for cities in the tropics.

In tropical regions, very high heat load exposure in urban areas will become more frequent. People living in informal structures may be more exposed to high temperatures. In Europe, the prevention of deaths in the community as a result of extreme high temperatures (heat waves) is now an issue of public health concern. It is likely that methods for addressing heat wave impacts upon health will be developed in Asian cities and some pilot projects have already been established in China.[40]

Global climate change may also exacerbate outdoor air pollution in Asian cities. Urban environmental problems such as outdoor air pollution have, in general, been decreasing steadily in developed countries because of active control measures. In low-income countries, increasing traffic and exhaust, as well as industrial emissions, are raising concentrations of sulphur dioxide (SO_2), nitrogen oxides (NO_x) and methane (O_3) and suspended particulate matter, which are known to be damaging to human health.[41] Delhi has high levels of urban pollution as a result of rapid industrialization and large numbers of small-scale industries in residential areas. Studies in Europe have shown that climate change may increase the number of days with high levels of tropospheric ozone (a secondary air pollutant).[42]

Longer-term changes and the future health of populations in cities

During recent decades, there have been improvements in the health of populations in cities; but these improvements are not equally distributed and high health burdens persist in the urban poor, particularly those living in informal settlements and slums.[43] The traditional approach to climate risk assessment – the top-down scenario-based approach – is undertaken at the regional or national level. Very few city assessments have been undertaken. Larger-scale studies rely on national projections of economic growth and do not address important inequalities within countries (or cities) and therefore do not focus on the impacts upon the most vulnerable populations.[44]

One approach, in the near term, is to assume that current trends in household income and health status will continue. For slum populations, this would mean a decline in health status and an increase in vulnerability to climate change. In the longer term (projections to the 2050s), one might assume some improvements in health and an improved capacity to adapt to climate change. An assessment of future health impacts should be undertaken using both optimistic and pessimistic assumptions about future health status. It is also important to consider that there are likely to be limits to the amount of climate change that can be managed (or adapted to). In particular, limits to water availability as a result of overexploitation and environmental degradation are likely to cause significant negative impacts upon health.

Responding to climate change: Adaptation and health at the city level

Urban populations, particularly poor urban populations, are currently not well adapted to climate and weather events. There is a particularly large burden of disease in urban poor populations due to temperature and rainfall extremes, and reducing this burden should be the priority for city governments.

A prerequisite for the prevention of adverse health effects from extreme events is public knowledge about the nature of the risk. Although public awareness increases following a natural disaster, it is often short lived. There is a clear need to develop and evaluate effective public health interventions for extreme weather events, such as heat health-warning systems to reduce the impact of heat waves. However, the implication of the French heat wave of 2003 was that not only were public health officers unprepared, but the entire infrastructure was also unprepared for such extreme temperatures. It will take many decades to adapt housing in order to maintain comfortable indoor temperatures in the face of prolonged extreme outdoor temperatures, especially in ways that will not increase energy consumption.

Many low-income countries have now begun to assess their needs for adaptation under the National Adaptation Programme of Action (NAPA) process of the United Nations Framework Convention on Climate Change (UNFCCC). The focus of the NAPAs has been on impacts in agriculture, forestry and water resources management. More recently, health effects are being addressed within the NAPAs – for example, in those of Bangladesh and Bhutan. The methods and tools for assessing the future risks to health from climate change are still being developed.[45] City-specific vulnerability assessments have also been undertaken in Dhaka[46] and in Cochin, India.[47]

There will always be uncertainties about the magnitude of adverse impacts of climate change, particularly relating to future changes in rainfall. We are confident, however, that the burden of ill-effects will most probably fall predominantly on those populations who have contributed little to greenhouse gas emissions.

More assessments of the impacts of climate change on health at the city level are needed in order to inform decision-making. We support the recent recommendations from the World Bank:[48]

- reliable and comprehensive assessments of risk vulnerabilities for exposed cities and the dissemination of such information;
- establishment of early warning systems and evacuation plans, including emergency preparedness and neighbourhood response systems;
- improved efficiency of the water supply management by minimizing leakages;

- improved health, educational and institutional capacity in urban environment management; and
- regularized property rights for informal settlements and other measures to allow low-income groups to buy, rent or build good-quality housing on safe sites.

Conclusions

Climate change represents a range of environmental hazards and will affect populations where the current burden of climate-sensitive disease is high – such as the urban poor in low- and middle-income countries. It is not the rapid development, size and density of cities that are the main determinants of vulnerability, but, rather, the increased populations in flood plains, coastal hazard risk zones and unstable hillsides vulnerable to landslides.[49] The scientific evidence, although limited for low-income populations, indicates that current weather extremes have significant impacts upon human health, particularly the impacts of heat waves, floods and heavy rainfall events. The methods for assessing the risks of climate change are undergoing development and there is a need to shift the focus from global and regional to local studies. Sectoral approaches to climate change impact assessments often ignore the effects on health. There is a need to better describe the risks to health as well as to improve the effectiveness of public health interventions. Improving the resilience of cities to climate change also requires improvements in the urban infrastructure, and such improvements may not be achieved quickly enough to avoid an increased burden of disease due to global climate change.

Notes

1. WMO (1996) *Climate and Urban Development*, WMO no 844, WMO, Geneva.
2. See reference 1.
3. Oke, T. R. (1973) 'City size and the urban heat island', *Atmospheric Environment*, vol 7, pp769–779; also Oke, T. R. (1997) 'Urban climates and global environmental change', in Thompson, R. D. and Perry, A. H. (eds) *Applied Climatology: Principles and Practice*, Routledge, London, pp273–287.
4. Kjellstrom, T., Friel, S., Dixon, J., Corvalan, C. F., Rehfuess, E., Campbell-Lendrum, D. et al (2007) 'Urban environmental health hazards and health equity,' *Journal of Urban Health*, vol 84, Supplement 1, May, pp86–97
5. Bull-Kamanga, L., Diagne, K., Lavell, A., Leon, E., Lerise, F., MacGregor, H. et al (2003) 'From everyday hazards to disasters: the accumulation of risk in urban areas', *Environment and Urbanization*, vol 15, no 1, April, pp193–204; also Gupta, I. and Mitra, A. (2002) 'Basic amenities and urban health in urban India', *National Medical Journal of India*, vol 15, Supplement 1, pp26–31.

6. Satterthwaite, D., Huq, S., Pelling, M., Reid, R. and Romero Lankao, P. (2007) *Adapting to Climate Change in Urban Areas: The Possibilities and Constraints in Low- and Middle-Income Countries*, Human Settlements Discussion Paper Series – Climate Change and Cities 1, International Institute for Environment and Development, London, 107pp.

7. IPCC (Intergovernmental Panel on Climate Change) (2007) *Climate Change 2007: The Physical Science Basis*, Contribution of Working Group I to the Fourth Assessment Report of the Intergovernmental Panel on Climate Change, Cambridge University Press, Cambridge and New York.

8. van Aalst, M. K. (2006) 'The impact of climate change on the risk of natural disasters', *Disasters*, vol 30, no 1, pp5–18; also Klein, R. J. T., Nicholls, R. J. and Thomalla, F. (2003) 'The resilience of coastal megacities to weather-related hazards', in Kreimer, A., Arnold, M. and Carlin, A. (eds) *Building Safer Cities: The Future of Disaster Risk*, World Bank, Washington, DC, pp101–120; and Confalonieri, U., Menne, B., Akhtar, R., Ebi, K., Hauengue, M., Kovats, R. S., Revich, B. and Woodward, A. (2007) 'Human health', in Parry, M., Canziani, O., Palutikof, J., van der Linden, P. and Hanson, C. (eds) *Climate Change 2007: Impacts, Adaptation and Vulnerability*, Contribution of Working Group II to the Fourth Assessment Report of the Intergovernmental Panel on Climate Change, Cambridge University Press, Cambridge and New York, Chapter 8, pp391–431.

9. Dhiman, R. C., Adak, T. and Subbarao, S. K. (2004) 'Impact of climate change on malaria in India with emphasis on selected sites', in Gosain, A. K., Sharma, S. K., Bhattacharya, S., Amit, G. and Rao, S. (eds) *Proceedings of the Workshop on Vulnerability Assessment and Adaptation due to Climate Change on Indian Water Resources, Coastal Zones and Human Health*, 27–28 June, Indian Institute of Technology, Delhi, and Ministry of Environment and Forests, Government of India, New Delhi, pp127–133.

10. Akhtar, R. (2007) 'Climate change and health and heat wave mortality in India', *Global Environmental Research*, vol 11, no 1, pp51–57; also Cruz, R. V., Harasawa, H., Lal, M. and Shaohong, W. with Anokhin, Y., Punsalmaa, B., Honda, Y., Jafari, M., Li, C. and Huu Ninh, N. (2007) 'Asia', in Parry et al (eds): see reference 8, Chapter 10, pp469–506.

11. See Chapter 4.

12. See Chapter 6.

13. See reference 8: Klein et al (2003); see also Chapter 2 and Nicholls, R. J. (1995) 'Coastal megacities and climate change', *Geojournal*, vol 37, no 3, pp1–11.

14. Nicholls, R. J. (2003) *An Expert Assessment of Storm Surge Hotspots*, Flood Hazard Research Centre, Enfield, UK.

15. Kosek, M., Bern, C. and Guerrant, R. L. (2003) 'The global burden of diarrhoeal disease, as estimated from studies published between 1992 and 2000', *Bulletin of the World Health Organization* vol 8, no 3, pp197–204; also Bhandari, N., Bahl, R., Taneja, S., Martines, J. and Bhan, M. K. (2002) 'Pathways to infant mortality in urban slums in Delhi, India: Implications for improving the quality of community and hospital-based programmes', *Journal of Health, Population and Nutrition*, vol 20, no 2, pp148–155.

16. See reference 10: Cruz et al (2007).

17. See reference 8: Confalonieri et al (2007).

18. Esrey, S. A., Potash, J. B., Roberts, L. and Shiff, C. (1991) 'Effects of improved water supply and sanitation on ascariasis, diarrhoea, dracunculiasis, hookworm infection, schistosomiasis and trachoma', *Bulletin of the World Health Organization*, vol 69, no 5, pp609–621.
19. Parkinson, J. (2003) 'Drainage and stormwater management strategies for low-income urban communities', *Environment and Urbanization*, vol 15, no 2, October, pp115–126; also Mitchell, G. (2005) 'Mapping hazard from urban non-point pollution: A screening model to support sustainable urban drainage planning', *Journal of Environmental Management*, vol 74, pp1–9.
20. Gabastou, J., Pesantes, C., Escalente, S., Narvez, Y., Vela, E., Garcia, L. et al (2002) 'Caracteristicas de la epidemia de colera de 1998 en Ecuador durante el fenomeno de El Niño' ['Characteristics of the cholera epidemic of 1998 in Ecuador during El Niño'], *Revista Panamerica de Salud Publica*, vol 12, no 3, pp157–164; also WHO (1998) 'Cholera in 1997', *The Weekly Epidemiological Record*, vol 73, pp201–208.
21. Ahern, M. J., Kovats, R. S., Wilkinson, P., Few, R. and Matthies, F. (2005) 'Global health impacts of floods: Epidemiological evidence', *Epidemiological Review*, vol 27, pp36–46.
22. Mondal, N. C., Biswas, R. and Manna, A. (2001) 'Risk factors of diarrhoea among flood victims: a controlled epidemiological study', *Indian Journal of Public Health*, vol 45, pp122–127.
23. Kunii, O., Nakamura, S., Abdur, R. and Wakai, S. (2007) 'The impact on health and risk factors of the diarrhoea epidemics in the 1998 Bangladesh floods', *Public Health*, vol 116, no 2, pp68–74; also Schwartz, B. S., Harris, J. B., Khan, A. I., Larocque, R. C., Sack, D. A., Malek, M. A. et al (2006) 'Diarrhoeal epidemics in Dhaka, Bangladesh, during three consecutive floods: 1988, 1998 and 2004', *American Journal of Tropical Medicine and Hygiene*, vol 74, no 6, pp1067–1073.
24. Hashizume, M., Armstrong, B., Hajat, S., Wagatsuma, Y., Faruque, A. S., Hayashi, Y. et al (2007) 'Association between climate variability and hospital visits for non-cholera diarrhoea in Bangladesh: Effects and vulnerable groups', *International Journal of Epidemiology*, vol 36, no 5, pp1030–1037.
25. Karande, S., Kulkarni, H., Kulkarni, M., De, A. and Varaija, A. (2002) 'Leptospirosis in children in Mumbai slums', *Indian Journal of Paediatrics*, vol 69, no 10, pp855–858.
26. Maskey, M., Shastri, J. S., Saraswathi, K., Surpam, R. and Vaidya, N. (2006) 'Leptospirosis in Mumbai: Post-deluge outbreak 2005', *Indian Journal of Medical Microbiology*, vol 24, Supplement 4, pp337–338.
27. See reference 26; also Karande, S., Bhatt, M., Kelkar, A., Kulkarni, M., De, A. and Varaija, A. (2003) 'An observational study to detect leptospirosis in Mumbai, India, 2000', *Archives of Diseases of Childhood*, vol 88, no 12, pp1070–1075.
28. See reference 21.
29. Young, S., Balluz, L. and Malilay, J. (2004) 'Natural and technologic hazardous material releases during and after natural disasters: a review', *Science of the Total Environment*, vol 322, pp3–20.
30. See reference 21; also Euripidou, E. and Murray, V. (2004) 'Public health impacts of floods and chemical contamination', *Journal of Public Health*, vol 26, no 4, pp376–383.

31. Koopman, J. S., Prevots, D. R., Marin, M. A., Dantes, H. G., Aquino, M. L., Longini Jr, I. M. et al (1991) 'Determinants and predictors of dengue infection in Mexico', *American Journal of Epidemiology*, vol 133, pp1168–1178.
32. MacDonald, G. (1957) *The Epidemiology and Control of Malaria*, Oxford University Press, UK.
33. Gubler, D. J. (1998) 'Resurgent vector-borne diseases as a global health problem', *Emerging Infectious Diseases*, vol 4, Special Issue, pp442–450.
34. Kovats, R. S. and Hajat, S. (2008) 'Heat stress and public health: a critical review', *Annual Review of Public Health*, vol 29, April, pp41–55.
35. Gaffen, D. J. and Ross, R. J. (1998) 'Increased summertime heat stress in the US', *Nature*, vol 396, pp529–530.
36. Kjellstrom, T. (2000) *Climate Change, Heat Exposure and Labour Productivity*, Proceedings of the 12th Conference of the International Society for Environmental Epidemiology (ISEE), 19–23 August, Buffalo, US.
37. Mairiaux, P. and Malchaire, J. (1985) 'Workers self-pacing in hot conditions: A case study', *Applied Ergonomics*, vol 16, no 2, pp85–90.
38. Jauregui, E. (1991) 'The human climate of tropical cities: an overview', *International Journal of Biometeorology*, vol 35, pp151–160.
39. Wilby, R. L. (2007) 'A review of climate change impacts on the built environment', *Built Environment*, vol 33, no 1, pp31–45.
40. Tan, J., Kalkstein, L. S., Huang, J., Lin, S., Yin, H. and Shao, D. (2004) 'An operational heat/health warning system in Shanghai', *International Journal of Biometeorology*, vol 48, no 3, pp157–162.
41. Health Effects Institute (2004) *Health Effects of Outdoor Air Pollution in Developing Countries in Asia*, Literature review, HEI Special Report 15, HEI, Boston.
42. Langner, J., Bergstom, R. and Foltescu, V. (2005) 'Impact of climate change on surface ozone and deposition of sulphur and nitrogen in Europe', *Atmospheric Environment*, vol 39, pp1129–1141; also Stevenson, D. S., Dentener, F. J., Schultz, M. G., Ellingsen, K., Noije, T. P. C., Wild, O. et al (2006) 'Multimodel ensemble simulations of present-day and near-future tropospheric ozone', *Journal of Geophysical Research*, vol 111, pD08301.
43. Phillips, D. R. (1993) 'Urbanization and human health', *Parasitology*, vol 106, ppS93–S107.
44. Kovats, R. S., Ebi, K. L. and Menne, B. (2003) *Methods of Assessing Human Health Vulnerability and Public Health Adaptation to Climate Change*, WHO/WMO/Health Canada, Copenhagen.
45. Ebi, K. L., Kovats, R. S. and Menne, B. (2006) 'An approach for assessing human health vulnerability and public health interventions to adapt to climate change', *Environmental Health Perspective*, vol 114, no 12, pp1930–1934; also McMichael, A. J., Campbell-Lendrum, D., Kovats, R. S., Edwards, S., Wilkinson, P., Edmonds, N. et al (2004) 'Climate change', in Ezzati, M., Lopez, A. D., Rodgers, A. and Murray, C. J. (eds) *Comparative Quantification of Health Risks: Global and Regional Burden of Disease due to Selected Major Risk Factors*, vol 2, World Health Organization, Geneva, pp1543–1649.
46. See reference 11.
47. Bindu, G., Chakrapani, S. B., Ensminger, J. T., Rajan, C. K., Simon, A., Natarayan, S. et al (2003) *Possible Vulnerabilities of Cochin, India, to Climate Change Impacts and*

Response Strategies to Increase Resilience, Oak Ridge National Laboratory, Tennessee, US, and Cochin University of Science and Technology, Cochin, India.

48. Bigio, A. G. (2003) 'Cities and climate change', in Kreimer, A., Arnold, M. and Carlin, A. (eds) *Building Safer Cities: The Future of Disaster Risk*, World Bank, Washington, DC, pp91–100.

49. See reference 6.

8

Climate Change and Urban Children: Impacts and Implications for Adaptation in Low- and Middle-Income Countries

Sheridan Bartlett

Introduction

There are many vulnerable populations in the context of climate change – the impacts are not spread equally in terms of location, economic status, gender or age. This chapter discusses the particular and often disproportionate risks to urban children in poverty from various aspects of climate change. It also explores the implications for adaptation, focusing on preparatory measures as well as responses to extreme events and to changes in weather patterns.[1]

Over the last 25 years, extreme weather events, including heavy rainfall, heat waves, droughts, floods, cyclones and hurricanes, have contributed to injury, illness, impoverishment, displacement, hunger and death for hundreds of millions of people, often with particular implications for children. Climate change is likely to have been a factor in many of these; but even if it was not, it is proof of the vulnerability of populations to events whose frequency and intensity is likely to increase in most places as a result of climate change. Climate change is also bringing higher temperatures, sea-level rise for all coastal cities and reductions in freshwater availability in many locations.[2] Even if an effective international agreement is reached soon on reducing greenhouse gas emissions sufficiently to slow and then stop global warming, much of the world's population will still face these changes over the next few decades because of the time-lag in the world's climate system. Attention to adaptation is needed as urgently as attention to mitigation.

Why children? Children, especially young children, are in a stage of rapid development and are less well equipped on many fronts to deal with deprivation and stress.[3] Their more rapid metabolisms, immature organs and nervous systems, developing cognition, limited experience and behavioural characteristics are all at issue here. In addition, their exposure to various risks is more likely to have long-term repercussions than with adults. Adaptations to climate change will be less than adequate in responding to the challenges if they fail to take into account both the particular vulnerabilities of children and the protective factors that can best support their resilience.

Almost all the disproportionate implications for children are intensified by poverty and the difficult choices low-income households make as they adapt to more challenging conditions. Events that might have little or no effect on children in high-income countries and communities can have critical implications for children in poverty. The likelihood of poor outcomes increases cumulatively with the number of risks that they face, whether physiological or psychological.[4] Children on the edge, like families on the edge, have fewer assets to draw on in every sense of the word and are more likely to be adversely affected by the various challenges imposed by climate change. In poor urban areas, these links can be especially striking.

Why urban children? Urban children are generally better off than their rural counterparts; but this is not true for the hundreds of millions living in urban poverty. Without adequate planning and good governance, poor urban areas can be among the world's most life-threatening environments.[5] In some informal settlements, one quarter of all children still die before the age of five.[6] Nor does the 'urban advantage' come into play in terms of education and life opportunities – the failure to complete, or even start, primary education is especially high among the urban poor, and prospects of upward mobility can be dim.[7] In many urban areas, the risks that children face are bound to be intensified by climate change. Most of the people and enterprises at most serious risk from extreme weather events and rising sea levels are located in urban slums in low-income countries, which are often in the most hazardous areas – floodplains or other areas at risk of floods, places at risk from landslides, sites close to industrial wastes, and areas unserved by the kind of infrastructure that can be strengthened and adapted to withstand more extreme conditions.[8] Although the urban poor are at highest risk of loss and harm, they are the least able to afford preventive measures and the least likely to have their needs for risk reduction taken seriously by local governments.

Children as resilient, active agents. Despite children's disproportionate vulnerability on many fronts, it is an oversimplification to think of them only as victims in the face of climate change. With adequate support and protection, children can also be extraordinarily resilient in the face of stresses and shocks. There is ample documentation, moreover, of the benefits of having older children active, informed and involved in responding to the challenges in their lives, not only for their own learning and development, but also for the energy, resourcefulness and knowledge that they can bring to local issues.[9]

An adaptation agenda with children in mind. It is increasingly recognized that effective adaptation to climate change in urban areas must address the development needs of the urban poor.[10] An adaptation agenda developed with children in mind broadens the terms of this discussion. Where infrastructure and basic services are concerned, for instance, it means taking account of the ways in which these affect children and those who care for them. For example, upgrading a road so that it is not washed away by flooding means considering the increased and more rapid traffic that will be generated and the effects for children playing or walking to school.

The issues go well beyond infrastructure, however. The lack of attention to children reflects a generally lower level of attention to the human implications of climate change – compared to the environmental and economic implications. Theory and practice regarding children have long stressed the importance of an integrated approach to development and well-being,[11] and this could well be more broadly applied. Adaptation, in these terms, means considering how to strengthen and support children's capacity to cope with the full range of risks and adversity associated with climate change, as well as that of the families and communities upon which they depend.

Understanding the impacts upon children of climate change

There is not enough knowledge on the implications of climate change for children to present a comprehensive picture. Even where there are projections for more general impacts, figures are seldom disaggregated by population group or age. However, it is possible to extrapolate from existing knowledge in related areas. Work on environmental health in urban areas, on disaster responses and household coping strategies, on the range of effects of urban poverty on children, the resilience of children and the beneficial effects of their participation in various efforts all contribute to a picture of the implications of disasters and responses to disasters, as well as more gradual change and the adaptations likely to be made to them. Table 8.1 provides an overview of likely changes in climate and their probable impacts upon natural and human systems.

Health and survival

The disproportionate health burden for children of challenging environmental conditions is well documented. According to the most conservative estimates, children under 14 are 44 per cent more likely to die because of environmental factors than the population at large. The same gap exists for morbidity and it increases greatly when the potential loss of healthy life years is considered.[12] The greater burden, especially for the youngest children, then, is not a minor matter of degree, and it is likely to be exacerbated in many places by climate change.

Mortality related to extreme weather events. Small children, along with women and the elderly, are most likely to be victims of such extreme events as flooding, high winds and landslides. A study of flood-related mortality in Nepal, for instance, found the death rate for children to be double that of adults, with

Table 8.1 *Some likely impacts of climate change upon natural and human systems*

Change	Impact upon natural systems, agriculture and water	Impact upon urban areas	Impact upon health and household coping	Implications for children
Warm spells and heat waves: frequency up in most land areas	Reduced crop yields in warmer regions; increased risk of wildfire; wider range for disease vectors	Heat islands with higher temperatures (up to 10° higher); often large concentrations of vulnerable people; air pollution worsens	Increased risk of heat-related mortality and morbidity; more vector-borne diseases; impact upon those doing strenuous labour; increase in respiratory diseases where air pollution worsens; food shortages	Greatest vulnerability to heat stress for young children; high vulnerability to respiratory diseases and vector-borne diseases; highest vulnerability to malnutrition, with long-term implications
Heavy precipitation events: frequency up over most areas	Damage to crops; soil erosion; waterlogging; water quality problems	Increased risk of floods and landslides; disruption to livelihoods and city economies; damage to homes, possessions and businesses, and to transport and infrastructure; loss of income and assets; often large displacements of population, with risks to social networks and assets	Deaths and injuries; increase in food-borne, water-borne and water-washed diseases; more malaria from standing water; decreased mobility, with implications for livelihoods; dislocations; food shortages; risks to mental health, especially associated with displacement	Higher risk of death and injury than for adults; more vulnerable to water-borne and water-washed diseases and to malaria; risk of acute malnutrition; reduced options for play and social interaction; likelihood of being removed from school/put to work, as income is lost; higher risk of neglect, abuse and maltreatment associated with household stress and/or displacement; long-term risks for development and future prospects
Intense tropical cyclone activity increases	Damage to crops, trees and coral reefs; disruption to water supplies.			

Increased area affected by drought	Land degradation; lower crop yields; livestock deaths; increased risk of wildfire and water stress	Water shortages; distress migration to urban centres; hydroelectric constraints; lower rural demand for goods/services; higher food prices	Increased food and water shortages; increased malnutrition and food and water-borne diseases; increased risk of mental health problems; respiratory problems from wildfires	Young children at highest health risk from inadequate water supplies; at highest risk of malnutrition, with long-term implications for overall development; risk of early entry into work exploitation
Increased incidence of extreme high sea level	Salinization of water sources	Loss of property and enterprises; damage to tourism; damage to buildings from rising water table	Coastal flooding; increased risk of death and injury; loss of livelihoods; health problems from salinated water	Highest rates of death for children; highest health risks from salinization of water supplies; long-term developmental implications

Source: Author and David Satterthwaite

pre-school girls five times more likely to die than adult men. Poor households were at six times higher risk than their better-off neighbours.[13] The distribution of deaths related to the 2004 Indian Ocean tsunami followed a similar pattern, as shown in Figure 8.1.[14]

In slower onset disasters such as droughts and famines, mortality rates are also more extreme for young children. A situation such as this is commonly defined as an emergency when crude mortality is 1 per 10,000 per day, and under-five mortality is double that.[15] This much higher rate for young children is not a departure from the norm in low-income countries;[16] but it still highlights a dismal reality – that higher mortality rates for young children, unthinkable in high-income countries, should be so routinely accepted as a baseline indicator of normality. Overall death rates for young children continue to drop in most parts of the world due to improved healthcare, immunization rates and environmental conditions. But for many of the children most at risk from the biggest killers – diarrhoeal and respiratory diseases, malaria and malnutrition – the situation is likely to worsen with some of the effects of climate change.

Water and sanitation-related illnesses. Inadequate access to clean water and proper sanitation increases the risk of a range of health problems. Globally, children under five are the victims of 80 per cent of sanitation-related illnesses and diarrhoeal disease, primarily[17] because of their less-developed immunity and because their play behaviour can bring them into contact with pathogens.

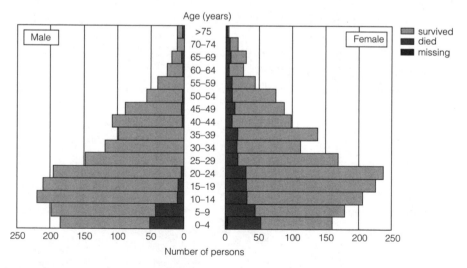

Figure 8.1 Age and gender distribution of tsunami-related deaths in Sri Lanka

Source: Nishikiori, N., Abe, T., Costa, D. G. M., Dharmaratne, S. D., Kunii, O. and Moji, K. (2006), 'Who died as a result of the tsunami? Risk factors of mortality among internally displaced persons in Sri Lanka: A retrospective cohort analysis', *BMC Public Health*, no 6, p7

Diarrhoeal disease also results in higher levels of malnutrition and increased vulnerability to other illnesses, with effects on overall development.[18]

Various conditions associated with climate change are likely to result in increased risks for young children. After extreme events, diarrhoeal illnesses related to breakdowns in piped water supplies and sanitation can take more lives than the initial disaster.[19] The risks in underserved urban settlements also increase with 'minor' events. During heavy or prolonged rains, blocked drains and flooded latrines can make contamination difficult to avoid, increasing the incidence of diarrhoeal illness in children.[20] Where the incidence and duration of rainstorms increases because of climate change, these conditions will become more prevalent.

Contamination of water supplies is also a risk during droughts. For small children's health, water quantity is generally considered even more important than its quality.[21] Unwashed hands, food, utensils, floors and cooking surfaces all contribute to higher levels of endemic illness. When water must be fetched from a distance, or when supplies are low or erratic, households make do with less than is necessary to meet children's routine health needs.[22] When they store water, the potential for contamination goes up. In a poor neighbourhood in Abidjan, Côte d'Ivoire, for instance, *E. coli* was found in only 1 per cent of water samples taken at the community source, but in 41 per cent of samples that had been stored at home.[23] The IPCC projects that climate change will increase the burden of diarrhoeal disease in low-income countries by approximately 2 to 5 per cent by 2020.[24]

Malnutrition. Malnutrition is related to food shortages resulting from reduced rainfall and other changes that affect agriculture, as well as to interruptions in food supplies in sudden acute events. Children in Africa born in drought years, for example, are significantly more likely to be malnourished or stunted (in Kenya, 50 per cent more likely to be malnourished, and in Niger, 72 per cent more likely to be stunted).[25]

But malnutrition is also closely tied to unsanitary conditions and to children's general state of health. Frequent bouts of diarrhoea and infestations of worms, for instance, mean impaired absorption and a loss of nutrients. When children are malnourished, their vulnerability to infection is greatly increased and a vicious cycle results.[26] A chronically malnourished three- or four-year-old may be at a permanent disadvantage, becoming both physically and mentally stunted.[27]

Nutritional risk as a result of disasters tends to be low if children were previously well nourished[28] and if the acute malnutrition associated with the event does not go on for too long. After Bangladesh's 1998 floods, when families were unable to compensate over time for the shortage of food and the deterioration in health conditions, flood-exposed children failed to experience the 'catch-up' growth common after a shock, remaining shorter than unexposed children from the same neighbourhoods.[29] Similarly significant impacts upon children's growth were found in Zimbabwe following a drought, in this case over a much longer term. Children in the critical 12- to 24-month-old age group during the drought in the early 1980s were found 13 to 16 years later to have had an average loss in stature of 2.3 inches. Their potential loss in lifetime earnings was calculated to be 14 per cent.[30] Malnutrition appears to be a greater risk among children of displaced families.[31] This may be related to the poor levels of sanitation in many temporary shelters as well as to the effects of displacement on household coping strategies. Infants are at particular risk. Stresses related to a crisis may affect mothers' breast milk production; at the same time, breast milk substitutes present a serious health risk in unsanitary environments.[32]

Vector-borne and infectious diseases. Increased temperatures and changes in precipitation are increasing the incidence and range of various vector-borne diseases and, with it, the level of exposure, with particular implications for children.[33]

The most serious threat is malaria. Fifty per cent of the world's population is now considered to be at risk, a 10 per cent increase in the last decade.[34] More than 90 per cent of the burden is in Africa, where 65 per cent of mortality is among children under five.[35] These numbers alone fail to capture the full implications for children. Malaria results in chronic anaemia, increases the severity of other diseases and more than doubles the mortality rates for children under five.[36] It contributes to impaired development in some children because of the insult to the brain during acute episodes; but this is also mediated by the effects of anaemia, repeated illness and under-nutrition related to the disease.[37]

Treatment measures are seldom adequate. A survey in Kampala, Uganda, found that children in 36 per cent of surveyed households had experienced fever in the previous two weeks, but less than 1 per cent received the recommended medical treatment despite the proximity of clinics and hospital. Only 11 per cent of households (the wealthiest) used treated nets.[38] Even this is high for Africa, where a multi-country survey found that treated nets were used by only 2 per cent of households with children under five.[39]

Respiratory illnesses. Respiratory illnesses cause 20 per cent of under-five deaths worldwide. A number of factors are involved, not all affected by climate change. However, changes in mean temperature and precipitation can increase the number of forest and bush fires, which affect air quality for thousands of kilometres, generally increasing the number of people experiencing respiratory difficulties.[40] Changing pollen counts, fungal growth and moulds related to flooding, and increases in ozone and other pollutants also increase the rates of pneumonia, upper respiratory disease and asthma. Asthma has doubled worldwide over the last 15 years, with the greatest increases among children,[41] and asthma deaths are expected to increase by 20 per cent by 2016.[42] Factors affecting the prevalence or severity of respiratory ailments are far from clear, however – the variables are too numerous.[43] Nor are children always those most affected.[44]

Heat stress. Those most at risk from increasingly frequent and intense heat waves are the elderly and the very young, who sweat less and have more surface area relative to body mass.[45] Research in São Paulo found a 2.6 per cent increase in mortality rates in children under 15 for every degree increase above 20°C – similar to the increase for those over the age of 65 (2.5 per cent).[46] For younger children, this increase is likely to be higher. The impact is most serious in cities, where the urban 'heat island' effect can mean differences of as much as 10°C between the city and surrounding areas.[47] Temperatures vary between neighbourhoods, with poorer groups more likely to live where temperatures are higher due to higher densities and less vegetation and open space.[48]

Injury. Children are particularly susceptible to injury – curious and driven to explore, yet lacking the capacity to understand and respond well to danger. Falls and burns, along with drowning, disproportionately affect children under five.[49] Children also experience more serious long-term effects from burns, fractures, head injuries and poisoning because of their size and physiological immaturity.[50] Injury rates are related to challenging conditions, overcrowding, complexity in the environment and higher levels of preoccupation on the part of adults[51] – all factors commonly experienced in the post-disaster context as well as in the context of gradually worsening conditions.

The quality of care. As changes in extremes and means create conditions that are more challenging to health, this also affects the burdens faced by caregivers. These problems are seldom faced one at a time. When inadequate water supplies are compounded by a lack of sanitation, overcrowded living quarters and an absence of safe play space, the difficulties can become overwhelming. Overstretched and exhausted caregivers are more likely to leave children unsupervised and to cut corners in all the chores that are necessary for healthy living, with potentially serious implications for children's health.

Learning and competence

For some children in some places, the challenges related to climate change could contribute to an erosion of both their mental capacity and their opportunities for learning and growth. The early years are the most critical time for brain development, which can be shaped by a range of environmental factors.[52] Good health is central, as sick or malnourished children lack the energy to be active learners.[53] Abundant research relates lower cognitive capacity and performance to undernutrition;[54] and behaviour and social relationships may also be affected.[55] The lack of specific nutrients such as iodine, iron or zinc, related to accessibility of certain foods, also hampers development.[56] Children's mental growth can also be affected by intestinal parasites, diarrhoeal disease and malaria,[57] all factors, as noted, that can be expected to increase with climate change. Maternal health, nutrition and stress levels during pregnancy are also related to children's lower cognitive performance and language ability later on.[58]

Children's learning also depends upon supportive social and physical environments. Their development of new skills and capacities takes place within a social and cultural context that is structured to help them acquire the experiences and competencies that they need to live their lives.[59] When young children lack easy access to social interaction and to safe, varied, stimulating surroundings for play, this can affect their development as capable problem-solvers and social beings.[60] Not all stimulation is positive for learning, however. High levels of noise and crowding and a lack of physical and temporal structure in daily life have been found consistently to have negative impacts upon children's development, distracting their attention and affecting the quality of their interactions with adults.[61] This is an accurate description of many post-disaster settings, where children may live for months on end in overcrowded emergency camps. Challenging events on a much smaller scale can also disrupt life repeatedly, diminishing the positive supports available to children and putting a damper on play and exploration.

For older children and also adolescents, opportunities for purposeful goal-directed activities and engagement in the world are primary avenues for the achievement of competence.[62] In the course of displacement, or in the disruption of routines and local environments that can accompany even 'minor' disasters, these opportunities, however minimal they may be, and whether formal or informal, can become seriously constrained. Schooling is an issue. After extreme weather events, schools may be destroyed, damaged, shut down or taken over as emergency shelters for weeks or even months.[63] Even when schools stay open, children may be pulled out because of displacement or because their disaster-affected families lack the resources for them to attend. Conditions for displaced children may also make it difficult to do homework, increasing the likelihood of their dropping out.[64]

The capacity to cope with adversity

The shock and distress of extreme events, as well as the deprivations and humiliations of displacement or slow recovery, can be profoundly debilitating. Children's psychological vulnerability and resilience in the face of hardship depend not only upon their health and internal strengths, but also upon household dynamics and levels of social support.[65] Age is just one of many factors mediating the experience of adversity: some children may actually be more resilient than their elders;[66] but their lack of social power within family and community can also leave them especially vulnerable to hardship. Children who have experienced success and approval in their lives are more likely to adapt well. Poverty and social status can play an important role in this regard. For older children, the effects of events on their social world and peer relationships are highly significant.[67] But without question, there can be numerous assaults on children's resilience after extreme events.

Especially in low-income countries, children may end up orphaned or separated from family. Extended family or other community members can provide a secure alternative; but too often even these bonds are frayed to breaking point and extra children can become a target for mistreatment.[68] Even where families remain intact, however, picking up the pieces can be extremely challenging. Basic requirements may be hard to come by, livelihoods may have disappeared, relief may be inequitably distributed, and community life and social supports may have collapsed. The disruption of play, school, daily chores, livelihoods and other familiar activities can leave children and adults more vulnerable to distress. Increased levels of irritability, withdrawal and family conflict are not unusual after disasters.[69] High stress for adults can have serious implications for children, contributing to neglect and even abuse.[70] Increased rates of child abuse have long been associated with factors that can become more prevalent after disaster or household upheaval – such as maternal depression, loss of property or a breakdown in social support. In the US, for instance, hospital records revealed that rates of traumatic brain injury inflicted on small children increased more than fivefold in the six months following a severe hurricane, when compared to the previous six months.[71] Children's anxious behaviour after disasters could contribute to abusive responses. Bed wetting, nightmares, aggressiveness or clinging behaviour can add to the stresses on parents attempting to deal with disaster-related problems.[72] Resilience in children in adversity has been related repeatedly, in part, to the presence of at least one actively supportive adult in their lives.[73] Even this can be hard to come by when adults are withdrawn and depressed, or angry and frustrated.

Displacement and life in emergency or transitional housing have been noted in many contexts to lead to an erosion of the social controls that normally regulate behaviour within households and communities. Overcrowding, chaotic conditions, a lack of privacy and the collapse of regular routines can contribute to anger, frustration and violence.[74] Sexual violence is commonly reported.[75] There have been numerous accounts of children and women enduring abuse of various kinds. Adolescent girls in particular complain of the lack of privacy around sleep, washing and dressing and of the sexual harassment they face.[76] The synergistic effects of such accumulated physical and social stressors have been found to affect children's development on all fronts.[77] As the numbers of displaced people grow, these dysfunctional environments are likely to become the setting within which more and more children spend their early years.

Disasters and long-term displacement are not unique, however, in terms of the stress they create. Even less extreme events can create havoc in people's lives, deepening the level of poverty – whether through short-term displacement, loss of work, reductions in food security, rising prices for basics, or just the time and energy drain associated with more challenging conditions. As Diagne describes in St Louis, Senegal: 'For those who live in flood-prone districts, each flood increases their poverty, depleting their incomes and meagre asset bases.'[78] The report from an African workshop points out that in the continuum between large-scale disasters and everyday hazards, it is the smaller-scale but more frequent events that cumulatively take the greatest toll on life, livelihoods and household well-being in many urban areas.[79]

Nor is it simply a matter of the shocks that households face. There is also the matter of anticipating and managing risk. This seldom presents simple choices, especially for the poor. Actions taken by households to limit their exposure to risk can result in substantial loss of income. Households in two flood-prone squatter settlements in Dhaka, for instance, were asked to consider the incentives that would encourage them to relocate to safer locations. Despite the extent and difficulty of their experience of coping with floods, many residents felt that relocation was simply not feasible without considerable incentives – including free land, non-repayable grants and long-term employment opportunities.[80] For those already in poverty, the costs of effectively managing risk may be excessive and can have long-term implications.

Gradually worsening conditions can undermine the precarious stability of households, and when the family system faces more pressure than it can easily adapt to, this can have critical consequences for children on all fronts. The stability of the household may be viewed as more important than the welfare of an individual child, as seen, for instance, in the allocation of food and other resources.[81] Many households make great sacrifices on behalf of their children; but in others, few of the benefits of what is earned or produced actually trickle down to reach children. Children can qualify as being in absolute poverty even in a household that does not.[82] When times are hard, children can become an asset that is drawn on to maintain the equilibrium of the household. They may be taken out of school in order to work or to take care of younger siblings, and some children may be considered more 'expendable' than others.[83] Many of Bombay's young prostitutes, for example, are from poor rural villages in Nepal, where inadequate crop yields lead families to sacrifice one child so others may survive.[84] Multidimensional definitions of poverty encourage broad thinking about the assets and risks that actually affect a family's capacity to cope and move ahead in the world. However, these definitions would be even more comprehensive if they took into account the extent to which families are drawing on their children as assets, or investing in them to ensure their optimal development.

The child-centred priorities of mothers are widely recognized;[85] but in difficult circumstances, these very priorities can result in levels of fatigue and stress that take a serious toll. Women in a Ghana town, for instance, spoke of the degree of their chronic anxiety, tiredness and physical aches and pains: 'What will the children eat? What will they wear? One of them is sick; she has to go to the hospital; where do I get the money? So every time you are thinking. When it's night and I lie down, I won't sleep.'[86] Mental health problems, which are increasingly acknowledged to be a significant health problem among the poor and especially among women, are closely tied to unpredictability, uncertainty and general insecurity.[87] These factors are likely to be exacerbated by climate change. There is growing evidence, for instance, of significant associations for women between food insecurity and anxiety and depression.[88] The combination of economic problems and psychological stress in a mother can result in significant risks for her children. Community-level supports are important here. Mothers who are involved in mutually supportive relationships through community institutions have been found to be less likely to have malnourished children, for instance, than those who are isolated within a family.[89]

Despite this litany of challenges, it is, again, misleading to think of children simply as victims. There are numerous accounts of their hardiness and resourcefulness in the face of both extreme events and everyday difficulties.[90] Children's capacity to cope well in difficult situations has frequently been related to their own active engagement and to opportunities to be involved in active problem-solving.[91] Repeated experience demonstrates how capable children are of looking critically at local problems and coming up with creative solutions that may not have occurred to adults.[92]

The implications for adaptation

In seeking to reduce vulnerability and enhance resilience in the face of various hazards and risks, how can the multiplicity of concerns for children of different ages be adequately represented without completely overwhelming any agenda?

In every aspect of adaptation – protection, preparation, relief and rebuilding – and at every level of response – including community, local government, NGO, national government and international agency – some basic principles can be taken into account:

- Children's requirements must be adequately understood. Unless various actors understand the implications for young people of various ages, the steps they take to respond to the crises of climate change are likely to be mis-targeted in some important ways.
- Children's priorities may differ from assumptions made by adults on their behalf. The information on which decisions are based must be information that can be trusted to represent children's experience.
- Incorporating a focus on children may mean changing the threshold at which an event or situation is considered potentially 'disastrous' or at which adaptation is considered necessary. It will also mean broadening the scope of adaptation to include issues that are not always considered to be central – but that, in fact, have benefits beyond those for children.
- As with gender, a consideration of age needs to be a routine feature of decision-making on every front, not a separate set of activities. The 'add-on' approach results in superficial band-aid solutions.

Within each aspect of planning for adaptation, whether in preparation or response, a concern for children means responding in four different areas, which can be considered in the appropriate detail at each level of action. Taking these guidelines into account, in other words, would mean something different to a donor agency and to local government agencies:

1   *Ensuring children's optimal health and nutrition.* Attention to children's health is important not only for the obvious and immediate benefits, but also because of the effects on enhancing children's resilience generally and supporting their long-term development on every front. For example, a period of nutritional deprivation that is short lived by adult standards may have far more critical implications for children. When disaster strikes, both the urgency of the response and its effectiveness will be affected by children's pre-existing levels of health. For donors, this may mean accepting that food aid programmes in response to a crisis are relatively ineffective compared to longer-term programmes. When children's health is already compromised by illness and malnutrition, they are more likely to sustain long-term damage to their development in the wake of a crisis, even with emergency food programmes.[93] For local government, a concern with children's health may become an additional reason for tackling environmental sanitation problems in underserved areas, as part of preparation for extreme events. For a community disaster preparedness committee, it might mean ensuring that information regarding risks to children's health of playing in flood waters is disseminated before the rainy season.

2   *Strengthening families' capacity to cope.* All adaptive measures geared towards the urban poor should ideally enhance their capacity to come through periods of shock without succumbing to major household catastrophe. But 'coping' in this context may take on broader meaning where children are concerned and will include the capacity of households to manage hardship without compromising the well-being of their children. NGOs, for example, might build child impact assessments into their microcredit activities, ensuring that loan repayments do not compromise children's nutrition; a healthcare system might allocate more of its resources to mental health supports; emergency response planning could include planning for the provision of temporary child care so that parents can have some hours each day to focus on recovery without worrying about their young children. Any supports focusing directly on children's health, safety and care will ease the burden on older family members.

3   *Maintaining, restoring and enhancing the potential for children's daily routines and activities.* Children need supportive functional adults in their lives; but they also rely on their daily routines and activities and on contact with their peers as a context for stability and optimal development. Other functions, more critical to survival, will inevitably be prioritized in preparing for, or responding to, crises on whatever scale – such as the protection of life and property or attention to food, health and livelihoods. But in the course of

addressing these things, it is important that children's spaces, activities and networks are not compromised – they should be identified, maintained and restored wherever possible. In paving and upgrading local streets to prevent them from washing away during increasingly common floods, for instance, speed bumps or sidewalks could be included to ensure that children are not endangered by faster traffic; in selecting space for emergency shelters, schools can be avoided where other possibilities also exist; in an emergency camp, a quiet space can be made available where children can do homework away from the noise and chaos of the camp.

4   *Respecting children's capacities; allowing them the chance for active involvement.* Despite the litany of challenges that children may face in the context of climate change, it is, again, misleading to think of them simply as victims. There are numerous accounts of their hardiness and resourcefulness in the face of both extreme events and everyday difficulties.[94] The chance to solve problems and to take action has been identified as a potent protective force for children in situations of adversity, allowing them some sense of control in situations where they might otherwise feel helpless and preoccupied by anxiety. Opportunities to demonstrate their competence and to contribute to a common effort can build confidence and a sense of effectiveness and camaraderie that can go a long way towards relieving distress. These opportunities do not need to be artificial attempts to include children; there are many real-life occasions for problem-solving and improvements in surroundings in both the post-disaster context and in the more 'everyday' context of urban poverty.[95] It should never be assumed that these are inappropriate for children. The contribution of young people is a potential community asset that is too seldom tapped in the process of development and adaptation. In the course of local risk assessment and monitoring, for instance, children's extensive knowledge of their own neighbourhoods could be recognized and drawn on; NGOs rebuilding after disasters could involve children along with adults in critiquing and modifying plans for relocated housing and community space, since they will inevitably point to concerns that adults will overlook.

Adding these concerns to the already long list of urgent priorities for adaptation may appear to be unrealistic. Fortunately, there is considerable overlap between the measures needed to protect and support children and those that are essential for reducing and responding to risk more generally. The most useful measures to protect children's health, for instance, also happen to be fundamental in reducing risks from potential disasters. Adequate provision for waste removal and drainage inhibits the potential for faecal contamination in the event of heavy downpours and reduces the likelihood of diseases that predominantly affect children – but it also protects communities from the chronic flooding that can result from

Table 8.2 *Adaptations and responses that take children into account*

	Reducing longer-term risks	Preparing for extreme weather events	Responding to immediate losses and threats following extreme weather events	Adapting to impacts and losses, and rebuilding to reduce future risks
Children's health, safety and nutrition	• Nutritional programmes to ensure children can withstand a crisis • Piped water, toilets and drains (with synergies for disaster reduction) • Measures such as mosquito nets	• Teach children basic survival skills (such as swimming in flood-prone areas) • Families develop strategies for avoiding separation, such as rendezvous points • Ensure adequate supplies of food and drinking water	• Reduce the risk of sanitation-related diseases in emergency camps • Attend to safety hazards in post-disaster environments • Reproductive health services for young girls as well as women • Support for breastfeeding mothers	• Ensure that rebuilding/upgrading is a chance to address environmental health issues • Rebuild in ways that make children's play and mobility possible without risk • Ensure adequate storage space in houses to keep hazardous items away from small children
Family and community coping strategies	• Child impact assessments to accompany poverty reduction measures • Financial incentives for managing risk, with a focus on children's vulnerabilities • Collaboration between child-focused agencies and those supporting community development	• Encouraging collaborative community measures rather than individualistic responses • Dissemination of local disaster preparedness information, with a focus on children's well-being	• Organize shelter so that family members and communities are kept together • Support children's resilience by supporting stable, functioning adults • Involve communities in post-emergency planning and decision-making; allow them to decide	• Location – access to jobs, markets, facilities, etc. • Local space flexible enough for small enterprises • Register house sites in women's names; women's involvement in decision-making • Housing design responsive to need for privacy

Children's daily activities and routines	• Placing speed bumps on upgraded roads • Planting shade trees where heat stress is an issue • Ensuring that accommodating to risks does not become a substitute for preventive adaptations	• Avoid selecting schools as emergency shelters	on their own needs and priorities • Get schools and child centres up and running again as soon as possible • Quiet space where children can do homework • Safe play space for young children • Keep children safe from harassment and abuse (e.g. lighting the way to the toilet) • Restore a sense of normalcy by recreating, as far as possible, daily chores and routines	• Vegetation, common space to encourage social interaction • Pockets of space where small children can play close to home • Community space that supports varied activities for older children • Space where girls can socialize without feeling exposed to criticism or harassment • Sidewalks, layouts, street lights that encourage safe mobility
Involving children in decision-making	• Involving children in environmental monitoring and assessment • Child-to-child health approaches (e.g. assessing patterns of diarrhoeal disease) • Supporting children's active stewardship through training and education	• Make disaster-related information available and understandable to children • Involve children in monitoring hazards, in disaster preparations and in risk-reduction measures	• Make relief information accessible and understandable to a 12-year-old child • Young people to have input on issues that concern them in emergency camps • 'Participation' that means genuine engagement, not tokenistic activities	• Giving children a genuine say concerning their own priorities • Embedding children's responses within more general planning

insufficient drainage or garbage-blocked drains. Making safe, appropriate land available for housing for low-income groups may diminish the risks associated with flooding or landslides that most seriously threaten children, but will also encourage greater investment in homes and neighbourhoods, further minimizing the likelihood of future damage.[96]

Risk reduction measures can even have unexpected benefits for children. In Bangladesh, for example, flood control embankment projects to protect people in low-lying areas and to stabilize riverbanks turned out to have highly significant effects on child mortality rates, which were 29 per cent higher outside these areas. Improvements in agriculture and fishery production, easier access by land to health centres, and a lower risk of drowning were all reasons in themselves to undertake flood control, and involved no additional investment.[97]

Table 8.2 provides a very brief summary[98] of some adaptations and responses that take children into account.

Conclusions

There are many vulnerable populations in the context of climate change – the poor, the elderly, pregnant women, those in particular locations. Children are not unique in this sense. However, they constitute an extremely large percentage of those who are most vulnerable and the implications, especially for the youngest children, can be long term. If speculation about the impacts of climate change fails to take into account the particular vulnerabilities (as well as capacities) of children at different ages, measures for disaster prevention and for adaptation may prove to be inadequate in critical ways and may even result in additional stresses for young minds and bodies.

Addressing these concerns for children may appear to be an unrealistic burden, adding unduly to the need for time and resources in the face of so many other compelling priorities. Fortunately, this is not a zero sum game. As stressed in this chapter, there are strong synergies between what children need and the adaptations required to reduce or respond to more general risks. The most useful measures to protect children's health are also fundamental in reducing risks from potential disasters – such as adequate drainage, waste removal and proper sanitation. Supporting adults so that they are better able to address their children's needs also leaves them better equipped to work collaboratively on reducing risks, preparing for disasters and rebuilding their lives after a crisis. Ensuring that children continue to have opportunities to play, learn and take an active role in finding solutions will prepare them to be the citizens we need in order to continue addressing the problems faced by their communities and by the planet. It has generally been found that neighbourhoods and cities that work better for children tend to work better for everyone, and this principle undoubtedly applies also to the adaptations that are being called for by climate change.

Notes

1. This chapter is a summary of a longer, more detailed working paper. See Bartlett, S. (2008) *Climate Change and Urban Children: Impacts and Implications for Adaptation in Low- and Middle-Income Countries*, Human Settlements Discussion Paper Series, Climate Change and Cities 2, IIED, London.
2. Wilbanks, T. and Romero Lankao, P. with Bao, M., Berkhout, F., Cairncross, S., Ceron, J.-P., Kapshe, M., Muir-Wood, R. and Zapata-Marti, R. (2007) 'Industry, settlement and society', in Parry, M., Canziani, O., Palutikof, J., van der Linden, P. and Hanson, C. (eds) *Climate Change 2007: Impacts, Adaptation and Vulnerability*, Contribution of Working Group II to the Fourth Assessment Report of the Intergovernmental Panel on Climate Change, Cambridge University Press, Cambridge and New York, Chapter 7, pp357–390.
3. Engle, P., Castle, S. and Menon, P. (1996) 'Child development: Vulnerability and resilience', *Social Science and Medicine*, vol 43, no 5, pp621–635.
4. See, for instance, Evans, G. W. and English, K. (2002) 'The environment of poverty: multiple stress exposure, psychophysiological stress and socioemotional adjustment', *Child Development*, vol 73, no 4, pp1238–1248; also Werner, E. and Smith, R. (1992) *Overcoming the Odds: High Risk Children from Birth to Adulthood*, Cornell University Press Ithaca, NY and London, for classic research exploring resilience longitudinally in a cohort of children in Hawaii.
5. See, for instance, Van den Poel, E., O'Donnell, O. and Van Doorslaer, E. (2007) 'Are urban children really healthier? Evidence from 47 developing countries', *Social Science and Medicine*, vol 65, no 10, pp1986–2003.
6. In Nairobi, for example, figures for 2002 show mortality rates of 62 per 1000 for children under five, compared to 113 per 1000 for Kenya's rural areas. Within the city's informal settlements, this rate rises to 151 per 1000, and in the Embakasi slum, to 254 per 1000 – four times as high as for the city as a whole. See APHRC (2002) *Population and Health Dynamics in Nairobi's Informal Settlements*, African Population and Health Research Centre, Nairobi, Kenya.
7. A recent case study of rickshaw pullers in Dhaka, for instance, shows that the adult children of these first-generation migrants were scarcely better educated than their fathers – 55 per cent had never attended school at all and only a small number were functionally literate. School attendance rates generally in Dhaka are only 58 per cent, compared to 73 per cent for villages. See Begum, S. and Sen, B. (2005) 'Pulling rickshaws in the city of Dhaka: a way out of poverty?', *Environment and Urbanization*, vol 17, no 2, October, pp11–26.
8. Satterthwaite, D., Huq, S., Pelling, M., Reid, H. and Romero Lankao, P. (2007) *Adapting to Climate Change in Urban Areas: The Possibilities and Constraints in Low- and Middle-Income Nations*, Human Settlements Discussion Paper Series, Climate Change and Cities 1, IIED, London.
9. A well-known overview of children's capacities in this regard is Hart, R. (1997) *Children's Participation: The Theory and Practice of Involving Young Citizens in Community Development and Environmental Care*, Earthscan/UNICEF, London.
10. See reference 8.
11. Bronfenbrenner, U. (1979) *The Ecology of Human Development: Experiments by Nature and Design*, Harvard University Press, Cambridge, MA.

12. Prüss-Üstün, A. and Corvalán, C. (2006) *Preventing Disease through Healthy Environments. Towards an Estimate of the Environmental Burden of Disease*, WHO, Geneva.

13. Pradhan, E. K., West, K. P., Katz, J., LeClerq, S. C., Khatry, S. K. and Shrestha, S. R. (2007) 'Risk of flood-related mortality in Nepal', *Disasters*, vol 31, no 1, pp57–70.

14. Nishikiori, N., Abe, T., Costa, D. G. M., Dharmaratne, S. D., Kunii, O. and Moji, K. (2006) 'Who died as a result of the tsunami? Risk factors of mortality among internally displaced persons in Sri Lanka: A retrospective cohort analysis', *BMC Public Health*, no 6, p7.

15. Sphere Project (2004) 'Humanitarian charter and minimum standards in disaster response', www.sphereproject.org/.

16. UNICEF (United Nations Children's Fund) (2007) *The State of the World's Children*, UNICEF, New York.

17. Murray, C. J. and Lopez, A. D. (1996) *The Global Burden of Disease: A Comprehensive Assessment of Mortality and Disability from Diseases, Injuries and Risk Factors in 1990 and Projected to 2020*, Harvard University Press, Boston, MA.

18. Bartlett, S. (2003) 'Water, sanitation and urban children: The need to go beyond "improved" provision"', *Environment and Urbanization*, vol 15, no 2, October, pp57–70.

19. WHO, www.who.int/entity/ceh/indictators/0_14disasterareas.pdf, accessed 15 October 2007.

20. See, for instance, Moraes, L. R., J. A. Cancio, S. Cairncross and S. Huttly (2003) 'Impact of drainage and sewerage on diarrhoea in poor urban areas in Salvador, Brazil', *Transactions of the Royal Society of Tropical Medicine and Hygiene* vol 97, no 2, pp153–158.

21. Shi, A. (2000) *How Access to Urban Potable Water and Sewerage Connections Affects Child Mortality*, Development Research Group, World Bank, Washington DC.

22. Victoria, C. G. et al. (1988) 'Water supply, sanitation and housing in relation to the risk of infant mortality from diarrhoea', *International Journal of Epidemiology*, vol 17, no 3, pp651–654; also Curtis, V., Kanki, B. et al (1995) 'Potties, pits and pipes: Explaining hygiene behaviour in Burkina Faso', *Social Science and Medicine*, vol 41, no 3, pp383–393.

23. Dunne, E. F., Angoran-Benie, H. et al (2001) 'Is drinking water in Abidjan, Côte d'Ivoire, safe for infant formula?', *Journal of Acquired Immune Deficiency Syndrome*, vol 28, no 4, pp393–398.

24. Confalonieri, U., Menne, B., Akhtar, R., Ebi, K., Hauengue, M., Kovats, R. S., Revich, B. and Woodward, A. (2007) 'Human health', Parry et al (2002): see reference 2, Chapter 7, pp391–431.

25. UNDP (United Nations Development Programme) (2007) *Human Development Report 2007/2008*, Palgrave Macmillan, New York.

26. Lechtig, A. and Doyle, B. (1996) 'The impact of water and sanitation on malnutrition and under-five mortality rates', *WATERfront*, vol 8, pp5–19.

27. Grantham-McGregor, S., Cheung, Y. B., Cueto, S., Glewwe, P., Richter, L. and Strupp, B. (2006) 'Developmental potential in the first five years for children in developing countries', *The Lancet*, vol 369, pp60–70.

28. Magkos, F., Arvaniti, F., Piperkou, I., Katsigaraki, S., Stamatelopoulos, K., Sitara, M. and Zampelas, A. (2004) 'Identifying nutritionally vulnerable groups in case of emergencies: experience from the Athens 1999 earthquake', *International Journal of Food Sciences and Nutrition*, vol 55, no 7, pp527–536.

29. Del Ninno, C. and Lundberg, M. (2005) 'The long-term impact of the 1998 flood on nutrition in Bangladesh', *Economics and Human Biology*, vol 3, no 1, pp67–96.

30. Alderman, H., Hoddinott, J. and Kinsey, B. (2004) *Long-Term Consequences of Early Childhood Malnutrition*, Mimeo, Department of Economics, Dalhousie University, Halifax, Canada.

31. See, for instance, Jayatissa, R., Bekele, A., Piyasena, C. L. and Mahamithawa, S. (2006) 'Assessment of nutritional status of children under five years of age, pregnant women and lactating women living in relief camps after the tsunami in Sri Lanka', *Food and Nutrition Bulletin*, vol 27, no 2, pp144–152; also Barrios, R. E., Stansbury, J. P., Palencia, B. and Medina, M. T. (2000) 'Nutritional status of children under five years of age in three hurricane-affected areas of Honduras', *Revista Panamericana de Salud Pública*, vol 8, no 6, pp380–384.

32. Caldwell, P. (1996) 'Child survival: Physical vulnerability and resilience in adversity in the European past and the contemporary third world', *Social Science and Medicine*, vol 43, no 5, pp609–619; also IFE Core Group (2006) *Infant and Young Child Feeding in Emergencies: Operational Guidelines for Emergency Relief Staff and Programme Managers*, http://ennonline.net.

33. Bunyavanich, S., Landrigan, C. P., McMichael, A. J. and Epstein, P. R. (2003) 'The impact of climate change on child health', *Ambulatory Pediatrics*, vol 3, pp44–52; also Ligon, B. L. (2006) 'Infectious diseases that pose specific challenges after natural disasters: A review', *Seminars in Pediatric Infectious Diseases*, vol 17, no 1, pp36–45; and Chapter 7.

34. Breman, J., Alilio, M. S. and Mills, A. (2004) 'Conquering the intolerable burden of malaria: what's new, what's needed: A summary', *American Journal of Tropical Medicine and Hygiene*, vol 71, no 2, Supplement, pp1–15.

35. See reference 34.

36. Snow, R. W., Korenromp, E. L. and Gouws, E. (2004) 'Pediatric mortality in Africa: *Plasmodium falciparum* malaria as a cause or risk?', *American Journal of Tropical Medicine and Hygiene*, vol 71, no 2, Supplement, pp16–24.

37. Holding, P. A. and Snow, R. W. (2004) 'Impact of *Plasmodium falciparum* malaria on performance and learning: review of the evidence', *American Journal of Tropical Medicine and Hygiene*, vol 71, no 2, Supplement, pp68–75.

38. Kemble, S., Davis, J. C., Nalugwa, T., Njama-Meya, D., Hopkins, H., Dorsey, G. and Staedke, S. G. (2006) 'Prevention and treatment strategies used for the community management of childhood fever in Kampala, Uganda', *American Journal of Tropical Medicine and Hygiene*, vol 74, no 6, pp999–1007.

39. See reference 34.

40. See reference 24.

41. See reference 33: Bunyavanich et al (2003).

42. WHO (2006) *Asthma Fact Sheet* no 307, August, WHO, Geneva.

43. Maynard, R. L. (2001) 'Asthma and air pollution: Editorial', *Clinical and Experimental Allergy*, vol 31, pp518–520.

44. For different relative effects on children and adults, see, for instance, Ko, F. W. S., Tam, W., Wong, T. W., Lai, C. K. W., Wong, G. W. K., Leung, T. F., Ng, S. S. and Hui, D. S. C. (2007) 'Effects of air pollution on asthma hospitalization rates in different age groups in Hong Kong', *Clinical and Experimental Allergy*, vol 37, pp1312–1319; also Mott, J. A., Mannino, D. M., Alverson, C. J., Kiyu, A., Hashim, J., Lee, T., Falter, K. and Redd, S. C. (2005) 'Cardio-respiratory hospitalizations associated with smoke exposure during the 1997 southeast Asian forest fires', *International Journal of Hygiene and Environmental Health*, vol 208, no 1–2, pp75–85.
45. Bytomski, J. R. and Squire, D. L. (2003) 'Heat illness in children', *Current Sports Medicine Reports*, vol 2, no 6, December, pp320–324; also Lam, L. T. (2007) 'The association between climatic factors and childhood illnesses presented to hospital emergency among young children', *International Journal of Environmental Health Research*, vol 17, no 1, pp1–8.
46. Gouveia, N., Hajat, S. and Armstrong, B. (2003) 'Socioeconomic differentials in the temperature–mortality relationship in São Paulo, Brazil', *International Journal of Epidemiology*, vol 32, pp390–397.
47. See Chapter 7.
48. Harlan, S. L., Brazel, A. J., Prashad, L., Stefanov, W. L. and Larsen, L. (2006) 'Neighbourhood microclimates and vulnerability to heat stress', *Social Science and Medicine*, vol 63, no 11, pp2847–2863.
49. Bartlett, S. (2002) 'The problem of children's injuries in low-income countries', *Health Policy and Planning*, vol 17, pp1–13.
50. Berger, L. R. and Mohan, D. (1996) *Injury Control: A Global View*, Oxford University Press, New Delhi.
51. See reference 50.
52. Walker, S., Wachs, T. D., Meeks Gardner, J., Lozoff, B., Wasserman, G. A., Pollitt, E., Carter, J. A. and the International Child Development Steering Group (2007) 'Child development: Risk factors for adverse outcomes in developing countries', *The Lancet*, vol 369, pp145–157.
53. See reference 27.
54. See reference 52.
55. Chang, S. M., Walker, S. P., Grantham-McGregor, S. and Powell, C. A. (2002) 'Early childhood stunting and later behaviour and school achievement', *Journal of Child Psychology and Psychiatry* vol 43, pp775–783.
56. See reference 3: Engle et al (1996).
57. Oberhelman, R. A., Guerrero, E. S., Fernandez, M. L., Silio, M., Mercado, D., Comiskey, N., Ihenacho, G. and Mera, R. (1998) 'Correlations between intestinal parasitosis, physical growth and psychomotor development among infants and children from rural Nicaragua', *American Journal of Tropical Medicine and Hygiene*, vol 58, pp470–475; also Niehaus, M. D., Moore, S. R., Patrick, P. D., Derr, L. L., Lorntz, B., Lima, A. A. et al (2002) 'Early childhood diarrhoea is associated with diminished cognitive function four to seven years later in children in a northeast Brazilian shantytown', *American Journal of Tropical Medicine and Hygiene*, vol 66, pp590–593; and Carter, J. A., Mung'ala-Odera, V., Neville, B. G. et al (2005) 'Persistent neurocognitive impairments associated with severe *falciparum* malaria in Kenyan children', *Journal of Neurology, Neurosurgery and Psychiatry*, vol 76, pp476–481.

58. See reference 52; also King, S. and Laplante, D. P. (2005) 'The effects of prenatal maternal stress on children's cognitive development: project ice storm', *Stress*, vol 8, no 1, pp1–3.

59. Valsiner, J. (1987) *Culture and the Development of Children's Action*, Wiley, New York; also Rogoff, B. (2003) *The Cultural Nature of Human Development*, Oxford University Press, Oxford and New York.

60. Wohlwill, J. and Heft, H. (1987) 'The physical environment and the development of the child', in Stokols, D. and Altman, I. (eds) *Handbook of Environmental Psychology*, Wiley & Sons, New York.

61. Wachs, T. and Corapci, F. (2003) 'Environmental chaos, development and parenting across cultures', in Raeff, C. and Benson, J. (eds) *Social and Cognitive Development in the Context of Individual, Social, and Cultural Processes*, Routledge, New York, pp54–83; also Stansfield, S., Haines, M. et al (2000) 'Noise and health in the urban environment', *Review of Environmental Health*, vol 15, no 1–2, pp43–82; and Evans, G. W., Lepore, S. J., Sejwal, B. and Palsane, M. N. (1998) 'Chronic residential crowding and children's well-being: an ecological perspective', *Child Development*, vol 69, no 5, pp1514–1523.

62. See, for instance, Chawla, L. and Heft, H. (2002) 'Children's competence and the ecology of communities: A functional approach to the evaluation of participation', *Journal of Environmental Psychology*, vol 22, pp201–216.

63. See, for instance, Diagne, K. (2007) 'Governance and natural disasters: Addressing flooding in Saint Louis, Senegal', *Environment and Urbanization*, vol 19, no 2, October, pp552–562.

64. Inter-Agency Network for Education in Emergencies, http://www.ineesite.org/standards/MSEE_report.pdf.

65. Boyden, J. and Mann, G. (2005) 'Children's risk, resilience and coping in extreme situations', in Ungar, M. (ed) *Handbook for Working with Children and Youth: Pathways to Resilience across Cultures and Contexts*, Sage Publications, London, pp3–27.

66. Palmer, O. J. (1983) *The Psychological Assessment of Children*, second edition, Wiley & Sons, New York.

67. See reference 65.

68. Tolfree, D. (2005) 'Community-based care for separated children: Responses to young children in post-emergency situations', *Early Childhood Matters*, vol 104, pp40–46, Bernard van Leer Foundation, The Hague, The Netherlands.

69. McFarlane, A. C. (1987) 'Family functioning and overprotection following a natural disaster: The longitudinal effects of post-traumatic morbidity', *Australian and New Zealand Journal of Psychiatry*, vol 21, no 2, pp210–218.

70. Curtis, T., Miller, B. C. and Berry, E. H. (2000) 'Changes in reports and incidence of child abuse following natural disasters', *Child Abuse and Neglect*, vol 24, no 9, pp1151–1162.

71. Keenan, H. T., Marshall, S. W., Nocera, M. A. and Runyan, D. K. (2004) 'Increased incidence of inflicted traumatic brain injury in children after a natural disaster', *American Journal of Preventive Medicine*, vol 26, no 3, pp189–189.

72. See reference 70.

73. See reference 3: Engle et al. (1996); see also reference 4: Werner and Smith (1992).

74. Gururaja, S. (2000) 'Gender dimensions of displacement', *Forced Migration Review*, www.fmreview.org/FMRpdfs/FMR09/fmr9.5.pdf.
75. Save the Children Sweden (2007) 'Bridging the gap – Save the Children's transitional housing project', www.crin.org/docs/BridgingtheGapfinal1.pdf.
76. Fisher, S. (2005) *Gender-based Violence in Sri Lanka in the Aftermath of the Tsunami Crisis*, MSc thesis, University of Leeds, UK.
77. Evans, G. and Saegert, S. (2000) 'Residential crowding in the context of inner-city poverty', in Wapner, S., Demick, J., Yamamoto, T. and Minami, H. (eds) *Theoretical Perspectives in Environment–Behaviour Research*, Kluwer Academic/Plenum Press, New York, Boston, Dordrecht, London, Moscow.
78. See reference 63: Diagne, K. (2007), p556.
79. Bull-Kamanga, L., Diagne, K., Lavell, A., Leon, E., Lerise, F., MacGregor, H., Maskrey, A., Meshack, M., Pelling, M., Reid, H., Satterthwaite, D., Songsore, J., Westgate, K. and Yitambe, A. (2003) 'From everyday hazards to disasters: The accumulation of risk in urban areas', *Environment and Urbanization* vol 15, no 1, April, pp193–204.
80. Rashid, H., Hunt, L. and Haider, W. (2004) 'Urban flood problems in Dhaka, Bangladesh: Slum residents' choices for relocation to flood-free areas', *Environmental Management*, vol 40, no 1, pp95–104.
81. Latapí, A. E. and González de la Rocha, M. (1995) 'Crisis, restructuring and urban poverty in Mexico', *Environment and Urbanization*, vol 7, no 1, April, page 70.
82. Gordon, D., Nandy, S., Pantazis, C., Pemberton, S. and Townshend, P. (2003) *Child Poverty in the Developing World*, The Policy Press, Bristol.
83. See reference 3: Engle et al (1996).
84. See http://www.speakout.org.za/about/child/child_childprostitution.htm.
85. See reference 3: Engle et al (1996).
86. Avotri, Y. A. and Wakters, V. (1999) '"You just look at our work and see if you have any freedom on earth": Ghanaian women's accounts of their work and their health', *Social Science and Medicine*, vol 48, p1126.
87. WHO (2001) *The World Health Report. Mental Health: New Understandings, New Hope*, WHO, Geneva; also Patel, V., Araya, R., de Lima, M., Ludermir, A. and Todd, C. (1999) 'Women, poverty and common mental disorders in four restructuring societies', *Social Science and Medicine*, vol 49, pp1461–1471.
88. Heflin, C. M., Siefert, K. and Williams, D. R. (2005) 'Food insufficiency and women's mental health: Findings from a three-year panel of welfare recipients', *Social Science and Medicine*, vol 61, no 9, pp1971–1982; also Hadley, C. and Patil, C. L. (2008) 'Seasonal changes in household food insecurity and symptoms of anxiety and depression', *American Journal of Physical Anthropology*, vol 135, no 2, pp225–232.
89. See reference 3: Engle et al (1996).
90. Hestyanti, Y. R. (2006) 'Resilience in children', *Annals of the New York Academy of Sciences*, vol 1094, pp303–307; also Boyden, J. (2003) 'Children under fire: Challenging assumptions about children's resilience', *Children, Youth and Environments*, vol 13, no 1, spring, http://colorado.edu/journals/cye.
91. See reference 65; also Norris, F. H., Friedman, M., Watson, P. J., Byrne, C., Diaz, E. and Kaniasty, K. (2002) '60,000 disaster victims speak. Part I: An empirical review of the literature, 1981–2001', *Psychiatry*, vol 65, pp207–239.

92. See reference 9; also Chawla, L. (ed) (2001) *Growing Up in an Urbanizing World*, Earthscan/UNESCO, London.
93. See reference 29.
94. See reference 90.
95. See reference 92: Chawla (ed) (2001).
96. See reference 8.
97. Myaux, J. A., Ali, M., Chakraborty, J. and de Francisco, A. (1997) 'Flood control embankments contribute to the improvement of the health status of children in rural Bangladesh', *Bulletin of World Health Organization*, vol 75, no 6, pp533–539.
98. A more detailed account can be found in the working paper on which this shorter chapter is based. See reference 1.

9

Unjust Waters: Climate Change, Flooding and the Urban Poor in Africa

Ian Douglas, Kurshid Alam, MaryAnne Maghenda, Yasmin McDonnell, Louise McLean and Jack Campbell

Introduction

Poor communities often live in the most hazardous and unhealthy environments in urban areas.[1] Many build their homes and grow their food on river floodplains in towns and cities. Others construct their shelters on steep, unstable hillsides or along the foreshore on former mangrove swamps or tidal flats. People suffering these poor conditions may find their difficulties compounded by the consequences of climate change. This chapter considers the implications for the vulnerability of the urban poor in Africa.

In the large cities of low-latitude countries, it is common for much of the low-income population to live in areas at risk from flooding[2] and this population is most likely to be affected by factors related to climate change.[3] Floods are natural phenomena; but damage and losses from floods are the consequences of human action. Although climate change is driven largely by modernization and development, all human activities, including land degradation by poor farmers and grazing flocks, contribute to environmental change. However, on a per capita basis, the poor in Africa are far more the victims of change than contributors to global warming and land degradation.

Flooding in urban areas is not just related to heavy rainfall and extreme climatic events; it is also related to changes in the built-up areas themselves. Urbanization restricts where floodwaters can go by covering large parts of the ground with roofs, roads and pavements, thus obstructing natural channels, and by building drains that ensure that water moves to rivers more rapidly than it did under natural conditions. Large-scale urbanization and population increases have led to large numbers of people, especially the poor, settling and living in floodplains in and around urban areas. In South Africa, for instance, Soweto-on-Sea near Port Elizabeth and Alexandra in Johannesburg illustrate this point.[4]

As people crowd into African cities, human impacts upon urban land surfaces and drainage intensify. Even moderate storms now produce quite high flows in rivers because of surface runoff from hard surfaces and drains. Water flowing through a series of culverts and concrete channels cannot adjust to changes in the frequency of heavy rain, as natural streams do. They are often obstructed by silt and urban debris, particularly when houses are built close to the channels. Such situations frequently arise when poor people build on low-lying floodplains, over swamps or above the tidewater level on the coast.[5] The effects of climate change are superimposed on these people-driven local land surface modifications.

Separating local changes from global climate changes is not always easy. The populations of towns and cities may be swollen by in-migration from rural areas in times of drought. This drought might be caused by climate change; but the local changes in the city stem from the activities of the migrants as they build homes, compacting the ground and altering the ways in which rainfall collects and flows towards streams and rivers. As floods begin to occur with greater frequency, local authorities and other agencies may take protective measures to avoid the movement of floodwaters into certain areas of towns and cities, often giving priority to the main business and administrative centres. In many cases, the floodwaters spread into other areas, often those occupied by the poorest communities for want of safer land. To establish how climate change will intensify the impacts of urban growth on flooding, especially flooding affecting the urban poor, it is necessary to look at how climate change is likely to influence rainfall that is intense and long enough to produce floods, as well as to examine how urbanization itself alters flood regimes, and to consider how sea-level rise affects settlements built on the shoreline and in former mangrove areas.

In much of the tropics, most rainstorms are highly localized, often covering less than $10km^2$; they are intense and of short duration, usually lasting an hour or less. The most intense thunderstorm, occurring, on average, once every two years, can deposit as much as 90mm of rain in just 30 minutes.[6] The volumes of water running off roofs and paved surfaces in urban areas from such storms are enormous. All too often, drains and culverts cannot cope and localized flash flooding occurs. These flash floods happen suddenly, with little lead time for warning; they are fast-moving and, generally, violent, resulting in a high threat to life and severe damage to property and infrastructure; and they are generally small in scale with regard to area of impact.[7] While European authors present flash floods as rare events in areas such as the Alps, often in association with landslides and mudflows,[8] tropical authors think in terms of the rapid flooding produced by major thunderstorms, which can occur several times a year. The latter are a major nuisance for urban residents in many African cities.

The changing climate in Africa

Africa is not a driver of climate change, but a victim.[9]

The weather is becoming increasingly volatile in Africa.[10]

Any analysis of long-term rainfall records in Africa reveals great variability from year to year.[11] There is also great spatial variability in rainfall on any one day or over any one month or year. Thunderstorms producing heavy downpours that cause localized flooding may extend over as little as $2.5km^2$.[12] In East Africa, rain can occur in isolated patches of less than 30km in diameter; but sometimes broad bands of varying rain up to 500km across can develop. This spatial variability makes precise forecasting difficult and poses problems for delivering good flood warnings. In a way, it is fortunate that the most widespread serious floods in major river basins such as the Zambezi are produced by widespread rain bands whose development and movement are readily detected by weather satellites. However, the more frequent flash floods in urban areas stem from the localized storms whose tracks and occurrence are difficult to predict. Urban areas can enhance the build up of thunderstorms through the urban heat island effect: as cities grow, the urban heat island becomes more marked, with possible increases in thunderstorm activity. Thus, even without the climatic changes due to global warming, urban extreme rainfall intensities may be increasing, along with their severe impacts upon society.

Examining the history of these long-term changes in Africa is complicated because of gaps and irregularities in some climate data that are the result of relocations of stations and changes in instruments. But when errors and inconsistencies can be reduced or eliminated through instrumentation changes, tests for changes in the intensity of extreme events can be made and tend to show significant increases in the intensity of extreme rainfall events.[13]

In the future, rising temperatures are projected to cause more frequent and more intense extreme weather events, such as heavy rainstorms, flooding, fires, hurricanes, tropical storms and El Niño events. It is likely that future tropical cyclones (typhoons and hurricanes) will become more intense, with larger peak wind speeds and heavier precipitation. Over most subtropical regions, rainfall is likely to decrease by as much as 20 per cent. There is likely to be quite marked winter drying in Southern and Northern Africa, but an increase in December, January and February rainfall in equatorial East Africa.[14] At the major river basin level, forecasting is more difficult.[15]

Trends in urban flooding in Africa

All countries are vulnerable to climate change and instability in weather patterns, but the poorest countries and the poorest people within them are most vulnerable, being the most exposed and having the least means to adapt.[16]

Climate change appears to be altering the pattern of flooding in Africa. Modelling shows that the pattern of rare large floods is going to change much more than long-term average river flows. Prolonged heavy rains may increase in volume and occurrence.[17] Many African cities have experienced extreme flooding since 1995.

Examples of flooding in urban areas

Heavy rains and cyclones in February and March 2000 in Mozambique led to the worst flooding in 50 years and brought widespread devastation to the capital city, Maputo, as well as to the city of Matola. Upwards of 1 million people were directly affected. Water and sanitation services were disrupted, causing outbreaks of dysentery and cholera. Newspaper reports described the disaster as destroying the rehabilitation efforts of what had been, until only a few years before, the world's poorest country.

In 2002, heavy rains caused by unusually high temperatures over the Indian Ocean killed more than 112 people in East Africa. Floods and mudslides forced tens of thousands of people to leave their homes in Rwanda, Kenya, Burundi, Tanzania and Uganda. Rwanda suffered the heaviest toll, with more than 50 dead in 10 days, many of the deaths caused by landslides. At least 1557 homes were destroyed and many cattle were killed. In Kenya, floods and mudslides killed 46 people in 2 weeks. In Tanzanian urban communities, hundreds of families were left homeless and damage to crops threatened food security. In August 2006, in Addis Ababa, floods killed more than 100 people and destroyed homes in eastern Ethiopia, after heavy rains caused a river to overflow.

There has also been damage in West Africa. Since 1995, floods have tended to cause increasing damage in Ghana, particularly in coastal areas. The cities of Accra and Kumasi have been particularly severely affected, with many forced to leave their homes. The perception of, impacts of and adjustments to urban flooding in Nigeria have been extensively studied.[18] Several studies of the hydrological changes associated with urbanization[19] have described the contribution of topographic conditions, rainfall characteristics, land-use changes (especially the expansion of paved impermeable areas), uncontrolled waste dumping and construction on the floodplain, to local flooding.[20] The roles of rainfall amount and intensity have also been discussed.[21]

The two drivers, *climate change* (affecting storm occurrence and intensity) and *local urban change* (due to alterations to the urban land surface and water pathways as a result of such activities as construction, paving, soil compaction and the removal of vegetation, but also due to blockage of drains and the diversion of natural flows) combine to produce increased local runoff and higher flood frequency, magnitude and duration. The urban poor are suffering more from these changes than other urban residents.

The clear messages emerging are that:

* Urban flooding is becoming an increasingly severe and more frequent problem for the urban poor.
* Climate change is altering rainfall patterns, tending to increase storm frequency and intensity, thus increasing the potential for floods.
* Local human factors, especially urban growth, the occupation of floodplains and the lack of attention to waste management and to the construction and

maintenance of drainage channels are also aggravating the flooding problem. Particularly problematic is the unwillingness of government at all levels to engage in the provision of integrated drainage systems in informal settlements, which are often regarded as being outside accepted urban regulation and planning systems.

Four types of urban flooding in African towns and cities

Human settlements may be affected by four types of flooding:

1   localized flooding due to inadequate drainage;
2   flooding from small streams whose catchment areas lie almost entirely within built-up areas;
3   flooding from major rivers on whose banks the towns and cities are built; and
4   coastal flooding from the sea or from a combination of high tides and high river flows from inland.

The first and second types of flooding occur much more frequently than flooding from major rivers. The fourth type of flooding occurs where settlements have been built on coastal wetlands and mangrove swamps.

Localized flooding. Localized flooding occurs many times a year in slum areas because there are few drains, most of the ground is highly compacted and pathways between dwellings become streams after heavy rain. Any drains and culverts that do exist are often blocked with waste and plastic debris because the slums lack adequate municipal waste collection and cleaning services.

Small streams. The small streams in urban areas rise quickly after heavy rain, but often pass through small culverts under roads. Although adequate enough to deal with the existing flood flows when they were designed, changes in urban areas and in storm intensity now produce flows that exceed the capacity of the culverts. The stream channels themselves may contain so much debris and urban waste that they are effectively smaller than they were two decades ago. These changes combine to make flooding more frequent.

Major rivers. Major rivers flowing through urban areas are affected by land-use changes and engineering works upstream. For example, dams can modify river flows. Most dams trap sediments, often causing rivers to erode their banks downstream more than they did in the past; and, although dam operation can lead to a greater regularity of flows, it may also lead to high flows when stored water is released suddenly to prepare for high flows upstream.

Often, natural levees along the river provide some protection to the towns and cities through which it passes. However, urban growth has usually expanded over some of the floodplain so that parts of the city are below flood level and the area into which floods can naturally overflow has also been reduced. Levees have been raised artificially, but with the risk that they may be breached and cause devastating urban flooding. Such flood events can cause severe losses and disrupt economic activity over large areas of the city. Depending upon the size of the river, flooding may last several days or several weeks.

In lowland and coastal cities, wet season flooding may affect some areas for two or more months because rain and river water combine to raise water levels in swamps that would naturally have been inundated at certain times of the year. Dumping of waste beneath dwellings in these areas tends to help raise levels further. Storm waves can also bring flooding to such areas.

Coastal flooding. More than one quarter of Africa's population resides within 100km of a sea coast,[22] with 12 per cent of the urban population living within the land area that may be affected by a 10m sea-level rise (the low-elevation coastal zone, or LECZ).[23] In coastal cities, many poor people live on former swamp land or in dwellings built on stilts in tidewater areas. Such communities are particularly vulnerable to increased storminess and rising sea levels. Modelling the effects of a 38cm mean global sea-level rise in 2080 gives estimates that the average annual number of people in Africa affected by flooding could increase from 1 million in 1990 to 25 million by 2050,[24] with a worst case scenario of 70 million by 2080.[25] Many, if not most, will be residents of poor urban communities. Examples of particularly vulnerable coastal lowland cities are Lagos and Port Harcourt in Nigeria[26] and the capital of The Gambia, Banjul.[27] There are also threats to coastal areas of Egypt[28] and to East African coastal settlements from sea-level rise.[29]

Local case studies of urban flooding

The 2003 World Development Report notes the pronounced difficulties the poor face when disaster strikes. Developing countries are particularly vulnerable because they have limited capacity to prevent and absorb ... effects [of natural disasters]. People in low-income countries are four times as likely as people in high-income countries to die in a natural disaster... Poor people and poor communities are frequently the primary victims of natural disasters, in part because they are priced out of the more disaster-proof areas and live in crowded, makeshift houses ... poor families are hit particularly hard because injury, disability and loss of life directly affect their main asset, their labour. Disasters also destroy poor households' natural, physical and social assets, and disrupt social assistance programmes.[30]

To ascertain the dimensions of flood problems in poor communities, ActionAid undertook participatory vulnerability analysis (PVA)[31] with people living in vulnerable areas in five capital cities representing different areas of Africa where ActionAid had representatives who were able to help with the enquiry. Policy analysis was also carried out as a part of PVA to understand whether there is a gap between poor urban people's experiences of climate change impacts and current disaster management policies. These analyses reveal much about the local factors that aggravate flooding and the views people hold about the causes of flooding and what might be done about it.

PVA is a tool developed by ActionAid that involves communities, local authorities and other stakeholders in an in-depth examination of what makes them vulnerable. PVA is essential to ActionAid's work on emergencies and conflict. The impact a disaster has upon the people who are affected will depend upon how vulnerable they are. By identifying the causes of their vulnerability, communities can set up their own coping mechanisms to mitigate the effects of hazards such as floods. In this study, the local ActionAid representatives met with focus groups they had already established in poor communities and discussed a pre-planned set of topics on the flood problems of urban areas: why floods occur; how members of the community adjust to them; who is responsible for reducing the flood risk; and what action the community itself can take. The responses covered a wider range of ideas than the planned topics, providing some vivid descriptions of how individuals reacted to flooding. Inevitably, the detail in the reports from the five cities differed; but altogether there is a story of human courage and endurance in the face of quite terrible conditions that often last for months rather than days or weeks. After a brief description of the situation in these cities, the focus groups' responses to these questions will be presented.

The worsening situation in the five cities

Accra, Ghana. Women in Alajo, Accra, observed that patterns of rain and flooding have become unpredictable since the 1980s: 'In some years the rain will fall greatly and destroy everything; and other times nothing will happen.' They noted that it used to rain heavily in June and July; but since 2000, the heavy rains sometimes start earlier than June or continue beyond July, making it difficult to prepare for flooding.

Men in Alajo described the impact of the flooding on their lives: 'Flooding makes the inhabitants of Alajo unable to do anything.' Slum dwellers' livelihoods depend upon such activities as small-scale commerce, petty trading and artisanal trades, which are disrupted by floods, thus affecting the capacity to buy food or pay bills, including those for children's education and healthcare: 'Flooding makes people go hungry for days.' Several Alajo residents spoke of engaging in petty trading and merchandising in wooden kiosks that cannot withstand the force of the floods.

Kampala, Uganda. In Kampala, construction of unregulated shelters by the poor in such slums as Kalerwe, Katanga, Kivulu and Bwaise has reduced infiltration of rainfall, increasing runoff to six times that which would occur in natural terrain. Some of the increase is probably due to climate change; but some is also the direct result of land cover change. Local people claim that floods are now more frequent and more severe. The flooding used to occur in predictable cycles in the two main rainy seasons of April–May and October–November; but now occurrences have become erratic and unpredictable.

Fifty-nine-year-old Masitula Nabunya of Bwaise III parish said that after the 1960 floods, a channel from Nsooba to Lubigi was dug and workers were employed to clean it regularly. There were no further flooding problems until the 1980s; but since then she has had to rebuild her house after being flooded six times. Flooding in these places is now much more frequent, with every small downpour appearing to produce intense flooding. Some of this is because the main drainage channel, originally 2m deep, is now only 30cm deep as a result of an accumulation of sediment and rubbish. The situation is also linked to the increased number of houses, yielding much more runoff from a given quantity of rain.

Lagos, Nigeria. Residents of the low-lying coastal slum settlement of Iwaya/Makoko in Lagos argue that the climate is changing and flooding is becoming more frequent. In these settlements, homes are built on stilts above swamps that are natural flood basins. The increasing peak flows, combined with higher spring tides, are affecting more homes, more frequently. Local people are concerned about property damage and the impact upon child health in an area with totally inadequate sanitation. Floodwaters can carry all sorts of organic waste into people's homes.

Maputo, Mozambique. In Block 40B of the Luis Cabral slum neighbourhood of Maputo, residents argue that flooding has become worse since 1980, pointing out that the 2000 floods completely destroyed the area. A single one-day rain event can cause floods that persist for three days. If the rains persist for three days to one week, the water depth rises to 1m and it may take a month to disappear.

Nairobi, Kenya. Flooding is a major problem in all informal settlements in Nairobi. In the Maili Saba slum, part of Dandora, next to the river, flooding is a normal occurrence. Poor people's houses are built of weak, inadequate building materials. Migration has led to more houses being built close to rivers, with consequent greater disruption when floods occur. To many residents, the El Niño-associated floods were particularly severe. Many local residents link increased flooding to both local activities and climate change. Many long-term inhabitants of slums such as Mabatini in Mathare agree that floods now occur in places where they did not two decades ago. Similar reports come from other African cities, whether inland or coastal. For the residents, floods are getting worse and climate change is contributing to this situation.

People's perceptions of the causes of flooding

Accra, Ghana. The poor residents of the district of Alajo in Accra were contacted in men's and women's groups and this provided a ranking of the importance of the causes of flooding, as they perceived them. Men pointed to:

- improper city planning with regard to layout of buildings and other structures;
- poor drainage;
- the lack of consultation by officials with the poor and an insensitivity to their problems:

> *Government and authorities take us for granted. Authorities do not respect us. They think they know it all and so will not ask for our opinion. They do not acknowledge the wisdom of the people. If they respected us and valued us, they will be sensitive to our plight and take simple but effective measures to solve the problem of flooding.*

- overpopulation:

> *Numbers of people and their houses, offices and businesses have increased in our community. If the drainage will be fixed, population will not be a problem. Without a good drainage system, population increase facilitates flooding.*

The women's group identified the same general issues, stressing the inadequate level of official attention to the problems of the poor:

> *In Alajo, there is no room created for floodwater to be properly contained. There is no way for the water to pass. The floods are not always caused by rains. Sometimes, even before the rains begin to fall, the drains are overflowing and the pathways obscured with wastewater flowing from other parts of the city and into Alajo from where there are no appropriate drains. So when it begins raining, things just worsen. At such times, if you want to take somebody to the hospital, he dies before your very eyes because you cannot carry him out.*

Kampala, Uganda. People sampled in the Bwaise, Kalwerwe and Katanga districts of Kampala view flooding problems as arising from poor drainage conditions and the general flat terrain and lowlands. Bwaise, in particular, is surrounded by the hilly locations of Kawempe, Nsooba, Kamwokya, Mulago and Makerere. People cited the following causes of flooding:

- Even when drainage channels are occasionally unblocked, the excavated silt is dumped alongside the channels and gets washed back in.
- Acute poverty means day-to-day survival takes much higher priority than care for the environment.
- Tree cutting for firewood, charcoal, mining and quarrying has contributed to changes in the weather patterns and, hence, to increased flooding.

- The expansion of commercial property and industrial developments in reclaimed wetlands where floodwaters used to drain has increased flooding elsewhere.
- The discriminatory enforcement of wetland policies that allow the rich to block natural drainage areas has greatly disadvantaged the poor through consequent flooding.
- Factory building on wetlands has blocked water flows and polluted the water.
- The unregulated construction of shelters has blocked many small drainage channels.
- The failure to de-silt the main drainage regularly has greatly reduced its capacity.
- Small culverts under road crossings are easily blocked by solid waste.
- Bank erosion along open drains produces silting, thus reducing their capacity.
- The stone linings and concrete banks of poorly constructed drainage systems have become degraded and have started to collapse.
- The failure to de-silt the lower end of the main drain into the swamp causes floodwater to flow backwards into Bwaise settlement.
- Rebuilding the main highway from Kampala to Gulu in a new location and the recent construction of the northern bypass road have interfered with water flows and aggravated flooding.
- The removal of eucalyptus trees along the main drainage channel that used to absorb some of the floodwater has led to increased flooding.
- The privatization of solid waste collection has led to much waste being dumped into the drainage channels, thus blocking them and aggravating flooding.
- Shelters built on hills around the city lack rain-harvesting facilities, which would have reduced the runoff water that contributes to flooding.

While the actual significance of some of these potential causes of flooding is not scientifically proven, this long list of locally perceived causes includes many drivers that could be dealt with by local action; but it also points to the lack of time the poor have to care for the environment.

Lagos, Nigeria. People in the Lagos PVA suggested the following causes of increased flooding:

- changes in the levels of high tides in the Lagos Lagoon and the Atlantic Ocean, affecting certain streets;
- the indiscriminate erection of structures by residents, leading to impediments to the flow of water;
- subsidence of coastal land;
- the indiscriminate dumping of wastes into the lagoon, leading to the blockage of drains (many of the participants were reluctant to agree that this was a cause, although a few did); and
- insufficient depth and capacity of the drainage channels to carry all the urban runoff, causing overflows and bank collapse.

The reluctance to accept waste dumping as a cause suggests an unwillingness to recognize personal responsibility. But lack of official attention to maintaining and improving an adequate drainage network for a rapidly growing megacity is also a major factor.

Maputo, Mozambique. In the Mafala neighbourhood of Maputo, residents noted both natural and local causes of flooding:

- although there was less rain overall, rare storms seemed more intense and led to more destructive flooding;
- a lack of adequate drainage infrastructure;
- no internal organization in the neighbourhood to maintain drainage channels, manage sewage, allocate land or assist in evacuation at flood times;
- an absence of land planning; and
- no assistance for flood victims.

Clearly, here again the lack of national or local government involvement in developing integrated drainage or in planning the settlement to minimize flood damage is readily apparent. However, there seemed to be no cohesion within the community to organize mutual self-help.

Nairobi, Kenya. The causes of flooding identified by respondents included:

- heavy rainfall – residents said that whenever there were heavy downpours, either in Mathare or even upstream in Central Province, they expected flooding;
- poor drainage systems – one woman commented that solid waste usually blocked the river, forming a dam that impeded the flow of water until it finally gave way and caused a flash flood;
- unplanned housing on the floodplain, which has restricted the capacity of the river;
- human activities near the river – for example, the Ngumba market in Mabatini is actually located in the river, which has been partly reclaimed by depositing sandbags in the channel;
- destruction of forests and lack of vegetation cover along river beds, with consequently reduced use of the river water; and
- changes in climatic conditions – one person commented that:

> *The presence of a lot of exhaust gases in the atmosphere has a negative impact on climatic conditions. This has led to erratic and unpredictable rains, with the quantities becoming either more or less during given periods.*

Within the five cities discussed in this section, focus group participants placed repeated emphasis on the lack of adequate drainage, poor management of existing drainage, the consequences of unplanned and unregulated urban development, lack of attention to the problem by governments, and changes in weather patterns. Those from coastal towns also emphasized changes on the shoreline, including subsidence, which often happens as coastal organic (peat) soils inland from mangrove swamps are drained and dry out. Some of the aggravating changes are seen as happening within the settlements themselves; but others are totally external to the settlements and beyond the control of flood victims.

Adaptations to urban flooding

Accra, Ghana. In the Alajo community in Accra, people dealt with the June and July 2006 floods in a variety of ways:

- using blocks, stones and furniture to create high places on which to put their most critical valuables;
- placing goods on top of wardrobes and in the small spaces between ceilings and roofs;
- sharing such high places with others who had no similar 'safe' sites; and
- temporarily moving away from the area to stay with friends and family.

One woman in Alajo described her experiences as follows:

> *As soon as the clouds gather I move with my family to Nima to spend the night there. When the rain starts falling abruptly, we turn off the electricity meter in the house. We climb on top of our wardrobes and stay awake till morning. Our house was built in such a way that ordinarily water should not flood our rooms; but this is not so. Our furniture has been custom made to help keep our things dry from the water. For instance, our tables are very high and so also are our wardrobes; they are made in such a way that we can climb and sit on top of them. These measures are adaptive strategies as old as I can recollect. I have two children but because of the flood, my first child has been taken to Kumasi to live with my sister-in-law.*

When residents of Alajo were in danger, they resorted to self-help or, for example, were rescued by other members of the community using locally manufactured boats, with no involvement by any government disaster agency. People said that their complaints to government authorities brought no results:

> *When the rain and the floods come, women and children suffer. You can be locked up for up to two days with the flood. Sometimes, we take our children out from the room to the rooftop. Then people bring boats to evacuate people.*

Kampala, Uganda. Individuals in slums in Kampala adopted similar strategies. The response to floods in July 2006 was characterized by *ad hoc* individual short-term efforts to survive and protect property. In addition, some residents undertook collective work to open up drainage channels; some permanent residents temporarily moved to lodges and public places such as mosques and churches until the water levels receded; many residents constructed barriers against water entry at doorsteps; and some created outlets at the rear of their houses so that any water entering their homes flowed out quickly.

There were limited collective efforts at the community level and virtually no significant intervention by the relevant local government at the divisional level. What helped the residents most was the fact that the rains that caused the flooding were not the continuous peak rains that last several days, such as those experienced in April and November. What limited the response of the residents was the fact that almost all activities are uncoordinated and are at the individual 'survival of the fittest' level. Another big limitation is the significant backflow of water from the direction that the floodwater would naturally take, as a result of silting.

Lagos, Nigeria. At present, individual coping strategies include 'bailing water out of the house with buckets'. Some wealthier community members use mechanical water pumps to remove water from their homes. People build temporary plank bridges between houses across the wetlands in order to be able to move about during flooding. The most helpful individual action at the household level has been to block water inlets with pieces of cloth to reduce the amount of water coming into the house and then to remove the blockage after the level of the water has gone down to allow the water already inside the house to flow out.

The community seems unable to mobilize community efforts to tackle the flood problem. But even if they were able to mobilize, they believe they would not be able to combat the hazard owing to its enormity.

Maputo, Mozambique. The comments of Maria Sebastião Tivane from the Mafalala settlement typify the responses of Maputo residents:

> *If it rains, water rapidly accumulates, flooding the area. Generally, water remains for about two months. During that period, for our safety we put our belongings on bricks – namely, beds and tables – to secure a place to sleep. Those who live in low areas suffer more. During the 2000 floods, I lost everything. My house was destroyed, including the latrine, and everything, that is why I do not have a bed. My neighbours suffered too; but they managed to save their goods. Because of my age and being without a husband, I couldn't remove my goods and leave the area. I suffered a lot and I continue suffering because of living conditions. I survive because of family support. We don't have any assistance or support from the government or non-governmental organizations.*

Nairobi, Kenya. In the slums of Nairobi, adaptations or responses to flooding include:

- bailing water out of houses to prevent damage to belongings;
- placing children on tables, initially, and later removing them to nearby unaffected dwellings;
- digging trenches around houses before and during floods;
- constructing temporary dykes or trenches to divert water away from the house;
- securing the structures with waterproof recycled materials;
- relocating to the highest parts of the dwelling that residents think are secure; and
- using sandbags to prevent the ingress of water.

Essentially, these are all individual coping strategies. Sometimes, people share protective storage or accommodation on higher ground. Spontaneous community action to unblock drainage channels is relatively rare. No coordinated action for emergency shelter or rapid response to flooding appears to exist in these cities. However, local people in poor communities have an acute awareness of the solutions that are necessary and are possible.

Perceptions of solutions to the flooding problem

Accra, Ghana. The key ideas expressed by community members were:

- The construction of a well-designed drainage system. The focus groups believe that:

  If there is proper drainage, then we will have no floods. We need proper engineers to work on it. We have to engage the services of competent engineers, even if they are from abroad and are qualified to do the job.

  It was also recognized that once the drains were constructed, the communities would have to take charge of keeping them clear, clean and well maintained.
- Education, advocacy and sensitization of the community, together with assistance from non-governmental organizations (NGOs).
- Advocacy with government and policy-makers to draw attention to the plight of residents in poor, flood-prone urban communities.
- The enforcement of municipal laws on planning and urban design. The community believes that the Accra metropolitan assembly is too lax in enforcing the removal of illegal buildings that make the area more susceptible to flooding.
- Proper waste disposal; ensuring the availability and regular emptying of waste receptacles; and eliminating the deliberate dumping of waste into drains.

Generally, when Accra slum residents think about solutions, it is in terms of medium- to long-term solutions that involve urban upgrading and major structural works that require relatively large capital expenditure.

Kampala, Uganda. Although opinions diverged about priorities and the order of remedial activities, there was an emerging consensus on what should be done:

- build planned new houses;
- construct a deeper and wider main drainage channel to accommodate the increased floodwaters;
- construct covered feeder channels to channel water into the main drainage system;
- have a permanent workforce to maintain and clean the drainage system;
- set up and promote the use and awareness of a proper garbage and solid waste disposal system;
- strictly enforce bylaws on the construction of houses and sanitation solutions;
- make stakeholders aware of their roles, responsibilities and duties in averting the floods and of the danger if they neglect these roles;
- build public toilets in slum areas built over wetlands, where the construction of individual private household toilets is expensive;
- prohibit the construction of human settlements in the remaining existing swamps;
- strengthen and de-politicize the building inspection unit of Kawempe division, allowing it to take impartial action;
- increase advocacy for increased budgets for improving drainage channels and flood-related control activities; and
- plant more trees along the main drainage channels, as had been done previously.

Lagos, Nigeria. In Lagos, both the slum dwellers and the mainland local government council believe that constant clearance of the drainage channel running through Iwaya/Makoko would prevent the ponding of water from other parts of the metropolis. Standard drainage facilities along major streets within Iwaya/Makoko would help to solve the flooding problem. The slum dwellers have also suggested using sand to raise the entire area to a higher level.

Maputo, Mozambique. Solutions here included:

- building secondary drains that link to the already existing main one;
- cleaning up the main drainage channel, which, at present, is partially silted up;
- removing all housing built on natural flood paths;
- improving the drainage culverts under the N4 Highway;
- ensuring that local drains feed effectively into the main drainage channel;
- conducting educational campaigns for communities on flood avoidance;
- creating industrial zones outside cities and towns; and
- increasing public participation and involvement in resolving environmental issues.

Nairobi, Kenya. Slum tenants thought there was limited potential for intervention on their part because of their high level of individual vulnerability and their exclusion from decision-making processes. However, they felt some measures were possible on their part:

- forming residents' associations to improve their welfare and responses to emergencies;
- partnering with others to plant trees along the riverbank and dig canals, trenches and drainage next to their houses; and
- prevailing on landlords to build humane and habitable houses and business premises, away from the river and able to withstand floods, as well as toilets to avert the outbreak of disease.

Recommendations for government at different levels included:

- government reform of housing policy to compel landlords to provide basic services such as toilets, drainage systems and other sanitation facilities;
- the inclusion of informal settlements in the city's waste management programmes;
- proper planning and provision of essential services that can sustain people's lives and their livelihoods;
- the development of infrastructure, including bridges, access roads and dykes along the riverbank;
- relocation by national government of people living along the river; and
- land reclamation, as in the case of the adjacent upgraded Mathare 4A project.

People are aware of the solutions and have strong views on who is responsible for taking action. However, there are different levels at which the various stakeholders in flood mitigation can operate to contribute to creating solutions. This requires an analysis of responsibilities and actions, which is the subject of the next section.

General guidelines on adaptations to climate change

The general literature on adaptations recognizes that flood warning systems are necessary for people living on floodplains; that human settlements should be planned to avoid flooding as far as possible; and that adequate evacuation procedures should be in place to assist flood victims. Integrated river basin planning incorporating flood storage into reservoirs is recommended for most large African river basins.

Flash floods require a different approach to reducing vulnerability than most other natural hazards, including other kinds of floods. Death and property loss per unit area can be very high, and flood mitigation strategies alone are not sufficient. Flash floods require a different way of thinking based on an informed public and a system for detecting a rain event that has the potential to cause a flash flood. For the most part, research efforts, whether basic or applied, have dealt with one or another of the components of the system and we have learned a great deal. Yet, uncertainty about individual elements of the system remains high.[32]

Coastal defence systems will require long-term investment for the future. Action should begin now because several African coastal areas are already experiencing significant impacts. Investment will help to safeguard the next generation of coastal residents; but that generation will have to continue the investment to protect its successors. Caring for the people and the environments of the future is an obligation that the people and the governments of today must not avoid. Failure will impose immense costs on our posterity.

For flooding, in general, three types of action[33] are particularly relevant to poor urban communities:

1   *Informed action at the local level.* Local initiatives to reduce vulnerability and increase community participation may be facilitated by training, capacity-building and resource transfers. These kinds of efforts may require outside support and can be sustained through a network of organizations engaged in economic, social, political and scientific action and inter-organizational learning.
2   *Maps of the decision processes for disaster mitigation, preparedness, response and recovery.* Such devices would identify critical actors at each jurisdictional level; their risk assumptions; their different types of information needs; and the design of an information infrastructure that would support their decisions. Only by making the complexities of environmental risk management explicit will it be possible to transform the destructive spiral of disaster into a learning process for responsible management of the environment.
3   *Enablement of affected populations.* Global initiatives for adaptation to climate change and for disaster reduction should be more specifically addressed towards assisting the people who face hazards to manage their own environments more responsibly and equitably over the long term. Flood victims often feel neglected by the authorities and cut off from major national and international initiatives to alleviate flood impacts and reduce the frequency of flood events.

While megacities can suffer large quantitative losses and damage to life and property, the proportion of the population and properties affected may be far greater in small urban settlements. If we compare the diverse sizes of towns that share similar political economies and communities of similar sizes with different political economies, a clear case can be made that small communities experience a far different exposure to hazard than do large metropolitan areas.[34]

In terms of poverty reduction, the Independent Evaluation Group (IEG) of the World Bank notes that:

> *Disaster risks do not make it into the CAS or PRSP[35] as often as country exposure to such risks would seem to warrant. When a CAS does discuss natural disasters, it is likely to discuss activities related to vulnerability reduction (such as strengthening disaster management, long-term planning and early warning systems).*[36]

The IEG also notes that the first challenge for the World Bank in relation to disasters is 'to ensure that the poor do not miss out on the recovery or, worse, lose the little they have left'.[37]

Responsibilities and actions

Following a disaster, solutions that will directly benefit the poor are found at the micro level. As one disaster expert interviewed by the study team put it, governments have 'thick fingers' for such fine-scale work.[38]

Responsibility: Theoretical framework

The principle of local, regional or national action at the appropriate scale applies to managing urban flooding. Where the problems are essentially internal to a specific community, then that community should manage them. Where they lie totally within the boundaries of a single local authority, then the local authority should manage them. Where they cut across many administrations, then national governments, or even international consortia, should manage them.

Applying this principle of management as close to the communities as possible, the management of localized flooding as a result of inadequate drainage should be undertaken by the local communities themselves. This is where local voluntary groups, assisted by national or international NGOs and with support from both local government and national disaster reduction organizations, could be highly effective. Local communities are stakeholders in the good drainage of, and the rapid water removal from, their own areas. They would benefit from improving and maintaining drainage channels, thus preventing the blocking of waterways and culverts by waste; from installing roof rainwater collection tanks for their own use; and avoiding construction on drainage lines. They could also organize local shelter for the people in their communities who are most affected by flooding.

Local authorities are best placed to cope with flooding from small streams whose catchment areas lie almost entirely within the built-up area. They administer the regulations and bylaws concerned with land-use planning and should be involved in local disaster management. However, most African local authorities lack the human resources and financial power to carry out such responsibilities effectively. They may be able to form partnerships with NGOs; but they should be supported by national governments and regional agencies to map flood risk areas, maintain urban stream channels, control building in flood channels and on floodplains, and provide emergency assistance.

Where towns and cities are flooded by major rivers overtopping their banks, their flood protection has to be seen in the context of the entire river basin, which may include more than one state. Where a river basin lies within a single nation state, integrated river basin management principles should be applied by an agency cutting across ministries concerned with both rural and urban interests to ensure that activities in upstream areas do not worsen the flood situation for towns and cities downstream. For large international rivers, river basin commissions are required to manage the water resources of the entire basin for the benefit of all communities in the different nations occupying the basin. Individual urban authorities may campaign for, or act to build, extra flood protection embankments. However, such works only serve to direct the floodwaters elsewhere. The natural floodplain should be retained to hold floodwaters and should not be built upon.

Cities faced with coastal flooding from the sea or from a combination of high tides and high river flows from inland have to integrate both river basin and coastal zone management, ensuring that the natural wetlands can continue to function as flood storage areas as far as possible. Where settlements already exist, filling those areas to prevent flooding may be desirable; but the implications for adjacent areas need to be considered. Social factors may lead people to move on to other nearby wetlands.

Required actions

More needs to be done to focus on the urban poor in international action on adaptation to climate change and disaster reduction. Seldom do the needs of the urban poor feature in responses to the National Adaptation Programme of Action (NAPA) on vulnerability to climate change, funded by the Global Environment Facility (GEF) for least-developed countries. The *Hyogo Declaration* (so named after the Japanese prefecture where the world conference on disaster reduction was held in 2005), in its international plan of action, points out that 'disasters in Africa pose a major obstacle to the African continent's efforts to achieve sustainable development'.[39] However, national Hyogo reports make scant reference to the needs of the urban poor. To achieve the inter-sectoral partnerships suggested by the Hyogo framework, steps are needed to create awareness and build capacity within city councils for the application of the framework and other relevant protocols and conventions for the needs of the urban poor.

Climate change is aggravating the problems caused by urban flooding that poor people in African towns and cities regularly face. The detailed reports from the cities studied by ActionAid confirm the general view in the literature on political ecology approaches, which demonstrate, for example, that when faced with a flood risk, residents of marginalized but risky areas have only a limited set of adaptation options.[40] As elsewhere, in some African countries the state allows such risks to exist as part of the politicized nature of urban planning and control. In some cases, the poor form associations to initiate some adaptations; but everywhere the poor need urgent help to increase their ability to avoid these problems. They need help at the local community level to improve their options for emergency action and evacuation. They need help at the municipal level to improve drainage, to regulate developments upstream and elsewhere that increase flooding in their communities, and to give them greater security of tenure so that they can invest in making their homes more flood resistant. They need help at the national level – particularly to ensure that their needs are included in national disaster reduction plans and that these and other impacts of climate change are included in poverty reduction strategies. They also need international help to see that funding for adaptation to climate change is directed towards their problems. If Africa generally is a victim of climate change, the African poor are where the outcomes of that victimization are mainly focused.

Notes

1. See, for example, Stephens, C., Timaeus, I., Akerman, M., Avle, S., Maia, P. B., Campanerio, P., Doe, B., Lush, L., Tetteh, D. and Harpham, T. (1994) *Environment and Health in Developing Countries: An Analysis of Intra-Urban Differentials*, London School of Hygiene and Tropical Medicine, 141pp; also Stephens, C. (1996) 'Healthy cities or unhealthy islands: The health and social implications of urban inequality', *Environment and Urbanization*, vol 8, no 2, October, pp9–30.
2. Hardoy, J. E., Mitlin, D. and Satterthwaite, D. (2001) *Environmental Problems in an Urbanizing World: Finding Solutions for Cities in Africa, Asia and Latin America*, Earthscan, London.
3. Adger, N. et al (2007) *Climate Change 2007: Impacts, Adaptation and Vulnerability, Working Group II Contribution to the Intergovernmental Panel on Climate Change Fourth Assessment Report, Summary for Policymakers*, Intergovernmental Panel on Climate Change, Geneva.
4. Viljoen, M. and Booyse, H. (2006) 'Planning and management of flood damage control: the South African experience', *Irrigation and Drainage*, no 55, ppS83–S91.
5. See, for example, Chapter 2.
6. Gupta, A. and Ahmad, R. (1999) 'Geomorphology and the urban tropics: building an interface between research and usage', *Geomorphology*, vol 31, pp133–149.
7. Gruntfest, E. and Handmer, J. (eds) (2001) *Coping with Flash Floods: Proceedings of the NATO Advanced Study Institute*, 8–17 November 1999, Ravello, Italy, NATO Science Partnership Sub-Series 77, Springer, Berlin.

8. See reference 4.
9. Commission for Africa (2005) *Action for a Strong and Prosperous Africa*, London, p249.
10. See reference 9: Commission for Africa (2005), p51.
11. See, for instance, Conway, D. (2005) 'From headwater tributaries to international river: observing and adapting to climate variability and change in the Nile basin', *Global Environmental Change*, vol 15, pp99–114.
12. Jackson, I. J. (1989) *Climate, Water and Agriculture in the Tropics*, second edition, Longman, London.
13. For instance, between 1931 and 1990 there were significant increases in the intensity of extreme rainfall events in about 70 per cent of South Africa. Increases in the intensity of high rainfall events have been greatest for the most extreme events. See Mason, S. J., Waylen, P. R., Mimmack, G. M., Rajaratnam, B. and Harrison, M. (1999) 'Changes in extreme rainfall events in South Africa', *Climatic Change*, vol 41, pp249–257.
14. IPCC (Intergovernmental Panel on Climate Change) (2007) *Climate Change 2007: The Physical Science Basis: Summary for Policymakers*, WHO, UNEP, www.aaas.org/news/press_room/climate_change/media/4th_spm2feb07.pdf.
15. For example, in the Blue Nile region of the Nile Basin, predictive models produce divergent results for rainfall changes in the crucial summer monsoon season. In the White Nile system, the various models agree on a winter increase in rainfall, but disagree on the size of that increase. They are inconsistent on how the summer monsoon will change. The models are consistent for small decreases in winter rainfall in the Nile Delta and for large decreases in the summer; but these are unlikely to be significant as rainfall is negligible in these months. See reference 13: Mason et al (1999).
16. IMF and World Bank (2006) *Clean Energy and Development: Towards an Investment Framework. DC2006-0002*, Environmentally and Socially Sustainable Development Vice-Presidency and Infrastructure Vice-Presidency, World Bank, Washington, DC, pviii.
17. Mason, S. and Joubert, A. (1997) 'Simulated changes in extreme rainfall over southern Africa', *International Journal of Climatology*, vol 17, pp291–301.
18. Ayoade, J. and Akintola, F. (1980) 'Flood perception in two Nigerian cities', *Environment International*, vol 4, pp227–280; also French, G., Awosika, L. and Ibe, C. (1994) 'Sea-level rise in Nigeria: Potential impacts and consequences', *Journal of Coastal Research* no 14, Special Issue, pp1–45; Muoghalu, L. and Okonkwo, A. (1998) 'Effects of urban flooding in Akwa, Anambra state, Nigeria', *Environmental Review*, vol 2, pp72–81; and Ologunorisa, E. (1999) 'Flood hazard perception and adjustment in Ondo, southwestern Nigeria', *Journal of Nigerian Affairs*, vol 4, pp172–193.
19. Akintola, F. (1994) 'Flooding phenomenon', in Filani, M. O. et al (eds) *Ibadan Region*, Rex Charles Publications in association with Connel Publications, Ibadan, pp244–255.
20. Babatolu, J. (1997) 'The June 24th 1995 flood in Ondo: Its antecedents and incidents', *Ife Research Publication in Geography*, vol 6, pp158–164; also Oriola, O. (1994) 'Strategies for combating urban flooding in a developing nation: A case study from Ondo', *The Environmentalist*, vol 14, pp57–62.

21. Olaniran, O. and Babatolu, J. (1996) 'Recent changes in rainfall pattern and its implications for flood occurrence in Ondo, Nigeria', *Ondo Journal of Arts and Social Sciences*, vol 1, pp125–136.
22. Singh, A., Dieye, A., Finco, M., Chenoweth, M. S., Fosnight, E. A. and Allotey, A. (1999) *Early Warning of Selected Emerging Environmental Issues in Africa: Change and Correlation from a Geographic Perspective*, United Nations Environment Programme, Nairobi, Kenya.
23. See reference 7.
24. Sachs, W. (2006) 'Climate change and human rights', *The Pontifical Academy of Sciences Scripta Varia*, vol 106, pp349–368.
25. Nicholls, R., Hoozemans, F. and Marchand, M. (1999) 'Increasing flood risk and wetland losses due to global sea-level rise: regional and global analyses', *Global Environmental Change*, vol 9, ppS69–S87.
26. For instance, parts of Lagos are 2m below sea level. Many slum dwellings are built on stilts over swamps and other wetlands. An extreme ten-hour rainfall in Port Harcourt on 14 July 2006 drove out 10,000 residents and caused widespread traffic chaos. The Niger Delta frequently experiences flood problems, aggravated by structures such as the Port Harcourt–Patani–Warri Highway that cuts across natural drainage lines and acts as a barrier to floodwaters. The blockage of channels by debris and the obstruction of flood paths by new construction were seen as the main obstacles contributing to the Port Harcourt flooding. See Abam, T., Ofoegbu, C., Osadebe, C. and Gobo, A. (2000) 'Impact of hydrology on the Port Harcourt–Patani–Warri road', *Environmental Geology*, vol 40, pp153–162.
27. Banjul could disappear in 50 to 60 years through coastal erosion and sea-level rise, putting more than 42,000 people at risk. See Jallow, B., Toure, S., Barrow, M. and Mathieu, A. (1999) 'Coastal zone of The Gambia and the Abidjan region in Côte d'Ivoire: Sea-level rise vulnerability, response strategies and adaptation options', *Climate Research*, no 6, Special Issue, pp137–143.
28. El-Raey, M., Dewidar, K. R. and El-Hattab, M. (2004) 'Adaptation to the impacts of sea-level rise in Egypt', *Mitigation and Adaptation Strategies for Global Change*, vol 4, pp343–361.
29. Magadza, C. H. D. (2000) 'Climate change impacts and human settlements in Africa: Prospects for adaptation', *Environmental Monitoring and Assessment*, vol 61, pp193–205.
30. Independent Evaluation Group (2006) *Hazards of Nature: Risks to Development: An IEG Evaluation of World Bank Assistance for Natural Disasters*, World Bank, Washington, DC, p48.
31. Smit, B. and Wandel, J. (2006) 'Adaptation, adaptive capacity and vulnerability', *Global Environmental Change*, vol 16, pp282–292.
32. Montz, B. E. and Gruntfest, E. (2002) 'Flash flood mitigation: recommendations for research and applications', *Environmental Hazards*, vol 4, pp15–22.
33. Comfort, L., Wisner, B., Cutter, S., Pulwarty, R., Hewitt, K., Oliver-Smith, A., Wiener, J., Fordham, M., Peacock, W. and Krimgold, F. (1999) 'Reframing disaster policy: The global evolution of vulnerable communities', *Environmental Hazards*, vol 1, pp39–44.
34. Cross, J. A. (2001) 'Megacities and small towns: different perspectives on hazard vulnerability', *Environmental Hazards*, vol 3, pp63–80.

35. CAS = Country Assistance Strategy; PRSP = Poverty Reduction Strategy Paper.
36. See reference 30: Independent Evaluation Group (2006), p35.
37. See reference 30: Independent Evaluation Group (2006), p67.
38. See reference 30: Independent Evaluation Group (2006), p49.
39. United Nations (2005) *Report of the World Conference on Disaster Reduction*, Kobe, Hyogo, Japan, 18–22 January 2005, A Conf 206/6, United Nations, New York, p19.
40. Adger, W., Huq, S., Brown, K., Conway, D. and Hulme, M. (2003) 'Adaptation to climate change in the developing world', *Progress in Development Studies* vol 3, pp179–195; also Pelling, M. (1999) 'The political ecology of flood hazard in urban Guyana', *Geoforum*, vol 30, pp240–261.

10

Urban Poverty and Vulnerability to Climate Change in Latin America

Jorgelina Hardoy and Gustavo Pandiella

Introduction

In Latin America, climate change and variability come to people's attention as extreme weather events such as floods, droughts, extreme temperatures, heavy rains and storms. These events are perceived as unusual and extraordinary and, over subsequent days, the media is full of press releases detailing how many people were killed, injured or displaced. Authorities and experts comment on the status of the situation, its causes and what should be done to prevent future disasters. However, a few days later everything is forgotten, although those who have been displaced or whose homes have been damaged continue to struggle with the situation. Much the same happens with the general coverage and information around disasters not caused by extreme weather. Many factors contribute to this kind of thinking. Some are related to old paradigms, which see disasters as occasional 'natural' extreme events rather than as caused by the lack of attention to risk reduction prior to the extreme event. Others have to do with the lack of rigorous data collection and analysis of the impact of disasters at country, regional and local level, so the information needed to justify actions and guide decisions on disaster prevention is not there. But much of it has to do with the long evident incapacity of governments to address risk and to integrate development with the reduction of vulnerability. In the city, hazards and vulnerability combine and reinforce each other, increasing the level of risk.

Much urban expansion in Latin America has taken place over floodplains or up mountain slopes, or in other zones ill suited to settlement, such as areas prone to flooding or affected by seasonal storms, sea surges or other weather-related risks. Mostly low-income groups occupy these dangerous sites. Usually, these areas were left vacant (and low-income households allowed to build on them) only because of the environmental conditions that make them so vulnerable and because of their lack of infrastructure and services. In most cases, the poor have no formal tenure of the land and face not only environmental risks, but also the risk of eviction. Left with no alternative, low-income groups inhabit overcrowded houses in neighbourhoods with high population densities, although, in many cases, informal settlements have been developed with layouts that include provision for road networks that would allow service installation and neighbourhood regularization in the future. In these neighbourhoods, houses are usually built with inadequate materials, making them damp and cold in winter and very hot in summer.[1] Meanwhile, within local governments there is generally an institutional incapacity to address this issue or to control pollution and protect natural resources, as well as a lack of accountability to the citizens in their jurisdiction and little or no scope for citizen participation.

The lack of attention to the risks faced by large sections of the urban population from extreme weather puts many people at high risk from the likely impacts of climate change, including storms, flooding, landslides, heat waves and drought, and overloaded water, drainage and energy supply systems. High levels of risk are particularly evident for those who inhabit dangerous sites and lack the resources and options to modify their vulnerability. Many urban inhabitants who lack safe and sufficient freshwater provision may face additional problems, as climate change contributes to constraints on freshwater supplies. Thus, climate change contributes another level of stress to already vulnerable cities and populations, adding to the inadequacies in water and sanitation coverage, poor solid and liquid waste collection and treatment, pollution, poverty and unemployment, lack of participation, and inadequate governance structures (including corruption). There are so many problems that there is an urgent need to address them in an integrated way.

Three-quarters of Latin America's population live in urban areas, a much higher proportion than in Asia and Africa.[2] In many countries in the region, a high proportion of the urban population lives in one or two very large cities. National economies, employment patterns and government capacities are also very dependent upon these large cities, which makes them extremely vulnerable. Any disruption can easily affect the whole country in terms of production, service provision, functioning of government institutions and the national economy. However, the growth of very large cities has been less than anticipated, with higher growth rates concentrating in mid-size or small cities and urban centres or on the periphery of metropolitan regions.

Latin American urban centres have developed within a great range of environments, from sea level to more than 3000m above sea level,[3] and in a variety of geographic and topographic locations. Although some have made considerable improvements regarding environmental risk management, these are the exceptions. In general, city governments have not implemented the controls and governance mechanisms that are essential to keeping environmental problems in check.[4]

A significant proportion of the region's population remains very poor. Estimates for 2006 indicated that 36.5 per cent of the region's population was living in poverty (194 million people) with 13.4 per cent in extreme poverty (71 million people) – although there has been a general trend towards poverty reduction up to 2008 (unlike the 1990s). By 2006, the number of people living in poverty in urban areas was nearly twice that in rural areas, while the number in extreme poverty was similar (35 million in urban areas, 36 million in rural areas).[5]

Most national governments have been unable to reduce absolute poverty levels or the very high disparities in income distribution, which have increased particularly since the 1970s. Within Latin America, the wealthiest 10 per cent of the population has between 40 and 47 per cent of a nation's income, while the poorest 20 per cent has only 2 to 4 per cent.[6]

The population that has been most affected by extreme weather events in the past provides a basis for identifying those most likely to be at risk from such events in the future.[7] But the available data on this are very limited. Although the combination of hazards and vulnerability generates environmental risks that are part of everyday life for large sections of the urban population, the number of deaths, serious injuries and loss of assets from these is not known. There are some data on the number of deaths and injuries for events registered as disasters; but this is known to be a small proportion of all those killed or injured by floods and storms, in part because the criteria for what constitutes a 'disaster' means that 'small' disasters go unregistered in official records. When flood deaths are recorded only for events in which at least 10 people died and/or at least 100 were reported as affected,[8] the number of deaths from floods is likely to be greatly underestimated.[9] Without adequate adaptation measures, climate change is likely to mean that the impact and frequency of small and not so small extreme weather disasters will increase.

The availability and quality of data on the impacts of extreme weather or other hazards is a problem throughout the region. Data from different sources exist – for instance, from each government agency, hospital, health and education centre or private firm – but are difficult to obtain and to compare because institutions manage their data in different ways and use different timeframes and geographic scales. This makes it difficult to build an accurate picture of impacts. For example, in Argentina, there is no agreed estimate of the population living in informal settlements. In 1995, researchers were already pointing to the limitations in the information needed to address risks – for instance, regarding tenancy, quality of housing and infrastructure, and access to basic services – and to the lack of studies or particular methodologies to study environmental conditions in low-income neighbourhoods and poor consolidated urban areas.[10] Also of concern then (as now) is that official data such as censuses are so aggregated that they are of little use to local-level action programmes. Non-governmental organizations (NGOs) may gather data in informal settlements where they work, and there are insights from numerous micro-level studies;[11] but, in general, there is little information on the different groups within the poor and on their different needs and priorities, and little of the kind of data needed to guide actions in ways that address root problems. Besides, situations change and it is difficult to keep track of these changes. Community mapping is interesting as it may provide a local perception of problems and an information base that can be updated and combined with local government data and perceptions, providing a much more accurate picture of reality at the local and micro-local level.

Vulnerability and adaptation in urban areas

Adaptations undertaken at community level, making use of traditional knowledge to reduce the effects of climate-related disasters, can be translated or improved in the face of climate variability and change. However, most of these examples are rural and include mechanisms for coping with droughts and floods. The agricultural sector has been adapting autonomously to climate variability using different seed varieties and technologies, adjusting times of sowing and harvesting, and moving spatially. But there is little evidence of adaptation in urban areas – perhaps not surprisingly in a context where national and local governments have never shown much interest in addressing vulnerability and managing risks.

The next section looks at six aspects of vulnerability:

1   Who lives or works in the locations most exposed to hazards related to the direct or indirect impacts of climate change (e.g. on sites at risk of flooding or landslides)?
2   Who lives or works in locations lacking the infrastructure that reduces risk (e.g. from serious floods where settlements lack drains)?
3   Who lacks the knowledge, capacity and opportunities to take immediate short-term measures to limit impacts (e.g. to move family members and assets before a flood hits)?
4   Whose homes and neighbourhoods face greatest risks when impacts occur (e.g. homes of poorer quality, which provide less protection for inhabitants and their possessions/physical assets so that there is more loss, often including death and serious injury)?
5   Who is least able to cope with impacts (illness, injury, death, loss of property, loss of income, lack of insurance or relation to government to get compensation)?
6   Who is least able to adapt to avoid impacts (e.g. by building better homes, getting government to install needed infrastructure and to provide needed disaster preparedness, and moving to a safer place)?

It must be recognized that adaptation cannot eliminate all risks from extreme events; so a critical part of adaptation lies in the resources, institutions and networks needed for rapid and effective immediate post-disaster response and for rebuilding homes and livelihoods.

Owing to the lack of local-level data, it has been difficult to find local case studies that illustrate all six of the above aspects. It is also difficult to separate processes and aspects of vulnerability when, in reality, these categories overlap and reinforce each other. For example, most of those who live or work in floodplains without the infrastructure to reduce risks are also poor and lack both the power to press for needed flood controls and suitable land and the insurance to protect their properties (houses and possessions) and health. Any case study can easily be relevant to several of the six aspects; but there may not be the data to illustrate each aspect. In addition, any of the adaptation measures implemented (autonomously or led by government) will have to compete with many other pressing needs.

Six aspects of vulnerability

Who lives or works in the locations most exposed to hazards related to the direct or indirect impacts of climate change?
In urban areas, when the land available for housing is scarce and/or unaffordable for low–income groups, the choices for location are limited. Individuals and households make choices that reflect priorities and trade-offs – for instance, with regard to location/accessibility, availability, type of ownership (private or state owned), security (i.e. the likelihood of eviction), possibilities of service provision and regularization, and cost. In some cases, land is occupied by organizations of dwellers who select a piece of land and prepare an urban plan with plots and streets. Once settled, they struggle for services, negotiate for regularization and, where natural and environmental conditions generate risks, demand solutions from government.

In most Latin American cities, there are concentrations of low-income households on land sites at high risk from extreme weather.[12] For example, an estimated 1.1 million people live in the *favelas* of Rio de Janeiro that sprawl over the slopes of the Tijuca Mountain range. Housing conditions here have improved over time, with better-quality building materials and public services such as electricity, water and sewerage. In many places, however, the paving of sidewalks has increased runoff in the rainy season to the point where water is ankle or knee-deep between houses. Water runs down from the mountain through cemented or quasi-natural watercourses, flooding lowlands. The accumulation of uncollected wastes also blocks drains and surface runoff. More intense or prolonged rains will increase risks in the area.[13]

The city of Santa Fe in Argentina (with a population of 489,595 in 2001[14]) has expanded increasingly onto the Río Salado floodplain. To defend itself from floods, it had to create embankments and dykes. A flood in 2003 displaced 139,886 people (one third of the city population) and 27,928 households were affected.[15] Official statistics indicate there were 23 deaths, although local sources suggest there were at least 100 more than this. There were also 180 cases of leptospirosis and 200 cases of hepatitis. Economic losses were estimated at approximately US$1 billion: US$752 million from losses in agriculture – cattle production, industry and commerce; US$180 million from infrastructure; and US$91 million in the social sector.[16] Actual losses were much larger than this but were hard to measure (e.g. work and school days lost and the impossibility of carrying out informal activities to generate income). Among the factors contributing to the flood were increased and more intense rainfall and deforestation and land-use changes around the city – but the flood caught the city authorities completely unprepared, even though the Instituto Nacional del Agua (INA) was monitoring water flows and had informed city and provincial government.[17] More floods during 2006 to 2007 also caught the government unprepared: there were several deaths, tens of thousands of people had to be evacuated, highways and roads were flooded and bridges brought down. Again, one third of the city became a shallow lake – the same part of the city that was hit by the 2003 flood (see below for how the lack of infrastructure and preparedness plans contributed to this). City authorities recognized that in the last 50 years there had been no official urban land policies and people had settled where and how they could, prioritizing proximity to work places or social networks. But the lack of policies is also a way of doing politics.[18]

Buenos Aires has had a significant increase in annual rainfall over recent decades and increasing numbers of intense rainfall events (e.g. more than 100mm in 24 hours).[19] According to DesInventar, between 1990 and 1998, 24 flood events occurred, affecting neighbourhoods of different income levels.[20] Other data indicate that between 1985 and January 2003, 35 flood events affected the metropolitan region.[21] The areas most at risk are the low-lying lands of the lower basins of the rivers Reconquista and Matanza-Riachuelo, and these lands have high concentrations of informal settlements.[22] No thorough studies have looked at flood events from the perspective of those most affected; but the location of informal settlements within the metropolitan area historically has been on disadvantaged lands, including low-lying coastal lands.

Quito, in Ecuador, is another city where hazards and vulnerability combine to create risk. The city is at the foot of the Pichincha volcano, on very steep slopes. Its population has increased fourfold over the last 30 years or so and a combination of problems (economic crisis, debt, population growing far faster than government can keep up, a lack of planning) has led to legal and illegal occupation of slopes. The costs of providing services and infrastructure to these areas are very high, especially for illegal settlements. The lack of sewers and drainage systems increases the risk of floods, while the lack of proper waste collection systems results in waste accumulation in ravines and gorges, which clogs natural water flow and generates floods and landslides.[23]

The metropolitan district of Caracas has suffered from recurrent disasters. Much of the city is built on slopes, with many gorges that lead to the main city river, the Guaire. In 1993, 41.5 per cent of the population lived in low-income neighbourhoods and, while the general population increased by 300 per cent between 1950 and 1990, the population in low-income neighbourhoods (*zonas de ranchos*) increased by 878 per cent, resulting in far higher population densities.[24] As the city has expanded, land has become more impermeable, increasing water runoff. Without planning, low-income neighbourhoods have occupied unstable land and gorges; together with waste accumulation, they act as barriers to water runoff.[25] In December 1999, Venezuela experienced a 1-in-100-year rainfall with massive landslides and floods that killed hundreds of people. The rainfall was unusual in its intensity, the time of year and in that it was not produced by either a hurricane or a tropical cyclone. The death toll among people settled on slopes and on low-lying lands was very high.[26] Eight states were affected, but especially Vargas. The area is heavily urbanized, with high population densities on a narrow strip between the mountains and the sea, and crossed by 37 rivers and 42 canyons. Rapid urban growth led to the occupation of slopes with no controls (the rich occupying floodplains and areas near riverbanks, while poor households settled on slopes and near ravines).[27] The metropolitan area of Caracas occupies a valley measuring approximately 30km east to west and 5km north to south. Although it is a relatively small area, coordination between different administrative units (municipalities) has proved difficult. Several efforts are under way; but there are difficulties in translating a theoretical model of risk management into practice.[28]

Intense rains in January 2006 affected several areas in Bolivia, including the city of Viacha, where the Río Pallina overflowed – a result of heavy rains combined with the dumping of city waste into the watercourse and a lack of cleaning and maintenance of the area. Settlements on the periphery of Viacha have expanded spontaneously, and regularization and basic services come after residents have settled; most houses do not have approved plans or legal tenure. Those most affected by the rains were low-income groups, with the disaster occurring at the same time as an economic and political crisis, making it very difficult to implement the needed actions in time. Residents recall former floods in 1985 and 1995, when sewage overflowed onto the streets and damp crept into house foundations; but none were as heavy as the 2006 floods. Demands on local government have been constant.[29] In Bolivia, 51 per cent of the urban population is poor. Migration from rural areas is an important part of the demographic and physical expansion of cities such as La Paz, Santa Cruz, Trinidad and Cochabamba, and in all of these there are risks of floods, hailstorms, droughts and landslides, with low-income groups settled in peri-urban areas being at particular risk. In January 2007, during floods in Cochabamba, 60 houses collapsed.[30]

During Hurricane Mitch, 30 per cent of the central district of Honduras, including the cities of Tegucigalpa and Comayaguela, was destroyed. Most damage was concentrated around the four rivers that cross these cities. Obsolete and inadequate city infrastructure, especially water, sanitation and drainage, a lack of zoning codes, the concentration of services and infrastructure in only a few centres, a lack of official prevention and mitigation strategies, together with inappropriate management of the river basins all combined to create the levels of vulnerability seen in Honduras' capital;[31] 78 per cent of Tegucigalpa's drinking water supply pipelines were destroyed.

Who lives or works in locations lacking the infrastructure that reduces risk?
Many of the urban neighbourhoods most at risk from extreme weather are made
even more vulnerable by the lack of infrastructure and services, and often by
physical changes to the site or its surrounds. The metropolitan region of Buenos
Aires has a large deficit in the infrastructure needed to keep risks to a minimum,
including provision for water, sanitation and drainage – although with large
disparities between the wealthier and the low-income municipalities in the quality
and extent of provision. Buenos Aires has an old drainage system, planned for half
the current population and designed to work in the context of open spaces and
vacant land that no longer exist. In 2001, record levels of precipitation caused large
parts of the urban infrastructure to collapse, a situation that has now become
recurrent.[32]

The devastating floods experienced by Santa Fe described above were due, in
part, to incomplete or unmaintained infrastructure. Infrastructure may also
generate a false sense of security, leading to a disregard of important non-structural
measures. In Santa Fe, where land use has not been regulated, recommendations
for avoiding the occupation of low areas were not enforced. A member of a local
foundation complained that local authorities favour the settlement of at-risk areas
by bringing piped water and electricity to the neighbourhoods 'where they have
their loyal voters'.[33] Infrastructure to defend certain city areas was supposed to be
in place shortly after 1998, but was never completed because of a lack of resources;
and the construction of road infrastructure, such as the highway connecting the
city with Rosario, created barriers to water runoff. Five years previously, studies
had pointed to the need to double the size of the highway's bridges. The pumps
and drainage systems installed to evacuate water in protected areas did not work
because of vandalism and lack of maintenance.[34]

The city of Pergamino in the Pampas of Argentina also faces more frequent
floods due to a combination of increased rainfall since the 1970s, land-use
changes without a proper urban plan, and the lack of drainage systems and proper
waste disposal.[35]

Besides the fact that basic services and infrastructure such as water and
sanitation and proper waste collection and disposal decrease health risks, when
they are in place, excess water drains more easily, cesspits do not overflow and
wastes do not clog drains and channels. In Latin America, sanitation has
improved; however, in 2004, 125 million people (14 per cent of the urban
population) still lacked a basic sanitation system[36] and a significantly higher
proportion lacked good-quality provision for sanitation and drainage.[37]

*Who lacks knowledge, capacity and opportunities to take immediate short-term
measures to limit impacts?*
The devastation caused in so many low-income settlements by extreme weather
is not necessarily a matter of lack of knowledge or capacities by their residents,

although this may be the case for some new migrants. For residents of informal settlements, there are often risks associated with moving away from their homes because of an approaching storm or likelihood of a flood, even when advised to do so – for instance, losing valuables to looters, uncertainty about provisioning for their needs in the places they move to, and the worry of not being allowed back if the settlement is damaged. There are also uncertainties about what the weather forecast actually implies for each home and household, so decisions are made in the context of stress and considerable uncertainty.

This uncertainty is not necessarily removed by official mechanisms to inform the population on how to prepare and react in case of disaster. In the case of the floods in Santa Fe, the accuracy of the information was doubtful. In addition, the lack of appropriate information and official evacuation mechanisms stopped many from evacuating promptly. The sense of insecurity for those living in informal settlements and the knowledge that looting usually accompanies flooding made many stay to protect their homes and assets. There is no official information regarding the post-disaster situation in Santa Fe, although different newspapers mentioned that many were not able to return to their houses or that government agencies intended to move them to other city areas far away from social and family networks, work and schools.

A case study of 15 disaster-prone 'slum' communities in El Salvador also shows the difficulties in getting appropriate risk reduction action at neighbourhood level. Households recognized the serious risk of flooding and landslides and took measures to lower risks. But various factors limited the effectiveness of community-wide measures, including the individualistic nature of households' investments, the lack of representative community organizations and the lack of support from government agencies, with most residents viewing local and national governments as unhelpful or even as a hindrance to their efforts.[38]

In the case of a low-income community (El Zanjon) on the banks of the Matanza Riachuelo River in Buenos Aires, the lack of advance warning has long hindered the community from taking appropriate action before floods arrive. In 2004, the neighbourhood was flooded and a few days later, filmmakers produced a video showing the situation and suggesting links to climate variability and change. Local inhabitants reported that they never knew in advance when the floods were coming even though there was official information regarding precipitation, tides and water levels. The video was used to generate awareness among the community and at different decision-making levels within government agencies, while a community early warning system was developed: a telephone line was installed so that port authorities could call a resident, and a system of whistles was set up to alert neighbours.[39]

There are examples of low-income populations that lack the knowledge to cope with risk. For example, in Brazil, new migrant populations from the arid north-east, with no personal experience of mudslides, arrive in Rio de Janeiro and settle on the hillsides. As they clear these areas for their homes, they remove the protective vegetation cover despite government efforts to protect these areas. The lack of personal knowledge of local risk and of appropriate building techniques hinders safer practices – although many other factors also contribute, including the prevalence of crime and violence that inhibit social cohesion. Over the last 15 years, there have been large public programmes to improve conditions in the *favelas*, including investment in basic infrastructure, health and education for half a million poor residents.[40]

Whose homes and neighbourhoods face greatest risks when impacts occur?

In informal settlements, houses are usually built incrementally over a number of years, with materials of diverse origin and quality and not always following accepted techniques. These houses rarely comply with official safety standards and there are no controls in place. Most buildings are used intensively – with high levels of overcrowding and a mix of living and working spaces. This is often combined with a lack of maintenance and with environmental conditions (e.g. humidity from proximity to river edges and coastal areas) that cause rapid deterioration. Houses are not as solid or as insulated as they should be and are often built on inadequate foundations (many on landfill or unstable land). In the suburbs of Buenos Aires, in low-lying lands, each resident contracts trucks to bring solid waste to their piece of land and later compact it as best they can. There is no coordination between neighbours, so plots end up on different levels; when it rains, some are flooded more than others. The natural drainage of the larger site has been totally modified without incorporating the necessary drainage infrastructure. Families often end up with water in their houses for up to a day when heavy (but not exceptional) rains occur. Houses built on stilts are rare in Buenos Aires – although there are examples, mostly in traditional low-income coastal areas (e.g. La Boca–Barracas, Isla Maciel and some neighbourhoods in Avellaneda, south of Buenos Aires, or Tigre, in northern Buenos Aires). Most relatively new low-income settlements have not incorporated such measures, although building two-storey houses would allow valuable assets to be moved to the higher floor. However, this cannot always be done because of the costs and skills necessary to build two-storey houses.

Most low-income groups live in housing without air conditioning or adequate insulation, and during heat waves, the very young, the elderly and people in poor health are particularly at risk.[41] In northern Mexico, heat waves have been correlated with increases in mortality rates; in Buenos Aires, 10 per cent of summer deaths are associated with heat strain; and records show increases in the incidence of diarrhoea in Peru.[42] Cold spells are also becoming more frequent, and without proper heating and housing insulation they are also difficult to cope with. In July 2007, it snowed in Buenos Aires for the first time in almost 100 years. There are no available data, however, on death tolls and health impacts related to unusual and extreme temperatures.

The expansion of dengue, malaria and other infectious diseases is related to changes in temperature and precipitation. No studies that we know of specifically associate disease risks and vulnerability to climate change. However, we can assume that low-income groups and, in particular, vulnerable age groups will be more at risk since they live and work in homes and neighbourhoods where public health measures to eliminate disease vectors are absent or ineffective. They also have to rely on overtaxed and often ineffective healthcare systems and lose school and work days to health problems that should have been prevented. Most work in the informal economy and, thus, lack insurance to cover lost workdays.

Who is least able to cope with impacts?

The most vulnerable groups (low-income groups, in general, women, children and the elderly) seldom have an influential voice with regard to disaster preparedness or responses. This applies, in particular, to those living in informal settlements where government agencies refuse to work. The needs of infants, children and the elderly often receive little attention. The same is generally true for women, who also have less scope to take action. In the case of the Santa Fe floods, although no precise data relate vulnerability to disaster, it has been recorded that, in general, those most affected live in flood-prone areas that also lack drainage infrastructure. Data from 2002 estimate that 63.7 per cent of the population of the city of Santa Fe were below the poverty line and there was an unemployment rate of 23 per cent. Certain indicators point to people's potential (or lack thereof) for coping with floods: in 2003, 46 per cent of Santa Fe's population were under the age of 18 and 93.8 per cent of those under 18 were poor; 41 per cent of the households had a female head; 80 per cent of the labour force worked within the informal economy; 41 per cent lived in informal settlements; and 60 per cent had no health insurance other than the public health system.[43]

A considerable proportion of the urban poor in Latin America are refugees, fleeing wars and conflicts (including guerrillas and drug warfare), disasters and environmental degradation. Even if many of these situations are unrelated to climate events, they highlight who is most affected. These people move to urban areas, leaving behind homes, social networks, family ties and assets. It takes a long time to insert themselves into local communities and build ties and participate in community organizations that can push for changes and negotiate with government and utilities for neighbourhood improvements. Recent floods in the city of Tabasco in Mexico generated between 60,000 and 100,000 refugees, who moved to Playa del Carmen and Cancun in search of jobs and a place to live.[44] It is impossible to know where these people will ultimately settle; but none of these cities were prepared to absorb so many migrants. Cancun, for example, was transformed over a period of 30 years from a fishing town of 500 inhabitants to the biggest tourist centre in Mexico, with 458,477 inhabitants. The city has a wealthy hotel area on a sand barrier, which is totally at risk from storm surges and hurricanes but which has appropriate services and resources for protection and recovery. The proper city, where most of the people serving the hotels or tourist trade live, is also at risk from hurricanes; but many neighbourhoods are impoverished and marginal, lacking services and adequate housing.[45]

In Colombia, between 1995 and 2005, 3 million people were displaced, mostly by paramilitary and guerrilla activity. According to the Consultoría para los Derechos Humanos y el desplazamiento Forzado (CODHES), women, children, Afro-American and native communities have been the most affected. The majority of the displaced move to nearby small urban centres or to mid-sized or large capital cities; but they usually lack the education and job skills suitable for urban life, and labour markets cannot absorb so many. Unemployment and low salaries are common. On average, in 2005, a displaced family earned 40 per cent of the minimum salary – evidence of the vulnerability of the displaced (who lose their land, assets, social and cultural networks) and the disruption of families in the process. Along with social and political unrest, much of Colombia is prone to flooding, landslides, tropical storms, droughts and seismic activity. Many of the displaced, already socially and economically vulnerable, move into marginal city areas (prone to flooding and landslides, near waste dumps) and are even more vulnerable than existing low-income city dwellers.

Migrants also take measures to address their vulnerability. In the suburbs of Buenos Aires, migrants from Peru organize savings groups that are used, among other things, for housing and household appliances. These savings groups are based on trust between friends and family. Migrants who have moved abroad often send remittances home – and remittance flows are greatly increased if family members at home are hit by a disaster. These funds are an important economic support for recovery.

Who is least able to adapt in order to avoid impacts?
Although Latin America has an abundance of freshwater resources, many cities depend upon local rivers, underground water, lakes and glaciers that may be affected by climate change. Considering city growth, environmental deterioration and possible climate change impacts, these sources might not be enough to meet demand. Cities such as Guadalajara in Mexico[46] and many Andean cities may face increasing water stress, and low-income groups who still lack adequate access to water will be even less likely to obtain it unless there is strong political commitment.

Cities located in semi-arid regions are particularly vulnerable. Glacier shrinkage reduces the storage of large quantities of water that are later released to river networks during the dry season. Many cities in the Andes will face water shortages during the dry season as a result of glacier retreat over the last few decades. Examples include Ushuaia in Tierra del Fuego, which obtains water from the Martial glacier, and Mendoza and San Juan in the Cuyo region in Argentina, where 2 million people live distributed in eight oases. A study from the central Andes of Peru indicates that the largest city in the region, Huancayo, with approximately 325,000 inhabitants, is already experiencing water shortages. Retaining walls and small dams have been constructed on nearby lagoons; but now these interventions are being called into question as they may have contributed to water shortages, along with the increased demands that come with population growth, land-use changes and deforestation. The situation is likely to become more acute with climate change. Structural measures have not provided expected outcomes, as they have been implemented within a framework of institutional weakness, overlapping functions between offices, corruption, political opportunism, weakened democracy and no stakeholder participation.[47]

Quito is another city that will face water shortages as a result of glacier retreat. According to official studies, climate change is affecting mountain glaciers and water availability through a reduction in surface and underground water, the sedimentation of waterways, land-use modification, the emergence of conflicts around water use, and increases in water use due to increased temperatures (see below for a discussion of how the local government is preparing an adaptation plan).[48]

The flooding in Santa Fe is also relevant to the issue of who is least able to adapt to avoid impacts. In this city, knowledge about the risks and about what needs to be done does not result in needed actions. The director of a local foundation in Santa Fe noted after the floods that 'there have always been heavy rains in the city of Santa Fe'; he also noted that the contingency plan for flooding was only on paper and that no one really knew what they were supposed to do. There was no alert and evacuation system in place, although everybody knew that more than 100,000 *santafesinos* were at risk and experts from INA had anticipated the weather conditions. No studies have monitored the actions taken in Santa Fe after the 2003 floods; but it seems that structural measures were proposed (although not necessarily implemented) and public resources were used with political aims.[49] Civil society groups (including groups of evacuees) have been unable to press government to implement the needed programmes and actions for overall city improvement and risk reduction. Floods in 2007 once again exposed the lack of official action. Recently, the municipality and the United Nations Development Programme (UNDP) invited local organizations to the presentation of a programme for the reconstruction of the city. The main proposal is the relocation of those most affected by the floods and the construction of social housing (1500 units) on vacant land in four different areas of the city near transportation networks, with services and infrastructure. However, who participates, who is relocated and which house prototypes are used are all decided by the city authorities. Selection criteria will be based on a family's vulnerability. The way in which the programme is implemented will result in new neighbourhoods with families from different places who will probably lose family support and social networks.[50]

An ambitious plan to address flooding in Buenos Aires is under way with support from the World Bank, which includes the modelling of drainage systems, the design of infrastructure works (structural measures) and the development of city norms (non-structural measures) and procedures (management system). The plan is based on historical climate records, with a 50-year horizon, and has not taken into account climate change variables. The reason given is that there is insufficient information to allow this, although the study recognizes that the floods have worsened over recent decades.[51] Meanwhile, an internal report from the International Development Research Centre (IDRC) suggests that the population at risk from flooding on coastal and estuary lands of the La Plata River could be 1.7 million by 2070, three times the current figure. The property and infrastructure losses for 2050 to 2100 could range from US$5 billion to US$15 billion. Meanwhile, low-income neighbourhoods and upper middle-income gated communities continue to settle on low-lying lands.[52]

In most Latin American cities, upper middle- and high-income neighbourhoods also settle in risk areas near rivers or coastal areas or on slopes; but they have a choice and the assets (capital, contacts, power, etc.) to reinforce their house structures, get protective infrastructure, and lobby for policies and actions that protect their homes, neighbourhoods and possessions are also protected by insurance.

Possible ways forward

A large and diverse body of promising experiences demonstrates how community-based actions in low-income settlements (sometimes supported by international agencies, local and national NGOs, state or national government bodies and charities) can address the risks described above. Even though many of these experiences are in response to risks that do not originate from the impacts of global warming, they show how local governments, communities and other social actors can work in collaboration or independently to reduce risks from extreme weather and other likely impacts of climate change.

Regional or national networks and risk management programmes

Central America is within the hurricane belt and has a long history of trying to cope with the effects. In 1998, Hurricane Mitch affected more than 1.2 million people, and conservative estimates suggest US$8500 million worth of losses, more than the annual GDPs of Honduras and Nicaragua combined. This set development back for more than a decade. More recently, the unprecedented hurricane season of 2005 shows how climate change may increase the intensity and frequency of these natural events.

A range of programmes and networks has been set up in the region to better prepare for disasters. In 1993, Costa Rica, El Salvador, Guatemala, Honduras, Nicaragua and Panama created the Centro de Coordinación para la Prevención de los Desastres en America Latina (CEPREDENAC). This centre coordinates development cooperation, information exchange and advice – seeking to contribute to the improvement of decision-making in the region regarding risk prevention and mitigation. In each country, a commission or national system for risk management and disaster prevention was set up.

In 2000, the government of Nicaragua created the Sistema Nacional para la Prevención, Mitigación y Atención de Desastres (SNPMAD), which integrates different government levels, social actors and municipal and regional committees for risk prevention and mitigation, with a clear focus on risk management. Nicaragua is the second poorest country in the region and 60 per cent of its labour force earns less than the amount needed to cover basic needs. Economic and political crises add to international context, droughts, floods and hurricanes. Estimates of economic losses between 1978 and 2000 are around US$4 billion. The system aims to articulate with municipal committees the work at the local level, strengthening networks and horizontal relations. A national fund has also been created to support the work.[53]

After Hurricane Mitch, El Salvador developed an early warning system and prepared the communities for emergencies. At the same time, it created an office for risk management.[54]

The Andean region is also working on disaster preparedness; although this is not specifically related to climate change, it may improve the potential to share knowledge and capacities, allowing countries to adapt more easily to climate change. Capital cities in the region[55] are taking part in a project to strengthen local capacities for risk management. During the last three decades, the Andean region urbanized rapidly, with the urban population rising from 30 to 75 per cent. Most low-income settlements are located on steep slopes. The Proyecto Regional de Reducción de Riesgos en Capitales Andinas (RLA/51467) is funded by the UNDP and DIPECHO.[56] It aims to establish alliances between local mayors and produce information exchange, tools and local norms and regulations that include risk management within local development plans.[57]

In terms of risk management, particularly after Hurricane Mitch and, later, Stan, Central American countries have recognized that disaster management is not the exclusive concern of civil defence institutions or a single organization, but, rather, an integral part of policies and actions at different government levels, involving different sectors and offices.[58] However, these programmes and networks have usually been set up at the national level, without sufficient coordination and implementation at the local level and with weak links to key sectors and institutions such as housing and urban planning. The emergency aspects of disaster remain deeply rooted within the institutions of the region.[59] Risk reduction is not really being addressed and many governments and international aid organizations continue to favour structural measures over non-structural, even though they have shown their limitations.

City-level risk management programmes or implementation of some of its components

Some of the cities that are best prepared for disasters are those affected periodically by seismic movements and hurricanes. During recent years, they have made improvements to include risk management within their local development plans and have set up warning systems.

Several municipalities (*alcaldías*) that are part of the metropolitan district of Caracas are undertaking actions to reduce risk within a broader framework of habitat improvement. The municipality of Chacao has developed an early warning system that aims to monitor gorges and alert dwellers about potential landslides, thus reducing damage and loss of life. The municipality of Bolivariano Libertador, where the Anauco neighbourhood is located (one of the areas that was most affected by 1999 landslides), is implementing a project of social and physical rehabilitation and a community warning system. Another municipality, El Hatillo, is working on community capacity, building in risk protection and prevention.[60]

Some cities are addressing problems of freshwater resources. In the cities of Jauja and Concepción, the implementation of such non-structural measures as incentives for proper land use and water resource use, taking advantage of the knowledge of the population, have shown good results for the rational management of water resources and other environmental concerns that together reduce risk.[61]

The city of Manizales in Colombia is well known for its ambitious environmental improvement process, which includes Biomanizales (the city's environmental policy, operating since 1995 and integrated within the city's development plan) and the Bioplan (the city's action plan to facilitate policy implementation). Perhaps the main achievement is the programme's integration of local and regional government, the private sector, universities and representatives of community organizations in a participative process that seeks to reconcile different priorities and interests. The programme includes a pilot project, Biocomuna Olivares, which was selected because of the area's vulnerable physical and social conditions. One of the activities involved relocating families living on steep slopes and at risk of landslides and flooding. However, a report mentions funding-related difficulties.[62] Since the 1980s, the local government has implemented a municipal disaster prevention system in line with its environmental action, with risk management as an integral part of local policies. A system of community preparedness and education, institutional coordination and research are in place. In addition, tax reduction is given to those who implement measures to reduce housing vulnerability. A system of collective voluntary insurance has also been implemented for lower-income groups.[63]

In response to Hurricane Mitch's impacts, the municipalities of La Masica,[64] Arizona, Esparta, San Francisco and El Porvenir in Honduras founded an inter-municipal association, Mancomunidad de los Municipios del Centro de Atlántida (MAMUCA), to create a platform for dialogue and cooperation in preparation for extreme natural events and to coordinate local responses. There are around 80,000 inhabitants in the MAMUCA region, about 20,000 in each municipality. The process involved participatory diagnosis and planning (taking stock of disaster risk management capacities and identifying relevant actors), awareness-raising, prioritization of strategic reconstruction activities, participation in local decision-making through *cabildos abiertos* (public meetings of citizens) and involving MAMUCA in the national disaster risk management system, COPECO (Comisión Permanente de Contingencias). One of the main outcomes is a significant improvement in evacuation action during rainstorms through community-based disaster reduction practices, and the possibility of sustaining a system of local emergency committees, CODELs (Comité de Emergencia Local), integrated within municipal emergency committees, CODEMs (Comité de Emergencia Municipal), and within COPECO. The CODEM is chaired by the mayor and involves the participation of representatives of the local council and local institutions (healthcare, police, fire department, Red Cross, etc.).[65]

Community organizations

In response to the rains and floods affecting the city of Viacha in Bolivia and the lack of government support, neighbours organized themselves. Each affected area (13 *barrios*) elected two representatives, from which seven were elected with different responsibilities, creating the 'association of those who suffered losses' (Asociación de Damnificados de Viacha, or ADV). This organization coordinates actions with the local government for resource distribution, housing reconstruction and upgrading. However, the work with some of the neighbourhood associations proved difficult as they ended up being indifferent to neighbours' claims.[66]

Floods in 1992 affected seven provinces in northeast Argentina and 123,000 people had to be evacuated. The national government received an emergency loan from the World Bank. A rehabilitation programme involved beneficiaries building their own houses in six provinces and a related flood protection programme included structural and non-structural measures. After ten years, more than 10,000 units had been built with services, on sites safe from flooding and constructed by the same community members who had been affected by the floods. One of the main assets was the transparency with which beneficiaries were selected and the funds managed. Overall, the process led to improvements in relations between different government levels and between government and community; it helped to regularize urban areas and created a sense of ownership, and it integrated those displaced by floods within the urban fabric through a participatory process.[67]

In the Barrio Parque Paso del Rey in the municipality of Moreno, Argentina, a local community organization with a strong leader has organized a soup kitchen that acts as an evacuation centre during floods caused by intense rains. The centre is becoming more and more organized, staffed with beds, mattresses, food and clothing. Evacuees have learned to read local conditions and know when to move to the evacuation centre. The occupation of marshlands and lagoons, coupled with individual practices such as elevating plots or building small walls to keep water out, has increased general flood risk in the *barrio* in successive years. Other localities in Moreno, such as Mariló, also have evacuation places managed by the community and an informal system for keeping track of river and stream water levels. When the situation overwhelms community action, demands are made on local government for mattresses, zinc sheets for roof replacement, etc.[68]

There are many examples outside the risk management sphere that involve neighbourhood organizations and local NGOs negotiating for water and sanitation, land regularization and environmental improvement. These are examples of how communities can organize and achieve a common goal.

Adaptation to climate variability and change

México and Cuba are implementing a regional three-year pilot project on climate change adaptation that aims to set up strategies, policies and adaptation measures. It is being implemented by the Centro del Agua del Trópico Húmedo para América Latina y el Caribe (CATHALAC) and coordinated by the UNDP. This initiative aims to identify priorities at the local, regional and national level, evaluating vulnerability and adaptation options.

The government of the city of Quito is putting in place several measures to prepare for the impacts of climate change. The plan, promoted by the mayor and set within the framework of the 2005 to 2009 government plan, includes emission controls, the creation of a legal framework for pollution control, a plant for methane catchment and treatment on the city's landfill, and a metropolitan system for risk management implemented by an emergency operation committee. They are also aware of the need to analyse vulnerability and adaptation in the face of climate change and to develop the institutional capacities needed to conduct these actions. One area is climate change and water services. The government is planning actions and projects to compensate for less freshwater availability, such as the reduction of water losses along the network; creating a culture of rational use of the resource; infrastructure works (dams); use of underground water sources; and the development of mechanisms to reduce conflicts generated around water use.[69] Despite being one of the few cities in the region that is taking climate change seriously and proactively, none of the actions suggested seem to integrate community participation within planning and implementation or within an analysis of the root causes of vulnerability – who, historically, has and has not had access to water, whether they will be better off with new government plans, etc.

An initiative fostered by the Spanish government aims to set up a regional network – Red Iberoamericana de Oficinas de Cambio Climático (RIOCC) (Ibero-American Network for Climate Change Offices) – to generate links and information exchange among the Spanish-speaking Latin American countries. This is intended to support the development of responses to climate change problems and facilitate consensus on responses.[70]

Relations between stakeholders

Although important advances have been made, the relationships between local communities, government and the private sector still need to mature. Since the 1980s, with the return to democracy of many Latin American countries, the election of national, provincial and local governments came with a wave of decentralization and municipalization, although not necessarily accompanied by decentralization of resources, capacities and control mechanisms. Local governments have had to assume increasingly diversified responsibilities while being confronted with new urban residents (mostly poor) each year. For municipal authorities, relations with different levels of government have proved complicated and time consuming, especially if they come from different political parties. In most Latin American nations, local government budgets depend heavily upon national and provincial/state budgets and allocations.

Few would say that governments are truly representative. It is common for presidents to concentrate power and control of resource allocations and for there to be difficulties in keeping the executive, legislative and judicial bodies operating independently.[71] In Argentina, for example, the electoral system is based on lists prepared by political parties in rather closed internal meetings, and citizens vote for a list, not an individual.

Municipal authorities' relations with their constituencies have also been complicated. Many local governments, with a mix of arrogance and practicality, find it easier to maintain tight control over what takes place within their boundaries in case demand overwhelms them. Neighbourhood leaders affiliated to political parties play an important role in the local community. Many manage social programmes and networks operating in the territory, but rarely with any accountability to the residents, and they may coerce citizens for support. It is difficult to overcome the jealousy and mistrust that often accompany this lack of accountability and transparency.

Another problem is the difficulty in integrating information, resources and capacities between offices of the same government level and between different government levels. In most cities, it is very difficult to put articulated and integrated programmes into practice.

The need for adaptation and development

Adaptive capacity in Latin America is low.[72] A background paper on impacts, vulnerability and adaptation to climate change in Latin America notes the difficulties in ensuring that adaptation assessment and planning move on to the implementation of concrete actions.[73] In part, this is due to the lack of certainty regarding likely impacts, especially local impacts; in part, it is because of a lack of resources and institutional capacities to address multiple and combined stresses and processes. Other reasons are the slow rate at which national policies have included climate change variables[74] and the difficulties in tackling root problems when decision-makers lack the training and access to information[75] (at different scales) in the context of fiscal constraints and conflicts between different levels of government. The difficulties in assessing vulnerability and adaptation options are also important.

Most of the attention and funding by national governments relating to climate change has been dedicated to preparing the national communications required by the United Nations Framework Convention on Climate Change (UNFCCC) and developing climate change mitigation options, mostly associated with greenhouse gas inventories and emissions reduction programmes. These also complement the governments' international negotiation strategies.[76] Much less research and action has concentrated on urban adaptation and resilience.

The *Global Report: Reducing Disaster Risk*[77] notes that the lack of capacity within governments to manage risks associated with past and present climate variability may also mean a lack of capacity to deal with the direct impacts of climate change. Taking advantage of lessons learned from climate variability and applying them to climate change adaptation could also avoid duplication of efforts. In practice, governments still tend to concentrate on emergency response and recovery and have been slow to adopt an integrated disaster prevention and preparedness approach, which needs an understanding of vulnerability and risk accumulation processes and a capacity and willingness to work with those who are vulnerable. So much of what has been learned about disaster prevention and preparedness has direct relevance for climate change adaptation.

Risk management – whether or not related to climate change and variability – should be an integral part of development policies. Most of the risks associated with likely climate change in the next few decades are not new: they are already evident although becoming more intense or frequent.[78] It may also be the case, however, that climate change and urban development can act to trigger new hazards in the region.[79]

Although Latin America contributes only a small proportion of total anthropogenic greenhouse gas emissions (between 4 and 5 per cent), by 2050, the region's share may grow to 9 per cent of global emissions.[80] This suggests a need to include some consideration of mitigation even if much more attention needs to be given to adaptation.

Actions that integrate an understanding of the links between environmental problems (including climate change and variability) and development have the greatest potential to generate multiple benefits and provide the kind of measures most needed in Latin America. Most of the best adaptation options are those that would be taken even in the absence of climate change because of their contribution to risk reduction and sustainable development.[81] Although in recent years there has been a change in the discourse of academics, technicians and policy-makers on this, few practical cases exist of an integrated approach to risk reduction. The norm is that research and risk management and development planning follow parallel tracks. The way in which disaster management is implemented in Argentina is a clear example of the difficulty of translating discourse into action, even though the Second National Communication emphasizes the need to address multiple stresses together.[82]

Addressing the root causes of vulnerability to climate change is a challenge not many in government are willing to face: 'The political costs of redirecting priorities from visible development projects to addressing abstract long-term threats are great. It is hard to gain votes by pointing out that a disaster did not happen.'[83]

However, there is a promising body of diverse experiences that shows the ways in which local governments, communities and other social actors can work in collaboration or independently to achieve improvements at city or neighbourhood level. This body demonstrates that community-based actions in low-income settlements (sometimes supported by international agencies, local and national NGOs, state or national government bodies, and charities) have made great strides in recent years.[84] Funds can be channelled effectively and efficiently to relatively inexpensive community-based initiatives – using a wide variety of schemes, from small loans or grants to small groups, to upgrading schemes, the installation of water supply and sanitation projects and even to full community development projects, including plans to manage risk related to water resources and water basins at local and city level. The guiding principles should be that they foster long-term solutions that respond to local needs, that they tackle more than one goal at a time, and that measures are undertaken within a broad risk management programme tied into long-term development goals.

Notes

1. See Hardoy, J., Mitlin, D. and Satterthwaite, D. (2001) *Environmental Problems in an Urbanizing World*, Earthscan, London, 448pp.
2. McGranahan, G., Balk, D. and Anderson, B. (2007) 'Cambio climático y asentamientos humanos en zonas costeras de baja altitud en América Latina y el Caribe', *Medio Ambiente y Urbanización*, no 67, pp5–24, IIED–AL, Buenos Aires.
3. Canziani, O., Diaz, S., Calvo, E., Campos, M., Carcavallo, R., Cerri, C. C., Gay-García, C., Mata, L. J. and Saizar, A. (2000) *Impactos Regionales del Cambio Climático. Evaluaciones de la Vulnerabilidad. Capítulo 6: América Latina*, Informe Especial, Grupo Intergubernamental de Expertos sobre el Cambio Climático (IPCC) WMO, UNEP.
4. UN-Habitat (2003) *Water and Sanitation in the World's Cities: Local Action for Global Goals*, Earthscan, London, 320pp.
5. CEPAL (Comisión Económica para América Latina y el Caribe) (2007) *Panorama Social de América Latina 2007*, CEPAL, Santiago de Chile.
6. Secretaría de Medio Ambiente y Recursos Naturales, Programa de las Naciones Unidas para el Medio Ambiente (2006) *El Cambio Climático en América Latina y el Caribe*, PNUMA–SEMARNAT, Mexico City.

7. See Chapter 3.
8. See http://www.em-dat.net/.
9. Examples of the scale of this undercount can be seen in the records of DesInventar, which is a data collection system and methodology created in 1994 by Red de Estudios Sociales en Prevención de Desastres en América Latina (LA RED) – the Network of Social Studies in the Prevention of Disasters in Latin America. It keeps track of disasters of different scales and impacts in 17 countries in the region. Records come from the media, national databases, government organizations, etc.
10. Hardoy, J. (1995) 'Urban research in Latin America', in Stren, R. (ed) *Urban Research in the Developing World, Volume Three: Latin America*, Centre for Urban Community Studies, University of Toronto, in collaboration with El Colegio de Mexico, Mexico City, the Instituto Universitario de Pesquisas do Rio de Janeiro (IUPERJ) and the Centre for Social Studies in Education (SUR) Santiago de Chile, University of Toronto Press, pp19–41.
11. See reference 10: Hardoy, J. (1995), p35.
12. See reference 1.
13. See Chapter 6.
14. INDEC (Instituto Nacional de Estadísticas y Censos) (2001) *Censo Nacional de Población y Vivienda*, INDEC, Buenos Aires.
15. Natenzon, C. (2006) 'Inundaciones catastróficas, vulnerabilidad social y adaptación en un caso argentino actual. Cambio climático, elevación del nivel medio del mar y sus implicancias', Paper submitted to EMF Workshop IX: Climate Change Impact and Integrated Assessment, 28 July 28–7 August, Snowmass, Colorado.
16. CEPAL (2003), cited in Natenzon (2006): see reference 15.
17. Asociación Civil Canoa, http://www.canoa.org.ar/DDHH02.html.
18. Asociación Civil Canoa, http://www.canoa.org.ar/PrPe-Recons.html.
19. See *Atlas Ambiental de Buenos Aires*, www.atlasdebuenosaires.gov.ar; also Rebagliati, R. (2003) 'Plan director de ordenamiento hidráulico y proyecto ejecutivo para el arroyo Maldonado del gobierno de la ciudad de Buenos Aires', *Contactar, Ciudades Saludables*, no 11, www.revistacontactar.com.ar/plan_director_nro11.htm.
20. Herzer, H. and Clichevsky, N. (2001) 'Perspectiva histórica: Las inundaciones en Buenos Aires', in Kreimer, A. et al (eds) *Inundaciones en el Area Metropolitana de Buenos Aires*, World Bank, Washington, DC; also see reference 4.
21. See reference 19: Rebagliati (2003).
22. See Re, M. and Menéndez, A. (2007) 'Impacto del cambio climático en las costas del río de la Plata', in *Revista Internacional de Desastres Naturales, Accidentes e Infraestructura Civil*, vol 7, no 1, April, Universidad de Puerto Rico, Recinto Universitario de Mayagüez, Puerto Rico, www.uprm.edu/civil/revistadesastres/vol7Num1/2%20Re%20y%20Menendez.pdf; also Frers, C. (2007) 'El cambio climático global y su influencia sobre la República Argentina. Impacto del cambio climático en la ciudad de Buenos Aires', www.internatura.org/estudios/informes/el_cambio_climatico.html; and Czubaj, F. (2007) 'Conclusiones del panel intergubernamental de las Naciones Unidas. Expertos advierten sobre los efectos del cambio climatico en la Argentina', *La Nación*, Sección Ciencia y Salud, 11 April, p16.
23. Zeballos Moreno, O. (1996) 'Ocupación de laderas: Incremento del riesgo por degradación ambiental urbana en Quito, Ecuador', in Fernández, M. A. (ed)

Ciudades en Riesgo, Degradación Ambiental, Riesgos Urbanos y Desastres en América Latina, LA RED, Lima; also UN-Habitat (2003) *Water and Sanitation in the World Cities: Local Action for Global Goals*, Earthscan Publications, London, p154.

24. Cilento Sarli, A. (2007) 'La vulnerabilidad urbana de Caracas', http://168.96.200 .17/ar/libros/venezuela/rvecs/3.2002/sarli.doc.

25. See reference 24.

26. Mata, J. L. and Nobre, C. (2006) 'Impacts, vulnerability and adaptation to climate change in Latin America', Background Paper presented at Regional Workshop on Latin American Adaptation, UNFCCC, 18–20 April, Lima, Peru.

27. See reference 4: UN-Habitat (2003), p149.

28. Jiménez, V. (2006) *Taller Vivencial de Intercambio de Experiencias Municipales en Reducción de Riesgos*, Report within the framework of Proyecto RLA/51467 Fortalecimiento Regional y Reducción de Riesgos en Ciudades Mayores de la Comunidad Andina, 9–12 November, Caracas, Venezuela.

29. 'Rehabilitación urbana en Viacha, La Paz, Bolivia', www.hic-net.org/document .asp?PID=238, accessed 4 December 2007.

30. UNDP–DIPECHO (2007) *Proyecto Regional de Reducción de Riesgos en Capitales Andinas. Documento Pais: Bolivia*, Mimeo, Brussels.

31. Mejia, F. Y. (2000) 'Construyendo una ciudad mas saludable y sostenible ambientalmente. Estrategia municipal para la superación de condiciones de vulnerabilidad del distrito central, capital de Honduras', Seminar on El Impacto de los Desastres Naturales en Areas Urbanas y en la Salud Publica Urbana en Centro America y el Caribe, ASIES, Guatemala.

32. Segunda Comunicación Nacional de la República Argentina a la Conferencia de la Partes de la Convención Marco de las Naciones Unidas sobre el Cambio Climático (CMNUCC) (2007) Secretaría de Medio Ambiente y Desarrollo Sustentable, Jefatura de Gabinete, Buenos Aires.

33. Valente, M. (2007) 'Cambio climático. Inundación Santa Fe: Aguas violentas, desidia humana', Buenos Aires, 2 April, (IPS) www.proteger.org.ar/doc621.html.

34. See reference 15.

35. Herzer, H. et al (2001) 'Grandes inundaciones en la ciudad de Pergamino: Eextraordinarias, pero recurrentes, análisis de un proceso de vulnerabilidad progresiva', *Realidad Económica*, no 175, pp92–116.

36. 'Noticias de Latinoamérica', *Boletín de Agua y Saneamiento*, no 20, July 2007.

37. See reference 4.

38. Wamsler, C. (2007) 'Bridging the gaps: Stakeholder-based strategies for risk reduction and financing for the urban poor', *Environment and Urbanization*, vol 19, no 1, April, pp115–142.

39. See Simms, A. and Reid, H. (2006) *Up in Smoke? Latin America and the Caribbean. The Threat from Climate Change to the Environment and Human Development*, Third report from the Working Group on Climate Change and Development, New Economic Foundation, p15.

40. See reference 13.

41. Bartlett, S. (2008) *Climate Change and Urban Children: Implications for Adaptation in Low- and Middle-Income Countries*, Human Settlements Discussion Paper Series, Climate Change and Cities 2, IIED, London.

42. See reference 26.
43. CEPAL (2003), cited in Natenzon (2006): see reference 15.
44. See http://www.migrantesenlinea.org/enlinea.php?c=1689.
45. Domínguez Aguilar, M. and García de Fuentes, A. (2007) 'Barriers to achieving the water and sanitation-related Millennium Development Goals in Cancún, Mexico, at the beginning of the twenty-first century', *Environment and Urbanization*, vol 19, no 1, April, pp243–260.
46. See Von Bertrab, E. and Wester, P. (2005) 'Gobernabilidad del agua en Méjico: La crisis de agua en Guadalajara y el destino del lago Chapala', *Medio Ambiente y Urbanización*, vol 21, no 62/63, pp143–160, IIED–AL, Buenos Aires.
47. Martinez, A. et al (2006) 'Vulnerability and adaptation to climate change in central Peruvian Andes cities: Report of a pilot study', in *Proceedings of the 8th International Conference on Southern Hemisphere Meteorology and Oceanography*, 24–28 April, Foz de Iguaçu, Brazil.
48. Neira Carrasco, J. A. (2007) 'Medidas asumidas por el municipio del distrito de Quito para afrontar los efectos del cambio climático', www.comunidadandina .org/desarrollo/cl_JuanNeira.pdf.
49. See reference 15.
50. See reference 17.
51. See reference 19: Rebagliati (2003).
52. Burone, F. (2007) *Vulnerable Communities Worldwide: Adaptation to Climate Change*, United Nations Climate Change Conference, 3–14 December, Nusa Dua, Bali, Indonesia.
53. Zilbert Soto, L. (2001) 'Material de apoyo para la capacitación en gestión local del riesgo', in *Formación de Recursos Humanos para la Integración de Sistemas Nacionales de Prevención, Mitigación y Atención de Desastres*, Implemented by Secretaría Ejecutiva del Sistema Nacional (SE–SNPMAD) and UNDP–Nicaragua with funds from Oficina para Ayuda Humanitaria de la Agencia Suiza para el Desarrollo y Cooperación (COSUDE) LA RED.
54. Lopez, A. D. (2004) 'Sistema de alerta temprana por inundaciones: Experiencia en El Salvador', hispagua.cedex.es/documentacion/documentos/cong_valencia2004/ PRESENTACIONES/SAT%20El%20Salvador.PDF.
55. La Paz, Lima, Quito, Caracas and Bogotá.
56. DIPECHO stands for Disaster Preparedness–ECHO, where ECHO is the European Commission's Humanitarian Aid Department.
57. See http://content.undp.org/go/newsroom/2007/june/pnud-comprometido-con-la-reduccin-de-riesgos-en-la-regin.es?lang=es.
58. Gavidia, J. (2006) 'Priority goals in Central America. The development of sustainable mechanisms for participation in local risk management', *Milenio Ambiental*, no 4, pp56–59, Journal of the Urban Environment Programme (UPE) of the International Development Research Centre (IDRC) Montevideo.
59. See reference 58.
60. See reference 28.
61. See reference 47.
62. Marulanda, L. M. (2000) 'El Biomanizales: política ambiental local. Documentación de la experiencia de gestión ambiental urbana de Manizales, Colombia', Instituto de

Estudios de Vivienda y Desarrollo Urbano (IHS) Dentro del Marco de Implementación del Proyecto Apoyo para la Implementación de Planes Nacionales de Acción del Habitat II (SINPA) Mimeo; also Velasquez, L. S. (1998) 'Agenda 21: A form of joint environmental management in Manizales, Colombia', *Environment and Urbanization*, vol 10, no 2, October, pp9–36.

63. UNDP (United Nations Development Programme) (2004) *Global Report: Reducing Disaster Risk – A Challenge for Development*, UNDP, Bureau for Crisis Prevention and Recovery, New York.

64. Even prior to Hurricane Mitch, la Masica had an early warning system in place that helped to save lives during the hurricane. See Lavell, A. (2000) 'Desastres urbanos: Una vision global', Seminar on El Impacto de los Desastres Naturales en Areas Urbanas y en la Salud Publica Urbana en Centro America y el Caribe, ASIES, Guatemala.

65. Bollin, C. and Mascher, F. (2005) 'Honduras: Community-based disaster risk management and inter-municipal cooperation', a review of experience gathered by the special inter-municipal association MAMUCA, GTZ., Eschborn.

66. See reference 29.

67. Programa de Protección contra las Inundaciones (PPI) Subprograma de Vivienda por Autoconstrucción, Esfuerzo Propio y Ayuda Mutua (2003) 'La experiencia en el programa de protección contra inundaciones', Ministerio de Planificación Federal, Inversión Pública y Servicios, IIED–AL, Buenos Aires.

68. Hardoy, J. and Pandiella, G. (2008) 'Consulta sobre los efectos del cambio climático en comunidades vulnerables. El caso del municipio de Moreno', Pcia. de Buenos Aires, Argentina, Prepared for Consulta Regional para Evaluar las Prioridades Regionales, Capacidades y Vacíos de Investigación en Cambio Climático y Reducción de la Pobreza en América Latina y el Caribe, Consulta Subregión Cono Sur, IDRC and DFID.

69. See reference 48.

70. See reference 26.

71. This is drawn from comments by Hermes Binner, governor of the province of Santa Fe, in *La Nacion*, 26 June 2008, p6, political section.

72. Magrin, G. and García, C. G. with Cruz Choque, D., Carlos Jiménez, J., Moreno, A. R., Nagy, G. J., Nobre, C. and Villamizar, A. (2007) 'Latin America', in Parry, M., Canziani, O., Palutikof, J., van der Linden, P. and Hanson, C. (eds) *Climate Change 2007: Impacts, Adaptation and Vulnerability*, Contribution of Working Group II to the Fourth Assessment Report of the Intergovernmental Panel on Climate Change, Cambridge University Press, Cambridge and New York, Chapter 13.

73. See reference 26.

74. See reference 1.

75. See reference 4.

76. See reference 26.

77. See reference 63.

78. Satterthwaite, D., Huq, S., Reid, H., Pelling, M. and Romero Lankao, P. (2007) *Adapting to Climate Change in Urban Areas: The Possibilities and Constraints in Low- and Middle-Income Nations*, Human Settlements Discussion Paper Series, Climate Change and Cities 1, IIED, London.

79. See reference 32.

80. See reference 39; see also references 26 and 3.
81. See reference 1.
82. See reference 32.
83. Christoplos, I., Mitchell, J. and Liljelund, A. (2001) 'Re-framing risk: The changing context of disaster mitigation and preparedness', *Disasters*, vol 25, no 3, pp185–198, http://dx.doi.org/10.1111/1467-7717.00171.
84. See reference 10.

3

CASE STUDIES ON ADAPTATION

11

Thinking Globally, Acting Locally: Institutionalizing Climate Change at the Local Government Level in Durban, South Africa[1]

Debra Roberts

Introduction

Durban is the largest port and city on the east coast of Africa with a total municipal area of 2300km² (see Figure 11.1). With a population of 3.5 million people and a budget of 23.4 billion South African rand,[2] it is one of South Africa's most important urban and economic centres. The local government structure responsible for managing the city is known as eThekwini Municipality and this municipality has become a leader in the field of local level environmental management.

Prior to the 1994 democratic transition in South Africa, environmental management at the local government level received very limited attention. After 1994, however, new local government structures began to emerge in response to the changing policy and legislative environment. Among these were structures with a specific environmental management mandate and focus. The process of democratization also resulted in a significantly revised development agenda. This was an agenda aimed at righting the wrongs of the country's apartheid past and ensuring that the basic needs (i.e. jobs, housing, education, etc.) of all South Africans, not just those of a select minority, were met in an equitable and just manner. Local government was, and is seen, as a critical player in meeting this objective given its direct interface with local communities and its pivotal role in service provision.

In many ways, this simultaneous elevation and revision of both the environmental and development agendas has created a significant dilemma for local government. This has manifested itself in a growing tension between the need to introduce environmental issues and concerns into planning and decision-making processes (often for the first time) and the need to expedite development to address significant socio-economic needs. This tension was exacerbated by the fact that environmental concerns are regarded as being of less significance than development priorities in South Africa. For these reasons, the emerging environmental management agendas of cities such as Durban were initially

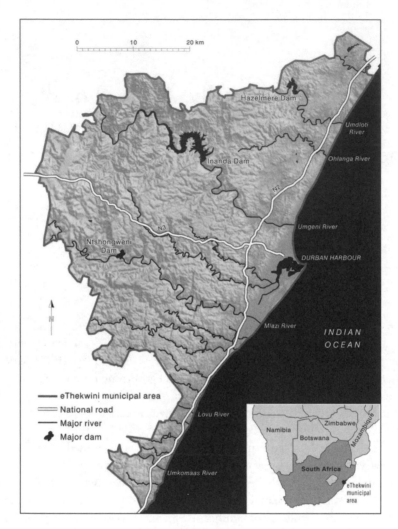

Figure 11.1 Location of the eThekwini municipal area

Source: Environmental Management Department, eThekwini Municipality

focused on issues that were relevant and related to local development pressures (such as addressing air pollution in strategic economic development nodes). Environmental matters that were of less immediate concern (i.e. that could not be related directly to the development agenda of the day) or that were of less local and political significance (such as biodiversity) tended to take a back seat during this transition period.

In Durban, this tension between the environmental and development agendas has never effectively resolved itself. It many ways, it has intensified due to the growing (rather than declining) range of development challenges facing the city. For example, Durban currently experiences:

- 43 per cent unemployment;[3]
- a housing backlog of 190,000 housing units;[4] and
- high levels of HIV/AIDS infection (e.g. one third of pregnant women attending public antenatal clinics are HIV positive).

There is also a growing (rather than declining) range of environmental challenges faced by the city. For example, Durban:

- is located in a global biodiversity hotspot that is being negatively affected by urban growth;
- has a manufacturing base that has caused significant environmental health challenges in local communities; and
- has seen the negative impact of rapid development on riverine and coastal ecosystems.

These challenges are both immediate and severe, and it is hardly surprising that climate change (an issue that appears more remote and global in nature) has remained – until relatively recently – a low priority on the municipality's agenda. In order to understand how the issue of climate change has become embedded in the local government dialectic in Durban, it is necessary to understand how the environmental management function of the city has evolved since 1994.

Climate change and the environmental management function

The environmental management function[5] was first established in eThekwini Municipality[6] in 1994. Although the staff servicing this function were aware of the climate change debate, the significant post-apartheid development challenges faced by the city meant that several years were to pass before climate change emerged as a significant issue on the municipality's environmental agenda.

The first serious discussions relating to climate change took place as part of the forward planning of the (then) Environmental Branch. In 1999, this led to the branch investigating the feasibility of establishing a climate protection programme. The lack of resources (human and financial) and technical skills and the need to deal with other 'higher priority' development matters, however, meant that the concept was temporarily shelved after initial investigation.

Renewed impetus was given to the idea as the result of a bilateral grant agreement signed between the national Department of Environmental Affairs and Tourism (DEAT) and the US Agency for International Development (USAID). This agreement focused on the implementation of a South African programme to address global climate change. One component of the programme aimed to engage a group of South African cities in actions that would address both their own urban service priorities and those of the global climate change agenda. The vehicle for achieving this goal was participation in the International Council for Local Environmental Initiatives' (ICLEI[7]) international Cities for Climate Protection campaign (CCP).

As part of the CCP campaign, the participating South African cities were required to commit themselves to five performance milestones:

1   conduct an energy and emissions inventory and forecast;
2   establish an emissions target;
3   develop and obtain approval for a local action plan;
4   implement policies and measures; and
5   monitor and verify results.

In 2000, the Environmental Branch received approval from eThekwini Municipality's executive committee to proceed with the project. The USAID-funded CCP campaign in South Africa effectively ended in 2006. The following outputs were achieved in Durban during the 2000 to 2006 period:

- The development of the municipality's first greenhouse gas emissions inventory. This recorded emissions that could be attributed to local government activities only and provided the catalyst for regular greenhouse gas emissions reporting within the municipality following the completion of the CCP campaign.[8]
- Based on the findings of the first greenhouse gas emissions inventory, a buildings energy efficiency pilot project was initiated. During the course of this project, the energy usage in two municipal buildings was audited. The findings of the audit indicated that the implementation of low-cost and no-cost energy saving interventions could result in annual savings in excess of 15 per cent of the combined energy usage in the buildings. The collective payback of the low-cost and no-cost options would be less than five months and the annual carbon dioxide (CO_2) savings would be approximately 340 tonnes. As a result, the timer controls on the air-conditioning plants in both buildings were trimmed. It is anticipated that this will yield a total annual CO_2 saving of 128 tonnes and an estimated financial saving of 53,400 rand per annum.
- Using the pilot project as a platform, nine additional municipal buildings were audited. During this roll-out phase, a number of energy efficiency opportunities were identified in the City Engineer's building. Two of the low-cost and no-cost interventions were subsequently implemented:
  - installation of timers on the fan-coil unit power supplies to eliminate out-of-hours usage of the air-conditioning plant; it was anticipated that this would yield a cost saving of 121,000 rand per annum and a CO_2 saving of more than 300 tonnes per annum; and
  - initiation of an energy efficiency awareness pilot project.

The need to build institutional understanding

Despite the municipality's involvement in ICLEI's CCP campaign, and the resultant mitigation spin-offs in terms of the buildings energy efficiency project, very little internal institutional momentum and knowledge was built around the issue of climate change *per se*. This was the result, in part, of the fact that the CCP campaign in South Africa did not offer the participating municipalities any in-depth opportunities to develop an understanding of climate change science and its local relevance. Subsequent experience in Durban has shown that without developing a meaningful understanding of the science, it is unlikely that climate change and its significance will be understood effectively at the local government level.

The implementation projects undertaken in Durban (i.e. the development of the greenhouse gas inventory and the buildings energy efficiency project) did not help to advance this understanding either. Involvement of municipal staff in the projects focused primarily on the delivery of the projects in terms of meeting funding and other administrative deadlines. In addition, the highly technical nature of the greenhouse gas inventory and the buildings energy efficiency project meant that the work was undertaken primarily by consultants hired to assist the Environmental Branch.[9] In reality, work was being overseen by municipal staff with very little real understanding of why this action was required in the first place. This situation was aggravated by the fact that, due to high workloads, staff involved in the CCP campaign did not have time to develop this understanding independently.

The net result was that even after the completion of the CCP campaign, the understanding of climate change among local government staff in Durban had not advanced significantly. An interesting observation is that this did not prevent further roll-out of climate change-related work by the (now) Environmental Management Department.

As part of the evaluation of the buildings energy efficiency project, the lead consultant recommended that in order to develop and enhance energy efficiency interventions throughout municipal operations, the development of a municipal energy strategy was a critical next step. On the basis of this recommendation, funding for the development of an energy strategy was sourced via the Danish International Development Assistance's (DANIDA) Urban Environmental Management Programme, initiated in South Africa in 2005. Given the focus of the project and the associated funding timelines, the development of the energy strategy has followed the same critical path as the buildings energy efficiency project (i.e. one whereby the municipal team has been guided technically by the lead consultant, with little meaningful opportunity to develop a more detailed understanding of the relationship between climate change and energy management).

Running in parallel, but not directly related to the CCP campaign, was the development of the municipality's first Clean Development Mechanism (CDM) project (initiated in 2002). This involved the establishment of landfill gas-to-electricity installations at three of the city's landfill sites (see Figure 11.2). Although the CDM project was initiated independently of the CCP campaign, given its significance in terms of mitigation impacts,[10] it was cited as an implementation measure in meeting the CCP campaign performance milestones.

The project manager of the CDM project was both vocal and passionate about establishing the link between climate change and the project. He invested a significant amount of time in understanding the science of climate change and presented this information as an introduction to the CDM project. He repeatedly emphasized that while the project was of financial benefit to the city, the real benefit lay in the reduction of greenhouse gases and the ability to reduce climate change. The impact of this outreach within the municipal structures was, however, limited due to the highly technical and specialized nature of the project, which meant that only a relatively small group of city officials was involved in project development and management. Nevertheless, the project was still significant in that it engaged a number of the city's lead decision-makers in the climate change debate for the first time.

Figure 11.2 Landfill gas-to-electricity installation

Source: Durban Cleansing and Solid Waste Department, eThekwini Municipality

Mainstreaming the climate change debate in Durban

From a local government perspective, the extent to which an issue such as climate change becomes successfully institutionalized in day-to-day operations, planning and decision-making can be evaluated by using institutional markers similar to the ones outlined below:

- the emergence of an identifiable political/administrative champion(s) for climate change issues;
- the appearance of climate change as a significant issue in mainstream municipal plans;
- the allocation of dedicated resources (human and financial) to climate change issues; and
- the incorporation of climate change considerations into political and administrative decision-making.

The following is a discussion of the extent to which these markers have been achieved in eThekwini Municipality.

Institutional marker 1: The emergence of an identifiable political/ administrative champion(s) for climate change issues

A key contribution to the mainstreaming of climate change within eThekwini Municipality occurred as a result of the participation of the head of the Environmental Management Department in an advanced semester-long environmental management programme at Brown University in Rhode Island (US) in 2004. The course is designed for professionals in leadership positions in the global South and provided the opportunity for an in-depth engagement with the science of climate change. This new understanding was to prove a critical factor in the subsequent initiation and development of the Municipal Climate Protection Programme (MCPP) and underscored the importance of capacity-building at the local government level in institutionalizing complex environmental issues such as climate change.

The information and understanding developed as a result of participating in this course has been shared subsequently with other stakeholders in Durban through a still ongoing series of seminars and presentations. In informal discussions with a researcher at the Council for Scientific and Industrial Research[11] at one of the early feedback sessions in 2004, questions were raised about what would be required to effectively mainstream the concept of climate change within local government's planning and decision-making processes. It was concluded that the biggest challenge was that the climate change debate was ostensibly a global debate, focusing on global level impacts, and that very little work had been done on determining and communicating an equivalent understanding of local-level impacts.

Given the significant development pressures that exist at the local level, particularly in cities of the global South, local government planners and decision-makers in many cases do not have the luxury of being concerned about global change. Realpolitick indicates that they are much more likely to be concerned about the local impacts of that change, particularly where those impacts affect or exacerbate local development needs and pressures. Therefore, key to any attempt to embed the climate change issue at the local government level is the ability to answer the question: 'What does it mean for my city, town or village?'

In Durban, the need to answer this question resulted in the Environmental Management Department initiating the MCPP. The development of this programme has been undertaken in a phased manner.

Phase 1: Climatic Future for Durban project. This initial phase of the programme saw a partnership established between the municipality and the Council for Scientific and Industrial Research, and the initiation of the Climatic Future for Durban project. This project focused on a review of global and regional climate change science and data sets and the translation of these into an understanding of the local-level impacts that would affect Durban. According to the findings of this work:

> *Local trends indicate that maximum and minimum temperatures are increasing, suggesting that Durban is getting warmer. It is predicted that for the period 2070 to 2100, Durban will experience an increase in the number of hot days with temperatures exceeding 30°C.*
>
> *Durban's rainfall patterns are also likely to be affected. Although it is likely that rainfall will increase slightly, the distribution of that rainfall will change, with longer periods of no rainfall and shorter periods of intense rainfall. These changes in temperature and rainfall may lead to numerous impacts on water availability, agricultural productivity and food security.*
>
> *Based on the analysis of Global Sea Level Observing System (GLOSS) data, results indicate that a number of economic and tourist areas may be affected by sea-level rise. Infrastructure, together with coastal vegetation, will be damaged. Damage can be expected from extreme events such as flooding, which may cause the high tide level to increase, thus resulting in potential impacts to infrastructure, increased flooding and coastal erosion and ultimately placing a significant portion of the population at risk.*
>
> *Climate change impacts are likely to increase the magnitude of existing problems linked to water availability, food security and health issues. Water availability in the Mgeni river catchment is predicted to decrease by 157.8 million cubic metres ... for the period 2070–2100. This will lead to a reduction in the water available for human and industrial consumption in Durban. It is also possible that migration of*

people from other dryer areas in the country will increase, placing a greater burden on already stressed resources. Agricultural production in Durban is also likely to be affected, particularly in subsistence farming areas where production yields are likely to decrease due to changes in rainfall and temperature.

Temperature increases may also cause the spread of malaria to previously unaffected areas in Durban. Infrastructure damage is likely to increase along the coast due to a higher mean sea level and an increase in extreme weather events (including sea storms). Major economic and tourist areas are likely to be negatively affected.[12]

Phase 2: Headline Climate Change Adaptation Strategy project. Once the range and extent of the local impacts of climate change were better understood, it became clear that climate change adaptation, rather than mitigation, was likely to be the immediate priority in the further development of the MCPP. This focus was confirmed at the presentation of the phase 1 work to the Economic Development and Planning Committee of the municipal council, where it became clear that political interest lay in reducing the impact of climate change upon the city rather than in reducing greenhouse gas emissions. As a result, phase 2 of the MCPP focused on the development of a 'headline adaptation strategy' for key municipal sectors. This is at odds with the mitigation focus of the majority of climate change funding streams available to local government.

The headline adaptation strategy made clear the relevance of climate change issues for virtually all departments and agencies within the municipality and listed the impacts of climate change upon key sectors such as infrastructure, human health, food security and agriculture, water, tourism/business, and biodiversity and the coastal zone. The strategy also outlined the kind of adaptation actions that might be appropriate in these sectors. The headline adaptation strategy is currently being used as the basis for the development of a more detailed Municipal Adaptation Plan (MAP) in two high-risk sectors (i.e. water and health). The key findings of the headline adaptation strategy are summarized below.

Human health. Some impacts in this sector are direct (e.g. heat waves and extreme weather disasters), while others arise through disturbances to ecological processes (e.g. the distribution of infectious diseases, freshwater supplies and food availability). Certain groups (e.g. the elderly, children and low-income and immuno-compromised individuals) are more vulnerable to these impacts than others. The municipality would thus have to respond to greater risks of heat-related deaths and illnesses, extreme weather (e.g. the vulnerability of sewage networks and of informal settlements to flooding), potentially reduced air quality and impacts of changes in precipitation, temperature, humidity and salinity upon water quality (e.g. an increase in diarrhoeal disease) and vector-borne diseases. There is a need for public education, to develop community response programmes, to ensure continued electricity supplies in all conditions, to promote the provision of more shade and increased water efficiency, to develop an extreme climate public early warning system, and to undertake research that improves the understanding of the link between health and climate change in Durban.

Water and sanitation. Durban already faces constraints on water supplies, with water resources under threat at present both in terms of quantity and quality. Climate variability affects water resources through periodic droughts, resulting in short-term water shortages at the local level. In addition, changes in rainfall distribution and increased temperatures will also reduce the capability of existing infrastructure (e.g. reservoirs) to store sufficient water. Management techniques, particularly those of integrated water resource management, can be applied to adapt to the hydrologic impacts of climate change, lessening vulnerabilities. Adaptive responses include both supply-side (i.e. changes in water supply) and demand-side (e.g. differential pricing, public awareness campaigns and statutory requirements) approaches. The municipality is already implementing some adaptation options to reduce the volume of freshwater needed (e.g. recycling sewage to potable standards).

Arguably for Durban, adaptation to changes in water availability is the most important adaptation measure. There is a need to evaluate the capacity of infrastructure to supply water within an uncertain climatic future so that it can cope with variable rainfall and increased flows during flooding events, as well as a need to understand future demands. Adaptation measures that require further investigation include increasing the water-absorbing capacity of the urban landscape; improving the urban drainage system; increasing the height of natural shoreline stabilization measures; utilizing storm water retention/ detention ponds and constructed wetlands; and adjusting storm sewer design and land-use planning and zoning to avoid locating structures/buildings in high risk areas.

Coastal zone. Coastal environments, settlements and infrastructure are exposed to a range of marine and land-based hazards such as storms, associated waves and storm surges, river flooding, shoreline erosion and an influx of biohazards (e.g. algal blooms). It is possible that these existing impacts will intensify under climate change. This is of particular concern in Durban given the city's naturally erosive coastline (see Figure 11.3). The municipality is investing heavily in developing the city's coastline for tourism, with key developments planned for the next 10 to 20 years. Increases in sea level could affect these developments if they are not taken into account properly. A series of extreme weather events in 2007 has already provoked discussions regarding the need to manage the strategic retreat of some existing coastal infrastructure from vulnerable areas.

Possible impacts of climate change upon Durban's coastline, particularly with regard to sea-level rise, have already been incorporated within the municipality's

Figure 11.3 Erosion of Durban's coastal zone

Source: Environmental Management Department, eThekwini Municipality, 2006

work over the last two decades and this is expected to continue. Mapping of 1:50 and 1:100 flood lines[13] for 90 per cent of rivers has been completed, with an associated programme to inform citizens. New developments need storm water management plans to ensure that excess runoff is contained on site. Development setback lines and potential erosion lines have been identified that incorporate 1:50 sea storms and a 50-year sea-level rise prediction. There is a need to map the 1:50 flood lines that have changed as a result of climate change. This will show sites at risk and can be used to develop plans to manage flood risks, identify the most vulnerable communities and avoid future developments in flood-prone areas.

Initial modelling of the local impacts of two Intergovernmental Panel on Climate Change (IPCC) scenarios of ~0.5m and ~0.9m sea-level rise, respectively, over the next 100 years resulted in predictions of probable maximum seawater levels of about 2.4m and 2.8m mean sea level along Durban's coastline. While the accuracy of these figures needs to be refined, they do suggest that low-lying areas such as the South Durban Basin (the manufacturing centre and economic heartland of the city) and the central business district could be negatively affected by sea-level rise in the future (see Figure 11.4).

Figure 11.4 Impact of sea-level rise on the South Durban Basin

Source: adapted from Environmental Management Department, eThekwini Municipality

Biodiversity. There is an urgent need to understand how local biodiversity will be affected by climate change and how these impacts could be managed and mitigated. Increased temperatures and the effect on water resources, water temperatures and river flows could have adverse effects on biodiversity through, for instance, increased evaporation from water bodies, loss of important habitats and changes in species' migratory patterns. Challenges faced by wetlands, such as development pressures, drainage and groundwater abstraction, could be exacerbated by changes in precipitation and its implications for water availability. The first step is to develop better data on the likely impacts upon biodiversity of the many effects of climate change.

Key infrastructure at risk. Built systems need to be able to endure greater exposure to extreme weather events, including extreme precipitation and windstorms. Infrastructure design is generally based on past climatic conditions; but these are no longer accurate indicators for planning, maintenance and upgrades. New guidelines are needed for municipal infrastructure in order to ensure safety and quality of life and to reduce long-term costs.

Electricity supplies. Gradual climate change does not pose a threat to electricity generation or supply for the municipality; but difficulties are likely in response to extreme events. There is a need to identify measures that ensure the availability of electricity in all conditions, especially in extreme climate situations. This is a sector where mitigation is an urgent need.

Transport. It may be necessary to revise road construction standards and avoid routes at high risk of flooding. There are also measures available to reduce emissions in the transport sector.

Food security and agriculture. Support is needed for local agriculture and attention should be given to the impacts of climate change upon commercial agriculture. Preliminary research undertaken during phase 3 of the MCPP suggests that 50 per cent of the food consumed by the rural poor is produced locally. Adaptation within this sector is therefore critical if food security is to be ensured in the future.

Disaster risk reduction. Durban has disaster management strategies; but these have largely focused on technological disasters (the city is an important industrial centre, including a nationally significant petrochemical sector) and natural disasters such as flooding. These strategies do not engage proactively with planning for extreme weather events or with developing the citywide health emergency plans required in response to climate change. There is also a need to shift from being responsive to disasters towards being proactive in minimizing hazard, reducing exposure and susceptibility, and enhancing coping and adaptive capacity. There is a need for more attention to be given to enhancing early warning systems, building more resistance into construction and infrastructure, and relocating people and infrastructure away from high-risk areas, as well as planning new development for less vulnerable areas.

Cross-sectoral municipal activities. There is a need to build awareness, encourage policy changes and develop strong public education and outreach. There should be support for local research and institutional capacity and for community-based adaptation.

Phase 3: Urban Integrated Assessment Framework. The outcomes of phases 1 and 2 of the MCPP highlighted the urgent need to incorporate climate change considerations within the municipality's various planning processes. The focus of phase 3 of the MCPP is therefore on the development of an urban integrated assessment framework – that is, a computer-based model that will facilitate the simulation, evaluation and comparison of strategic development plans and policies in the context of climate change.

Such an integrated assessment framework will provide strategic input into the ongoing development of the city's integrated development plan (IDP),[14] allowing the municipality to factor climate change considerations into its long-term planning and budgeting and to develop appropriate responses in terms of adaptation and mitigation plans. Because of the pioneering nature of the work being undertaken, the eThekwini municipal team has established research collaboration with the Tyndall Climate Change Research Centre in the UK. The Tyndall team is working independently on the development of a similar model for the City of London. This collaboration provides valuable opportunities for peer review for both teams even though the priority sectors being modelled are different due to the differing development contexts of the two pilot cities. Involvement in the project is also helping to build further the capacity of staff within the Environmental Management Department in the areas of climate change science and climate change impact assessment.

Institutional marker 2: The appearance of climate change as a significant issue in mainstream municipal plans

As a result of the work done in phases 1 to 3 of the MCPP, climate change concerns are increasingly influencing the strategic planning undertaken by the municipality. At the level of short- to medium-term plans, climate change appears as a strategic issue to be addressed in the municipality's IDP. This is reflected in the requirement for the development of an MCPP within the IDP.[15]

Also at the short- to medium-term level, the city's open space system plan (known as the Durban Metropolitan Urban Space System Plan) (see Figure 11.5) is currently being remapped. As part of this process, a first attempt is being made to 'climate proof' the biodiversity resources that the system protects. This is being done through the application of a number of climate-specific design principles – for example, planning for the creation of corridors that will facilitate the southern and altitudinal migration of species; enlarging existing core conservation areas (to increase the size and range of altitudinal gradients protected); and identifying areas for improved matrix management (i.e. where improved management of the more formal urban landscapes can help to improve the ecological viability of the core conservation areas). Given that the open space system already covers an area of approximately 64,000ha, it is clear that any change to the spatial footprint of this system will have a significant impact upon land acquisition, development planning and natural area management within the municipality.

In terms of longer-term planning, the issue of climate change has also begun to feature significantly in the stakeholder discussions taking place within the context of the Imagine Durban campaign. Imagine Durban is a municipality-led project focusing on integrated long-term planning. It is being implemented in conjunction with Sustainable Cities, a non-governmental organization (NGO) from Vancouver, Canada, and the PLUS Network (a network of 35 cities sharing experiences in sustainability planning), which have received funding from the Canadian International Development Agency to support the project. Imagine Durban is a process that is mobilizing stakeholders (including government, non-government and civil society organizations, faith-based groups, tertiary institutions, business organizations and ordinary residents) to imagine where they would like to be in the future. It emphasizes that planning choices made today will affect generations still to come. From this perspective, the current generation of Durban residents bears a unique responsibility in terms of climate protection planning. Climate protection is therefore a key consideration in the environmental work stream of the Imagine Durban campaign.

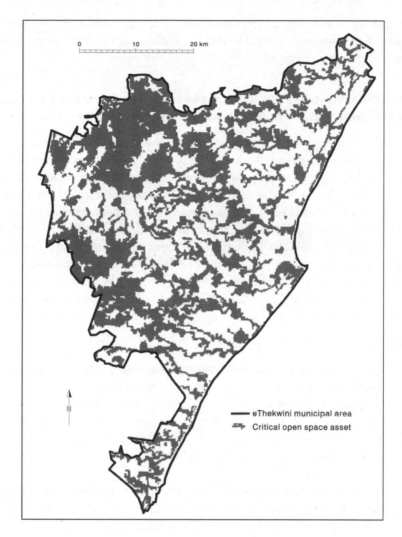

Figure 11.5 The Durban Metropolitan Urban Space System Plan

Source: Environmental Management Department, eThekwini Municipality

Institutional marker 3: The allocation of dedicated resources (human and financial) to climate change issues

A further outcome of the work undertaken during phases 1 to 3 of the MCPP was the realization that successful development and roll-out of the MCPP would require that the task be appropriately resourced, both from a human and financial perspective. This required institutional change as no formal climate change mandate existed anywhere within the prevailing municipal structures. As a result, a new branch has been created within the Environmental Management Department to deal specifically with the issues of climate change and climate protection. This change to the city's institutional structures was approved in 2007 and funds have now been secured to fill the management position in the Climate Protection Branch as a first step in establishing the branch.

Institutional marker 4: The incorporation of climate change considerations within political and administrative decision-making

While the issue of climate change is not yet noticeably affecting day-to-day decision-making in the municipality, it is clear that local government leaders in Durban are beginning to acknowledge the likely significance of the matter. In 2007, for example, the executive committee of the municipality responded to the call by the South African Local Government Association to address climate change issues by asking the city manager to compile a detailed report on the effects of climate change on the city. This provided an opportunity to profile the work being undertaken within the MCPP and to inform the politicians of its significance. Further weight was given to the need to prioritize the issue of climate change as a result of its inclusion in the statement made by the president of the African National Congress (ANC), Jacob Zuma, on 8 January 2008:

> *As we work to grow and transform our economy, we must recognize that climate change is a new threat on a global scale that places an enormous burden on especially the poor. We must therefore proceed without delay to implement our resolutions on climate change, particularly with respect to the reduction of greenhouse gas emissions and the promotion of renewable energy sources.*

It is interesting to note that adaptation does not feature in this statement. This is a reflection of the disjuncture that exists between national- and local-level policy-makers in South Africa around the issue of climate change.

The interest of decision-makers in climate change has also been enhanced in Durban as the result of a series of extreme weather events during 2007 (i.e. a series of storms and high tides), which resulted in extensive infrastructural damage due to flooding and coastal erosion. Although not directly attributable to climate change, these events have raised general awareness of the kind of impacts that may be experienced in a climatically changed future. As a result, there has been increased political and administrative support for climate change-related work in the municipality. One should not, however, be naive and imagine that the integration of climate protection considerations within political and administrative decision-making is likely to be a smooth process. Based on past experience, anything that affects budget lines and the city's current desired development path is likely to result in contestation between the various parties involved.

Conclusions

Using the four institutional markers defined here, it can be concluded that reasonable progress (given the development challenges and resource constraints faced by the municipality) has been made in Durban in mainstreaming climate change concerns at the local government level. The key to unlocking this process was capacity-building of key local government personnel. This kind of capacitation holds the potential to unlock endogenous resources and interest in climate change – ultimately making the likelihood of sustainable climate protection interventions greater. A significant drawback, however, is the fact that while strong climate change champions have emerged within the city's administration, no equivalent political champions have yet emerged. Plans are currently being developed to address this shortfall and to build capacity and political interest in the climate change issue.

In Durban, capacitation has also produced institutional change and the mainstreaming of climate change concerns within various municipal short- and long-term planning processes. Furthermore, it has been the catalyst for the development of a new assessment tool, which is intended to facilitate a more comprehensive incorporation of climate change concerns within the city's long-term planning. Such an approach should assist in reducing the prevailing tensions that exist between development and environmental priorities within the city by allowing decision-makers to better understand the long-term development consequences of short-term decisions that exacerbate climate change risk.

It is interesting to note that the need for local government to prioritize adaptation over mitigation interventions, given the kind of development threats faced by the municipality as a result of unavoidable climate change, emerged very early on in the development of the MCPP.[16] This suggests that in cities of the global South, donor monies may be better spent on capacitating people, especially around issues of climate change adaptation, rather than on supporting often *ad hoc* climate change mitigation projects.

Experience with the development of the MCPP has also indicated that embedding the concept of climate change within local government activities requires not only that the global debate is made relevant locally, but that this information is framed within a broader social/environmental justice framework. This would ensure that the development agenda of local government and the climate protection agenda are meaningfully and sustainably linked. Only in this way will climate protection concerns affect decision-making and resource allocation at the local level. In South Africa, this local-level action is critical, as past experience has shown that municipal innovation is often a key factor in catalysing meaningful activity by both provincial and national governments.

Notes

1. This chapter represents the views of the author and does not necessarily represent the views of eThekwini Municipality.
2. For the 2008/2009 financial year; US$1 = 7 to 8 South African rand.
3. This figure does not include those employed in the informal sector.
4. The backlog is calculated as follows: informal settlement dwellings + informal backyard dwellings + rural dwellings (from the 2001 population census). A 1.5 per cent growth rate is applied to this total and the number of houses built since the census is subtracted. This excludes a figure for overcrowded formal dwellings, which is difficult to estimate given changes in the census since 1996.
5. This function has taken a variety of institutional forms over the years, first being known as the Environmental Branch (1995–2003) and subsequently becoming the Environmental Management Department (2003 onwards).
6. In a smaller precursor entity known as Durban Municipality.
7. Now renamed ICLEI–Local Governments for Sustainability.
8. The third greenhouse gas inventory was completed in 2007 and, for the first time, includes both municipal and community contributions to greenhouse gas emissions.
9. Later to become the Environmental Management Department in 2003.
10. In total, the project will achieve a reduction of 7.6 million tonnes of CO_2 and is currently the largest Clean Development Mechanism project in Africa.
11. The Council for Scientific and Industrial Research is a parastatal research organization in South Africa.
12. Shamini, N., Hounsome, R. and Iyer, K. (2006) *Climatic Future for Durban*, prepared by CSIR NRE, edited by D. Roberts, A. Mather and M. Maganlal, Durban, April.
13. These lines indicate the maximum level likely to be reached by floodwaters, on average, once every 50 or 100 years, respectively.
14. An integrated development plan (IDP) is the product of a process by which South African municipalities prepare five-year strategic plans that are reviewed annually in consultation with communities and stakeholders. These plans seek to promote an integrated response by balancing social, economic and ecological pillars of sustainability without compromising the institutional capacity required in the implementation and by coordinating actions across sectors and spheres of government.
15. Plan 1: Sustaining our built and natural environment; Programme 7: Develop and implement municipal pollution reduction and climate protection.
16. It is, however, acknowledged that mitigation is the only successful long-term form of adaptation.

12

Developing a Municipal Adaptation Plan (MAP) for Climate Change: The City of Cape Town

Pierre Mukheibir and Gina Ziervogel

Introduction

Scientific evidence confirms that climate change is already taking place and that most of the warming observed during the past 50 years is due to human activities.[1] In Southern Africa, climate change projections suggest increased variability in rainfall, more frequent extreme events and increased temperatures.[2] These will occur even if global emissions were to be reduced in accordance with the Kyoto Protocol. In Cape Town, a significant number of past disasters and events have been associated with weather conditions and the concern is that these may occur more frequently in the future.[3]

In recent years, reducing vulnerability to climate change has become an urgent issue internationally. In low- and middle-income countries there has been a lag in significant response to this challenge, although it is clear that it should be at the forefront of any sustainable development policy agenda. Adaptation to climate change is a process whereby individuals and communities seek to respond to 'actual or expected climatic stimuli or their effects'.[4] This process is not new and throughout history people have adapted to changing climate conditions. What is new is the incorporation of climate change and its potential impacts into policy-making and planning on a range of scales.[5]

National Adaptation Programmes of Action (NAPAs) have been developed recently under the United Nations Framework Convention on Climate Change (UNFCCC) for least developed countries (LDCs).[6] However, to date, there has not been a consolidated or coordinated approach to adaptation at the sub-national scale, with few municipalities assessing projected climate impacts in developing countries. This needs to be addressed urgently as it is at this level that many people are directly affected by climate-induced impacts and it is at this level that institutional solutions can be introduced that target wide numbers of people.

This chapter presents an overarching framework for a municipal-level approach to adapting sectors to climate impacts by highlighting examples of potential impacts for the city of Cape Town. Some adaptation actions and possible interventions have been suggested. However, as this is a more conceptual framework for developing and implementing a plan, no stakeholder consultation or assessment of the city's capacity to plan and implement an adaptation programme has been made, although they are currently exploring how to implement it.

Background to climate change

In this chapter, both climate change and climate variability are considered and therefore it is important to understand the distinction between the two.

Climate variability can be thought of as the way in which climatic variables (such as temperature and precipitation) depart from some average state, either above or below the average value. Although daily weather data depart from the climatic mean, the climate is considered to be stable if the long-term average does not significantly change. On the other hand, climate change can be defined as a trend in one or more climatic variables characterized by a fairly smooth continuous increase or decrease of the average value during the period of record.[7]

Current research would suggest that the political and planning response is lagging behind in the understanding of climate change, particularly in how it deals with the uncertainty that is an intrinsic part of climate change science. This does not mean that there is no confidence in the understanding or that the understanding is not certain enough to allow for the development of appropriate adaptation strategies and policies for resource management – rather, that types of uncertainty should be acknowledged and factored in accordingly. Four sources of uncertainty currently limit the detail of the regional projections:[8]

1   *Natural variability*: due to the finite historical records from which the range of natural variability at different scales of time and space has been defined, it is not possible to set the definitive limits of natural variability or to establish how much of the change in variability is due to anthropogenic factors.
2   *Future emissions*: much of the projected change depends upon how society responds to reducing greenhouse gas emissions.
3   *Uncertainty in the climate systems*: current understanding of the regional dynamics of the climate system of the African sub-continent is limited.
4   *Downscaling*: this is the development of regional and local-scale projections of change from the global models. These projections maintain the uncertainty of the global models although they incorporate local climate dynamics. For this reason, downscaled projections are starting to be used more widely to represent patterns of climatic change.

Using the regional downscaled projections from the Climate Systems Analysis Group, the most relevant change in atmospheric circulation expected for the Western Cape is a decrease in the frequency of low pressures typically associated with winter storms during early winter. This has been observed in spatially varying trends in precipitation. Furthermore, the trend of fewer low pressure systems during early winter can lead to weaker synoptic forcing and conditions conducive to brown haze and smog in the Cape Town area.[9]

Towards a framework for adapting to climate change at the municipal level

The political discourse on climate change has been debated internationally through the UNFCCC; but in the past the agenda has focused mainly on mitigation of greenhouse gas emissions. Recently, there has been a shift in focus, where policy-makers and academics have begun to debate the issues surrounding adaptation to future climate impacts and to consider the implications for the future.[10] In addition, all parties to the convention, including South Africa, agreed to adopt national programmes for mitigation and adaptation, and to describe these in 'national communications'.[11] However, this has been focused mainly at the national level, and the resources and capacity at local level to deal with the implementation and operational issues are not always considered. For the city of Cape Town, for example, the only relevant published study has been the climate impact assessment for the Western Cape commissioned by the provincial government.[12]

There is a clear need to develop a framework for adaptation to climate change at the municipal level in order to prioritize the most urgent local adaptation activities and to identify the required local human and financial resources. If climate variability is to increase, it is necessary to understand how climate affects the different sectors and their resultant vulnerabilities. This will focus attention on where priority intervention might reduce the impacts of climate change and help cities to adapt rather than react when the damage has already been done, although it should be recognized that the reduction of greenhouse gases through mitigation is necessary as well.

The adaptation policy framework developed by the United Nations Development Programme (UNDP) is structured around four major principles from which actions to adapt to climate change can be developed: [13]

1   adaptation to short-term climate variability and extreme events is included as a basis for reducing vulnerability to longer-term climate change;
2   adaptation policies and measures are assessed in a development context;
3   adaptation occurs at different levels of society; and
4   both the strategy and the process through which adaptation is implemented are equally important.

These principles should be reflected upon continually to ensure adaptation activities are achieving their desired goals.

A number of methodologies have been developed that are either national level in scale, such as the NAPA, or project focused, such as the SouthSouthNorth Adaptation Project Protocol (SSNAPP) methodology developed by SouthSouthNorth.[14] However, these methodologies do not institutionalize the approach at a local level.

The following ten steps are presented to guide the development of an appropriate local level or Municipal Adaptation Plan (MAP) (see Figure 12.1):

1 Assess current climate trends and future projections for the geographical region.
2 Undertake a climate vulnerability assessment of the municipal area. Many cities will not have collected and analysed this information and would therefore have to develop this assessment from scratch:
  • identify current sectoral and cross-sectoral vulnerabilities based on current climate variability risks and trends;
  • identify future potential vulnerabilities based on future projected climate scenarios and future climate risks;
  • capture this information on local vulnerability maps using geographic information systems (GIS) and other tools – the climate impact assessment would include sea-level rise, drought and flood-prone areas.
3 Review current development plans and priorities. Most municipalities would be able to find this information in their various strategic plans.
4 Overlay development priorities, expected climate change, current climate vulnerability and expected future climate vulnerability using GIS for spatial interrogation and other participatory and quantitative assessments for further analysis. These various overlays will assist in identifying hotspots where adaptation activities should be focused.
5 Develop adaptation options using new and existing consultative tools. These options should integrate climate-sensitive responses with development priorities and focus on areas that are highly vulnerable to climate variability.
6 Prioritize the adaptation actions using tools such as multi-criteria analysis (MCA), cost-benefit analysis (CBA) or social accounting matrices (SAMs).
7 Develop programme and project scoping and design documents together with associated budgets. This document will be the MAP (see Figure 12.1).
8 Implement the interventions prioritized in the MAP.
9 Monitor and evaluate the interventions on an ongoing basis.
10 Regularly review and modify the plans at predefined intervals.

These ten steps should be complemented by two cross-cutting processes:

1 *Stakeholder engagement*: stakeholders should be engaged with in order to identify vulnerable sectors and existing and potential adaptation initiatives.

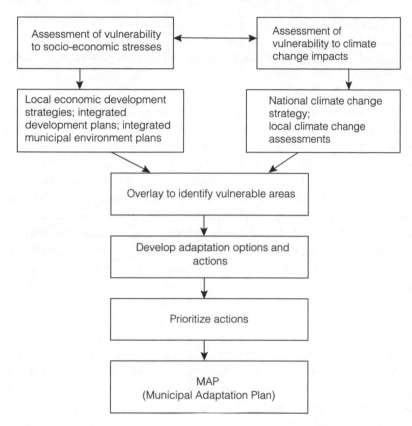

Figure 12.1 Process for developing a Municipal Adaptation Plan (MAP)

This engagement process is also necessary to bring politicians and decision-makers on board and to give them insight into the projected impacts and potential adaptation actions. Since some of the actions will be capital intensive or politically unpopular, it is necessary to build political will to fund and support adaptation measures. Furthermore, some actions may require certain trade-offs upon which the stakeholders would need to deliberate.

In developing the MAP, various products would be produced, including a vulnerability assessment, a climate impacts assessment and a vulnerability map, highlighting hotspots where developmental priorities intersect with climate impacts. It is important that a broad range of expertise is drawn on to gather this evidence.

2   *Adaptive capacity assessment*: the capacity to adapt of the various sectors that would be affected by the impacts of climate change needs to be assessed. Adaptive capacity can be defined as the potential or ability of a system to adapt to impacts of climate change. There are currently no methodologies for assessing the adaptive capacity of a sector; but this is a gap that should be addressed in the future.

This process should also include an assessment of the local government's capacity to implement adaptation actions in terms of budgetary and personnel constraints, with and without explicit climate change adaptation strategies.[15]

Many tools and methods exist for undertaking vulnerability and adaptation assessments, both qualitative and quantitative. O'Brien et al[16] explain that the definition of vulnerability determines how it is assessed. Vulnerability can be viewed as an 'end point', where climate change results in vulnerability, or as a 'starting point', which determines adaptive capacity and the impact that climate change will have. Eriksen and Kelly[17] provide an assessment of the different types of vulnerability indicators developed for climate policy assessments and highlight the fact that some approaches emphasize the physical more than the social aspects and vice versa. What is apparent is that the understanding of the causes of vulnerability is not always clear and vulnerability assessment methods need further development and clarity. It is important that any assessment of vulnerability at the metropolitan scale should be clear about what is being measured and how this relates to the causes of vulnerability. The information needed from a metropolitan vulnerability assessment should help to determine the appropriate tools. For example, the assessment of how one group or sector might be vulnerable to different types of climate variability might make use of matrices and expert opinion or focus groups. Formal assessments might include the use of vulnerability maps and agent-based models.

Assessing vulnerability to current climate variability is challenging because of the range of factors, in addition to climate, that contribute to vulnerability. Assessing vulnerability to climate change is even more challenging because of the dynamic nature of vulnerability. Although some attempts to evaluate adaptive capacity provide an indication of the ability to adapt to future change, it is impossible to definitively define future vulnerability – although some tools, such as scenarios, may help to evaluate future pathways of vulnerability.

Once the key vulnerabilities are identified, it is necessary to formulate an adaptation strategy consisting of a range of adaptation actions. These adaptation actions need to be developed for the local context in conjunction with key stakeholders, including those directly affected, experts in the sectors and climate specialists who can comment on the nature of the climate variability. This is necessary in order to assess the secondary impacts of certain adaptation actions and to ensure that there is equity and sustainability given the complex institutional arrangements of the city and its inhabitants. For example, in the city of Cape Town, Swilling highlights how infrastructure has been emphasized as key to economic growth and social development policy; yet the sustainability of this infrastructure planning is seldom engaged with at the level needed.[18] This critique provides important information that can be helpful in evaluating Cape Town's current and future infrastructure vulnerability, and can contribute to an assessment of infrastructure vulnerability to climate change.

Once adaptation actions have been identified, they need to be prioritized. One method of evaluating which actions might be pursued first is MCA. This allows options to be evaluated using a range of criteria that include the analysis of unquantifiable factors, especially when distributional implications need to be considered. The purpose of using MCA is to aid decision-making rather than to evaluate options on monetary terms. It is useful in assessing options for adapting to climate change as there are many factors that need to be considered, including equity, efficiency, short- or long-term benefits as well as many other non-monetary factors. Tools such as CBA and SAMs are useful when determining the financial implications of an intervention in terms of both cost and benefit to society. Issues such as the impact on gross domestic product (GDP) and employment can be assessed. At the same time, the limitations of these methods should be addressed. For example, although MCA might enable non-cost factors to be assessed, the stakeholders defining and evaluating the criteria may have biases. More flexible methods can therefore also be explored for choosing priority adaptation actions.

One of the first steps towards developing a MAP would be to consolidate and integrate existing adaptation initiatives in order to avoid duplication, and to work within budgetary and capacity constraints. A holistic approach to developing a MAP should also include reviews of both the direct impact on natural resources, and the secondary impacts on the socio-economic environment and the livelihood of communities. Through stakeholder consultation and prioritization, these and other sectors could be included.

A key component of a framework for the climate change strategy is the ongoing monitoring of the programmes and projects that are prioritized and implemented. The effectiveness of the interventions should be regularly assessed and modifications made if necessary. Adaptation to climate change is not an event; rather, it is an ongoing process of social learning. The development of a MAP should lead to adaptation actions being integrated within development policy and planning at every level. It should not be an add-on or an afterthought. Development itself is key to adaptation since adaptation should be an extension of good development practice and should reduce vulnerability. All levels of government should ensure that policies, programmes, budget frameworks and projects take account of climate change since critical economic, social and ecological challenges can only be addressed effectively on a regional scale.[19] However, there is little evidence of this kind of integration since low- and middle-income countries face two key barriers on this front: institutional constraints and technical capacity.[20] These are discussed further in the conclusion.

Examples of potential current and future municipal climate-induced impacts for the city of Cape Town

This section provides a few examples of current and future vulnerability to climate variability and change for the city of Cape Town. Due to the limited nature of this study, this has been based on a desktop assessment of existing reports. Some potential actions and possible interventions have been suggested. No stakeholder consultation or assessment of the city's capacity to plan and implement an adaptation programme has been undertaken.

Urban water supplies

The supply of water services in Cape Town faces a number of challenges, including eradicating a backlog in basic services, reducing demand, meeting wastewater effluent standards (thereby reducing impact upon the water quality of urban rivers), managing assets and ensuring that development growth demands are met.[21] The greater Cape Town area has been identified by the Department of Water Affairs and Forestry (DWAF) as the first major urban region in South Africa where the demand for water will exceed the total potential yield for the area if the economic and population growth scenarios are realized or the expected impact of projected climate change manifests itself.[22]

Figure 12.2 shows projected demand and also illustrates the relief that the Berg Water Project will bring under the 'low water demand' scenario. The commissioning of a dam on the Berg River in 2007 enabled an increase in the available supply by about 25 per cent. Under the 'low water demand' scenario, however, the city will have a water deficit by 2013. Domestic consumption accounts for two-thirds of the city of Cape Town's demand. Any demand-side management strategy should focus initially on this sector. As shown by the 'actual demand' curve, demand-side management initiatives, such as step tariffs and water restrictions during the recent drought periods, have reduced consumption quite considerably.

Impacts and vulnerabilities. Recently, the Western Cape experienced a drought that can be attributed to climate variability. Climate variability is expected to alter the current hydrological resources in Southern Africa and to place added pressure on the adaptability of future water resources. During the past 20 years, most of Southern Africa has experienced extensive droughts, the last four being in 1986–1988, 1991–1992, 2000–2001 and 2004–2005. As shown in Figure 12.3, dam levels in the Western Cape were at their lowest in five years during 2005. This drought-induced water shortage placed stress on the water supply and management in the city of Cape Town and resulted in a demand-side management response.

Adaptation initiatives. Current water management practice was developed to ensure that the existing supply of water meets the growing projected demand. Some of the mechanisms may be appropriate to deal with the future intermittent

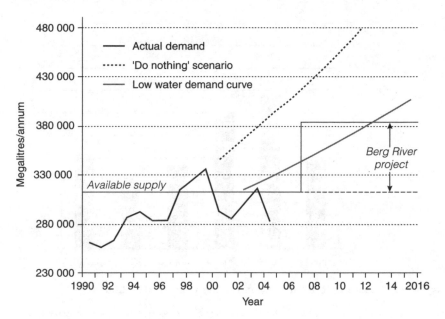

Figure 12.2 Water supply and demand projections for Cape Town

Source: adapted from City of Cape Town (2006) *Draft Water Service Development Plan 2006/07*, 8 February

shortages that will be brought about by climate variation; but robust long-term strategies are required to ensure that water demand matches supply even in times of reduced availability. In addressing future projected climate change impacts, some of the proposed measures may need to be introduced sooner than originally planned.

The Integrated Water Resource Planning Study, commissioned by the former Cape Metropolitan Council (CMC), identified the need to adopt an integrated water resource planning approach to manage the changing water demand, as well as to address the effects of population, economic growth and stresses on the supply of water.[23] The stresses on the supply of water should include projected climate impacts. In addition, there should be a strong focus on defence of the ecological reserve to ensure sustainability of wetland and river ecosystems. It has been proposed in the Berg Water Management Area (WMA) assessment study that no development or investment decisions should be made without taking into account the actual or potential effects of climate change on water resources.[24]

In addition, it is important that the impacts due to the changes in climate be monitored as a precautionary measure. Special attention is to be given to long-term monitoring of hydro-meteorological parameters in selected benchmark sub-catchments. Water planners and managers need to use the available climate data to make strategic decisions on an ongoing basis.

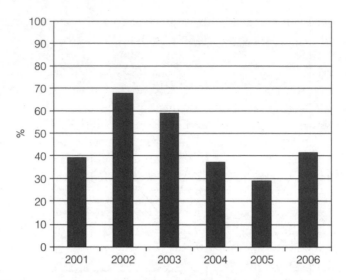

Figure 12.3 Storage levels on 1 May for the years 2001–2006

Source: City of Cape Town (2006) 'Weekly dam levels', www.capetown.gov.za/water/water resources.asp, accessed 9 May 2006

It would be strategic to establish effective water demand-side management before undertaking further capital expenditure on developing additional sources of water. To this end, the CMC accepted in 1997 the following policy statement:

> ... *to develop and manage, in a participatory manner, the implementation of a socially beneficial, technically feasible, economically effective, ecologically sustainable water demand management strategy, which will reduce the (DWAF 1994) projected demand in greater Cape Town by 20 per cent (or more) by the year 2010.*[25]

The city of Cape Town has since (in 2004) outlined a ten-point plan for achieving greater water conservation to complement the existing city of Cape Town's water demand management strategy and to achieve the objectives of the long-term sustainable water conservation strategy currently being developed by the city of Cape Town in partnership with the Department of Water Affairs and Forestry.[26]

These initiatives include the following:

- *Water restrictions*: in the past, the city of Cape Town has used measures such as restricting the use of water for some activities to specific times and disallowing other activities in order to reduce the demand on the limited water resources.

- *Water tariffs*: market-based allocations are able to respond more rapidly to changing supply conditions and also tend to lower the water demand, conserve water and consequently increase both the robustness and resilience of the water supply system.[27] Water tariffs were effectively used during the 2005 water shortage to reduce demand by the city of Cape Town.
- *Reducing leaks*: in Cape Town, the unaccounted-for water was estimated at 23 and 18 per cent for 2000 and 2001, respectively.[28] The upgrading and improvement of water supply lines, as is taking place in Khayelitsha through the Water Leaks Project, would bring these losses to within acceptable limits. Furthermore, the efficient use of water would reduce treatment and distribution costs.
- *Pressure management*: with the introduction of pressure management systems, as in Khayalitsha, water lost from undetected leaks is reduced by lowering the off-peak water pressure in the pipes. This also reduces the water lost (unused) through leaks from pipes on private property.[29]
- *Awareness campaigns*: through the media and knock-and-drop pamphlets, the city of Cape Town has embarked on an awareness campaign in an attempt to reduce the consumption of domestic water.

A number of policies and measures could be implemented by the city of Cape Town to reduce water demand. The cost implications of these would require further investigation:

- *Incentives*: these could be in the form of rebates for ratepayers and businesses that install rainwater tanks, reuse their grey water and install low-flush toilets.
- *Regulations*: building regulations should require that all new buildings be equipped with water-saving devices, such as low-flush toilets and rainwater tanks.

Given the high growth rates projected for the area and the already insufficient resource capability, water demand management alone will not be sufficient to meet future water requirements. Other potential supply-side interventions will have to be resorted to. Some of these are discussed below:

- *Berg WMA schemes*: two schemes located on the Berg river are being developed, as described in a report by BKS.[30]
- *The Table Mountain group aquifer*: the current belief is that the Table Mountain group aquifer has great potential for water productivity; it is already significantly utilized for irrigation and for municipal use throughout the Western Cape. This option is also being considered for water supply to the Cape Town Metropolitan Area. However, much uncertainty still exists regarding the productivity, rate of recharge and sustainability of the aquifer.

- *Other augmentation schemes*: other schemes that could be developed in the short to medium term include the Cape Flats aquifer, the Lourens River diversion scheme and the Eerste River diversion scheme.[31]
- *Reuse of effluent*: the city of Cape Town reuses 9 per cent of its treated effluent.[32] There should be incentives to encourage industries and other wet-processing systems to recycle their wastewater. At a domestic level, the re-use of grey water should be encouraged.
- *Water harvesting*: the installation of rainwater tanks in homes and commercial buildings for use in gardens, swimming pools and sewerage could be encouraged with incentives.
- *Modification of catchment vegetation*: the Working for Water Programme aims to remove invasive alien tree species (wattle, pine, etc.) from catchments in South Africa. By modifying the vegetation in catchments where water-thirsty vegetation with high transpiration rates has reduced the stream flow, the available water supply could be increased. Invading alien plants cause the loss of some 7 per cent of the flow in South Africa's rivers each year.[33]
- *Seawater*: the supply of seawater for certain domestic uses (e.g. swimming pools and sewerage) should be investigated further.
- *Desalination*: the energy intensity and high financial costs of production have, so far, made this technology unviable. However, the unit price of desalinated water internationally is dropping continually as technology improves. The major stumbling block, however, is that the Western Cape will be faced with an 'energy crunch' in the future.[34]
- *Improved integration of climate variability information into decision-making*: a Water Research Commission-funded project, Climate for Water, is exploring ways to enable water resource managers to integrate information about climate variability on an annual timescale in order to better manage resources, given the expected seasonal variation. Adapting to annual variability can be seen as an adaptation to climate change.

Storm water

The damaging floods in March 2003 and April 2005 were due to heavy rainfalls over a short period of time. The extent of the damage in the Western Cape province during this period exceeded 260 million rand.[35] Furthermore, storm water drains in the area are prone to blockages – sand from the Cape Flats is blown into the drains during the dry summer months and then obstructs rainwater drainage during the rainy winter season and, more specifically, during times of unpredicted heavy storms and intense rainfall. In the 'leafy' suburbs, leaves block the drains, particularly in the autumn, with the same result. These blocked drains cause flooding and damage to property and infrastructure. This is also true in areas where there is no drainage infrastructure, such as informal settlements (mostly on the Cape Flats). Poor drainage also has other adverse impacts upon the livelihoods and health of low-income households.

Impacts and vulnerabilities. The intensity of rainfall in the Western Cape can be expected to change due to climate variability. An increase in the number of extreme events will have the effect of substantially increasing the losses to the public and private sectors, as well as increasing personal hardship for the people directly affected.

Adaptation initiatives. The city has an extensive storm water and flood risk infrastructure and an elaborate hydrological monitoring network.[36]

Further risk reduction initiatives would include:

- ongoing monitoring and warning of impending disaster risks, with the help of the provincial weather and hydrological monitoring stations;
- reducing the impacts of these natural hazards through infrastructural means such as flood detention ponds and weirs;
- increasing the flood event return period that structures are designed to accommodate;
- the ongoing maintenance of storm water drains to clear them of sand build-up and rubbish; and
- the development of resilient infrastructure to include appropriately designed and constructed low-income homes, and storm water drainage and sewage treatment installations to cope with flash floods.

Fires

There are large areas of natural vegetation (mainly *fynbos*) within the city's municipal boundary, including the Table Mountain National Park, which are subject to bushfires. These bushfires normally occur, on average, every 15 years or so, with actual intervals between fires ranging between 4 and 40 years. The prevailing warm, dry summers are conducive to fires, which are common between November and March each year, especially when hot, dry, windy conditions prevail for several days.[37] These fires, while necessary for the regeneration of the *fynbos* and *renosterveld*, sometimes get out of control and cause damage to urban infrastructure.

Impacts and vulnerabilities. Based on modelling, the frequency and intensity of wildfires is expected to increase substantially due to lower rainfall (reducing the moisture content of fuels), lower relative humidity, longer droughts and higher wind speeds. High fire risk conditions are projected to almost triple in the west of the province. This will have a negative effect on biodiversity, soil structure and the spread of fire-adapted alien invasive plants, which would further alter and enhance fuel loads, making wildfires more intense. Plantations and buildings will be subject to increased risk.[38]

The soil erosion caused by winter rains after the summer fires further reduces the chances of indigenous vegetation recovering. For example, a study conducted in the Western Cape revealed that 6 tonnes of soil per hectare were lost following fires in pine stands compared to 0.1 tonnes per hectare following a fire in an adjacent *fynbos* area.[39]

Adaptation initiatives. Since management strategies to influence the frequency and intensity of fires in *fynbos* have been unsuccessful in the past, it may be appropriate to adopt defensive measures as well.

Some adaptation responses to fire risks would include:

- increased training in ecological fire management to improve control of the necessary burning of *fynbos* vegetation;
- increased fire-fighting capabilities, including greater training and investment in capacity for fire-fighting, as well as rapid and effective response to fires using aircraft;
- removal of plantations, especially in areas where future climate change might make them less productive;
- control of alien invading plants as a specific focus for managing the risk of damage by wildfire;
- appropriate fire breaks between vegetation and residential areas; and
- erosion protection to avoid loss of top soil due to post-fire rains.

Coastal zones

A change in global surface temperature is likely to be accompanied by worldwide sea-level rise through three main mechanisms: the warming and associated thermal expansion of the oceans, the melting of glaciers and, to a much lesser extent, the polar ice balance (Greenland and the Antarctic).[40]

It is suggested that specific locations be carefully evaluated in terms of their vulnerability to the following five potential impacts:[41]

1   increased exposure to extreme events (which themselves might increase in frequency or intensity);
2   increased saltwater intrusion and raised groundwater tables;
3   greater tidal influence;
4   increased flooding (frequency and extent); and
5   increased coastal erosion.

Impacts and vulnerabilities. The city of Cape Town's coastline, for example, has many sandy areas with a high potential for erosion as a result of the high-energy wave regime. In addition, the most significant impacts of sea-level rise are expected in those areas where problems are already being experienced. In most cases, these are areas where development has taken place too close to the high-water line or at too low an elevation above mean sea level.

A case study conducted by Hughes[42] in 1992 showed that a 1m rise in sea level would cause damage to private property in Muizenberg and on Woodbridge Island in the order of tens to hundreds of millions of South African rand (property values have since risen sharply). A new study, commissioned by the City of Cape Town in 2008, suggests that rising sea levels and increasingly frequent storms could affect developments proposed for coastal sites, making Cape Town 'particularly vulnerable' to the effects of climate change.[43]

Adaptation initiatives. Proposed planning and mitigation measures to manage the potential coastal impacts should include:

- The development of a coastal vulnerability map using GIS, where sites are assessed according to the scale of potential impacts with respect to sea-level rise. A point-rating system, whereby the vulnerability of sites can be evaluated objectively, should be initiated.
- The development of a shoreline management plan to include the protection of the ecological water reserve for estuaries. Ribbon development close to the shore should be avoided and buffer zones should be maintained.
- There should be a review of the existing regulations and bylaws – for example, more stringent set-back lines for developments.
- A maintenance and monitoring programme for existing coastal infrastructure should be established.[44]
- The design of structural mitigation measures, such as coastal protection/ developments/ structures specifically to compensate for the effects of sea-level rise. These would include breakwaters, revetments and sea walls, which protect infrastructure such as housing, promenades, pavements and parking areas from direct wave action and under-scouring.

The question arises as to when and to what extent coastal protection measures should be implemented to deal with possible future sea-level rise.

Conclusions

This chapter presents a methodology for municipalities to develop an integrated adaptation plan. However, the MAP should not be seen as a one-off process. It should be used initially to educate planners concerning these potential impacts and to develop both sectorally based and cross-sectoral interventions. With time, the integration of climate-sensitive actions into development planning should become commonplace in all municipal departments and their strategic plans.

An integral part of the MAP is the inclusion of an early warning system, where daily and seasonal weather forecasts are monitored to identify any pending impacts and potential disasters. A communication protocol is required to ensure that early warnings from the relevant entities are effectively communicated to the affected authority and communities so that appropriate interventions can be initiated.

A number of potential barriers to implementing a MAP do, however, exist. Issues such as low local human capacity to undertake this kind of planning and the limited knowledge and understanding of climate issues at local and municipal level are some of the more obvious obstacles. Limited financial resources and competing priorities often result in medium- to long-term planning being sidelined, while projects that do not fit into the short political life of decision-makers are not implemented. It is difficult to convince decision-makers to consider the need for a climate strategy when the climate projections cover a longer time horizon than the political and development framework and are associated with high uncertainty. Finally, in the absence of a legislative framework, not all municipalities will undertake comprehensive and consistent adaptation planning.

The case study of the city of Cape Town has shown that although it has no formal adaptation strategy in place, there has been enough momentum to initiate a framework that can then, ideally, be used to leverage implementation action. Gaining political support could help to provide the necessary resources to ensure that the MAP is taken seriously and is implemented. Although there are not many activities in the city that currently are called adaptation actions, there are many ongoing activities which already facilitate adaptation to climate variability in that they reduce the impacts of climate variability, and that could therefore be supported as climate change adaptation actions that contribute to the climate change strategy of the city of Cape Town. Developing a thorough methodology will require integrating the expertise of government stakeholders, researchers, civil society and the private sector. This integration may prove challenging and will depend upon the level of support. Yet, it is clear that Cape Town is vulnerable to climate change, and finding ways to adapt should be adopted sooner rather than later, when the costs of recovery or change to infrastructure and planning will be even higher.

This chapter serves as an initial broad overview of the problems posed by projected climate change and requires further attention to detail in many areas before a clear adaptive strategy can be developed. Further focused study is required, both to reduce uncertainties in many areas relating to the climate projections themselves and to improve understanding of the implications of impacts and sectoral and cross-sectoral vulnerabilities. More detailed assessments of the vulnerability of key threatened areas, together with likely timelines of impacts, should be undertaken. Along with this is the need to better understand how institutions might 'adapt' to enable climate-sensitive development to become the norm, not only in order to respond to projected climate impacts, but also to ensure resilience to current climate variability.

Notes

1. IPCC (Intergovernmental Panel on Climate Change) (2001) *Climate Change 2001: Synthesis Report*, Cambridge University Press, Cambridge, UK and New York, US.
2. Hewitson, B. C. and Crane, R. G. (2006) 'Consensus between GCM climate change projections with empirical downscaling: Precipitation downscaling over South Africa, *International Journal of Climatology*, vol 26, no 10, pp1315–1337.
3. DiMP (2000) 'Draft risk and vulnerability assessment for the Western Cape', Commissioned by the Department of Local Government, Province of the Western Cape.
4. McCarthy, J. J., Canziani, O. F., Leary, N. A., Dokken, D. J. and White, K. S. (eds) (2001) *Climate Change 2001: Impacts, Adaptation, and Vulnerability*, Contribution of Working Group II to the Third Assessment Report of the Intergovernmental Panel on Climate Change (IPCC) Cambridge University Press, Cambridge, UK and New York, US, p72.
5. Adger, W. N., Arnell, N. W. and Tompkins, E. L. (2005) 'Successful adaptation to climate change across scales', *Global Environmental Change*, vol 15, pp77–86; also Füssel, H.-M. and Klein, R. J. T. (2006) 'Climate change vulnerability assessments: an evolution of conceptual thinking', *Climatic Change*, vol 75, pp301–329.
6. LEG (Least Developed Countries Expert Group) (2004) *National Adaptation Programmes of Action (NAPA): Selection of Examples and Exercises Drawn from Regional NAPA Workshops*, UNFCCC LEG, UNDP, UNEP and UNITAR, Bonn and Geneva.
7. See reference 1.
8. Midgley, G. F., Chapman, R. A., Hewitson, B., Johnston, P., De Wit, M., Ziervogel, G., Mukheibir, P., Van Niekerk, L., Tadross, M., Van Wilgen, B. W., Kgope, B., Morant, P., Theron, A., Scholes, R. J. and Forsyth, G. G. (2005) *A Status Quo, Vulnerability and Adaptation Assessment of the Physical and Socioeconomic Effects of Climate Change in the Western Cape*, Report no ENV-S-C 2005-073 to the Western Cape Government, Cape Town, CSIR, Stellenbosch.
9. Pers comm with M. Tadross, Climate Systems Analysis Group, University of Cape Town, June 2006.
10. See reference 6.
11. DEAT (2004) *A National Climate Change Response Strategy for South Africa*, Pretoria, September.
12. See reference 8.
13. Lim, B., Spanger-Siegfried, E., Burton, I., Malone, E. and Huq, S. (2005) *Adaptation Policy Frameworks for Climate Change: Developing Strategies, Policies and Measures*, Cambridge University Press, Cambridge.
14. See reference 6; also Alam, M. and Mqadi, L. (2006) 'Designing adaptation projects', *Tiempo*, vol 60, July, pp21–24.
15. Smit, B. and Pilifosova, O. (2001) 'Adaptation to climate change in the context of sustainable development and equity', in McCarthy et al (2001): see reference 4.
16. O'Brien, K., Eriksen, S., Schjolden, A. and Nygaard, L. P. (2004) *What's in a Word? Conflicting Interpretations of Vulnerability in Climate Change Research*, CICERO Working Paper 2004:04.

17. Eriksen, S. and Kelly, M. (2006) 'Developing credible vulnerability indicators for policy assessment', *Mitigation and Adaptation Strategies for Global Change*, www.springerlink.com/content/kr6481642w504335/fulltext.pdf, 22 May 2006.

18. Swilling, M. (2006) 'Sustainability and infrastructure planning in South Africa: A Cape Town case study', *Environment and Urbanization*, vol 18, no 1, April, pp23–50.

19. Intergovernmental Integrated Development Task Team for the Cape Town Functional Region (2006) 'A proposed agenda for action: An intergovernmental approach to the development challenges of Cape Town', South African Government, Western Cape Provincial Government and City of Cape Town, 28 February.

20. Mukheibir, P. and Sparks, D. (2006) *Climate Variability, Climate Change and Water Resource Strategies for Small Municipalities*, Report 1500/1/06, Water Research Commission, Pretoria, January; also Stern, N. (2006) *Stern Review: The Economics of Climate Change*, HM Treasury, London; and Burton, I., Huq, S., Lim, B., Pilifosova, O. and Schipper, E. L. (2002) 'From impacts assessment to adaptation priorities: The shaping of adaptation policy', *Climate Policy*, vol 2–3, pp145–159.

21. City of Cape Town (2006) *Draft Water Services Development Plan 2006/07*, 8 February.

22. DWAF (Department of Water Affairs and Forestry) (2004) *National Water Resource Strategy*, first edition, September.

23. Geustyn, Loubser, Streicher and Palmer Development Group (2001) *Water Services Development Plan, City of Cape Town*, Cape Town, December.

24. BKS (Pty) Ltd (2003) *Berg Water Management Area: Overview of the Water Resources Availability and Utilization*, Report no 19/000/00/0203, Department of Water Affairs and Forestry (DWAF) Pretoria, September.

25. ARUP (2002) 'Berg water project background information', http://www.tcta.co.za/projects/berg_bid.htm.

26. See reference 21.

27. Schulze, R. and Perks, L. (2000) *Assessment of the Impact of Climate Change on Hydrology and Water Resources in South Africa*, ACRUcons Report 33, School of Bioresources Engineering and Environmental Hydrology, University of Natal, Pietermaritzburg, January.

28. See reference 23; see also reference 21.

29. City of Cape Town (2005) 'Cape Town announces strategies to ensure future water supply', *Cape Gateway*, 15 September.

30. See reference 24.

31. See reference 21.

32. See reference 23.

33. Kasrils, R. (2000) 'A water perspective on invasive species', Presented at The Best Management Practices Symposium, 22–24 February, Kirstenbosch, South Africa.

34. See reference 8.

35. Holloway, A. (2005) *Risk Reduction and Emergency Management Component, Strategic Infrastructure Plan*, Province of the Western Cape, Second Draft, DiMP, University of Cape Town, 5 December.

36. See reference 35.

37. See reference 8.

38. See reference 8.
39. Scott, D. F., Versfeld, D. B. and Lesch, W. (1998) 'Erosion and sediment yield in relation to afforestation and fire in the mountains of the Western Cape province, South Africa', *South African Geographical Journal*, vol 80, pp52–59.
40. See reference 1.
41. See reference 8.
42. Hughes, P. (1992) *The Impacts of Sea-Level Rise on the South African Coastal Environment*, PhD thesis, Department of Oceanography, University of Cape Town.
43. Brundrit, G., Cartwirght, A. and Fairhurst, L. (2008) *Global Climate Change and Adaptation – A Sea-Level Rise Risk Assessment*, Study reference no R030800032, Global Climate Change, prepared for the city of Cape Town, July.
44. City of Cape Town (2003) *Coastal Zone Management Strategy*, Department of Environmental Planning, Cape Town, 31 October.

13

Adapting to Climate Change: Water Management for Urban Resilience

Mike Muller

Introduction

It is anticipated that global warming and related climate changes that are predicted to occur over the next century will significantly increase the weather-related risks facing human settlements. However, while significant attention has been focused on actions to mitigate climate change, less has been done to adapt to a future that many believe is already beginning. Nor is it clear how such adaptation can be promoted most effectively.

At the World Bank's 2006 Conference on Development Economics in Tokyo, Professor Michael Grubb of the UK Carbon Trust complained that scientists and economists were talking past each other about the challenges of climate change:

> *To date, this debate on impacts between economists quantifying specific, potentially measurable and monetizable impacts, and scientists focused on risk indices and scenarios, has been largely a dialogue of the deaf.*[1]

The same may be said about the engagement in climate policy discussions of the community of built environment practitioners, particularly the engineers who conceive, design, build and operate the physical infrastructure that sustains our urban societies.

The approach to the provision and management of that infrastructure will, in substantial measure, determine the future vulnerability or, to use the inverse, the resilience of urban communities to climate-related disasters. Despite this, relatively little work has been done on the potential impacts of climate change upon urban settlements in high-income nations, and even less in low- and middle-income nations that are most vulnerable. The principal focus has remained on the contribution of urban activities to climate change, mitigating their effects rather than adapting to them.[2]

There is an important debate about the relative importance for different societies of mitigation, which addresses the drivers of climate change, versus adaptation, which considers the measures necessary to accommodate such changes.[3] The 'development rather than mitigation' view has been most succinctly expressed by environmental 'dissident' Bjorn Lomborg, who recommended that:

> *... we should not spend vast amounts of money to cut a tiny slice of the global temperature increase when this constitutes a poor use of resources and when we could probably use these funds far more effectively in the developing world.*[4]

A further consideration, particularly in poorer countries, is whether it is necessary to distinguish between adaptation-specific activities and 'normal' development.

A strong case can be made for the allocation of additional development funds to address the impacts of climate change in poorer countries on the basis of the 'polluter pays' principle. However, if resources are to be usefully directed to adaptation, there will have to be clarity about the strategies proposed to do this as well as some evidence of their efficacy. It is thus important to consider how adaptation efforts can fit within the mainstream of development strategies. In this, the water sector may provide some useful indicators and guidance in the broader debate.

It is urgent to move beyond the mitigation and adaptation debate if only, as Professor Grubb said, because the infrastructure we build today locks us into patterns of behaviour for many years to come. He further noted that: '"Leapfrogging" in infrastructure, by trying to make choices at the leading edge for the long term, is ... a huge opportunity in the course of development.'[5]

Grubb was addressing primarily energy and development issues, which are where the main mitigation challenges lie. Yet, the point is even more valid in the water environment, which arguably will be most affected by climate change in such key parameters as river flow.[6] Furthermore, unlike energy infrastructure, the useful life of large water infrastructure is often measured in hundreds of years, and investments that are made today will still be operating under the new climates of the 22nd century.

While the role of water management in mitigating flood and public health disasters is well recognized,[7] its effective execution may also have a role in preventing less obvious slow onset disasters that are more insidious but arguably as damaging, since they may lead to the collapse of the social, political and financial viability of urban settlements.

This chapter considers the physical and financial implications for urban areas of the potential impacts of climate variability and change on water resources. The issues are illustrated in the context of sub-Saharan Africa, which is predicted to be one of the regions most affected and is certainly among the most vulnerable. Some potential impacts upon urban communities are outlined, and areas in which different practice could achieve better outcomes for city dwellers are identified. Information and instruments required to translate the desirable interventions into practical programmes of adaptation are highlighted which, if given the same priority as climate change mitigation, could help to make urban settlements more resilient to many types of disaster. Finally, a brief review is made of the financial and institutional approaches that will have to be addressed to promote effective adaptive action.

Instruments to manage variability, reduce vulnerability and build resilience

Building resilience to manage the impacts of variable climates on human activity is the day-to-day business of water managers, whether in planning for weather extremes or optimizing long-term resource utilization. This has been done throughout the history of human settlements. Much of the simplest traditional water infrastructure – the household rainwater cistern, the 'tank' in the Indian town – enables households and communities to manage the variability of the water resources upon which they depend, which, in turn, reflects their local climate. The same is true for the simple river training, floodwalls and flood diversion canals that protect many of the world's towns and cities.

Over time, quantitative climate information and assumptions have been embedded more formally into the design of this essential infrastructure, as well as that of the water distribution and waste collection networks, roads and storm water drains, and human settlements, more generally.

One way to manage the impacts of climate variability on water resources is to capture and control river flows. Dams are built to retain and store flows that are in excess of user requirements and to release them during periods when low flows are not sufficient to meet user needs, a practice that can also serve to maintain aquatic ecosystems. Alternatively, during floods, peak flows can be stored for later release, avoiding flood damage by reducing maximum flows. Both functions are important to sustain urban settlements and to avert disasters caused by floods and droughts.

A further important function of dams is to store water as a form of potential energy to generate electricity, without which healthy urban life is difficult to sustain as settlements increase in size. Nineteen per cent of the world's electricity is currently generated from hydropower and there is substantial potential to expand this, particularly in low- and middle-income countries.[8] A specific benefit of hydropower is that it does not usually generate significant quantities of greenhouse gases and thus allows economic and social development to occur without aggravating global warming.

Other important waterworks include canals, tunnels and pipelines, which not only supply human demands directly but, less obviously, create linked systems that, by virtue of their multiple sources, suffer less variability and therefore offer enhanced supply security. Equally, wastewater disposal and storm water drainage systems contribute to the ability of communities to maintain their activities and protect public health during extreme weather events.

The design of all these structures reflects formal quantitative assumptions about climate since it takes into account likely variations in rainfall and stream flow as well as likely storm intensities and maximum flood sizes.

The water managers' armoury for addressing variability is not restricted to infrastructural means. As important are the institutional mechanisms that, again more or less formally, help to deal with climate variability and achieve such goals as supplying water for people, industries and farms, and protecting communities from flooding while sustaining ecosystems.

An obvious example is rules on water allocation that prioritize different uses of water at different times. In many countries, water law and management practice apply categories such as 'winter water' and 'surplus flow' to determine who can use how much water and when. From this perspective, organized drought restrictions should not be seen as supply failures, but, rather, as institutional mechanisms to manage variability by prioritizing different water uses during times of supply stress.

Beyond direct water management, institutional instruments such as land-use planning can substantially reduce the vulnerability of communities to water-based natural disasters if they are supported by reliable flood data that can be provided by water managers. There is often a choice from a suite of hard and soft instruments that can be applied to enhance resilience. In the case of floods, resilience can be achieved by building infrastructure such as floodwalls; alternatively, communities can be designed to be resilient by planning approaches that do not allow settlements to be located in vulnerable areas; often, a mix is most appropriate.

The development context and constraints before climate change

It might be expected that the threat of climate change would encourage greater attention to building the capacity to manage the impacts of general climate variability upon water resources. This is not (yet) to say that such specific action is required in water resources management concerning climate change, although the case is growing stronger. A risk-based approach would suggest that the evident uncertainty about the climatic future should mean more explicit attention to mechanisms that could help to manage it; from there, it is a small step to recognizing that the bounds of variability may be changing.

It is not clear whether that is happening yet, precisely because water resources management is already so focused on dealing with climatic and weather variability and there is, as yet, only limited scientific evidence for increased variability beyond historic norms. It has been noted that most human societies are inherently adaptive; however, it is anticipated that climate change will test these coping capacities, which will need to be strengthened.[9]

Meanwhile, many poorer countries are not even able to manage their current variability, not because the necessary strategies are unclear, but because the means to implement them are lacking. They may reasonably ask why they should address tomorrow's climate change if they cannot afford to manage today's drought.

This is evident in the challenge of maintaining reliable urban water supplies. In low- and middle-income countries, generally, and in sub-Saharan Africa, in particular, both industrial and domestic consumption are growing and more water will be needed. The nature of urban living and modern industry requires those sources to be reliable in the short term and assured over longer time periods.

At first sight, sub-Saharan Africa's challenge is not so great. Of the 295 million urban residents in Africa, 254 million are reported to already have 'improved' water supplies[10] (although, currently, these services are often not functioning effectively).[11] Assuming that the volumes consumed remain the same, only a manageable 15 per cent increase in the amount supplied would be required to reach 100 per cent. However, urban growth of at least 50 per cent, or 150 million people, is predicted between 2000 and 2015.[12] If this occurs, a 60 per cent increase in water volumes would be required if all urban residents were to be adequately served.

The challenge – and the opportunity – is to meet these needs in a manner that 'leapfrogs' the current approaches and puts the countries and cities concerned into a position that allows them not just to meet these new needs, but to do so in a manner that leaves them more resilient to the potential impacts of climate change. This would involve such 'soft measures' as conservation programmes that would moderate the growth in demand. Another effective approach would be to design cities with denser housing (rather than larger gardens), which has been shown to reduce water use.[13] In poorer countries, however, this might be at the expense of domestic food security.

Whatever strategy is chosen, substantial investments will be required. An important question is, thus, what impacts climate change could have upon the nature and costs of the investments required to meet urban water needs in Africa and other poor regions.

The challenges of climate change for water resources management

To address this question in the water sector, it is necessary first to consider the potential impacts of climate change upon water resources and their management.

It has been suggested[14] that if energy generation and use is the focus of mitigation, water management will be at the centre of adaptation to climate change. The general picture of global warming is reasonably clear and agreement is growing about its regional dynamics and scale. However, moving from temperature predictions to reliable predictions of seasonal rainfall and its distribution in time is already a big leap. The current rainfall predictions are indicative rather than definitive and are still relatively general, which limits their utility for indicating the type of strategic challenges that may arise. Similar caveats apply to the other key dimension of climate variability that has an impact upon water resources and their management – namely, the predictions that there will be significant changes in weather extremes, with more powerful, intense storms and longer, more intense droughts.[15] This would be consistent with the underlying analyses of energy flows that underpin predictions of global warming and are of great importance for water managers who necessarily focus on extreme events.

The more difficult questions relate to the impacts of changing temperatures and rainfall upon water availability. To fully understand the impacts of climate change upon urban communities, it is necessary to be able to predict average rainfall and stream flows (to determine water availability and storage requirements), as well as extreme flows and storms (to design infrastructure to withstand them), as well as to predict potential changes in groundwater yields.

The effects of climate change on available water (as opposed to rainfall) are more difficult to predict because a number of effects combine. Crudely put: if temperatures increase, there will be more evaporation from the soil and transpiration from plants and less water will flow into rivers or seep into the underground aquifers; but if rainfall is more intense, a larger proportion of water will flow off the ground as floods or infiltrate through the soil into the deeper groundwater.

Changes in carbon dioxide concentrations, temperature and rainfall will have an impact upon plant cover and land use which will, in turn, substantially affect the behaviour of water when it falls as rain. And there are direct anthropogenic impacts to be considered – changes in land use (e.g. cropping systems) will also affect the availability of water and add a further layer of complexity to the uncertainty about the 'natural' processes.

It is thus clear that the prediction of stream flows and groundwater regimes under climate change scenarios is an ambitious undertaking; although efforts have been made for some regions, they still provide a relatively wide range of possible outcomes.[16]

The important conclusions for the purposes of this chapter are as follows:

- Changes in temperature and rainfall will usually be amplified in the response of water resources systems, with relatively small (10 to 20 per cent) changes in rainfall leading to large (up to 75 per cent) changes in perennial stream flow.

- Uncertainty grows as extrapolations are made from climate models related to temperature predictions, to rainfall predictions and, finally, to predictions of the stream flow consequences.

Paradoxically, one consequence of the wide uncertainty is that water managers still use historic climate data to design water infrastructure. Thus, in order to determine the likely yield of a dam, the usual approach is either to:

- use an historic record of the flows in relevant streams and rivers to determine how much water can reliably be made available; or
- use rainfall and runoff data from a similar area and 'synthesize' an artificial 'record' of flows.

In both cases, parameters derived from historic information will be used to generate a series of predictions of possible stream flow sequences against which the performance of the structure will be evaluated. The details of these approaches are not important for the purposes of this chapter, save to say that both are dependent upon local or related historic records of stream flow and rainfall and, equally important, upon the ability to use the data and translate them into useful information.

A practical example of the challenges posed by climate change is the decision that will have to be taken in South Africa within the next decade concerning the source of the next major increment in water supply to the metropolitan area of Johannesburg and its surrounding industrial heartland. There are two main options:

- expand the existing Lesotho Highlands Water Project, taking more water from the Orange River system that rises in the mountains of Lesotho and flows to the Atlantic Ocean on the border with Namibia and putting it into the Vaal system; or
- capture water from the other side of the divide, from the Thukela and other shorter, smaller rivers that flow to the Indian Ocean on the east coast and transfer it into the Vaal Basin.

Whichever option is chosen, this will be an expensive project, costing over US$1 billion and taking up to a decade to plan and build, so decisions cannot be taken lightly. The comparative costs of the alternatives are not dissimilar.

Factors that will affect the decision include differences in operating costs, since one solution will require less pumping than the other; and political considerations, since the existing treaty between Lesotho and South Africa provides for further phasing of existing transfers, and a further phase would bring a substantial cash injection to Lesotho. Capital costs will, however, always be an important determinant of the lifetime cost of water delivery, so the comparative costs of the alternatives are an important issue. But apparent differences in the unit cost of water calculated for each scheme may be meaningless if the hydrological forecasts upon which they are based are not reliable or comparable.

Climate science offers only limited help in making this decision. Thus, it is currently suggested that for South Africa, in terms of rainfall, the west and south-western parts will become drier and the east of the country will stay the same and may even become wetter.[17]

In this case, climate predictions would suggest that it might be less risky to opt for an eastern river source, which is predicted to be less affected by climate change (less risky) and would have the advantage of maintaining a balance between different sources – a more resilient system. But it is not clear how much weight should be given to these criteria. Nor is it known how firm the numbers will be when the decisions have to be made and firm information – about, say, project costs – traded off against what is, at present, far less precise climate information.

This example illustrates why many practitioners argue that it is not yet possible for water managers, particularly in low-income countries, to take climate change into account in their designs. Yet, the logic remains that water investments should be designed to perform under future climate regimes. The present challenge is thus to improve the descriptions of those possible regimes by reducing the uncertainties that multiply at each step of the hydrological cycle, from temperature predictions to estimates of rainfall, evaporation, infiltration and runoff, in order to obtain reasonably reliable predictions of stream flow and groundwater availability. If these flows can be predicted better, they can be managed better.

The underlying concern remains that if rainfall changes, if the increased variability and event intensity that is predicted actually occurs, this will impose substantial costs upon poor countries. The next step is thus to gain some indication of the magnitude of those costs and then to consider how they might be addressed.

Water resources costs: The added burden of adaptation

For policy purposes, it is important to distinguish between the costs of managing 'normal' climatic variability and those of managing the new impacts of climate change. If climate change is driven by the activities of certain communities or countries, it may be appropriate to apply the polluter pays principle, which would have significant implications for financing the costs that may be incurred. However, the boundary between 'normal' and 'new' variability is not obvious. It is thus difficult to determine what proportion of a dam helps to manage 'normal' variability and what proportion of the 'new' variability is 'created' by climate change.

Preliminary estimates of some of the additional costs that may be imposed on cities in sub-Saharan Africa have been made by the author[18] in an attempt to determine their order of magnitude, as well as to identify some of the underlying issues. Changes in rainfall patterns and stream flows will have a direct impact upon cities, some of which are very obvious:

- Water supply is costly and, if availability of water is reduced by climate change, larger conurbations will have to change their consumption patterns or bring their water from further afield.
- Standards for wastewater treatment typically depend upon the extent to which effluents can be diluted when they are discharged; so if stream flows are reduced, treatment must be intensified to maintain the same environmental standards. Municipal wastewater collection and treatment is already the most costly element of infrastructure required to meet the Millennium Development Goals (MDGs) for health, water and environmental protection[19] and, since treatment costs increase exponentially with the degree of purification required, climate change could add substantially to the burden of meeting these MDGs.
- Any increase in the intensity of rainfall and, therefore flooding, as a consequence of climate change will increase the cost of roads and storm water drainage, as well as of flood protection works.
- Many cities in sub-Saharan Africa are dependent upon hydropower for their electricity, and power failures can lead to more general 'urban failure'.

There are also less direct effects:

- Flood risk affects the area of land available for settlement as well as the cost of protecting vulnerable land from flooding (the challenge of sea-level rise, which is relevant for many coastal cities, is not considered here).
- Bringing water from further afield not only increases the cost of water, but also expands the area affected by competition with cities for water. This will have economic impacts upon the cities themselves, whether through higher prices for rural products or the aggravation of rural unemployment, leading to urban migration.

Accurate costings of these impacts will obviously depend upon the details. However, in order to obtain an order of magnitude estimate of the potential cost implications of climate change for African cities, the following first-order assumptions have been made:

- The reliable yield from dams will reduce at the same rate as stream flow: a 30 per cent reduction in average stream flow will result in 30 per cent less yield and the unit cost of water will go up by more than 40 per cent.

- Where waste is disposed into a stream, if stream flow is reduced by 30 per cent, the pollutant load must be reduced by 30 per cent. Since in order to achieve lower pollution levels, treatment costs increase rapidly, it is reasonable to assume that the overall cost of wastewater treatment could double.
- Power generation reduces linearly with stream flow (the true situation is somewhat more complex and depends upon the way in which schemes are operated); a 30 per cent reduction in stream flow will result in a 30 per cent reduction in electricity production.

Applying these assumptions, and using unit costs derived from actual project experience,[20] the costs of adapting existing urban water infrastructure in Africa have been estimated at between US$1050 million and US$2650 million annually:

- urban water storage: US$500 million to $1500 million (capital cost); US$50 million to $150 million (annual equivalent);
- wastewater treatment: US$100 million to $200 million annually;
- electricity generation: US$900 to $2300 million annually (this does not include the cost of rehabilitating deficient infrastructure).

The costs of new development are also likely to rise by between US$990 million and US$2550 million annually. In general, the marginal unit cost of water resources development for water supply to urban areas increases with each new increment of supply. It is therefore conservative to assume that the costs of adapting to climate change for new developments will be similar to those for existing systems:

- urban water storage: US$150 million to $500 million (capital cost);
- (new water supplies for 150 million): US$15 million to $50 million (annual equivalent);
- wastewater treatment: US$75 million to $200 million annually (assuming an additional 100 million served);
- electricity generation: US$900 to $2300 million annually (assuming installed capacity doubles).

There are many other costs that will be imposed upon urban areas through the water cycle. The economic impacts of rural water shortages upon urban areas are particularly difficult to quantify. However, urban migration is a management challenge for almost all African cities and any declines in rural production will certainly have second-order impacts upon city economies.

There will also be additional costs incurred in the construction of roads and storm drainage, from the loss of use of land that is threatened by floods, and for additional flood protection for existing settlements. These and other indirect effects are site specific and less easy to cost on a regional level.

The issue of flooding highlights the fact that climate change may not always be negative, as the availability of land for urban settlement may be positively affected by a reduction in rainfall. However, if the frequency and intensity of extreme storms rises, flood lines may not change significantly in a drier future, which would counter any possible expansion of habitable area. All of these effects call for elucidation and quantification to enable communities to understand what will be needed to deal not just with current variability, but also with changes in its nature.

While this discussion has focused on the costs of actions to address the potential water-related impacts of climate change, a final critical point needs to be made. If the actions identified to make urban settlements more resilient are not taken, flood disasters, water and electricity supply interruptions, with the resulting economic public health and economic implications, will occur. The costs of such disasters will almost certainly be greater than the costs of prevention through appropriate adaptation measures. At the extreme, if disasters place unsustainable financial burdens on urban societies, this could lead to the collapse of public services, and climate change will have created 'failed cities'.

Some practical challenges and responses

Financial challenges

The additional costs outlined above (US$2 billion to $5 billion annually) could feasibly be met from national sources given current levels of expenditure, supplemented by aid funding which, in the case of sub-Saharan Africa, reached US$23,276 million in 2004.[21] They do, however, demonstrate that climate change could add substantially to the overall cost of urban management and of doing business in urban areas (which is already high and, arguably, underfunded). This will have an impact upon the ability of urban centres in low-income nations to compete in an increasingly globalized economy and will undermine their ability to sustain themselves. In this more generic manner, the impacts of climate change through water threatens to leave them more vulnerable to disaster. Specific responses are therefore needed to the challenges that are emerging.

This concern is shared in a working paper of the UK government's Stern Review:

> ... *the adverse impacts of climate change will be felt most acutely and soonest by poor people in developing countries, in particular in Africa, because of their geographical and climatic conditions, their high dependence on agriculture and the natural environment, the deficiencies in their infrastructure, and their limited capacity and lack of financial and technical resources to adapt.*

> *An equitable international response to climate change must include not just action on mitigation, therefore, but also finding ways of working with the most vulnerable countries and regions to ensure their growth and poverty reduction goals are not compromised.*[22]

Another recent review of the challenges of funding the costs of adapting to climate change asked whether these should be funded through the 1992 United Nations Framework Convention on Climate Change (UNFCCC) or through other channels, and concluded that a twin-track approach would be appropriate.[23]

Certain institutional interests would seek to ring-fence funds for climatic adaptation purposes. Given the difficulty in distinguishing between adaptation and normal development, this is likely to lead to suboptimal investments. The present approach of the UNFCCC, which tends to separate climate adaptation from the 'normal' development and management activities, has been questioned. The result, say Bouwer et al, is that 'most of the proposed funding ... is limited to capacity-building (such as joint research and knowledge exchange) and does not include the provision of funds for the implementation of adaptation'.[24]

On efficiency grounds, the objective should be for adaptation efforts to be integrated within the mainstream of development rather than kept in a climate and sustainability 'ghetto'. For low-income countries that are aid dependent, particularly in sub-Saharan Africa, the objective should be to place additional funding in appropriate national budgets and support the planning and budgeting processes to ensure that new investments are 'climate proofed'. This would be consistent with the 2005 Paris Declaration on Aid Effectiveness,[25] although it may frustrate those who wish to see quick and dedicated climate-related action.

The Paris Declaration offers a more elegant and integrated approach; but to take advantage of the opportunities it offers, the countries concerned will need to put credible planning and budgeting processes in place. It would also be necessary to build into existing monitoring and reporting mechanisms ways to track expenditure related to adaptation activities. The objective should be to keep governments (on both sides) honest about the processes of resource mobilization and allocation, as well as to focus continued attention on the need to integrate climate adaptation within normal development activities.

Institutional challenges

Considerations of finance for adaptation lead logically to the institutional issues. One relevant institutional response is the emergence of the philosophy and methodology of integrated water resources management (IWRM). Although some advocates see it as a 'soft' alternative to infrastructure development, relying solely on instruments such as demand management, IWRM promotes a holistic approach to water management and recognizes that there are multiple pathways to building resilience. The methodology seeks to identify and then to achieve trade-offs between different water management objectives, including environmental sustainability, economic efficiency and social equity, all of which have implications for disaster mitigation. It encourages the structured engagement of communities and sectors affected by water in its management to ensure both that optimal (direct and indirect) mechanisms are identified, considered and applied, and that an understanding of water constraints and challenges is diffused into the society.[26]

The potential contribution of an IWRM approach to the achievement of sustainable development was emphasized by world leaders at the 2002 World Summit on Sustainable Development, where they agreed that all countries should establish water management plans by 2005 (a target that has proved to be aspirational and motivational rather than practical, but no less important for that).[27] The challenge is now to undertake the institutional and technical work that will make it possible to translate the policy aims of IWRM into practice, in disaster management as well as in other dimensions. The mainstreaming of adaptation or 'climate proofing' into national development plans is a key institutional action for which IWRM offers a potentially useful channel.

Technical challenges

There are serious practical challenges facing climate scientists and water managers who seek to build the resilience of urban settlements to climate change. The quality of the climate and hydrological information needed to design new water management infrastructure is grossly deficient. In poorer developing countries, this has not been particularly obvious over the past decade because of the decline in investment in water infrastructure during the period. This was a result of financial constraints as well as donors' attempts to achieve greater private-sector investment and their concerns about the social and environmental impacts of large water projects.[28] It is now recognized that additional investments are required and that public channels are appropriate, particularly for large, long-term investments, which, historically, in order to be undertaken, have required public finance by virtue of the long-term nature of their returns.[29]

A natural consequence of the drought in water investments over the past few decades is that less priority has been attached to collecting and processing the hydrological data that are used to support them. This has contributed to a marked decline in hydrological networks over recent decades.[30] This trend has been exacerbated by progress in the use of remote systems in other dimensions of observation, which has reduced dependence upon terrestrial networks; detailed hydrological observation has yet to benefit from such remote platforms.[31]

Thus, many poorer countries have limited information to support the planning, development and management of water. This situation cannot be reversed overnight since, to be most useful, hydrology requires long, relatively complete records and there is a danger that when the investment tide turns, it will not be possible to use the new funding flows optimally. There is a growing awareness that existing design standards are perhaps no longer applicable. As one practitioner commented:

> *Marked changes in design floods are possible ... with potentially serious repercussions in design hydrology. In the absence of more comprehensive understanding, it is not possible to make reliable predictions at present, so practitioners are faced with the risk of either over-designing their infrastructure or incurring potentially unacceptable levels of risk.*[32]

> *Design hydrology will, therefore, in all likelihood, have to be re-evaluated in the light of anticipated climate change and the enhanced climatic variability associated with this change.*[33]

The rehabilitation of hydrological monitoring infrastructure and the recovery and use of existing as well as new data to provide hydrological design parameters that reflect the risk of climate change-induced variability are among the areas where 'leapfrogging' into the future is possible. But while the development of methods for remote monitoring of stream flow is on the global climate agenda, there is little urgency, perhaps because the promised water investments have yet to create the demand. Similarly, many countries have yet to begin to review their design standards from a climate change perspective. Delays in this area will leave urban communities and poor countries more vulnerable to natural disasters than they need to be.

Conclusions: Water resources management could be a lead sector in building urban resilience to climate change

Over the past two decades, energy has rightly taken centre stage in the climate change debates, with a focus on mitigation. The stakes are high since mitigation measures affect the very structure of the world's energy and industrial economies. While mitigation was correctly the initial focus, because prevention is always better than cure, attention must necessarily turn to adaptation as yesterday's predictions become today's realities. This will mean a growing focus on water, as is evident in urban areas where a failure to address the impacts of climate change upon water resources will leave their inhabitants vulnerable to a range of immediate acute and slow-onset disasters.

These include:

- flood damage to urban settlements;
- water and electricity supply failures affecting public health as well as the economic performance and sustainability of urban communities; and

- financial costs that will render water and related services unaffordable, potentially causing their collapse, with the same results.

While the costs are high, as illustrated by the costings presented earlier, they are not nearly as high as those required to meet the challenges of mitigation, estimated by the Intergovernmental Panel on Climate Change (IPCC) to be between US$60 billion and US$240 billion.[34] Adaptation measures will, in many cases, be integral to the process of achieving the social goals established in the Millennium Declaration.[35] And beyond the MDGs, building resilience into water management systems will also be critical in meeting the needs of economic water users upon whom urban economies depend.

For these reasons, the water sector may provide practical opportunities, at a realistic scale, to begin to make progress towards the goals of adaptation while the debates about the restructuring of the world's energy and industrial technology platforms continue. Water could become a lead sector in the process of developing appropriate models for financing the implementation of adaptation.

The sooner a start is made, the easier it will be to accommodate adaptation into 'normal' development. Conventional public finance approaches, if applied globally, would invest in adaptation now to avoid later crisis spending. In the context of the reform of overseas development assistance, the most effective approach would be to link additional budget support transfers to planning and budgeting processes that are enhanced to identify adaptation elements of existing spending items. In a world where rules were just and fair, a substantial proportion of these incremental costs would be met by those whose actions have imposed them, in terms of the polluter pays principle.

Effective action for adaptation has hardly begun; but there are many opportunities. Climate change is a slow-onset disaster that offers communities and nations time to adapt. The water cycle offers its own natural learning opportunities; it can be a patient teacher for those who are willing to learn.

Notes

1. Grubb, M. (2006) 'Climate change impacts, energy, and development', Paper presented at the Annual World Bank Conference on Development Economics, 30 May, Tokyo, p9.
2. Gagnon-Lebrun, F. and Agrawala, S. (2006) 'Progress on adaptation to climate change in developed countries: an analysis of broad trends', ENV/EPOC/ GSP(2006)1/FINAL, OECD, Paris.
3. Tol, R. S. J. (2005) 'Adaptation and mitigation: trade-offs in substance and methods', *Environmental Science & Policy*, vol 8, pp572–578.
4. Lomborg, B. (2001) *The Skeptical Environmentalist: Measuring the Real State of the World*, Cambridge University Press, Cambridge, 540pp.
5. See reference 1: Grubb, M. (2006), p26.

6. IPCC (Intergovernmental Panel on Climate Change) (2001) *Summary of Climate Changes and Likely Impacts on Water Resources*, Report of Working Group II, Intergovernmental Panel on Climate Change, Cambridge University Press.
7. UN (United Nations) (2002) *Plan of Implementation of the World Summit on Sustainable Development*, www.un.org/esa/sustdev/documents/WSSD_POI_PD/English/WSSD_PlanImpl.pdf.
8. UNESCO (United Nations Educational, Scientific and Cultural Organization) (2003) *Water for People, Water for Life; the First UN World Water Development Report*, UNESCO and Berghahn Books, Paris.
9. Adger, W. N., Huq, S., Brown, K., Conway, D. and Hulme, M. (2003) 'Adaptation to climate change in the developing world', *Progress in Development Studies*, vol 3, no 3, pp179–195.
10. See reference 8.
11. Thompson, J., Porras, I. T., Wood, E., Tumwine, J. K., Mujwahuzi, M. R., Katui-Katua, M. and Johnstone, N. (2000) 'Waiting at the tap: Changes in urban water use in East Africa over three decades', *Environment and Urbanization*, vol 12, no 2, October, pp37–52.
12. UN (2006) *World Urbanization Prospects: the 2005 Revision*, United Nations Population Division, Department of Economic and Social Affairs, CD-ROM edition – data in digital form (POP/DB/WUP/Rev.2005), United Nations, New York.
13. Jansen, A and Schulz, C. E. (2006) 'Water demand and the urban poor: A study of the factors influencing water consumption among households in Cape Town, South Africa', Working paper no 02/06 in Economics and Management Series, January, Department of Economics and Management, Norwegian College of Fishery Science University of Tromsø, Norway.
14. Muller, M. (2007) *Climate Change Adaptation and Integrated Water Resource Management – An Initial Overview*, TEC Policy Brief 5, Global Water Partnership, Stockholm.
15. IPCC (2001) *Climate Change 2001: Impacts, Adaptation and Vulnerability*, Report of Working Group II of the Intergovernmental Panel on Climate Change, Hydrology and Water Resources Section, Cambridge University Press.
16. See, for instance, Hewitson, B., Engelbrecht, F., Tadross, M. and Jack, C. (2005) 'General conclusions on development of plausible climate change scenarios for Southern Africa', in Schulze, R. E. (ed) *Climate Change and Water Resources in Southern Africa: Studies on Scenarios, Impacts, Vulnerabilities and Adaptation*, Water Research Commission Report 1430/1/05, WRC, Pretoria, Republic of South Africa, Chapter 5, pp75–79; also de Wit, M. and Stankiewicz, J. (2006) 'Changes in surface water supply across Africa with predicted climate change', *Science Express*, www.sciencemag.org/sciencepress/recent.dtl, p1/10.1126/science.1119929.
17. See reference 16: Hewitson et al (2005).
18. Muller, M. (2006) 'Living with climate: Can the water sector lead in building resilient societies?', Paper presented at the Conference on Living with Climate Variability and Change: Understanding the Uncertainties and Managing the Risks, 17–21 July, Espoo, Finland, www.livingwithclimate.fi/linked/en/Muller_text.pdf.
19. Camdessus, M. (chair) (2003) *Financing Water for All*, Report of World Panel on Financing Water Infrastructure, Global Water Partnership/World Water Council Third World Water Forum, 16–23 March, Kyoto.

20. See reference 18.
21. OECD (Organisation for Economic Co-operation and Development) (2006) *DAC Development Cooperation Report 2005*, Development Assistance Committee, OECD, Paris.
22. Stern, N. (2006) *Review of the Economics of Climate Change: What is the Economics of Climate Change?* Discussion Paper, Her Majesty's Treasury, UK Government, 31 January.
23. Bouwer, L. M., Jeroen, C. and Aerts, J. (2006) 'Financing climate change adaptation', *Disasters*, vol 30, no 1, pp49–63.
24. See reference 23: Bouwer et al (2006), p56.
25. Paris High Level Forum (2005) *Paris Declaration on Aid Effectiveness, Ownership, Harmonization, Alignment, Results and Mutual Accountability*, OECD/Development Assistance Committee, Paris.
26. Global Water Partnership (2000) *Integrated Water Resources Management Background Paper*, no 4, Technical Advisory Committee, GWP, Stockholm.
27. See reference 7; also Global Water Partnership (2006) *Setting the Stage for Change*, Second informal survey by the GWP network giving the status of the 2005 WSSD target on national integrated water resources management and water efficiency plans, GWP, Stockholm, February.
28. Muller, M. (2007) 'Parish pump politics – the politics of water supply in South Africa', *Progress in Development Studies*, vol 7, no 1, pp33–45.
29. See World Bank (2004) *Water Resources Sector Strategy*, World Bank, Washington, DC; see also reference 2.
30. WMO (World Meteorological Office) (2003) 'Networks, availability and access to hydrological data', Memorandum by Dr W. Grabs, Chief, Water Resources Division, WMO (retrieved from Global Runoff Data Centre, www.grdc.bafg.de., September 2006); also Washington R., Harrison, M. and Conway, D. (2004) *African Climate Report*, Commissioned by the UK government to review African climate science, policy and options for action, DFID, London.
31. See reference 18.
32. Schulze, R. E. (2005) 'Case study 2: potential impacts of shifts in hydroclimatic zone on design hydrology from small catchments in Southern Africa', in Schulze, R. E. (ed) (2005): see reference 16, Chapter 13, pp241–247.
33. Schulze, R. E. (2005) 'Adapting to climate change in the water resources sector in South Africa', in Schulze, R. E. (ed) (2005): see reference 16, Chapter 27, pp423–449.
34. IPCC (2001) *Summary for Policymakers: The Economic and Social Dimensions of Climate Change*, Report of Working Group III, Intergovernmental Panel on Climate Change, Cambridge University Press.
35. UN (2000) *United Nations, Millennium Declaration*, A Res 55/2, September 2000, New York.

4

MOVING FORWARD

14

Climate Change Risk: An Adaptation and Mitigation Agenda for Indian Cities

Aromar Revi

Introduction

India is one of the more vulnerable and risk-prone countries in the world.[1] Over the centuries, its population has learned to cope with a wide range of natural and human-made hazards. Rapid population growth, high densities, poverty and high differentials in access to housing, public services and infrastructure have led to an increase in vulnerability over the last few decades, especially in India's urban centres.

Climate change is expected to increase the frequency and intensity of current hazards and the probability of extreme events, and to spur the emergence of new hazards (e.g. sea-level rise)[2] and new vulnerabilities with differential spatial and socio-economic impacts. This is expected to further degrade the resilience of poor, vulnerable communities, which make up between one quarter and one half of the population of most Indian cities.[3] Climate change is set to become an increasingly important strategic economic and political concern as it starts to eat into India's high economic growth rates and affect the lives and livelihoods of millions of people.

Overall risk in Indian cities is typically associated more with vulnerability than with hazard exposure. It is therefore important to understand a number of processes that are rapidly changing India's urban landscape, altering livelihood opportunities and wealth distribution, which, in turn, affect the vulnerability of many communities and stakeholders, and their capacity to adapt to long-term risks.

This analysis focuses on an adaptation-led strategy to reduce climate change risk and increase urban resilience in keeping with India's development priorities and challenges. It shifts the emphasis from the mitigation and techno-centric response that has come to dominate the Organisation for Economic Co-operation and Development (OECD)-led climate crisis discourse and suggests a more independent route to a more sustainable future.[4]

Climate change in India can be seen from the perspective of a three-part transition: a demographic transition that will see India's population stabilizing at about 1.6 billion in the 2060s; a simultaneous rural to urban (*RUrban*) transition, which will add nearly 500 million people to the country's urban settlements over this period; and a simultaneous environmental transition – brown (water, sanitation and environmental health), grey (air and water pollution) and green (climate change).[5] Multiple sub-regionally nuanced strategies will be needed to respond to the climate crisis, drawing on considerable local experience of coping with uncertainty and with systems far from equilibrium.

India's *RUrban* transformation (2000–2050)

Unlike most of the rest of the world, South Asia has been marked by low levels of urbanization despite being one of the most urbanized pre-colonial regions of the eighteenth century.[6] Only about 30 per cent of India's population lived in urban areas in 2006;[7] but given its 1.1 billion-plus population, its urban population still exceeds that of Japan, the European Union and most other regions of the world except for the US and China.[8] Over the next 40 years, India will experience one of the most dramatic settlement transitions in history as its urban population grows from about 300 million to more than 700 million.[9] By 2025, an estimated 70 Indian cities are expected to have a population in excess of 1 million. Three mega-urban regions – Mumbai–Pune (50 million), the national capital region of Delhi (more than 30 million) and Kolkata (20 million) – will be among the largest urban concentrations in the world.[10] By mid-century, India could have both the largest urban and rural populations of the time. This will have an important bearing on global climate vulnerability and the potential for mitigation and adaptation. Hence, the future direction of Indian urbanization is not only an important domestic concern, but also a major international opportunity to demonstrate the viability of a more sustainable development.

Urban India overtook rural India in its share of gross domestic product (GDP) in the late 1990s, and urban per capita incomes are more than three times those in rural areas.[11] India's agricultural sector currently contributes only 18 per cent of GDP, although it provides livelihoods to almost 60 per cent of the population as well as the biomass and ecosystem services that enable the 'metabolism' of most Indian cities to function.

Climate change-induced disruptions and the pre-emption in net primary productivity by human systems[12] could force many Indian cities to adapt in the medium term by altering their extractive relationship with the countryside. *RUrbanism*, or 'keeping the balance between rural and urban areas', will become increasingly important in India, as rural–urban and inter-urban resource and socio-economic conflict became sharper in the future.[13]

Migration in India has been constrained by a number of factors, including:

- a crisis in creating new urban formal-sector livelihoods in an era of globalization;
- dismal living and working conditions for the poor in cities;
- high urban poverty levels driven by high costs of living;
- poor improvements in rural education until the late 1990s; and
- a slow process of social transformation.[14]

It is possible, however, that climate change may force the pace of rural–urban migration over the next few decades. The ongoing agrarian crisis in rural India[15] could be catalysed by climate change into a migratory rout, driven by increases in extreme events, greater monsoon variability,[16] endemic drought, and flooding and resource conflict.[17] These scenarios have only been broadly articulated but not systematically investigated with fine-grained geographic information system (GIS)-linked models.[18]

Alternatively, severe stresses induced in urban areas due to a combination of water scarcity, the breakdown of environmental services, flooding and consequent water-borne diseases and malaria-type epidemics, along with a rapid rise in health expenditure, could maintain the low current level of rural–urban migration. A greater mobility of the backward castes and women could also, in time, alter the migration dynamics across demographically dominant northern and eastern India. This indicates the potential for climate change (along with other driving factors) to induce bifurcation behaviour in migration and, hence, urbanization trends – questions that need to be investigated further.

Maintaining two-way flows of food, biomass, water, energy, livelihoods, products and services across the *RUrban* continuum will be crucial to India's 'development transition' and medium-term sustainability. Climate change adaptation in both cities and their embedding countryside is an undiscovered near-term policy concern – intimately connected with livelihoods and drought, biomass and energy security.[19]

India, like China in the 1990s, is starting to massively ramp up infrastructure investment in the energy, water, transportation and telecommunications sectors to support their growth and expansion. These systems have a typical service life of 50 to 150 years. More importantly, they are difficult to replace (if damaged or destroyed in extreme weather events), challenging to relocate (if necessary for effective adaptation) and may spur significant greenhouse gas contributions (if executed using business-as-usual technologies and management methods).

The challenge for India is to re-examine whether its current development trajectory and growth framework may be more appropriate than an exclusive engagement with mitigation and greener systems and production. A climate policy that has a closer fit with India's initial conditions, strengths and capacities may serve both the country and the world's purposes better than a 'recycled' programme of action from a rather different context.

Urban renewal, disaster management and climate change mitigation

India made a late start in engaging with questions of climate change despite early environmentalist and academic positions on these questions.[20] While climate change has started to creep into the post-Rio (1992)[21] global policy agenda, India has been preoccupied with pressing poverty, economic and social development and political challenges.

India has undertaken four officially supported national technical assessments of climate change risks, impacts, adaptation and mitigation options since 1992.[22] These assessments were all largely externally funded and driven; they were coordinated by the Ministry of Environment and Forests, which is far from being a politically powerful ministry; and they were primarily focused on the 'science' of climate change, closely allied to the Intergovernmental Panel on Climate Change (IPCC) agenda and trends of analysis.[23] They were therefore weak in engaging with the complex nature and intensity of vulnerability in India, probably the most critical factor in risk mitigation.[24]

The official Indian position on climate change has been strongly tied to fixing responsibility for correcting historical emissions by the OECD countries.[25] Hence, it is focused largely on the greenhouse gas–energy nexus, its impact upon energy security and technology transfer[26] and the post-Kyoto opportunities for financial leverage from expected cross-national flows of capital; or as a fringe issue taken up by environmental non-governmental organizations (NGOs) and activists that has little to do with the mainstream economic 'development' agenda.[27] The debate on adaptation has been weak despite a moderate Indian scientific presence in the IPCC process and an Indian IPCC chair since 2002.[28]

A great missed opportunity in the last 15 years was the chance to connect the official climate change adaptation agenda with the rapid development of natural hazard risk assessment, management and mitigation capacity after devastating disasters in the 1990s and the early 2000s. A series of moderately successful post-disaster reconstruction and mitigation programmes, especially after the Orissa super-cyclone (1999), the Kachchh earthquake (2001) and the Indian Ocean tsunami (2005), dramatically altered perceptions and the institutional and technical capacity to address vulnerability reduction and risk mitigation in India. India is one of the few large countries that have a central authority to address disaster management and similar well-developed institutions at state level.

The devastation wrought by the 2005 tsunami also brought a long-simmering concern to the fore – the integrated management of India's coastal zone, balancing environmental and biodiversity conservation, livelihood and economic development, and risk mitigation concerns. A series of integrated coastal zone management plans are now in progress, along with a review of the principles for managing the coastal regulation zone. This will provide an important stepping stone for a more evidence-based set of climate mitigation and adaptation measures for coastal India and its cities – a key driver of medium-range economic growth and development.[29]

The other important post-2004 development is the reappearance of urban development, urban renewal and governance as a significant public policy agenda after a decade-long hiatus. The Jawaharlal Nehru National Urban Renewal Mission (JNNURM) was initiated in 2005 to target 60 of the most important cities with a US$10 billion challenge fund to address infrastructure development, urban poverty and urban governance.

A chasm exists between the official urban 'city building' development agenda and vulnerability reduction for those most at risk in these urban areas. The Indian state and its elite have been ambivalent in accepting the centrality of the poor in the process of urban development and economic growth. The imperative of delivering adequate services (water, sanitation, solid waste, drainage, power) and equitable access to land and housing to the bulk of city residents is still a matter of contention. This ongoing institutional and cultural failure has been documented for decades; but the current scale of demolitions and relocations is compounding the vulnerability of many urban residents.

Breaking this impasse will be central to the next conceptual leap of political and bureaucratic attention – from the state provisioning of basic services and access to livelihoods and housing, to alternative mechanisms for ensuring their sustainable provisioning, functioning and financing. This can be supported through multiple variants of community–public–private partnerships. The role of risk reduction and climate change adaptation in lowering the mounting social costs of recurrent disasters will need to be situated around action in this space. However, no JNNURM component addresses either urban vulnerability or risk mitigation. This will call for advocacy by the climate change community and would need to be linked to sustainable city and regional development initiatives.[30] Otherwise, urban adaptation and mitigation could be limited to signing operationally meaningless memoranda of understanding between Indian and OECD cities, official junkets and press releases, with little impact upon the most vulnerable.

An important post-1990 factor is the emergence of city-level political processes – community and people's movements – that have started contesting from 'below' for 'space' for the poor within many cities. This has been accompanied by NGO and judicial activism on a range of environmental questions, which unfortunately have had little impact upon more proletarian concerns such as environmental health, which could dramatically reduce the risk exposure of poor households. These currently fractured forces, if adequately mobilized, could provide a base for future citywide, community-based risk mitigation efforts that are crucial to the success of climate change risk adaptation. A parallel but often conflicting development is the increasing concern of the elite with the quality of urban life, security and the sustainability of various urban services. But here again, enlightened self-interest has not come to terms with the challenges and opportunities that the transformation of India's cities presents. Concerns for 'carbon neutral' lifestyles and enterprises and for higher quality of life must converge with harsh realities on the ground. This remains a largely unexplored area.

India's climate change risk exposure

Most Indian communities and institutions have a history of coping with uncertainty and extreme events with great equanimity. However, the current pressure on resources, high population densities and ongoing rapid economic, technological and slower social changes imply that a mix of institutional, market- and community-led mitigation and adaptation interventions will be necessary if future losses are to be within tolerable bounds. The poor and vulnerable, who suffer the most in extreme events, should be the first priority.

The following sections explore India's climate change-related risk exposure, unbundling first- and second-order risks and defining a coherent set of adaptation and mitigation measures that could converge with ongoing natural hazard risk reduction and urban renewal interventions.

Temperature and precipitation changes

While there is little scientific 'doubt' about the emergence of climate change as an important risk in the Indian subcontinent over this century, there is still considerable uncertainty concerning precise mechanisms and impacts, especially related to precipitation and sea-level rise, as presented in Table 14.1.

In spite of the uncertainty, there is broad consensus on the envelope of first-order climate change impacts in South Asia over the 21st century:

Table 14.1 *Climate change projections for India based on an ensemble of four General Circulation Model (GCM) outputs*

Year	Temperature change (°C)			Precipitation change (%)			Sea-level rise (cm)
	Annual	Winter	Monsoon	Annual	Winter	Monsoon	
2020s	1.36 ± 0.19	1.61 ± 0.16	1.13 ± 0.43	2.9 ± 3.7	2.7 ± 17.7	2.9 ± 3.7	4–8
2050s	2.69 ± 0.41	3.25 ± 0.36	2.19 ± 0.88	6.7 ± 8.9	−2.9 ± 26.3	6.7 ± 8.9	15–38
2080s	3.84 ± 0.76	4.52 ± 0.49	3.19 ± 1.42	11.0 ± 12.3	5.3 ± 34.4	11.0 ± 12.3	46–59

Source: Agarwal, D. and Lal, M. (2001), *Vulnerability of Indian Coastline to Sea-level Rise*, Centre for Atmospheric Sciences, Indian Institute of Technology, New Delhi

- There has been a general increase in both mean minimum and maximum temperatures of 2° to 4°C, depending upon the realized atmospheric greenhouse gas concentrations,[31] with an impact upon evapo-transpiration levels and therefore agriculture, horticulture and forestry and human activities, especially in arid, semi-arid and mountain zones.

- This could lead to a mean surface temperature rise of 3.5° to 5°C by the end of the century, which would imply changes in the location and viability of some settlements (especially in the arid and semi-arid zones) and in the pattern of building across the subcontinent, with an increasing role for passive solar and energy efficient design.[32]

- This regional temperature rise, along with changes in the global climate system and the Indian Ocean monsoon system, may lead to a mean increase of 7 to 20 per cent in annual precipitation. A 10 to 15 per cent increase in monsoon precipitation in many regions, a simultaneous precipitation decline of 5 to 25 per cent in drought-prone central India and a sharp decline in winter rainfall in northern India are also projected.[33] This implies changes in the output of winter wheat and mustard crops in north-western India, which could have a significant impact upon national food security, regional crop mixes and resultant demand for irrigation. This is a most serious risk to rural India and the hope of an agricultural resurgence.

- The substantial spatial differences in precipitation changes imply adaptation of sub-regional agriculture, changes in water supply arrangements and a strong policy emphasis on water conservation and efficiency in most cities, as more rain could fall in more intense spells and drought intensity could increase. This increase, combined with a shorter wet season, will imply a change in the hydrology of many river systems and therefore a modification in the storage capacity and management regime of many dams and reservoirs, thus affecting urban water systems.

- A decrease in the number of rainy days (5 to 15 days on average) is expected over much of India along with an increase in heavy rainfall days and in the frequency of heavy rainfall events in the monsoon season.[34] These changes are expected to increase the vulnerability of Indian agriculture and natural resource-linked livelihoods and also that of the urban poor who typically reside in areas more prone to pluvial flooding and who are most vulnerable to water scarcity as they largely depend upon informal water markets.

- The substantial increase in extreme precipitation (similar to Mumbai in 2005 and the 2005 and 2006 Gujarat flood events) expected over a large area of the west coast and central India[35] will require a significant revision of urban planning practices across city and neighbourhood scales to integrate flood and climate change mitigation and adaptation measures within day-to-day urban development and service delivery activities.[36]

Drought

The most serious climate change risk to the Indian economy and its people is the increased intensity, frequency and geographical coverage of drought. Drought typically makes up one half to two-thirds of the natural hazard risk exposure.[37] Its primary impact is in rural areas, where agriculture, animal husbandry and, to a lesser extent, forestry[38] and fishing are significantly affected, leading to cycles of seasonal and distress migration, and increasing rural debt and a spate of farmer suicides across much of semi-arid India over the last few years.[39]

Drought has two typical first-order impacts upon Indian cities: drinking water shortages and increases in food and biomass fuel prices. It also has a number of important second-order impacts: depressed demand for urban-produced secondary goods and services because of depressed agricultural demand; and increasing seasonal and distress migration from rural areas.[40] Continuing severe climate change-induced drought that makes subsistence agriculture uneconomical in large parts of semi-arid central, western and southern India could catalyse a sharp increase in migration. This, apparently, is not factored into current economic development or national security strategy.

Climate change is expected to increase the severity of drought, especially in western India where five river basins are expected to face acute to severe water shortages, affecting a large number of cities in Gujarat. Land uses, cropping patterns and poor water resource management in the 20h century have resulted in a 50 per cent reduction in the surface water discharge of the Ganga over the last 25 years and in a sharp drop in groundwater tables across the entire Indo–Gangetic plain.[41] The Ganga, Narmada, Krishna and Kaveri rivers are expected to experience seasonal or regular water stress, affecting western, northern and eastern India.[42] If the political and economic consequences of the Kaveri dispute and the Narmada struggle[43] are an indication, within the next decade Indian federalism could be severely challenged by these changes.

Climate change is expected to increase drought in semi-arid peninsular and western India, forcing more of the landless and small and marginal farmers to migrate to cities. They often form the most vulnerable groups in cities – having limited skills, education, capital and access to the social networks that underpin much of economic and social mobility in urban India. They often live in illegal, unserviced settlements exposed to a wide range of environmental risks, from flooding to fire, and continual cycles of demolition and eviction by civil authorities. They are, therefore, dual victims of existing natural hazards and emerging climate change – displaced from their original places of residence and occupations and challenged by urban risks in their new urban places of residence.

The most serious regional impact of climate change would be changes in the river hydrology in the Indo–Gangetic plain and the Brahmaputra Valley due to glacial melt and regression of the Himalayan glaciers.[44] Ongoing transboundary conflicts between India and Pakistan, and Nepal, India and Bangladesh may be compounded by a possible China–India conflict over the use of the Yarlung Tsang-po/ Brahmaputra waters as river flows decline and inter-basin transfers are increasingly suggested as solutions to challenges of urban and regional water stress.[45]

Four of the ten largest mega-urban regions of the 21st century – namely, Delhi, Dhaka, Kolkata and Karachi – lie on the banks of these great rivers along with more than 30 other million-plus cities. Significant changes in river hydrology and the availability of irrigation and drinking water could have a dramatic impact upon the growth and development of the many small- and medium-sized towns and million-cities that are expected to mushroom across these fertile plains in the next three decades, adding an unprecedented resource dimension to the social and economic transformation of northern and eastern India.

The bulk of the water extraction from these river systems is for irrigation to provide food for close to 1 billion people. Hence, an emerging conflict is brewing between cities and the rural areas from where the urban water supply is drawn and to where city water pollution is discharged. Since the 1980s, multiple environmental struggles have been fought over the extraction of surface water from remote watersheds where many relatively poor people have been displaced by exploding urban demand.[46] This will surely accelerate and become an increasing constraint on the current resource-inefficient pattern of urban development – if Delhi's long saga with Haryana and Uttar Pradesh on drinking water transmission is an indication of the future.[47]

The national capital region of Delhi faces a severe water shortfall of 200 million gallons per day (MGD), or more than 32 per cent of its production.[48] Drinking water is being transported from more than 300km away to meet the demands, and unaccounted-for water losses are more than 44 per cent.[49] Rising temperatures and energy demand for cooling, increasing precipitation variability, fewer rainy days, the unsustainable mining of groundwater and a river system that has been polluted to death could all make the Delhi mega-urban region, with a projected population of more than 30 million, highly unsustainable in spite of rapid growth in its income and wealth. These questions are far from the minds of both planners and politicians as they prepare to 'green' the city for the 2010 Commonwealth Games.

Delhi is simultaneously experiencing the 'brown', 'grey' and 'green' environmental transitions[50] over a period of less than 50 years; but water availability rather than economic and social development challenges may be its undoing, as with two other great capital cities of this region: Mohammed-bin-Tuglak's (1325–1351) Tuglakabad, near Delhi, and Akbar's (1556–1605) Fatehpur Sikri, near Agra.

River and inland flooding and extreme rainfall events

The next most important climate change risk is increased riverine and inland flooding, especially in northern and eastern India and adjoining Nepal and Bangladesh. Tens of millions of people are currently affected by floods for three to six months of the year in eastern India.[51] Increased precipitation and higher peak monsoon river flows due to glacial regression could exacerbate the situation for additional tens of millions. This is largely due to the high population densities across this region, combined with very high vulnerability due to a mix of poorly designed and executed flood management systems, complex land and water tenure regimes and high levels of poverty, which over the last few decades have severely degraded the coping capacity of millions of residents of eastern India.[52]

Climate change is expected to increase the severity of flooding in many Indian river basins, especially those of the Godavari and Mahanadi along the eastern coast.[53] Floods are also expected to increase in north-western India, adjoining Pakistan, and in most coastal plains in spite of existing upstream dams and 'multipurpose' projects. Extreme precipitation is expected to increase substantially over a large area of the west coast and central India.[54] Gujarat, one of India's most prosperous states, has experienced severe flooding for three consecutive years since 2004, causing large economic losses in its cities.[55]

The devastating Mumbai floods of 2005 were caused by an extreme weather event. Most city services were shut down for the first time in recorded history for almost five days, with no contact via rail, road or air with the rest of the country. More than 1000 people lost their lives in the region and economic life in the city came to a halt[56] due to a combination of institutional failures, lack of preparedness and extremely high vulnerability of the poor.[57]

Cyclonic storms, storm surge and coastal flooding

The third most important risk is that of cyclonic storms, storm surge and accompanying coastal inundation. A sea surface temperature rise of 2° to 4°C, as anticipated in the Indian Ocean over the century, is expected to induce a 10 to 20 per cent increase in cyclone intensity.[58] Since the frequency of cyclones in the Bay of Bengal is about five times that of the Arabian Sea,[59] India's east coast is clearly at more risk in spite of the fact that the north Indian Ocean Basin is one of the least intense cyclone/hurricane basins in the world.

The high concentration of population on India and Bangladesh's eastern coasts has led to extremely high vulnerability in this region, leading to devastating loss of life and property. The 1999 Orissa super-cyclone killed more than 10,000 people and devastated buildings, lifeline infrastructure and economic assets across ten coastal and six inland districts; this was due to a mixture of devastating storm surge, cyclonic winds and coastal flooding.[60] A 1991 cyclone killed more than 139,000 people in Bangladesh and caused a significant compression of its GDP.[61]

Cyclones and storm surge could have a devastating impact upon such large urban centres as Mumbai and Chennai and the million-cities of Vishakapatnam, Surat, Bharuch, Bhavnagar and Jamnagar, as well as causing critical bottlenecks in important ports such as Kandla.[62] Storm surge, when accompanied by coastal flooding and cyclonic winds, is the second most devastating rapid-onset hazard in Gujarat, accounting for 12 per cent of the risk to the state and a potential loss of more than 11,000 lives for a probabilistic 100-year event.[63] Losses could rise considerably with increased migration to the coast, drawn by huge investments in coastal infrastructure, settlements and enterprise; but these are located largely unmindful of future risk distribution.

Mean and extreme sea-level rise

Data over the last century indicate a mean sea-level rise (SLR) of less than 1mm per year along the Indian coast. More recent observations suggest an SLR of 2.5mm per year since the 1950s. An SLR of between 30cm and 80cm has been projected over the century along India's coast based on multiple climate change scenarios.[64]

Two more recent studies have placed between 6 million and 40 million of the coastal population at risk in South Asia. A World Bank-funded study[65] used multiple scenarios ranging from 1m to 5m of sea-level rise based on evidence of increased rates of deglaciation in Greenland and Antarctica and the resultant increased probability of extreme climate scenarios. Up to 1 per cent of India's urban areas could be inundated by a 3m SLR, and just under 2 per cent with a 5m rise. A 3m SLR is expected to affect more than 1 per cent of the population, and a 5m rise is expected to affect 2.5 per cent of the population. The spatial databases used in this study may leave room for inaccuracies – but it provides a basis for a broad comparative analysis. The overall regional compression of GDP as a result of losses directly due to SLR is estimated at 0.6 per cent from a 1m SLR, 1.6 per cent from a 3m SLR, and 2.9 per cent from a 5m SLR for South Asia. The relative impact upon India would typically be lower than in Bangladesh, where up to 10 per cent of the area and population are at high risk; but serious adaptation and mitigation measures will be required, especially for coastal cities and ports, which are expected to produce a high share of GDP and underpin India's growing manufacturing exports. There is a clear case for a macroeconomic analysis of risk for India, as has been undertaken for Bangladesh[66] and the UK.[67]

A second study, led by the International Institute for Environment and Development (IIED),[68] examined vulnerability within the low-elevation coastal zone (LECZ) (i.e. settlements and facilities at risk of a 10m SLR) – probably the outer boundary of catastrophic climate change.[69] Using a more robust methodology than the World Bank study, it estimated that Asian countries contain three-quarters of the global LECZ population and two-thirds of the global LECZ urban population, with a higher concentration in cities over 5 million in size. India is estimated to have the second largest LECZ population, with about 3 per cent of national area at risk.[70]

In short, irrespective of the form and method of assessment, SLR is a serious risk for a number of cities along India's coast. It is clearly in the national interest to invest in more and better science in order to assess possible risks at various levels of climate change. The costs of inaction on this count alone could outstrip that investment by many orders of magnitude.[71]

The stretches along the western Indian coast that are most vulnerable to SLR are Khambhat and Kachchh in Gujarat, Mumbai and parts of the Konkan coast, and South Kerala. The deltas of the Ganga, Krishna, Godavari, Cauvery and Mahanadi on the east coast are expected to be lost, along with significant settlement areas and irrigated land and a number of urban settlements that are situated there.[72] The loss of these important economic and cultural regions could have a considerable impact upon the states of West Bengal, Orissa, Andhra Pradesh and Tamil Nadu.

No estimates of the impact of climate change upon saltwater intrusion in the coastal zone and upon coastal agriculture and fisheries, and, therefore, upon agricultural, pastoral and fishing communities, are available, but these are expected to be significant.

SLR, combined with an increased frequency and intensity of tropical cyclones, is expected to lead to an increase in extreme sea levels due to storm surge.[73] The fact that India's coast and especially its western seaboard and stretches along the Bay of Bengal are expected to grow dramatically in terms of population, infrastructure and industrial investment in the next two decades implies a non-linear increase in coastal SLR vulnerability. The primary driving factors are differential population densities along the coast and in coastal deltas; a greater openness of the Indian economy to trade; a sharp upturn in energy imports, almost exclusively traded by sea; and strong public investment incentives to coastal development.

Environmental health risks

Climate change is expected to accentuate environment-related health risks, including those from water-washed diseases (e.g. diarrhoea, cholera and typhoid), due to water scarcity and malaria. Malaria is expected to expand from its currently endemic range in eastern and north-eastern India to western and southern India, thereby placing a large incremental population at risk.[74] Given that Indian cities have become major reservoirs of vector-borne diseases such as malaria and dengue fever, it can be expected that morbidity risks would increase. Additional research needs to be undertaken on the potential impact of water scarcity and flooding upon environmental health conditions in cities and their consequent impact upon morbidity, mortality and productivity.

Composite multi-hazard risk adaptation

Addressing a complex of six major risk groups – temperature and precipitation variability; drought; flooding and extreme rainfall; cyclone and storm surge;

sea-level rise; and linked environmental health risk – is a serious public policy and adaptation management challenge for India.

An important new method that can help to address these concerns is composite risk assessment and adaptation planning. This enables a geographically explicit estimation of probabilistic hazard risk, vulnerability and the imputed composite multi-hazard economic risks. Risk prioritization by hazard, element at risk and location can thereafter be undertaken, assisting in creating evidence-based investment, regional and urban development policies and building a bridge between public agencies, communities and the private sector.[75]

Some capacity has been built nationally and in about one quarter of Indian states to address single rapid onset (e.g. earthquake) and long onset (e.g. drought) risk; but managing a complex portfolio of hazard risks and vulnerabilities is beyond both the current mix of public institutions and the nascent private reinsurance and insurance industry.

India has no robust national estimates of composite economic risk due to natural hazards, unlike Bangladesh.[76] A national vulnerability atlas,[77] updated to assess district-level building vulnerability to cyclone, storm surge, earthquake and flood risk exposure, does not use probabilistic methods of risk assessment, and the fragility functions used are based on a very limited analysis of loss. Furthermore, no economic loss estimates have been derived. The only robust state-level estimates of composite risk indicate an annual gross state domestic product compression of about 2 per cent for Gujarat, of which drought makes up 57 per cent, cyclone and storm surge 12 per cent and inland flooding 5 per cent over a 100-year time horizon.[78] This assessment breaks new ground by unbundling risk for urban and rural areas. This is one of the most detailed sub-regional risk assessments in the world, reaching sub-district level for eight crops, animal husbandry, fisheries, industry, services and critical infrastructure. Yet, even though it was completed in 2005, it does not take into account increased hazard risk due to climate change because of the low awareness of climate risk exposure in India.

Urban populations and elements at risk

The most vulnerable populations and elements in a typical Indian city are:

- slum, squatter and migrant populations resident in traditional and informal settlements, which are often located in the most vulnerable locations;
- industrial and informal service sector workers, whose occupations place them at significant risk of natural hazards;
- buildings, especially traditional and informal housing that is especially vulnerable to wind, water and geological hazards;
- industrial units, their in-house infrastructure, plant, machinery and raw materials;

- lifeline public and private infrastructure, which includes roads, bridges, railways, ports, airports and other transportation systems; water, sewage and gas pipelines; drainage, flood and coastal defence systems; power and telecommunication infrastructure; and critical social infrastructure such as hospitals, schools, fire and police stations and first responder's infrastructure; and
- ecosystems and the natural environment, especially wetlands, riverine, estuarine and coastal ecosystems, and surface and groundwater systems.

Risk adaptation and mitigation measures need to address particular populations and elements at risk within a *RUrban* landscape to be effective in responding to a heterogeneous field of constraints and opportunities. Hence, decentralized adaptive management strategies that engage with a political, policy and implementation continuum from the neighbourhood, city and region to the national level have proved to be more effective than centralized top-down interventions.[79] A coherent framework, within which public policy, private sector and civil society urban development and planning actions are taken can reduce vulnerability and risk in a steady iterative manner over a period of decades.[80] This, in turn, requires a new set of incentives and structures that link short-run priorities with long-run strategic actions – a major shift in the current urban management paradigm.

Urban vulnerability to climate change

Ironically, but not surprisingly, the urban residents most vulnerable to climate change are the poor slum and squatter settlement dwellers and those who suffer from the multiple insecurities that poor governance, the lack of serious investment in the commons, and a strong nexus between the political class, real estate developers and public agencies bring to cities. Through a long process of loss accumulation, they are multiply challenged by even small events that affect their livelihoods, income, property, assets and, sometimes, their lives. Because of systematic exclusion from the formal economy of the city – basic services and entitlements and the impossibly high entry barrier into legal land and housing markets – most poor people live on hazardous sites and are exposed to multiple environmental health risks via poor sanitation and water supply, little or no drainage and solid waste services, air and water pollution, and the recurrent threat of being evicted. Yet, they survive, add considerable economic value to the city and 'subsidize' the better-off via their poor living and working conditions.

Until basic entitlements, services and quality of life are ensured for the bulk of India's urban residents and the vulnerability of the rest is reduced to acceptable levels, little or no public and community-based structural mitigation action is likely. Urban mitigation activities typically will be led by enterprises and large public utilities that seek carbon offset-linked financial and economic incentives.

In the near term, the focus in Indian cities, neighbourhoods and communities will need to be on adaptation to climate change. The primary challenges here will lie in better and more accountable city governance, democratic decentralization improving the functioning of public institutions, and the recreation of the 'commons' through multiple political and institutional struggles. Technical, purely economic or even institutional 'fixes' typically will fail to deliver results unless local democratic, political and socio-cultural processes are engaged with around the themes of equity, social transformation, local 'voice' and 'agency'. Given the 'distance' between these concerns and those of the global climate change debate, a rather different set of strategies should probably emerge in India than those currently envisaged.

A possible urban climate change adaptation framework

Developing a climate change adaptation framework for urban India will require opening a dialogue on urban development and growth, vulnerability, risk unbundling, the redirection of ongoing investments and programmes, and the building of new alliances between a wide range of actors not often in engagement. Together, this can help to transform existing cities to make them more inclusive and productive, thereby reducing structural vulnerability.

A pragmatic way forward is to build upon the existing momentum of hazard risk management and mitigation efforts. This is most effectively done by mainstreaming them into urban redevelopment initiatives, such as the JNNRURM, and mobilization from below via NGOs, community-based organizations (CBOs) and political processes in particular cities. Given that a number of these stakeholders have little or no knowledge of climate change issues, the development of a framework linking dialogue, engagement and action would be a useful step.

This framework would need to provide a link between national, state and city-level policy, political institutional arrangements and interventions at city and neighbourhood levels. It would also serve as a platform for dialogue between government functionaries, political leaders, CBOs and NGOs who are active in trying to channel citizen and community energy towards productive ends and private entrepreneurs who could provide the motive power for adaptation implementation.

A sketch for a possible framework at multiple levels, involving various stakeholders and institutions, is presented below.

National level. India has not developed a National Adaptation Programme of Action (NAPA) to address urban climate change risk reduction partly because of institutional fractures within the government of India and its status as an emerging middle-income state. The primary responsibility currently lies with the Ministry of Environment and Forests, which has weak traction with more key sectoral ministries. To integrate a cross-cutting climate change agenda within the overall planning and investment process of the government of India would imply a possible relocation of this function to the Cabinet Secretariat or the Planning Commission, with strong support from the Ministry of Finance. This would require an amendment to the Allocation of Business Rules (1961)[81] and the establishment of a climate change secretariat to address cross-cutting issues. This would enable the coordination of adaptation policies and programmes across key line ministries and functions and the mobilization of state governments and cities for adaptation planning and implementation.

The Ministry of Finance could play a central role in defining fiscal and financial measures to 'incentivize' both mitigation and adaptation, based on a 'NAPA-like' rollout schedule. This could include the creation of a domestic market for carbon credits linked via appropriate institutions to the global carbon market, enabling the financing of state-led, pro-poor adaptation.

The National Disaster Management Authority (NDMA), within the Ministry of Home Affairs, is the apex disaster management agency although the bulk of this responsibility and action lies with state governments.[82] The climate change agenda could build a bridge between current NDMA priorities and medium- and long-term climate adaptation.

The Ministry of Environment and Forests, along with the Department of Ocean Development, engages with coastal zone regulation in coordination with state-level ministries. This is another locus of convergence that a cabinet secretariat-based climate change cell could address.

The departments of urban development and poverty alleviation, which jointly manage the JNNURM, should be the fulcrum of urban climate change risk mitigation at the national level and the primary agency for urban climate policy and programme design once appropriate state and city capacities are built. An integration of concerns within long-range city development plans, infrastructure development and poverty reduction interventions at city level is crucial. Disaster management is one of the many elements of the JNNURM that is poorly resourced at city level. It needs to be scaled up and broadened to encompass a wider climate adaptation agenda.

The creation of a National Technical Mission on Urban Climate Change Adaptation to deliver time-bound outcomes may be a useful way to focus energies and put the climate crisis onto the public policy agenda. Specific priority tasks for the government of India could include the development of a *National Risk and Vulnerability Atlas* that includes climate change-related risks and estimates of potential losses to economic activity and capital stocks. This will enable the identification of priority cities and sectors for intervention and thereby open appropriate windows of opportunities within the JNNURM. A new series of national building and lifeline infrastructure risk mitigation standards will be necessary, taking into account climate-related risks. This can be taken forward by the NDMA, the Ministry of Urban Development and the Bureau of Indian

Standards, based on the pattern of the national earthquake mitigation standards.[83]

A series of insurance instruments for short- and medium-term risk coverage to urban infrastructure enterprises and incentives for public–community–private partnerships need to be put into place, similar to initiatives in the agricultural sector.

Apex institutions that bring together public- and private-sector enterprises, civil society and academic institutions (especially science and technology, management and social science research) will need to be activated at national level to build research and action-oriented networks in and between their sectors of competence. Education, training and capacity-building at schools and universities for public functionaries, managers and the media will need to be launched.

State level. Each state needs to establish a state disaster management authority along the lines of the Gujarat State Disaster Management Authority, especially in urban areas. This can build on existing flood, cyclone and surge and drought risk reduction efforts. Considerable capacity-building will be required to prepare these agencies to take on these additional responsibilities and develop actionable state-level adaptation programmes of action.

The boards of the departments of state finance and planning will need to integrate climate change adaptation within their medium-term planning and expenditure frameworks and enable synergy between cross-sectoral adaptation and mitigation investments.

Changes are necessary in the appropriate state housing and urban development, town planning and infrastructure legislation to integrate disaster and climate change mitigation concerns within urban planning and development. Training and capacity-building of state public functionaries and bureaucrats in climate change risk assessment and adaptation is an important human resource investment.

A process of catalysing entrepreneurial activity around climate adaptation and mitigation is best led in some states by the government, while in others a private sector lead will be most appropriate. Once beyond a critical threshold it could well be spun off.

City level. Current legal, regulatory and governance structures and the institutional culture of most cities are inadequate to address the challenge of climate change adaptation and mitigation.

An urban governance, planning and service delivery framework, as well as institutional arrangements, will be necessary to link urban renewal and development with short- and medium-term hazard risk reduction, as well as to climate adaptation. An important first step is the development of public entitlements and service delivery to the poor and vulnerable to ensure that existing asymmetries and structural vulnerabilities are addressed. This will involve strong interventions in real estate and housing markets and public service delivery, and a supportive policy and institutional environment at state level.

This is best operationalized via a re-examination of city development plans that attempt to link a long-term vision for urban development with an action plan for infrastructure upgrading, poverty reduction and better governance. An appropriate urban platform to enable multi-stakeholder engagement with strategic risk-sharing and adaptation will help to create appropriate fiscal and financial incentives for adaptation linked to neighbourhood-led processes, especially in informal settlements. An outcome could be a politically mandated city adaptation programme of action linked to private-sector and community-led adaptation that focuses on the primary urban greenhouse gas flux sectors (i.e. transportation and building and energy systems).

Within this larger framework, a city Disaster Management Plan (DMP) and zonal DMPs need to integrate climate change and other hazard mitigation concerns within the primary land-use and zoning instruments, within city structure and development plans and within zonal development plans and appropriate building regulation and infrastructure development guidelines.

A critical support activity would be a multilingual GIS-based city DMP and zonal DMPs on the internet, possibly linked to a public database that records property and real estate information, building permissions and public investments in infrastructure. This would provide a framework within which neighbourhood urban renewal and planning are coordinated with risk mitigation.

A public–private–resident partnership to finance, build and retrofit housing and infrastructure to disaster-resistant standards at neighbourhood level, and a public–private partnership to develop strategic flood, cyclone, storm surge and sea erosion defences at city level will need to be explored for each city.

Neighbourhood level. Each city will need a network of climate change-related community-based disaster management and risk mitigation initiatives, especially for slum, squatter and informal settlements in vulnerable locations. This would provide a basis for a citywide dialogue on appropriate adaptation and mitigation involving all population groups and stakeholders. This will be critical to developing implementable city adaptation programmes of action.

The private sector. Given the availability of a public domain risk adaptation framework, the private sector should be encouraged to develop appropriate risk assessment, adaptation and mitigation plans for clusters of enterprises in vulnerable areas. This would enable a rebalancing of demand and supply-side initiatives – that is, greenhouse gas emission abatement, decentralization and dematerialization of supply and service chains. Development of private enterprise-led building and infrastructure upgrading, retrofitting and technical support initiatives to enable and scale adaptation will also be important.

Civil society organizations. These need to take the lead in advocacy and mobilization and adaptation centred on the provision and extension of basic services and entitlements. They can also lead on neighbourhood pilot projects to test new methods of community-based adaptation, specifically for slum and informal settlements and vulnerable populations. NGOs can provide independent feedback and checks and balances on the functioning of public- and private-sector institutions working on natural hazard and climate change risk mitigation.

Key instruments that could help to mitigate climate change-related risks include:

- *New construction and development.* This should be executed to incremental standards for land use, planning, construction, and operations and maintenance (O&M) that enable fully built development to meet climate change vulnerability norms and enable poor residents living in self- or artisan-built construction to upgrade at an appropriate pace and cost. This will require changes in legal, regulatory, planning and design guidelines along with a recognition of the rights of residence and economic participation for all residents of the city. Considerable enterprise and institutional development inputs will be required to make this a reality. If structured imaginatively, this could well be funded in part by carbon credits.
- *Retrofitting and strengthening buildings.* A large proportion of a typical Indian city building stock does not meet contemporary standards of building safety. Technical measures to strengthen and retrofit these buildings are cost effective (typically 5 to 15 per cent of capital investment) but have never been implemented across an Indian city except in Bhuj, after the 2001 Kachchh earthquake. For this to be possible would take considerable institutional and financial innovation and well-considered incentives.
- *Lifeline infrastructure development and strengthening.* Building the energy, water, wastewater, transportation, telecom and information technology (IT) infrastructure for a city typically takes decades. Given current growth trends, it will happen in many Indian million-cities over the next two to three decades and will need to last for a century or more. Appropriate climate change-related adaptation and mitigation measures will need to be integrated within the design of these systems.

    Since they involve lumpy investments and require massive annual expenditure on O&M, adequate attention needs to be paid to risk-adjusted least-lifecycle costs. Some of these services are best provided by public providers; others, given possible quantum leaps in technology and distributed network development, may be better managed privately. There is a need to explore appropriate forms of regulation and management to mitigate climate risk. This is also a prime case for carbon offset financing.

    Sequencing of these interventions should ideally be prioritized by their strategic impact and vulnerability reduction potential, especially in slum and informal settlements. The priorities of the poor and the affluent can vary considerably. A pro-poor process of climate change-related priority setting needs to provide adequate 'voice' to more vulnerable groups.
- *Hazard modification.* A number of pre-colonial and colonial drainage, urban surge and flood protection systems have been in operation in various parts of

India. The rapid pace of urban development has often made them dysfunctional or irrelevant. Repairing and strengthening strategic flood, storm surge and coastal defences are important city-level interventions. Detailed economic, social and environmental cost-benefit analysis will be needed to assess whether these investments are appropriate vis-à-vis relocation and other adaptation options.

Water use efficiency and conservation measures are the best strategic defence against drought on the demand side, in conjunction with appropriate water management practices. Enabling the conceptualization and implementation of such vulnerability reduction and hazard modification interventions will need to be explored through pilot projects in different cities with varying ecological regimes.

- *Relocation and rehabilitation.* Relocation should emerge as a policy option only after all other options have failed. Typical measures include the relocation of particular settlements, parts of a city or an entire city system depending upon the expected level of risk. Changes in the economic structure of cities will be necessary in order to move out of sensitive economic activities, as well as changes in systems of governance to enable a more rapid response to emerging risk within both the public and the private sectors. Planning, market and financial instruments will be needed to address adequately local relocation and associated rehabilitation needs, with recognition of the rights of residents to compensation. Relocating part of a city is clearly a huge political decision that needs to be equitable, transparent and participative in its execution – few such precedents are available in India. The moderately progressive national rehabilitation policy does not address climate change-related concerns.

  A first step in spatial adaptation would be to shift settlements out of highly vulnerable areas, especially the inter-tidal zones, riverine, estuarine and low-lying areas. If this is inadequate, then the relocation of a particular section of a city and, finally, the relocation of an entire urban system to a new location can be considered. Relocation at this scale is unprecedented other than for reservoir submergence in independent India. This would be a major economic and political challenge, apart from being difficult to implement in an equitable manner.

- *Joining up with ongoing hazard risk reduction programmes.* The most important ongoing climate change-related risk mitigation programme is the National Cyclone Risk Mitigation Programme, which is being implemented across India's coastal states. The governments of Orissa, Andhra Pradesh and Gujarat have made progress in its implementation in rural settlements.[84] A similar initiative needs to be developed for urban areas that combines natural hazard risk mitigation and climate change adaptation.

  The 2005 Tsunami Rehabilitation Programme, active in the southern coastal states of Tamil Nadu, Andhra Pradesh and Kerala, is specifically focused on coastal zone management and the mitigation of cyclone, storm surge and sea erosion hazard risk. A climate change-related agenda needs to be introduced expeditiously into this programme before it comes to a close.

A number of independent flood risk mitigation interventions have been launched by state governments and for specific cities in Maharashtra, Gujarat, Orissa, Uttar Pradesh and Bihar. A common method of addressing inland flood risk mitigation is still to be evolved. This is a crucial concern that could influence the lives of tens of millions of people. The integration of climate change adaptation measures within flood mitigation interventions will probably first take root in Gujarat, which has suffered three seasons of extreme rainfall since 2004. This can then be adapted and scaled to other parts of the country.

• *Strengthening regional and rural–urban linkages.* Conventional disaster management and mitigation planning have focused typically either on urban areas or villages. The increasing integration of the Indian economy has led to the strengthening of the forward–backward linkages between urban and rural settlements. The risks to which cities and their embedding countryside are exposed need to be addressed together by integrating climate change-related adaptation into regional and *RUrban* sectoral and investment planning.

This is particularly important in India, where agriculture is highly sensitive to monsoon variability as 65 per cent of the cropped area is rain fed. Changes in temperature and precipitation could have a significant impact upon more than 350 million people who are dependent upon rain-fed agriculture.

Changes in the flows of food and biomass are especially important because the metabolism of Indian cities is still dominated by flows of unprocessed food and traditional biofuels. Similarly, drinking water and renewable biofuels, hydropower and possibly wind energy flows could be affected by climate changes, causing moderate to severe disruption in urban systems. Hence, instead of an exclusive focus on cities, regional climate change risk adaptation strategies and action plans are needed, especially for mega-urban regions and metropolitan cities.

Institutional capacity for urban climate risk adaptation

A fundamental challenge to Indian climate risk adaptation is the declining quality of urban governance and the weak institutional capacity to manage urbanization, ensure equitable and quality public service delivery, and access to housing markets via appropriate planning and regulation. Without these institutional changes, the structural vulnerability of large populations cannot be addressed, providing a weak foundation on which to build climate adaptation.

Since the mid 1990s, India has developed significant natural disaster management and risk mitigation capacity at national and state levels. The national *Vulnerability Atlas of India*[85] was the first such attempt at identifying and mapping vulnerability at district level across the country; but risk unbundling for specific urban centres was weak. Subsequent efforts have attempted to take the process of hazard risk modelling, vulnerability assessment and composite risk assessment to finer resolution (i.e. block, *taluka* and settlement levels).[86]

The NDMA has been established, but the most extensive risk mitigation experience lies with state-level agencies in Andhra Pradesh, Gujarat, Orissa and Tamil Nadu, which have been active in disaster mitigation planning, investment and, to a lesser extent, community-based disaster mitigation.

A number of interventions are currently being implemented in various cities to mitigate natural hazard risk, especially from flood, sea erosion and storm surge. These are, however, responding to a contemporary perception of risk based on historical experience and records. They have little or no capacity to engage with emergent risks induced by climate change. The ability to conceptualize and integrate these measures within existing plans and programmes will need to be developed at state and city level and, if they are of any great magnitude, supported by the government of India.

The government of Maharashtra developed India's first urban disaster management plan for Mumbai in the late 1990s, identifying flooding as a significant risk and pinpointing bottleneck locations in each ward as well as vulnerable slums and settlements.[87] But there was little follow-up and these bottlenecks became the primary cause of the 2005 Mumbai deluge,[88] pointing to the need for a drastic revamp of Mumbai's institutional capacity.[89]

Addressing in a practical way the differential vulnerabilities of population groups within cities is a serious challenge. Improvements in access to affordable housing and land markets and in lifeline infrastructure, along with more appropriate zoning regulations, are important interventions with strong co-benefits for the poor today and climate change risk tomorrow if they are planned and executed in a pro-poor manner.

A great risk in market-driven adaptation policy is the possibility of a slew of anti-poor interventions leading to a vicious cycle of displacement resettlement and increasing vulnerability in many cities. A number of successful programmes have demonstrated that the cost of *in situ* risk mitigation is often a fraction that of relocation, typically less than 10 per cent of the capital cost of new development. This needs to be integrated within the urban planning process and legal framework.

Building a mitigation agenda for Indian cities

India became a signatory to the Kyoto Protocol in 2002, which gave it some latitude in initiating mitigation activities because of its developing country status. The impact of the measures taken, for instance in pollution control, conservation and promotion of renewable energy,[90] is expected to be relatively small, primarily because India's energy intensity is growing rapidly from a very small base. Almost half of India's households lack access to electricity and energy demand can be expected to grow at a faster rate than India's annual growth in GDP.[91] Given that India's energy security can only be assured in the medium term by using coal-based thermal power generation, a domestic debate on greenhouse gas mitigation at the expense of expanding energy services will be challenging in the short term.

A series of macro-policy incentives will be required to reduce the carbon intensity of India's energy system and its economy. Debates around city sustainability and greening have opened up in the last decade and limited progress has been made on strong interventions that would enable the development of more compact cities, mixed land use, a radical improvement in public mobility systems, greater resource efficiency and recycling in buildings and services, and a break with India's 20th-century engagement with colonial and Western-oriented planning standards.

Much of the high energy and resource-intensive real estate and building boom is driven by corporations and the urban upper-middle classes who wish to participate in a replication of the 'American dream' in India. This is clearly unsustainable both in the short and medium terms, and voluntary and public restraints on wasteful consumption and effective resource management using market-based, technological and legal instruments are in order. The private and public sectors will lead much of this mitigation agenda as they make good business sense.

Conclusions

Although the level of exposure to hazard in India is high, vulnerability typically contributes more to overall risk in India's cities. Reducing this vulnerability will mean a shift in public policy, mobilization and enterprise from mitigation towards adaptation. This needs to be grounded in the institutional, socio-cultural and political realities of India, and needs to focus on the poor and most vulnerable through a mix of policy, regulatory, fiscal and financial, and institutional and mobilization instruments.

This is probably best implemented by mainstreaming climate change risk assessment and adaptation and mitigation measures into ongoing national hazard mitigation programmes and building a tangible set of links with urban renewal interventions that are being taken up in many of India's largest cities.

To accomplish this, a multilevel climate adaptation framework is necessary, which works at national, state, city and neighbourhood levels and brings together the state, private and civil society sectors. Robust adaptation programmes in a set of pilot cities will allow for the exploration of the important linkages between adaptation and mitigation.

Notes

1. IFRC (2005) *World Disasters Report*, Geneva; also Parasuraman, S. and Unnikrishnan, P. V. (2000) *India Disasters Report*, Oxford University Press, New Delhi.
2. Nicholls, R. J. and Lowe, J. A. (2006) 'Climate stabilization and impacts of sea-level rise', in Schellnhuber, H. J., Cramer, W., Nakicenovic, N., Wigley, T. and Yohe, G. (eds) *Avoiding Dangerous Climate Change*, Cambridge University Press, pp195–202.
3. Satterthwaite, D., Huq, S., Pelling, M., Reid, H. and Lankao Romero, P. (2007) *Adapting to Climate Change in Urban Areas: The Possibilities and Constraints in Low- and Middle-Income Nations*, IIED Climate Change and Cities Series, Working Paper 1, London, 110pp.
4. De Vries, H. J. M., Revi, A., Bhat, G. K., Hilderink, H. and Lucas, P. (2007) *India 2050: Scenarios for An Uncertain Future*, Netherlands Environment Assessment Agency (MNP) Bilthoven.
5. See Chapter 2.
6. Revi, A., Dronin, N. and de Vries, B. (2002) 'Population and environment in Asia since 1600 AD', in deVries, B. and Goudsblom, J. (eds) *Mappae Mundi: Humans and Their Habitats in a Long-Term Socio-Ecological Perspective*, Amsterdam University Press, The Netherlands; also Banga, B. (ed) (2005) *The City in Indian History: Urban Demography, Society and Politics*, Manohar, Delhi.
7. Census of India (2006) *Population Projections for India and States 2001–2026*, Office of the Registrar General and Census Commissioner, New Delhi.
8. UN (United Nations) (2006) *World Urbanization Prospects: The 2005 Revision*, United Nations, New York.
9. Hughes, B. and Hillenbrand, E. E. (2006) *Exploring and Shaping International Futures*, Paradigm, London.
10. Dyson, T. and Visaria, P. (2004) 'Migration and urbanization: retrospect and prospect', in Dyson, T., Cassen, R. and Visaria, L. (eds) *Twenty-First Century India, Population, Economy, Human Development and the Environment*, Oxford University Press, New Delhi, Oxford, pp108–157; also Revi, A. (2006a) *Long-range Macro-dynamics of Indian Urbanization in a Globalizing World*, Proceedings of the Conference on India and China in a Global Perspective, April 2006, New School, New York; and see reference 7.
11. CSO (2006) *National Accounts Statistics*, Central Statistical Organization, New Delhi; also Reserve Bank of India (2006) *Handbook of Indian Economic Statistics*, Mumbai.
12. Fischer-Kowalski, M. and Haberl, H. (2007) *Socioecological Transitions and Global Change: Trajectories of Social Metabolism and Land Use*, Edward Elgar, Cheltenham.
13. Revi, A., Prakash, S. and Mehrotra, R. (2006b) 'Goa 2100: The transition to sustainable design', *Environment & Urbanization*, vol 18, no 1, April, pp51–65.
14. See reference 10: Revi (2006a).
15. Sainath, S. (2002) *Everybody Loves a Good Drought: Stories from India's Poorest Districts*, Penguin, New Delhi.
16. Zickfeld, K. et al (2005) 'Is the Indian summer monsoon stable against global change?', *Geophysical Research Letters*, vol 32, L15707, Potsdam Institute for Climate Impact Research, Potsdam, Germany.
17. Gosain, A. K. et al (2006) 'Climate change impact assessment on hydrology of Indian river basins', *Current Science*, vol 90, no 3, 10 February, pp346–353; also

Mall, R. K. et al (2006) 'Water resources and climate change: An Indian perspective', *Current Science*, vol 90, no 12, 25 June, pp1610–1626; and Ramesh, R. and Yadava, M. G. (2005) 'Climate and water resources of India', *Current Science*, vol 89, no 5, 10 September, pp818–824.

18. Rupa Kumar, P. et al (2006) 'High-resolution climate change scenarios for India for the 21st century', *Current Science*, vol 90, no 3, 10 February, pp334–345; also GSDMA/TARU (2005) *Gujarat Vulnerability and Risk Atlas*, Gandhinagar.

19. See reference 10: Revi (2006a).

20. Agarwal, A., Narain, S. and Sharma, A. (1993) *Green Politics: Global Environmental Negotiations*, Centre for Science and Environment, New Delhi.

21. IPCC (Intergovernmental Panel on Climate Change) (1995) *Second Assessment – Climate Change*, Geneva.

22. The first was supported by the Asian Development Bank; the second, the Asian Least Cost Greenhouse Abatement Study (ALCGAS) – ADB (2002) *Asian Least Cost Greenhouse Abatement Study (ALGAS)*, Manila – was supported by the Global Environment Facility (GEF); the third was a climate impact assessment study funded by the UK Department for Environment, Food and Rural Affairs (Defra); and the fourth was the recently concluded National Communication Project supported by the GEF. See Sathaye, J. et al (2006) 'Climate change, sustainable development and India: Global and national concerns', *Current Science*, vol 90, no 3, 10 February, pp314–325. There have also been a number of long-range resource, energy and sustainable development studies; but these have had limited impact on the government of India agenda. See TERI (1998) *Looking Back to Think Ahead: GREEN India 2047*, Tata Energy Research Institute, New Delhi; also Planning Commission (2002) *India Vision 2020*, New Delhi.

23. TERI (Tata Energy Research Institute) (2004) *India Specific Impacts of Climate Change*, Tata Energy Research Institute, New Delhi.

24. Revi, A. (2005) 'Lessons from the deluge: priorities for multi-hazard risk mitigation in Mumbai', *Economic and Political Weekly*, vol XL, no 36, September 3–9, pp3911–3916.

25. Parikh, J. K. and Parikh, K. (2002) *Climate Change: India's Perceptions, Positions, Policies and Possibilities*, OECD, Paris.

26. Socolow, R. and Pacala, S. (2004) 'Stabilization wedges: Solving the climate problem for the next 50 years with current technologies', *Science*, vol 305, no 5686, 13 August, pp968–972.

27. Planning Commission (2006) *Report of the Expert Committee on an Integrated Energy Policy*, New Delhi; also see reference 22: Sathaye et al (2006); Sharma, S., Bhattacharya, S. and Garg, A. (2006) 'Greenhouse gas emissions from India: a perspective', *Current Science*, vol 90, no 3, 10 February, pp326–333; Shukla, P. R. (2006) 'India's GHG emission scenarios: Aligning development and stabilization paths', *Current Science*, vol 90, no 3, 10 February, pp384–395; Shukla, P. R. et al (2003a) *Development and Climate – An Assessment for India*, Indian Institute of Management, Ahmedabad; and Gupta, V. (2005) 'Climate change and domestic mitigation efforts', *Economic and Political Weekly*, vol 40, no 10, 5 March, pp981–987.

28. Shukla, P. R. et al (2003b) *Climate Change in India: Vulnerability Assessment and Adaptation*, Hyderabad University Press.

29. Government of India (2006) *Report of M S Swaminathan Committee to Review the Coastal Regulation Zone Notification 1991*, New Delhi, <http://mssrf.org/rm/reports/crz_report_prof/crz.htm>, accessed 4 July 2007.
30. See reference 13.
31. See reference 27: Sharma et al (2006).
32. See reference 27: Planning Commission (2006).
33. See reference 17: Ramesh and Yadava (2005).
34. See reference 18: Rupa Kumar et al (2006).
35. See reference 18: Rupa Kumar et al (2006); also IITM (1989) *Probable Maximum Precipitation Atlas*, Indian Institute of Tropical Meteorology, Pune.
36. See reference 24.
37. See reference 18: GSDMA/TARU (2005).
38. Ravindranath, N. H. et al (2006) 'Impact of climate change on forests in India', *Current Science*, vol 90, no 3, 10 February, pp354–361.
39. See reference 15.
40. See reference 18: GSDMA/TARU (2005).
41. Kumar, R. et al (2005) 'Water resources of India', *Current Science*, vol 89, no 5, 10 September, pp794–811.
42. See reference 17: Gosain et al (2006).
43. Murty, K. S. (2002) 'River water sharing: India's problems', *International Association of Hydrological Sciences Publication*, no 274, pp323–328; also Dreze, J., Samson, M. and Sarkar, S. (eds) (2003) *The Dam and the Nation: Displacement and Resettlement in the Narmada Valley*, Oxford University Press, New Delhi.
44. Tangri, A. K. (2003) 'Impact of climate change on Himalayan glaciers', in *Proceedings of V&A Workshop on Water Resources, Coastal Zones and Human Health*, NATCOM, 27–28 June, Indian Institute of Technology (ITT) New Delhi.
45. See reference 17: Mall et al (2006); also Chellaney, B. (2007) 'Averting water wars in Asia', *International Herald Tribune*, 26 June.
46. See reference 1: Parasuraman and Unnikrishnan (2000).
47. Zérah, M. H. (2000) *Water: Unreliable Supply in Delhi*, Manohar Publishers, New Delhi.
48. Daga, S. (2005) 'Private supply of water in Delhi', Centre for Civil Society, http://www.teri.res.in/teriin/news/terivsn/issue35/water.htm, accessed 4 July 2007; also Delhi Jal Board, www.delhijalboard.nic.in/, accessed 4 July 2007.
49. Government of NCT of Delhi (2002) *Economic Survey (2001–2002)*, New Delhi.
50. McGranahan, G. and Mercutollio, P. J. (2007b) *Scaling Urban Environmental Challenges: From Local to Global and Back*, Earthscan, London.
51. Mishra, D. K. (1999) 'Flood protection that never was: Case of Mahananda Basin of north Bihar', *Economic and Political Weekly*, vol XXXIV, no 29, July, pp2013–2018.
52. See reference 4.
53. See reference 17: Gosain et al (2006).
54. See reference 18: Rupa Kumar et al (2006).
55. See reference 18: GSDMA/TARU (2005).
56. Government of Maharashtra (2005) *Maharashtra Floods 2005*, Department of Relief and Rehabilitation, http://mdmu.maharashtra.gov.in/pdf/Flood/statusreport.pdf, accessed 4 July 2007.
57. See reference 24.

58. Aggarwal, D. and Lal, M. (2001) *Vulnerability of Indian Coastline to Sea-level Rise*, Centre for Atmospheric Sciences, Indian Institute of Technology, New Delhi.

59. India Meteorological Department (1979) *Tracks of Storms and Depressions in the Bay of Bengal and the Arabian Sea 1877 to 1970*, New Delhi; also India Meteorological Department (1996) *Tracks of Storms and Depressions in the Bay of Bengal and the Arabian Sea 1971 to 1990*, New Delhi; and TARU (2005) *Disaster Management Plan Blueprint for the Hazira Area Development Committee*, Gandhinagar.

60. TARU/BMTPC (1998) *Rapid Damage Assessment of Cyclone-affected Areas of Kachchh and Saurashtra in Gujarat*, New Delhi.

61. Benson, C. and Clay, E. (2002) *Bangladesh: Disasters and Public Finance*, World Bank, Washington, DC.

62. See reference 18: GSDMA/TARU (2005); see also reference 59: TARU (2005).

63. See reference 18: GSDMA/TARU (2005).

64. See reference 58.

65. Dasgupta, S. et al (2007) *The Impact of Sea-Level Rise on Developing Countries: A Comparative Analysis*, World Bank Policy Research Working Paper no 4136, February.

66. See reference 61.

67. Stern, N. (2007) *The Economics of Climate Change: The Stern Review*, Cambridge University Press.

68. See reference 5.

69. Diamond, J. (2005) *Collapse: How Societies Choose to Fail or Succeed*, Penguin, London.

70. See reference 5.

71. See reference 67.

72. See reference 58.

73. Unnikrishnan, A. S. et al (2006) 'Sea-level changes along the Indian coast: Observations and projections', National Institute of Oceanography, Goa and the Indian Institute of Tropical Meteorology, Pune, *Current Science*, vol 90, no 3, 10 February, pp362–368.

74. Bhattacharya, S. et al (2006) 'Climate change and malaria in India', *Current Science*, vol 90, no 3, 10 February, pp369–375.

75. See reference 18: GSDMA/TARU (2005).

76. See reference 61.

77. BMTPC (1997) *Vulnerability Atlas of India*, Building Materials and Technology Promotion Council, New Delhi.

78. See reference 18: GSDMA/TARU (2005).

79. Moffat, S. (2003) *CitiesPLUS*, Project for Greater Vancouver, Sustainable Urban Systems Design Competition, Tokyo.

80. See reference 24.

81. Government of India (1961) *The Government of India (Allocation of Business) Rules*, New Delhi, http://cabsec.nic.in/abr/abr_odr.htm, accessed 4 July 2007.

82. Planning Commission (2007) *Report of the Working Group on Disaster Management for the XI Plan*, New Delhi.

83. NDMA (2007) *Earthquake Disaster Guidelines*, New Delhi, http://ndma.gov.in/wps/wcm/resources/file/ebfb870f7a208c7/Guidelines%20for%20Management%20of%20Earthquakes.pdf, accessed 4 July 2007.

84. Government of Andhra Pradesh (2000) *Andhra Pradesh Cyclone Contingency Plan of Action*, Hyderabad.
85. See reference 77.
86. See reference 18: GSDMA/TARU (2005).
87. Government of Maharashtra (1999) *Mumbai Disaster Management Plan*, http://mdmu.maharashtra.gov.in/pages/Mumbai/; also Vatsa, K. and Joseph, J. (2003) 'Disaster management plan for the state of Maharashtra, India: Evolutionary process', *Natural Hazards Review*, vol 4, no 4, November, pp206–212.
88. See reference 24; also Conservation Action Trust (2006) *Mumbai Marooned: An Enquiry into Mumbai Floods 2005*, Mumbai.
89. Government of Maharashtra (2006) *Chitale Committee Report on the Mumbai Floods of 2005*, Mumbai.
90. See reference 27: Shukla, et al (2003a).
91. TERI (2006) *National Energy Map for India: Technology Vision 2030*, The Energy and Resources Institute, New Delhi.

15

International Funding to Support Urban Adaptation to Climate Change

Jessica Ayers

Introduction

While estimates of the costs of adaptation to climate change remain vague, especially for low- and middle-income countries, recent approximations of current needs are in the range of tens of billions of dollars per annum[1] and well in excess of levels of official development assistance (ODA). The World Bank estimates that climate-proofing development investments (including ODA and concessional finance, foreign direct investment and gross domestic investment) in low- and middle-income countries alone will cost between US$10 billion and US$40 billion annually.[2] This figure has since been criticized for not taking into account the costs of climate-proofing existing supplies of natural and physical capital where no new investment is planned, the costs of financing new investments specifically to deal with climate change, or the costs to households and communities to fund their own adaptation needs.[3] More recent estimates by Oxfam that do acknowledge these factors put the costs of adaptation closer to US$50 billion annually,[4] while the United Nations Development Programme (UNDP) suggests this could spiral to US$86 billion annually by 2015.[5] The longer it takes to implement an effective international agreement to reduce and then halt greenhouse gas emissions, the higher these costs of adaptation will be and the more likely that the limits to adaptation will be reached and exceeded.

The costs of adaptation in cities will account for a significant proportion of this average, largely because of the expense required to adapt (or, in the case of many low- and middle-income countries, to build new and resilient) infrastructure and services for densely populated areas. The United Nations Framework Convention on Climate Change (UNFCCC) estimates that adapting infrastructure worldwide could require US$8 billion to US$30 billion in 2030, one third of which would be for low- and middle-income countries.[6] Yet, this wide-ranging estimate is at the conservative end of the scale because it is based on adapting existing infrastructure without taking into account the large deficit in basic infrastructure in most urban centres in low- and middle-income nations.[7]

Existing international funding to support adaptation needs in low- and middle-income countries comes from two main sources: first, dedicated climate change funds under the UNFCCC and, second, through ODA. Currently, both of these avenues fall significantly short of meeting the costs of adaptation in low- and middle-income countries. This chapter will begin by exploring the opportunities and challenges for financing adaptation through the UNFCCC mechanisms and will consider recent innovative proposals that could help to bring these funds closer to the amounts that are required. Recognizing that UNFCCC channels alone cannot meet the full costs or the full scope of supporting activities to build resilience to climate change, the role of ODA and potential tensions and complementarities with the UNFCCC will be discussed. Finally, it will be noted that raising funds for adaptation at the international level is not enough while barriers for accessing and using these funds for the most vulnerable groups in the most vulnerable countries exist. The political and institutional constraints for accessing international funds by vulnerable urban stakeholders will be considered and options will be proposed for ensuring that funding for adaptation reaches those who need it most and can use it well.

Funding for adaptation under the United Nations Framework Convention on Climate Change (UNFCCC)

The structure of funding under the UNFCCC

At the first meeting of the Conference of the Parties[8] (COP 1) to the UNFCCC in 1995, the Global Environment Facility (GEF) was established as the financial mechanism of the UNFCCC and was given responsibility for the transfer of funds under the UNFCCC from high-income to low- and middle-income countries. The original mandate for the GEF in relation to climate change adaptation was to support studies, assessments and planning on vulnerability and adaptation in low- and middle-income countries, as well as capacity-building.

At COP 7 in 2001, Decision 6 of the Marrakech Accords further requested that the GEF should fund 'pilot or demonstration projects to show how adaptation planning and assessment can be practically translated into projects that will provide real benefits'.[9] This led the GEF to establish the Strategic Priority 'Piloting an Operational Approach to Adaptation' (SPA) under the GEF Trust Fund. COP 7 also gave rise to three new and additional funds beyond those contributed to by the GEF: the Least Developed Countries Fund (LDCF), established under the convention to support the 49 nations designated as the least developed countries (LDCs)[10] to adapt to climate change and initially used to support the design of National Adaptation Programmes of Action (NAPAs); the Special Climate Change Fund (SCCF), to support a number of climate change activities, including mitigation and technology transfer, but intended to prioritize adaptation; and the Kyoto Protocol Adaptation Fund (AF) to support concrete adaptation projects in low- and middle-income countries that are party to the protocol. This fund sits under the Kyoto Protocol and is financed from a levy on the Clean Development Mechanism (CDM).[11]

Following lengthy negotiations since Marrakech on how to operationalize the LDCF and the SCCF, and despite some reluctance from low- and middle-income countries (for reasons outlined below), it was decided at the end of COP 9 that both these funds should be brought under the guidance of the GEF.[12] This gave rise to the current structure of international funding for adaptation under the UNFCCC: three funds managed by the GEF (SPA, LDCF and SCCF), and the AF.

There are a number of reasons why the existing funds managed by the GEF are not adequate for meeting adaptation needs in low- and middle-income countries and this chapter will focus on three of them. First, levels of funding do not amount to anywhere near enough. All three GEF-managed funds are based on ODA-type voluntary pledges and bilateral contributions from donors. This type of contribution is unlikely to ever be able to generate the required levels of funding – especially given that contributions are meant to be additional to ODA – when many high-income nations are failing to meet their 0.7 per cent commitments to ODA in the first place. As of March 2008, the total resources pledged to the LDCF, the SCCF and the SPA totalled US$298 million (US$172.8 million to the LDCF, US$75.6 million to the SCCF and US$50 million to the SPA).[13] Furthermore, donors are delaying on meeting their pledged commitments because of an alleged lack of adequate and accountable mechanisms in low- and middle-income countries for receiving and disbursing money. This means that the actual funds contained in the LDCF total US$91.8 million, in the SCCF US$59.9 million and in the SPA US$50 million.[14] This leaves almost US$100 million pledged to the UNFCCC still outstanding. To illustrate the trivial scale of these contributions, a recent report by Oxfam International pointed out that the total funds delivered to the LDCF are less than the amount spent in the US on suntan lotion in one month.[15]

Second, the governance structure of the GEF has come under criticism from non-governmental organizations (NGOs) and the academic community for undermining any ownership of adaptation funds by low- and middle-income countries.[16] Under Article 11 of the UNFCCC, the GEF is required to have 'an equitable and balanced representation of all Parties within a transparent system of governance'.[17] While decisions of the GEF council are taken by consensus of all parties to the convention, if no consensus is available then a majority of countries, weighted by donation, is required to carry a vote. This means that GEF council members from countries that make the largest contributions carry the most weight, essentially giving veto power to the group of five largest donor countries.[18] This has raised concerns, particularly from low- and middle-income nations represented in the Group of 77,[19] regarding the decision-making procedures of the GEF, which have eroded its political acceptability. The lack of 'one country, one vote' procedure has resulted in a 'democratic deficit',[20] giving rise to the impression that key decisions are being made by the representatives of powerful countries, beyond the control of weaker constituents.[21]

Third, many low- and middle-income countries have expressed concern over the unclear guidance and high transaction costs attached to GEF funding mechanisms. For example, in their comprehensive review of GEF-managed funds for adaptation, Klein and Möhner[22] show that the GEF does not provide adequate operational guidance (in the form of programming papers), making it difficult for low- and middle-income countries to apply for project funding. In addition, although funding through the GEF is not formally conditional, requirements attached to funding include burdensome reporting and co-financing criteria. Finally, funding through the GEF is disbursed through implementing agencies such as the UNDP, the United Nations Environment Programme (UNEP) and the World Bank, which adds further bureaucracy to the process; for example, many LDCs have expressed concern over the functional relationships with implementing agencies inhibiting access to funding for NAPAs from the LDCF.[23]

Therefore, funding under the GEF is inadequate to meet the current costs of adaptation in low- and middle-income countries, both fiscally and in terms of accessibility.

The Adaptation Fund (AF)

The AF offers a much more promising approach to adaptation funding. It is unique in that it has a novel democratic governance structure, decided upon at COP 13 in Bali in December 2007. It is not managed by the GEF, but has its own independent board with representation from the five United Nations regions, as well as special seats for the LDCs and small island developing states. The GEF provides secretariat services to the AF on an interim basis. Countries can make submissions for funding directly to the AF rather than go through a designated implementing agency (as is the case with the GEF-managed funds), and countries also have the authority to designate their own implementing agencies, such as NGOs, to make submissions for funding directly under the AF. It is hoped that the unique structure of the AF will be able to overcome, or at least minimize, the problems of accessibility currently faced with the GEF funds and will increase the effectiveness of climate change financing on adaptation.

In addition, the AF has the greatest potential to generate adequate levels of international funding for adaptation. The revenue generated from the CDM levy alone is projected to be between US$160 million and US$190 million, and potentially much more depending upon the volumes traded and prices as targets are set.[24] This mechanism for generating funding sets the AF apart from the GEF funding streams. Resources do not come from bilateral donations, thus avoiding the 'domestic revenue problem';[25] in other words, money raised domestically is likely to be regarded as nationally owned and therefore its allocation could face political resistance. Instead, funds are collected from private-sector actors by the CDM executive board, an international, not national, body. This means funds are independent from national treasuries and other domestic agencies.[26]

Finally, there is potential to significantly scale up financing under the AF mechanism by applying the levy to other activities.

The potential for new and innovative funding under the UNFCCC

The need to increase the scale of funding for adaptation has been recognized internationally and a variety of new and innovative mechanisms for doing so have been, and continue to be, proposed. Two of the most promising[27] are discussed here: applying a levy on bunker fuel[28] activities; and the international auctioning of assigned amounts units (AAUs)[29] under the Kyoto Protocol.

Müller[30] suggests that the most 'natural' way to generate funding for the AF would be to extend the 2 per cent levy to other non-emissions-trading activities. This would be favoured over increasing the levy on the CDM or applying it to other emissions-trading mechanisms, which would increase CDM transaction costs and potentially discourage investment in the CDM.

One idea launched in 2006 was to create an International Air Travel Adaptation Levy (IATAL), which has the potential to generate an estimated US$4 billion to US$10 billion per annum of additional funding for adaptation in low- and middle-income countries.[31] Based on the fact that the aviation industry is a significant contributor to global emissions totals, coupled with the need to increase funding for adaptation, the IATAL represents a politically, ethically and economically attractive option for generating funding for adaptation.[32] The IATAL has a twofold advantage: it will discourage flying and it will raise significant funds for adaptation, particularly from long-haul flights. This presents an equitable option because the costs of the levy would inevitably fall on passengers who, by the very fact that they are passengers, have a high carbon footprint and also have the capacity to pay. As stated by Müller: 'both conditions ... apply to air passengers quite generally: subsistence farmers from Bihar are generally not found on airplanes and people who fly will generally have a significant carbon footprint'. [33] As such, the option of IATAL has been given serious consideration by legislators and the G8+5.[34]

The levy could also be applied to maritime bunker fuels through an International Maritime Emissions Reduction Scheme (IMERS). Discussions around IMERS began in 2006 based on the concept of establishing a 'maritime greenhouse gas fund' under the auspices of the International Maritime Organization (IMO), with revenues from an upstream fuel levy, with the aim of spending around 50 per cent (equating to approximately US$2 billion) of the annual revenue for adaptation in low- and middle-income countries. At the 57th session of the Marine Environment Protection Committee in April 2008, a global levy scheme on ships was endorsed as a means of reaching maritime greenhouse gas reduction targets by using funds to purchase carbon emissions credits instead. Under this scheme, all ships engaged in international voyages would be subject to a bunker levy established at a given cost per tonne of fuel bunkered. Such a scheme would both encourage a reduction in the baseline of fuel used and also fund carbon credit purchases.[35] If some of the revenues are also applied to adaptation, this would again have the dual benefit of contributing to both global adaptation and mitigation agendas.

The essential feature of all levies on bunker fuels is that they can be designed to deliver genuinely international revenues: funds that cannot readily be tied down to a country, thus resolving the problem of 'domestic revenue'. Furthermore, one of the chief motivations behind IATAL is that it assigns responsibility to individuals rather than countries. This is particularly significant in low- and middle-income countries with high inequality and growing populations of wealthy individuals, where governments and industry have been accused of 'hiding behind the poor'[36] in avoiding national emissions reduction targets.

Another way of raising funds for adaptation would be to apply the levy to international auctioning of AAUs. As noted, applying the levy to carbon trading schemes could result in higher transaction costs, inhibiting the success of carbon markets. However, one solution to this has recently been submitted to the UNFCCC by Norway. The suggestion is that a levy be applied to the International Emissions Trading Scheme, through which Annex 1 countries[37] under the Kyoto Protocol are allowed to trade AAUs with each other. The Norwegian proposal suggests that the adaptation levy could be extended to the carbon market at the point of issuance of AAUs, and therefore the levy would not increase transaction costs when AAUs are traded. Rather, a small portion of permits would be withheld from national quota allocation and then auctioned by the appropriate institution. The resulting revenue could then be placed in a fund to be used for adaptation.[38] Müller suggests that this proposal is one of the few workable suggestions for applying the levy to other international trading schemes, as well as one that may be able to generate significant additional funding to meet the costs of adaptation in low- and middle-income countries.[39]

While these proposals do represent an opportunity to generate significant funding for adaptation under the UNFCCC, they are still being debated and are likely to be slow coming to fruition. Furthermore, funding adaptation through the UNFCCC has other limitations. UNFCCC support for adaptation addresses adaptation in the narrowest sense – that is, adaptation to climate change as distinct from climatic variability. At the level of climate negotiations, this distinction is important because such information informs political questions surrounding costs and burden-sharing.[40] Funding for adaptation is the responsibility of high-income, high-emitting countries, to be paid to countries most vulnerable to the impacts of those emissions. It is therefore relevant for the negotiations to distinguish between funding for building resilience to climate change (which is additional to ODA contributions) and funding for building resilience to climate variability, more generally (which could be included in ODA contributions). This UNFCCC approach is supported by many low- and middle-income countries in order to prevent industrialized countries incorporating adaptation funding within development assistance and thereby avoiding providing new and additional funding for adaptation under the UNFCCC. Therefore, as recently as the June 2008 meeting for the subsidiary bodies to the UNFCCC, low- and middle-income countries called for the measurable, reportable and verifiable use of new and additional funding for climate change-specific activities (as opposed to more general resilience building).[41]

However, building adaptive capacity requires actions that focus not only on the measurable and verifiable impacts of climate change, but also on a wide range of factors that contribute to a broader reduction in vulnerability to climate variability and climate change.[42] It is important that funding is made available for adaptation activities that can also address other, non-climatic, aspects of vulnerability. Such activities have traditionally been the focus of development practitioners; yet the climate regime has not conventionally engaged many of the agencies and actors whose participation in adaptation is essential.[43] Given these limitations to assistance for adaptation under the UNFCCC, a second, significant, international source of finance for adaptation must come from ODA.

The role of official development assistance (ODA) in funding adaptation

The objectives of development overlap considerably with those of adaptation because vulnerability depends upon the capacity of a society to cope with and adapt to climate-related hazards; this is constrained by factors such as lack of resources, poor institutions, governance, inadequate infrastructure and other economic constraints related to a lack of development.[44] Given this close relationship, supporting adaptation through development pathways makes sense.[45] This section discusses two key ways in which development assistance can finance adaptive capacity in recipient countries: first, through the generation of specific bilateral or multilateral climate change funds that are independent (but supposedly supportive) of the UNFCCC and intended to fund targeted adaptive initiatives for capacity-building and protective infrastructure; and, second, through mainstreaming climate change into development. This involves integrating climate change within ongoing development planning to 'climate proof' existing development investments, maximize the potential of development projects to enhance adaptive capacity, and avoid maladaptation.[46]

Multilateral and bilateral funds for adaptation

Generating funds through bilateral and multilateral institutions can capitalize on the experience of development agencies in reducing vulnerability and channelling funding for international development objectives. The largest and most recent (and controversial) example of such a fund can be drawn from the World Bank Climate Investment Funds (CIFs).

The overall objective of the CIFs is to provide concessional loans for policy reforms and investments that achieve development goals through a transition to a low carbon development path and a climate-resilient economy.[47] There are two trust funds under the CIFs: the Clean Technology Fund, essentially focusing on mitigation and investment in low carbon technologies; and the Strategic Climate Fund, which is broader and more flexible in scope and serves as an overarching fund that can support various programmes to test innovative approaches to climate change. The first of these programmes, intended to fund adaptation activities, is the Pilot Programme on Climate Resilience (PPCR), with a target size of US$1 billion, aimed at increasing climate resilience in low- and middle-income countries.

The development of the CIFs, in general, and the PPCR, in particular, has been shrouded in controversy. First, the governance structures of the CIFs and PPCR (see Box 15.1) have been heavily criticized as being donor driven,[48] potentially undoing the progress made with the AF, which had only been decided upon a few months prior to the announcement of the PPCR. Indeed, the PPCR was originally entitled the Adaptation Pilot Fund, widely interpreted as a move to compete with the AF under the Kyoto Protocol.[49] However, a recent revised proposal included a more balanced representation of donor and recipient countries and includes the chair of the AF board (see Box 15.1) in an attempt to link the World Bank initiative to the UNFCCC. At the time of writing, these arrangements were still under discussion.

Box 15.1 The governance structures of the World Bank Climate Investment Funds (CIFs) and the Pilot Programme on Climate Resilience (PPCR)

The Strategic Climate Fund would be governed by a trust fund committee with six representatives from donor countries, six representatives from eligible recipient countries, a representative from the World Bank and a representative from partner multilateral development banks. The Pilot Programme on Climate Resilience (PPCR) operations and activities would be overseen by a PPCR subcommittee with two members of the Strategic Climate Fund Trust Fund Committee, six representatives from donor countries, six representatives from recipient countries and the chair of the Kyoto Protocol Adaptation Fund (AF) board. Decisions would be by consensus.

Source: CCCD (2008) *Financing Mechanisms for Adaptation*, Secretariat to the Commission on Climate Change and Development, Stockholm, Sweden

The main criticism of the PPCR is now regarding the fact that most of the funding under the PPCR will be made available through loans, not grants, and that these loans are to be counted as ODA. The World Bank has justified this decision by reinterpreting the concept of 'new and additional', stating that funds 'are new and additional to existing levels of ODA' but that 'it is expected that most donors will include contributions to the CIFs in their ODA reporting'.[50] Criticism against the PPCR on this basis raises an important point about funding for adaptation: that responsibility for assisting the most vulnerable countries in coping with the impacts of climate change must be additional to existing aid commitments and based on the polluter pays principle, pointing towards responsibility-based rather than burden-based criteria.[51] Financing for adaptation is not owed to poor countries as 'aid' but, rather, as compensation from high emissions countries for those that are most vulnerable to the impacts.[52] This principle is specifically recognized by the UNFCCC through Article 4.4, which specifies that developed countries have committed to helping 'particularly vulnerable' countries meet the costs of adaptation,[53] and this principle is upheld in the decisions regarding the allocation of the UNFCCC funds but not by funding adaptation through ODA.

Mainstreaming into ODA

In the context of ODA, mainstreaming adaptation means working through existing channels of ODA to integrate adaptation concerns across the full range of support. Mainstreaming is seen as making more sustainable, effective and efficient use of resources than is the case when climate policies are designed and managed separately from ongoing activities.[54]

One way of mainstreaming climate change into development processes is through screening of development portfolios.[55] Portfolio screening involves the systematic examination of an agency's set of policies, programmes or projects, with the aim of identifying how concerns about climate change can be integrated within an agency's development priorities.[56] Such screening helps both to identify existing development projects that are particularly threatened by climate change and to identify opportunities for incorporating climate change more explicitly within future projects and programmes. A review of the screening activities of donor portfolios by Klein and colleagues[57] concluded that between 2001 and 2007, six development agencies screened their development portfolios (Box 15.2 presents a case study of mainstreaming adaptation into World Bank operations). The authors concluded that while most agencies already consider climate change as a real but uncertain threat to future development, they tend to have given less thought to how different development patterns might affect vulnerability to climate change.

Box 15.2 Mainstreaming climate change into World Bank operations

Burton and Van Aalst suggest that climate risk assessment should become a routine component of World Bank activities where there are significant climate risks, and propose a screening tool to select which projects merit further risk assessment. At the country level, the risks of climate change and variability should be recognized alongside other risks that are routinely assessed, such as environmental impacts, economic risks and political risks, as reflected in Country Assistance Strategies and sector work.

These suggestions fall mostly within the scope of regular World Bank work; but their implementation could be facilitated by the emerging international regime for climate change adaptation, particularly in the financing opportunities under the UNFCCC.

Recommendations for mainstreaming into the Bank's work include:

- Mainstreaming adaptation through the routine incorporation of climate risk management within World Bank work at the country and project level. The climate risk management should target the whole spectrum of climate change, climate variability and extremes.
- A preliminary screening of projects for climate risk could be quick and straightforward, provided that the appropriate climate risk information is readily available. The World Bank could establish a Climate Risk Management Knowledge Base to facilitate this.
- Only for projects at risk would further risk assessments be performed. Tools for such an assessment, best practice examples and access to networks of expertise and experience could also be included in the Climate Risk Management Knowledge Base.
- At the country level, climate risks should routinely be assessed in Country Assistance Strategies and sector work, alongside other risk assessments.
- The development of climate risk screening tools and methods for risk assessment can build upon recent and current World Bank work in the regions. Further development could initially take place on a pilot basis.
- While the development of tools and the collection of information can only happen in the context of particular countries and sectors, and should go hand in hand with ongoing World Bank work, there is a need for central support and coordination.

The World Bank has since begun to develop a screening tool to help project developers to assess whether proposed investments face significant climate risks. The computer-based package would also provide sources of information and expertise on ways to reduce a project's vulnerability. The Bank suggests that in the longer term it could become a standard tool for screening new projects for climate risk early in the project cycle.*

Note: * See Burton, I., Diringer, E. and Smith, J. (2006) *Adaptation to Climate Change: International Policy Options*, PEW Centre on Global Climate Change, Arlington, VA

Source: adapted from Burton, I. and Van Aalst, M. (2004) *Look Before You Leap: A Risk Management Approach for Incorporating Climate Change Adaptation into World Bank Operations*, Working Paper 100, Environment Department, The World Bank, Washington, DC

Mainstreaming adaptation into climate change is not a 'one-stop shop' for financing both adaptation and development priorities in vulnerable low- and middle-income countries. First, development activities are sensitive to a range of climate variables, only some of which can be reliably projected by climate models. Second, there is a mismatch between the temporal and spatial scales of information required for development and climate change planners, particularly where development interventions take place at the local scale, where accurate climate data are lacking.[58] It is difficult to develop adaptation plans for any urban centre if there is little certainty as to what climate change implies for that particular locality.

Furthermore, there may be trade-offs between development priorities and the actions required to deal with climate change at all levels,[59] and climate-proofed agendas of development institutions may find themselves competing with institutions and constituencies whose overriding priorities are economic and social development. In this case, efforts to fully mainstream adaptation into ODA may encounter political and institutional resistance, especially if they entail new conditionalities. Objections by recipient countries may be particularly strong where new measures are not accompanied by increased assistance, so that it appears that existing aid flows are being diverted to needs other than development.[60] In such instances where conflicts arise, adaptation would involve designing and implementing measures that are more targeted to specific threats than development interventions tend to be, and mainstreaming would then ensure that development activities themselves are not maladapted to climate change.[61] However, it should be recognized that much of what is part of a pro-poor development agenda will contribute to reduced risks and vulnerabilities to most of the likely impacts of climate change – for instance, as provision for good-quality piped water, sanitation, storm and surface drainage, all-weather roads and paths and healthcare are extended to 'slums' and informal settlements.[62]

Given that there can be trade-offs between development and adaptation priorities, ODA cannot be seen to 'plug the gap' left by inadequate climate change finance under the UNFCCC.[63] Funding for adaptation must be in addition to ODA funds, and not all development choices can be dictated by climate change priorities. From a political standpoint, it is most plausible to pursue adequate financing for adaptation within the UNFCCC. In addition, given that future adaptation needs are closely tied in with the achievement of international greenhouse gas reduction targets, it makes sense to build on, rather than compete with, the climate change apparatus already established under the convention.[64] ODA certainly has a role to play in supporting the UNFCCC[65] by funding adaptation activities beyond the narrow remit of the convention; however, this role is additional (but related) to the obligations of the formal climate change management frameworks of the UNFCCC.

Access to adaptation finance by urban stakeholders

Within the international climate change arena, there seems to be a preoccupation with estimating the costs for adaptation and raising the funds to meet those costs. Underpinning this concern over funding amounts is an apparent assumption that, were adequate funding available for low- and middle-income countries to adapt, then adequate adaptation could take place. However, this overlooks the fact that there is a significant deficit in 'absorptive capacity'[66] of many low- and middle-income countries and the most vulnerable groups within them to access these funds and then to use them for their intended purposes. Problems with accessing funds at the international level have already been discussed and highlight the need to support capacity-building initiatives to ensure that vulnerable low- and middle-income countries are able to access funding when it is available. At the country level, there is a need to think carefully about the receiving of funds and the delivery mechanisms through which this funding can be disbursed for the purposes of adaptation. There are obviously key roles for city and municipal governments.

Experience with adaptation funding under the UNFCCC has shown that in-country, institutional responsibilities for adaptation are unclear and sometimes in competition.[67] With the increasing proliferation of bi- and multi-donor and convention funds available, it is vital to avoid duplication of efforts and to ensure consistency in approach. One solution that is currently being piloted in Bangladesh is the development of a country-owned Multi-Donor Trust Fund (MDTF) through which all funding for adaptation could then be channelled. The fund would pool money obtained from different national and multilateral climate change funds and be managed by a board of trustees. To date, the UK government's Department for International Development (DFID) has pledged UK£75 million in grant funding to initiate this fund and this has been matched by a national pledge by Bangladesh of US$45 million to demonstrate its commitment to the progress of the MDTF.[68] It is hoped that such a framework could significantly reduce transaction costs for global and bilateral funds and pave the way for large fund flows in the future, while ensuring proper institutional structures, governance, management and targeting of funds at the national level.

The scale and scope of the MDTF are still under discussion at the time of writing; but it is hoped that the fund would be accessible to the government agencies, NGOs and private sector actors who work with vulnerable communities at the local level. However, a recent announcement that the World Bank is likely to take at least interim (two years) responsibility for the governance of the fund has raised alarm bells, particularly from NGOs concerned that this may result in bureaucratic and functional problems similar to those already faced with the international and, in particular, the GEF-managed adaptation funds.[69] Discussions concerning MDTF governance remain ongoing.

It is also important that the institutions and agencies through which funds are channelled to the people most at risk from climate change are given careful consideration. Given that most of those most vulnerable to climate change are the poorest people in low-income countries, in order for adaptation funding to be effective in reducing vulnerability these groups must be targeted by adaptation resources. Adaptation to climate change at this level requires local knowledge, local competence and local institutional capacity.[70] However, the success of adaptation at the local level relies heavily on supportive institutional environments created by the levels above. Successful adaptation requires both the involvement of local groups and civil society organizations with the knowledge and capacity to act, and a willingness among local and national governments to work with and support low-income and vulnerable groups.[71] Achieving such synergies among this range of stakeholders depends critically upon how (or, in many cases, whether) adaptation funding is made accessible to those who need it on the ground. An ongoing study by the International Institute for Environment and Development (IIED)[72] has identified five main strategies for channelling resources to adaptation:

1   integrating adaptation within national planning;
2   social transfers for building adaptive capacity;
3   multi- and bilateral-funded projects for adaptation;
4   international and national or local NGO-managed adaptation; and
5   private-sector provision of adaptation goods and services.

The authors of the study recognize that these are not mutually exclusive or competing means of addressing adaptation; rather, the aim of the study is to consider in which contexts different combinations of channels can be most effective. The study, furthermore, evaluates each of these channels against their ability to achieve 'adaptation by the poorest'. Each 'channel' was assessed against its scale, impact upon indicators of adaptive capacity (including poverty, health, education and governance)[73] and 'pro-poor' effectiveness.

Early findings from the review demonstrate the need to use different funding strategies in combination under varying circumstances to ensure adaptation that benefits those most at risk and most vulnerable. For example, channelling funds through government institutions can be advantageous in terms of scale and efficiency of resource allocation and this can also have beneficial impacts upon the governance indicators of adaptive capacity. However, significantly, achieving adaptation that benefits the poorest groups requires government capacity and willingness to work with them and their organizations. In a review of constraints on the adaptive capacity of urban areas in low- and middle-income countries, Satterthwaite and colleagues[74] show that in the most vulnerable cities in low- and middle-income countries, one third or more of the population and workforce live and work in illegal settlements that local governments often refuse to work with or even recognize. The authors argue: 'you cannot fund a pro-poor adaptation strategy if the city government refuses to work with the poor, or sees their homes, neighbourhoods and enterprises as "the problem"'. The authors conclude that the capacity of local governments to ensure provision for infrastructure and for disaster risk reduction and preparedness is pivotal in avoiding catastrophic impacts of climate change; and yet this capacity is lacking in the urban areas that need it most.

Conversely, while civil society actors, particularly NGOs, are sometimes lauded for their ability to access and support local-level and community-based approaches, the benefits that NGOs can achieve are largely dependant upon the political context in which they operate. Civil society efforts require practical structures for collaboration with government; and where the agenda of NGOs conflicts with that of the state, NGOs are obliged to respect the priorities of national development strategies in deciding where to place and how to handle their resources. Furthermore, accountability towards funders rather than beneficiaries can result in NGOs marginalizing the lowest-income groups that they claim to represent.

However, financing adaptation through governments while also supporting civil society can increase the effectiveness of both. Increasing NGO capacity can strengthen lobbying of low- and middle-income country governments on behalf of the poor and help to hold governments accountable for service delivery, which can provide some assurance to donors of the effectiveness of aid channelled through national systems. Likewise, linking NGOs to national planning processes can increase accountability of the NGOs and the processes that they manage. Furthermore, NGOs are well placed to encourage uptake of services provided by other channels to the poorest groups, given their access to local communities and capacity to communicate messages in locally appropriate contexts. Finally, simultaneously supporting adaptation through NGOs and government systems can encourage state support for civil society actions and encourage the scaling-up of community-based approaches.[75] But NGOs also need to be accountable to low-income groups and recognize the knowledge, resources and capacities that they can bring to adaptation.

In an urban context, in areas where vulnerability can be ascribed to the failures or limitations of local government, financing adaptation should be used both to address this problem and work around it. Funding could be channelled through civil society organizations that do have direct access to, and a history and knowledge of working with, the poorest, as well as private-sector initiatives that can offer goods and services not provided by the government. There are also channels through which funding can support community-driven 'adaptation + development' directly – for example, through local grassroots–local NGO–local government partnerships.[76] In addition, institutional support for local-level adaptation needs attention. Any fiscal support must be accompanied by, or used for, the strengthening of institutional capacity and accountability at the city and sub-city levels of government in order to reduce these gaps between local and national processes and to ensure that financial resources reach those who can use them best.

Clearly, the relative weight and combinations of different adaptation finance strategies will depend upon the specific local and wider contexts of climate change vulnerabilities. While these conclusions are seemingly commonsense, political expediency often results in an overemphasis on one funding strategy at the expense of others;[77] for example, adaptation projects financed through large multilateral agencies are currently being prioritized over other mechanisms, while streamlining adaptation through national plans is widely regarded as a win–win option for climate-proofing national development. There is a need for further research into how, and under what circumstances, combinations of different channels can be best designed to facilitate access to funding for adaptation by the most vulnerable groups.

Conclusions

The costs of adaptation to address current and near-term future risks arising from climate change are huge; at present, the formal funding mechanisms under the UNFCCC for meeting these costs fall far short of what is needed. Innovative proposals are being discussed currently, which have the potential to bolster UNFCCC funds, and there is some optimism about the scale and capability of the AF to become the key avenue through which international commitments on adaptation should be channelled. However, it is unlikely, certainly in the near future and probably ever, that finance for adaptation under the UNFCCC can meet all the adaptation needs of low- and middle-income countries. International funds through development assistance can contribute to meeting this shortfall. Yet, financing adaptation through overseas development assistance raises its own set of political and ethical problems concerning the responsibilities of high-income countries to pay for the costs of climate change in addition to aid commitments. Furthermore, discussions on how to finance adaptation tend to overlook the local and national political and institutional constraints on achieving adaptation, even with adequate finance, and bypass considerations of how to channel funding to those who need it and can be most effective in addressing it.

These conclusions do point to an opportunity for complementarity between UNFCCC and ODA international funding streams for adaptation. Given the overlap between development and adaptation objectives, there must be a role for ODA in financing adaptation, independent but supportive of the UNFCCC. Development assistance takes a more inclusive approach to vulnerability reduction and therefore can be used to address the underlying drivers of vulnerability associated with poor institutional capacity. Convention funds could be packaged with ODA assistance to support broader climate risk management strategies in vulnerable low- and middle-income countries.[78] International donors are well positioned to strengthen national capacity, while development practitioners and disaster risk reduction practitioners also have a wealth of experience in dealing with reducing vulnerability to climate hazards and extremes at local, sub-national and national scales.[79] ODA therefore has a role in funding adaptation, and channelling funds through development organizations can help to build the necessary local and national institutional capacity to receive and use UNFCCC funds appropriately, as and when they become available to any reasonable degree.

Notes

1. Müller, B. (2008) *International Adaptation Finance: The Need for an Innovative Strategic Approach,* Background Policy Paper for the Climate Strategies Project on Post-2012 Policy Framework: Options for the Tokyo G8 Summit, Oxford Institute for Energy Studies, UK.
2. World Bank (2006) *Clean Energy and Development: Towards an Investment Framework,* ESSD-VP/I-VP, World Bank, Washington, DC, 5 April, x+38pp.
3. ActionAid (2007) *Compensating for Climate Change: Principles and Lessons for Equitable Adaptation Funding,* Action Aid, Washington, DC.
4. Oxfam International (2007) *Adapting to Climate Change: What's Needed in Poor Countries, and Who Should Pay,* Oxfam Briefing Paper 104, Oxfam, Washington, DC, Brussels, Geneva and New York.
5. UNDP (United Nations Development Programme) (2007) *Human Development Report 2007/2008: Fighting Climate Change: Human Solidarity in a Divided World,* UNDP, New York.
6. UNFCCC (United Nations Framework Convention on Climate Change) (2007) 'Analysis of existing and planned investment and financial flows relevant to the development of effective and appropriate international response to climate change', Background paper, UNFCCC, Berlin.
7. Satterthwaite, D., Huq, S., Pelling, M., Reid, R. and Lankao Romero, P. (2007) *Adapting to Climate Change in Urban Areas: The Possibilities and Constraints in Low- and Middle-Income Nations,* Human Settlements Discussion Paper Series – Climate Change and Cities 1, IIED, London.
8. The COP is the association of the UNFCCC. It meets once a year at each COP to review the UNFCCC's progress. To date, there have been 14 COPs.

9. UNFCCC (United Nations Framework Convention on Climate Change) (2001) *The Marrakesh Accords and the Marrakesh Declaration*, http://unfccc.int/cop7/accords_draft.pdf 30.

10. The term least developed country (LDC) is used by the UN, including the UNFCCC, to describe the world's poorest countries according to the criteria of low income, human resource weakness and economic vulnerability.

11. The Clean Development Mechanism (CDM) is a carbon trading mechanism under the Kyoto Protocol that allows countries with greenhouse gas reduction targets to generate emissions reductions by investing in clean development in low- and middle-income countries.

12. Mace, M. J. (2006) 'Adaptation under the United Nations Framework Convention on Climate Change: the international legal framework', in Adger, W. M., Paavola, J., Huq, S. and Mace, J. (eds) *Fairness in Adaptation to Climate Change*, MIT Press, Boston.

13. GEF (Global Environment Facility) (2008) *Status Report on the Climate Change Funds as of 4 March 2008*, Report from the Trustee, GEF, Washington, DC, GEF/LDCF.SCCF.4/Inf.2.

14. See reference 13.

15. Oxfam International (2008) *Climate Wrongs and Human Rights: Putting People at the Heart of Climate Change Policy*, Oxfam Briefing Paper 117, Oxfam, Washington, DC, Brussels, Geneva and New York.

16. See reference 3; also Müller, B. (2006) 'Nairobi 2006: Trust and the future of adaptation funding', www.oxfordenergy.org/pdfs/EV38.pdf.

17. UNFCCC (United Nations Framework Convention on Climate Change) (1992) 'Article 11', in *United Nations Framework Convention on Climate Change*, New York, May.

18. Streck, C. (2001) 'The global environment facility: a role model for global governance?', *Global Environmental Politics*, vol 1, pp17–18.

19. The Group of 77 is a large negotiating alliance of low- and middle-income countries that focuses on numerous international topics, including climate change, and seeks to harmonize the negotiating positions of its 131 member states. The name comes from the Joint Declaration of the Seventy-Seven Countries in 1964 formed during international trade negotiations.

20. See reference 16: Müller (2006).

21. See reference 3.

22. Klein, R. J. T. and Möhner, A. (2008) 'Governance limits to effective global financial support for adaptation to climate change', Paper presented at the conference Living with Climate Change: Are There Limits to Adaptation?, Royal Geographical Society, 7–8 February 2008, London.

23. Ayers, J. (2008) 'Implementing NAPAs: Are we there yet?', *Tiempo*, vol 69, pp15–19.

24. Müller, B. (2007) 'The Nairobi climate change conference: a breakthrough for adaptation funding', in *Oxford Energy and Environment Comment*, Oxford Institute for Energy Studies, Oxford.

25. See reference 1.

26. See reference 1.

27. See reference 1.

28. These are fuels consumed for international marine and air transport.

29. Parties with commitments under the Kyoto Protocol have accepted targets for limiting or reducing emissions. These targets are expressed as levels of allowed emissions, or 'assigned amounts', over the 2008 to 2012 commitment period. The allowed emissions are divided into 'assigned amount units'.

30. See reference 1.

31. See reference 1.

32. Müller, B. and Hepburn, C. (2006) *IATAL – An International Air Travel Adaptation Levy*, European Capacity Building Initiative, Oxford.

33. See reference 1.

34. The Group of 8 Plus 5 is an international forum for the governments of Canada, France, Germany, Italy, Japan, Russia, the UK, the US and the European Union, and five developing countries: Brazil, China, India, Mexico and South Africa.

35. IMO (International Maritime Organization) (2008) 'IMO environment meeting approves revised regulations on ship emissions', IMO Newsroom, http://www.imo .org/Newsroom/mainframe.asp?topic_id=1709&doc_id=9123.

36. Greenpeace (2007) *Hiding Behind the Poor*, Report by Ananthapadmanabhan, G., Srinivas, K. and Gopal, V. for Greenpeace India.

37. Annex 1 countries are high-income countries (non-Annex 1 countries are low- and middle-income countries).

38. UNFCCC (2008b) *Finance – AWGLCA: Norway's Submission on Auctioning Allowances*, UNFCCC, Bonn, http://unfccc.int/files/kyoto_protocol/application/ pdf/norway_auctioning_allowances.pdf.

39. See reference 1.

40. Huq, S. and Ayers, J. (2008) 'Streamlining adaptation to climate change into development projects at the national and local level', in European Parliament (ed) *Financing Climate Change Policies in Developing Countries*, European Parliament, Brussels, PE 408.546-IP/A/CLIP/A/CLIM/ST/2008-13.

41. Klein, R. J. T. (2008) 'Mainstreaming climate adaptation into development policies and programmes: a European perspective', in European Parliament (ed) *Financing Climate Change Policies in Developing Countries*: see reference 40.

42. Adger, W. N., Huq, S., Brown, K., Conway, D. and Hulme, M. (2003) 'Adaptation to climate change in the developing world', *Progress in Development Studies*, vol 3, no 3, pp179–195; also Agrawala, S. (ed) (2005) *Bridge Over Troubled Waters: Linking Climate Change and Development*, OECD, Paris; Klein, R. J. T., Schipper, E. L. and Dessai, S. (2003) *Integrating Mitigation and Adaptation into Climate and Development Policy: Three Research Questions*, Working Paper 40, Tyndall Centre for Climate Change Research, University of East Anglia, UK, www.tyndall.ac.uk/publications/working_ papers/working_papers.shtml, accessed 3 September 2006; and Klein, R. T. J., Eriksen, S. E. H., Naess, L. O., Hammill, A., Tanner, T. M., Robledo, C. and O'Brien, K. L. (2007) *Portfolio Screening to Support the Mainstreaming of Adaptation to Climate Change into Development Assistance*, Working Paper 102, Tyndall Centre for Climate Change Research, University of East Anglia, UK.

43. Burton, I., Diringer, E. and Smith, J. (2006) *Adaptation to Climate Change: International Policy Options*, PEW Centre on Global Climate Change, Arlington, VA.

44. See reference 41; see also reference 40.

45. Dodman, D., Ayers, J. and Huq, S. (2009) 'Building resilience', in *State of the World 2009: Into a Warming World*, Worldwatch Institute, Washington, DC.

46. Maladaptations are actions or investments that enhance rather than reduce vulnerability to impacts of climate change. This can include the shifting of vulnerability from one social group or place to another; it also includes shifting risk to future generations and/or to ecosystems and ecosystem services. In many cities, investments being made are, in fact, maladaptive rather than adaptive. Removing maladaptations is often the first task to be addressed, even before new adaptations.

47. World Bank (2008b) 'Q&A: Climate investment funds', World Bank, Washington, DC, 1 July.

48. CCCD (Commission on Climate Change and Development) (2008) *Financing Mechanisms for Adaptation*, Secretariat to the Commission on Climate Change and Development, Stockholm, Sweden; also Müller, B. and Winkler, H. (2008) 'One step forward, two steps back? The governance of the World Bank climate investment funds', in *Oxford Energy and Environment Comment*, Oxford Institute for Energy Studies, Oxford, February.

49. See reference 1.

50. See reference 47.

51. Thompson, M. and Rayner, S. (1998) 'Cultural discourse', in Rayner, S. and Malone, E. L. (eds) *Human Choice and Climate Change Volume 1: The Societal Framework*, Batelle Press, Ohio.

52. See reference 3; see also reference 4.

53. See reference 40.

54. See reference 42: Klein et al (2003).

55. See reference 40.

56. See reference 42: Klein et al (2007).

57. See reference 42: Klein et al (2007).

58. See reference 42: Agrawala (ed) (2005).

59. See, for instance, the discussions on Durban's adaptation programme in Chapter 11.

60. See reference 43; also see reference 41.

61. See reference 42: Klein et al (2007).

62. See reference 7.

63. See reference 40.

64. See reference 43.

65. See reference 40.

66. See reference 1.

67. See reference 22.

68. UK/Bangladesh Climate Change Conference organized by the UK Department for International Development, 10 September 2008, Royal Geographical Society, London.

69. See reference 68.

70. See reference 7; see also Chapters 3 and 11.

71. See reference 7.

72. IIED (forthcoming) *Adaptation by the Poorest*, Report funded by the World Wildlife Fund (WWF) UK, IIED, London.

73. Acknowledging that direct measurement of adaptive capacity is inherently problematic, the authors assessed it on the basis of other indicators that exhibit a

strong statistical relationship with successful responses to climate-related events. Summarizing the work of Adger et al, which identifies 18 indicators as statistically significant, the authors developed four broad categories of indicators related to income, health, poverty and governance. See full report for more details: Adger, W. N. et al (2005) 'Social-ecological resilience to coastal disasters', *Science*, vol 309, no 5737, 12 August, pp1036–1039.

74. See reference 7.
75. See reference 72.
76. Mitlin, D. (2008) 'With and beyond the state; co-production as a route to political influence, power and transformation for grassroots organizations', *Environment and Urbanization*, vol 20, no 2, October, pp339–360.
77. See reference 72.
78. See reference 43.
79. See reference 40.

16

Conclusions: Local Development and Adaptation

David Satterthwaite, David Dodman and Jane Bicknell

Introduction

We hope that this volume helps to establish that urgent attention needs to be given to climate change adaptation in urban areas in low- and middle-income nations. While there are some careful studies showing the risks in particular cities, and who is most at risk, these have not generated a broader acceptance among national governments and international agencies of the scale and nature of risk faced by urban populations. Indeed, most discussions of adaptation do not deal with urban areas at all. This is surprising given not only the number of people whom they house, but also the number of urban dwellers at risk from climate change and the economic importance of urban areas in virtually all national economies.

The chapters in this volume illustrate the challenges faced by urban citizens and governments in low- and middle-income countries as a result of climate change. The scale of the challenge is substantial: hundreds of millions of urban dwellers are likely to be at risk from the direct and indirect impacts of climate change over the next few decades. But the research findings presented in this volume also help to translate these abstract figures into the experiences that will affect individuals and communities, the very young and elderly people, households and businesses in towns and cities as a result of climate change.

This concluding chapter draws out some of the key themes identified by the contributors to this volume and uses these as the basis for suggesting future directions for research and action. This approach reflects a recognition that the effects of climate change are already being felt and that unless actions are taken soon, the consequences could be a growing number of catastrophic events. It is also likely that there will be a large increase in the number of disasters that are not logged in international disaster databases (whose cumulative impacts may be greater than those that are logged) and also a large increase in less dramatic but nonetheless damaging changes – for instance, greater health risks from certain diseases and serious constraints on freshwater supplies. In part, this approach can be taken because of the growing acceptance of the basic facts of climate change and a growing realization that there is a necessity to move beyond describing people's vulnerability to them, to creating more resilient human settlements. Of course, building resilience and facilitating adaptation need to take place within a broader context of measures to reduce greenhouse gas emissions.

Key themes

Reading the chapters in this volume brings to the fore certain key themes:

1 The very large numbers of urban dwellers at risk from the impacts of climate change. This is best documented with regard to floods and storms – see, for instance, the cases of Mombasa in Chapter 3, Dhaka in Chapter 4, Mumbai and Shanghai in Chapter 6, various cities in Africa in Chapter 9, Santa Fe, Caracas and Buenos Aires in Chapter 10 and many cities in India in Chapter 14. Certain chapters also highlight the vulnerability of cities or particular city populations to sea-level rise, including the global overview of urban populations in the low-elevation coastal zone (LECZ) (Chapter 2), Cotonou (Chapter 5) and Shanghai and Mumbai (Chapter 6); Chapter 14 notes the large stretches of the coast in India at risk from sea-level rise, which include many heavily populated areas. Many chapters point to the worries about changes in freshwater resources for cities – including cities in the Andes (Chapter 10), in Asia (Chapter 7), in sub-Saharan Africa (Chapter 12), in India (Chapter 14) and in Durban (Chapter 11). This discussion of changes in freshwater availability recognizes that climate change's impact is not necessarily increased water scarcity but, rather, increased stresses on regular supplies in local contexts where much of the population lack safe and sufficient provision for reasons that have little or nothing to do with water scarcity. As Kovats and Akhtar note in Chapter 7: 'The impact of climate change upon water availability is likely to be one of the most significant for the health of populations. However, due to the complexity of the factors that determine access to clean water (social, political and environmental), the impacts upon health are not well addressed in the literature on climate impacts.'

2 Getting more attention to avoiding extreme weather disasters. The number of extreme weather disasters and the scale of their impact have grown rapidly in urban areas in low- and middle-income nations even though it is likely that there are large undercounts in the number of disasters and their total impact (see Chapters 1, 9 and 10). It may not be possible to ascribe this to climate change or to identify climate change's contribution relative to other factors. In many urban centres, this growth in the number and impact of extreme weather events has much to do with the growth of urban populations concentrated on sites at risk. But this is evidence of how vulnerable large sections of the urban population are to extreme weather events whose frequency and/or intensity is likely to increase as a result of climate change. Two chapters in particular, Chapters 8 and 10, raise the importance not only of action now to avoid disasters (as better-quality homes, neighbourhoods and infrastructure and services prevent floods that cause death and injury, as well as limiting damage to properties), but also of being prepared for them (to limit their impacts) and being able to respond rapidly in ways that quickly and effectively address the needs of those who are affected and displaced. Chapter 10 also points out how it is more difficult politically to get action to limit the impact of extreme weather (or other disasters) because it is not possible to show in advance how many deaths could be avoided by doing so. Many of the measures needed to reduce vulnerability to extreme weather require working with low-income groups on what can be politically difficult issues, such as providing infrastructure and services to those living on land that is illegally occupied or subdivided. Although Chapter 10 is on Latin America, its opening paragraph has wider relevance:

> ... *climate change and variability come to people's attention as extreme weather events such as floods, droughts, extreme temperatures, heavy rains and storms. These events are perceived as unusual and extraordinary and, over subsequent days, the media is full of press releases detailing how many people were killed, injured or displaced. Authorities and experts comment on the status of the situation, its causes and what should be done to prevent future disasters. However, a few days later everything is forgotten, although those who have been displaced or whose homes have been damaged continue to struggle.*

Chapter 14 highlights how, in India, a great missed opportunity over the last 15 years was the chance to connect the official climate change adaptation agenda with the rapid development of natural hazard risk assessment, management and disaster risk reduction capacity after the devastating disasters during the 1990s and early 2000s.

3 The variations in risk and vulnerability within the population of any urban centre. The fact that there are large differentials in risk and vulnerability within urban centres is an issue covered in virtually all the chapters. This can be seen in how certain locations within an urban area are affected most, and how often these are locations with high concentrations of low-income households – often illegal or informal settlements with poor-quality housing and a lack of protective infrastructure. See, for example, the extent to which low-income groups have no alternative but to settle on land at risk from floods or landslides (Mombasa in Chapter 3; Dhaka in Chapter 4; Mumbai and Rio de Janeiro in Chapter 6; Santa Fe in Chapter 10); the lack of protective infrastructure (many chapters, but particularly Dhaka in Chapter 4; Mumbai in Chapter 6; and Santa Fe in Chapter 10); and the lack of land-use planning and building control (many chapters; but see Chapter 4 for details of how natural drains are lost to building expansion in Dhaka).

Chapter 8 highlights the differentials in risk and vulnerability within urban populations for different age groups, and between women and men (and girls and boys), for avoiding disasters, for avoiding death and injury when they occur, and for coping after disasters have occurred. This includes a concern for understanding the implications of these risks for children's long-term development, as well as children's resilience and their potential contribution to solutions.

All chapters, with Chapter 6 having this as a particular focus, cover the complex range of factors that contribute to risk and vulnerability in each location.

4 Adaptation needs to be locally driven and to involve those most at risk. The particular ways in which climate change will affect particular urban centres and particular population groups within them is very much influenced by local contexts, including the quality of buildings, the availability of infrastructure, urban forms and topographies, land uses around the urban centre, local institutional capacities. Indeed, one of the first ways for any urban centre to start planning for adaptation is to begin building a more detailed picture and map of who is most at risk to extreme weather and disasters, and why (see Chapters 3, 10 and 11, in particular). This includes understanding the current impact of weather and climate variability on health (Chapter 7), and drawing together relevant information from different sources and government agencies (Chapters 9 and 10). Local knowledge and widespread local consultation are necessary – in order to gauge the concrete and particular ways in which women and men of different age groups and in different places are at more serious risk, as well as to establish what everybody can contribute to risk reduction (Chapter 8).

5 Linked to this point about locally driven adaptation is the importance of two key actors – local governments and community-based organizations. It is impossible to conceive of an effective adaptation programme for any major urban centre without a competent, capable local government that is able and willing to work with the inhabitants of the settlements most at risk – which in most nations means working with the residents of informal/illegal settlements. This does not mean that the local government is the only actor – but it has to provide the framework and policies that encourage and support the contributions of individuals, households, community-based organizations, non-governmental organizations (NGOs) and private enterprises – and provide the needed local coordination for the actions and policies of different agencies from higher levels of government. Most chapters consider these issues, with Chapters 11 and 12 making this their central focus. Chapter 11 reports on the city of Durban's programme for adapting to climate change. This is of interest not only because it describes the development of an adaptation plan by the city government (and the information base it needs), which is very unusual (very few city governments in low- and middle-income nations have taken this step), but also because it discusses the difficulties that developing such an adaptation programme faces, even within a city government committed to development and poverty reduction. Many government agencies (and politicians and senior civil servants) see climate change adaptation as potentially drawing resources from their budgets – and this to address risks that they see as too uncertain or too far into the future. As Debra Roberts stresses, each city needs an information base to make climate change relevant to its locality and requires support for developing this. But many international agencies concerned with climate change are prioritizing mitigation, not adaptation (see also Chapters 1 and 14). Roberts also stresses the need to go beyond the easy, almost symbolic, project (e.g. reducing methane emissions from landfills), and notes how external funding would be better spent capacitating people rather than implementing often *ad hoc* climate change-related projects.

6 Many chapters describe actions and precedents that show some movement towards adaptation. There is much to be learned from the experience in Durban (Chapter 11); Chapter 12 describes the kind of municipal adaptation programme that needs support in Cape Town; Chapter 13 notes ways to take forward water management for greater urban resilience to climate change. Chapter 8 has some strong examples of the means by which the risk and vulnerability of children are reduced in disaster response; and Chapter 10 has examples of city and national governments in Latin America that are addressing adaptation issues, usually driven by responses to the devastating impacts of recent extreme weather events.

Conclusions

The central role of local governments

Perhaps the main message of this volume is that adaptation is not possible without knowledgeable, accountable, better resourced and technically competent local authorities who are willing and able to work well with the groups most at risk. This is a point that has resonance far beyond the specific context of climate change: well-governed towns and cities have populations and economies that are resilient to a broader range of shocks and stresses, including the extreme weather and other events that can bring disasters that should have been avoided. Well-governed urban centres should be able to protect their inhabitants from floods and storms and ensure a high quality of life through the provision of infrastructure, services, public space, a planning framework and accountability. They should be able to understand the very location-specific, place-specific local needs for this – through strong local information, careful consultation and accountable political and administrative systems. Planning, land-use management, and building and land-use standards should ensure that sufficient land is available for housing (including low-cost housing) without urban expansion over land that is dangerous or needed for city or regional flood protection. Obviously, one important adaptation strategy is to ensure sufficient supplies of legal serviced land for housing that serves low-income households both in its location and in its price – and that avoids dangerous locations. This is something easily stated, but almost always difficult politically.

As many chapters in this volume make clear, there are very substantial synergies between successful adaptation to climate change and successful local development, including poverty reduction. Reductions in poverty, including improvements in housing and living conditions and provision for infrastructure and services, are central to adaptation. Successful well-governed cities greatly reduce climate-related risks for low-income populations; unsuccessful badly governed cities do not and may greatly increase such risks. And one of the key predictors for resilience at the level of the individual, household and community is access to safe, secure housing with the necessary infrastructure and services. Although building standards and regulations are necessary and are intended to ensure the safety of homes, schools and offices, simply making these more rigorous or enforcing them more stringently is likely to have negative impacts upon the ability of the urban poor to find or build safe shelter. These standards are intended for finished buildings; yet the financial constraints faced by most low-income groups mean that they are seldom able to build or purchase an entire structure at a single time. Thus, what is required is a more flexible system of standards that encourages and supports low-income urban residents to construct incrementally in a safe way, rather than using standards that deem illegal all their efforts.

It is not surprising that most city governments and most ministries and agencies at higher levels of government in low- and middle-income countries have given little attention to climate change adaptation within their urban policies and investments. This is not only because of limitations in city and municipal governments – even where such governments are competent, representative and accountable to poorer groups, they generally have more pressing issues, including large backlogs in provision for infrastructure and services, and with much of their population living in poor-quality housing. They are also under pressure to address a range of immediate needs – to improve education, healthcare and security – and are looking for ways to expand employment and attract new investment. It is difficult to engage them when risks are uncertain and perceived as being in the future.

Unless adaptation to climate change is seen to support and enhance the achievement of development goals and to be relevant to the ministries or agencies responsible for housing, planning, infrastructure and public works, it will remain marginal within most government plans and investments. Perhaps as importantly, the need for adaptation highlights the importance of strong, locally driven development that delivers for poorer groups and is accountable to them. Similarly, the extreme vulnerability of large sections of the urban population to many aspects of climate change reveals the deficiencies in 'development'. Unless these deficiencies are addressed, there is no real basis for adaptation. It is very difficult to conceive of how to get pro-poor and effective adaptation in nations with weak, ineffective and unaccountable local governments. This is especially so in the many nations that also have civil conflicts and no economic or political stability. Many of the nations or cities most at risk from climate change lack the political and institutional base to address adaptation. Even if we can conceive of how this might be addressed, it is difficult to see how existing international institutions as they are currently configured can do so. Discussions on the framework for international funding for adaptation may still be far from providing the necessary funding (as discussed in Chapter 15); but understanding how this can support locally determined, locally driven adaptation that serves, and works with, those most at risk, is even further off.

The importance of community-based adaptation and its limits

For community-based adaptation, there is a danger that its relevance will be both overstated and underplayed at the same time. It will be overstated because community-based organization and action cannot provide the citywide infrastructure and service provision and city–region management that are central to adaptation. Many of the risks and vulnerabilities that low-income groups face come from deficiencies or inadequacies in infrastructure provision that they alone cannot address. For instance, they may be able to help construct or improve drainage and collect solid waste within their settlement; but this needs a larger drainage and solid waste collection system into which to feed; or investments and actions are needed 'upstream' from them – for instance, to reduce the volume and speed of floodwaters.

But the relevance of community-based adaptation is also underplayed in that the policies and practices of governments and international agencies do not recognize the capacity of community-based organizations to contribute to adaptation, or, if they do, they lack the institutional means to support them. Low-income urban residents can affect many risk-reducing measures, individually or collectively, while well-organized, representative community organizations are important for representing their interests to local governments and external funders. Also important is the possibility for these local organizations to form broader coalitions to undertake work on a larger scale, and to influence local and international views on effective adaptation and international strategies for adaptation financing.[1]

The work of community-based action to install and maintain sewers and drains in Karachi and other urban centres in Pakistan can illustrate this. With the support of a local NGO, the Orangi Pilot Project–Research and Training Institute, the residents of small streets (lanes) were able to work together to design and manage the installation of good-quality sewers and drains; some also installed piped water. By keeping down unit costs, the costs could be covered by payments made by the residents. This also allowed a much larger-scale initiative since no external funding had to be negotiated. These community-managed initiatives have greatly improved conditions in low-income settlements all over Karachi and in many other urban centres; but to be effective, they need to be integrated within a larger system of water, sewer and drainage mains. What made this model so much more effective and large scale was the capacity of the local NGO not only to support community action, but also to get local government to support this – and so local government provided the larger infrastructure framework into which all the community-managed interventions could fit.[2]

There are increasing numbers of examples of partnerships between local governments and community-based organizations formed by the urban poor that have greatly reduced environmental health risks – for instance, by improving housing and installing or improving piped water, sanitation and drainage.[3] Although these are not in response to climate change (although many are in response to extreme weather), they show what is possible. There is also a 40-year experience of upgrading 'slums' and informal settlements that has nothing to do with climate change and, although the extent of success is very varied, where it works, it certainly reduces poorer groups' vulnerabilities to flooding and other extreme weather events. Many city governments support 'slum and squatter' upgrading.[4] In some nations, these receive considerable support from national government – as in the Baan Mankong (secure tenure) programme in Thailand, supported by the Thai government's Community Organizations Development Institute,[5] and in the PRODEL programme in Nicaragua.[6] The best 'slum and squatter' upgrading programmes can be seen as good examples of the necessary combination of community-based adaptation and supportive local governments; they may focus on addressing 'everyday' hazards and protection against extreme weather, but addressing climate change is often simply an extension of this.

Another important set of experiences relevant to community-based adaptation is community-managed enumerations and surveys.[7] In many cities, federations of slum/shack dwellers and local NGOs have undertaken surveys and mapping of all informal settlements at a citywide scale – for instance, in Johannesburg and Cape Town[8] in South Africa, in Kisumu and Nairobi[9] in Kenya, and in Phnom Penh[10] in Cambodia. This has also been done for all of Karachi's informal settlements by the Orangi Pilot Project–Research and Training Institute, and this detailed mapping contributed to the innovations noted above in sewers and drainage construction.[11] The advantage of these initiatives is that not only do they identify risk, but they also focus on populations who are particularly vulnerable and engage these populations in developing this information base and identifying appropriate responses. In many cities, the slum/shack dweller federations and their support NGOs have also undertaken surveys of vacant land to identify safe and appropriate sites for relocation when *in situ* upgrading is not possible.[12]

In addition, the slum/shack dweller federations and their support NGOs have undertaken many detailed household surveys in informal settlements – covering every household and producing very detailed maps showing plot boundaries and existing infrastructure provision. This provides the information base needed for investment plans for infrastructure and services and for upgrading housing – and often for plot regularization and land tenure provision for households. These are often the first surveys, plans and maps ever produced for these informal settlements – even when such settlements comprise a significant proportion of a city's population. They have also provided the means by which the residents of these settlements and their community organizations have engaged with local governments in discussing development plans for their settlements[13] – for instance, in Nairobi,[14] Dar es Salaam[15] and Mumbai.[16] But almost all of the valuable precedents noted above were only possible because of representative organizations formed by urban poor groups within informal settlements, in which women had central roles. In most informal settlements, these organizations are not present or face strong local opposition.

Mitigation and the distribution of adaptation costs

Discussions of adaptation must also remember the profound unfairness globally between those who cause climate change and those who are most at risk from its effects.[17] This can be seen from three different aspects.

The first concerns nations. It is within the wealthiest nations that most greenhouse gases have been emitted; but it is mostly low- and middle-income nations that are bearing, and will bear, most of the costs. Figure 16.1 gives some idea of the scale of the differentials between nations with regard to carbon dioxide emissions per person from fossil fuel use and the manufacture of cement. For many low-income nations, emissions per capita can hardly be seen on the graph because they are less than 0.1 metric tonnes, i.e. less than 1/200th that of the US and Canada. In 2004, per capita carbon dioxide emissions were around 20 tonnes in the US and Canada, 6 to 10 tonnes in most European nations – and less than 0.25 tonnes for many nations in sub-Saharan Africa and Asia. Several sub-Saharan African nations have per capita emissions of less than 0.1 tonnes, including Niger, Burkina Faso, Malawi, Uganda, Rwanda, Central African Republic, Mali, Burundi and Chad. Several low-income Asian nations have per capita emissions below 0.25 tonnes, including Cambodia (with less than 0.1 tonnes), Nepal, Myanmar, Lao PDR and Bangladesh; many more have between 0.25 and 0.5 tonnes. These nations' per capita figures are also far below the world average targets sought for 2030 or 2050 to slow and then stop the increase in carbon dioxide concentrations in the atmosphere.

The differentials between high-income nations and low- and middle-income nations would be even larger if each nation's historic contribution to carbon dioxide in the atmosphere was considered. For the other greenhouse gas emissions,

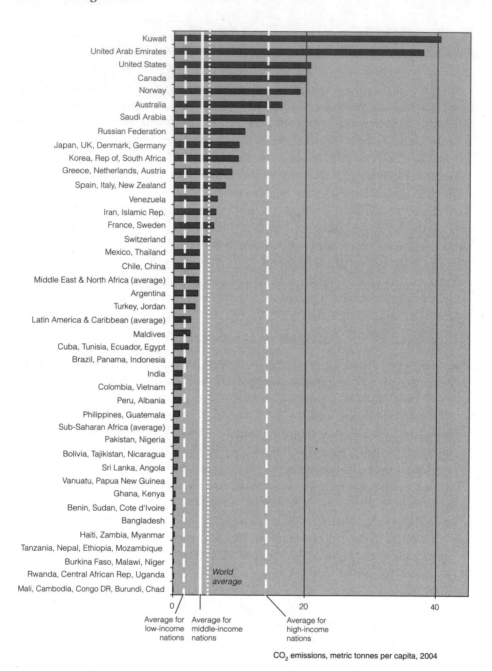

Figure 16.1 Comparisons between nations and groups of nations for carbon dioxide emissions per capita (metric tonnes) in 2004

Note: The statistics in Figure 16.1 are for carbon dioxide emissions stemming from the burning of fossil fuels and the manufacture of cement. They include carbon dioxide produced during the consumption of solid, liquid and gas fuels and gas flaring. Carbon dioxide emissions from these sources represented only 57 per cent of global anthropogenic greenhouse gas emissions in 2004.[a]

The most important omissions are carbon dioxide emissions from forestry (mostly deforestation and land-use changes associated with it) and methane and nitrous oxide (mostly arising from agriculture). It would be more useful to be able to compare nations in terms of total anthropogenic emissions for all greenhouse gas emissions (including methane, nitrous oxide and fluorocarbons); but there is no up to date data on this for most low- and middle-income nations. There is also the complication that land use, land-use changes and forestry are major contributors to total anthropogenic greenhouse gas emissions in some nations (e.g. in Indonesia and Brazil), but act to remove carbon dioxide emissions in many nations to the point where, when these are considered within total emissions, they produce negative figures for many low-income nations.[b]

[a] Rogner, H.-H., Zhou, D., Bradley, R., Crabbé, P., Edenhofer, O., Hare, B., Kuijpers, L. and Yamaguchi, M. (2007) 'Introduction', in Metz, B., Davidson, O. R., Bosch, P. R., Dave, R. and Meyer, L. A. (ed) *Climate Change 2007: Mitigation*, Contribution of Working Group III to the Fourth Assessment Report of the Intergovernmental Panel on Climate Change, Cambridge University Press, Cambridge.

[b] See UNFCCC (2008) *National Greenhouse Gas Inventory Data for the Period 1990–2005*; also 'Note by the Secretariat', United Nations Framework Convention on Climate Change, FCCC/SBI.2007/30, 28pp; UNFCCC (2005) *Sixth Compilation and Synthesis of Initial National Communications from Parties not Included in Annex I to the Convention*; and 'Note by the Secretariat', United Nations Framework Convention on Climate Change, FCCC/SBI/2005/18/ Add.2, 20pp.

Source: World Bank, *World Development Indicators On-line*, accessed 1 November 2008

including carbon dioxide emissions from deforestation and land-use changes, and other important greenhouse gas emissions, including methane, nitrous oxide and fluorocarbons, the picture is less clear because country data on these are less certain and less complete. It is also complicated by the contributions of land-use changes and forestry, which can be large contributors to total aggregate emissions or large greenhouse gas sinks (and therefore reduce a country's aggregate emissions). Data for 1994 for low- and middle-income nations suggest that many low-income nations in Africa and some in Asia and Latin America were removing more greenhouse gases than they were emitting.[18]

The second aspect of unfairness concerns people – it is the high-consumption lifestyles of the wealthy (and the production systems that meet their consumption demands, wherever these are located) that drive climate change;[19] it is mostly low-income groups in low- and middle-income nations, with negligible contributions to climate change, who are most at risk from its impacts.

The third aspect of unfairness relates to who has the capacity to move from urban centres or urban sites at risk. Larger companies and corporations can easily adjust to new patterns of risk induced by climate change, and move their offices and production facilities away from cities or other urban sites at risk. Wealthier households can also move. But cities cannot move. And all cities have within them the homes, cultural and financial assets and livelihoods of their inhabitants, much of which cannot be moved. Climate change is likely to threaten the very viability of some major cities – including cities with very low greenhouse gas emission levels.

The statistics in Figure 16.1 actually understate the scale of these differentials. Greenhouse gas emissions in high-income nations are kept down by the fact that many of the energy-intensive goods used or consumed by their citizens and businesses are imported. If greenhouse gas emissions were allocated to the consumer whose demand for goods or services was the root cause of the emissions, the differentials between high-income nations and low-income nations in average per capita emissions would be even higher.[20] As Walker and King note:

> ... *many of the countries in the Western world have dodged their own carbon dioxide emissions by exporting their manufacturing to ... China. Next time you buy something with 'Made in China' stamped on it, ask yourself who was responsible for the emissions that created it.*[21]

In addition, comparing 'averages' for nations obscures just how much wealthy groups drive the problem. The differentials in greenhouse gas emissions per person between rich and poor groups can be much larger than the differentials between rich and poor nations. For instance, the greenhouse gas emissions generated as a result of the high-consumption lifestyle of a very wealthy person are likely to be hundreds of thousands of times more than that generated by many low-income households in low-income nations. For a proportion of low-income households in urban areas in low-income nations, their contribution to greenhouse gas emissions may be negative since their consumption levels, including fossil fuel use, are so low, and these are more than compensated for by their work recovering materials from waste and returning these into production.

The very survival of some small-island and some low-income nations (or their main cities) is in doubt as much of their land area is at risk from sea-level rise and storms; yet their contributions to global greenhouse emissions have been very small. Hundreds of millions of rural and urban dwellers who contribute very little to greenhouse gas emissions are likely to face very serious constraints on freshwater availability for their livelihoods and their domestic consumption – for instance, as rainfall patterns change, as freshwater sources close to coasts become salinated or as glaciers recede.[22] There are also tens of millions of people in low- and middle-income nations whose homes and livelihoods are at risk from sea-level rise and storms, although they have made very little contribution to global warming. The economic cost of losing certain cities for which adaptation costs are considered 'too high' may be relatively small for many national economies. But what will happen to international relations as increasing numbers of people lose their homes, assets, livelihoods and cultural heritages to climate change-related impacts – especially when the main causes of this are strongly associated with the lifestyles of high-income groups in high-income nations, and the reason for their loss is the failure of high-income nations to cut back their emissions? Would the US government have opposed the Kyoto Protocol's modest targets for emissions reductions if Washington DC, New York and Los Angeles faced risks comparable to those facing Dhaka, Mumbai, Lagos, Bangkok and Male – as a result of greenhouse gas emissions that the US had not generated?

Although this volume has focused on adaptation (except for Chapter 14, which looks at both adaptation and mitigation), the priority for the urban populations most at risk from the floods, storms, heat waves, water supply constraints and other impacts that climate change is likely to bring is actually mitigation – an avoidance of these impacts and, thus, of the need to adapt. This means governments in high-income nations must focus on the reductions in greenhouse gas emissions needed within their borders and on measures that reduce the greenhouse gas emission implications of their citizens' consumption patterns, which underpin emissions beyond their borders. Almost all adaptation implies costs and these are likely to rise rapidly without effective mitigation – as will the numbers of homes, livelihoods, settlements, cities and, ultimately, lives that adaptation is unable to protect.

In discussions on climate change during the 1990s, the priority given to mitigation and the lack of attention to adaptation was justified by the hope that mitigation would mean that dangerous impacts would be avoided. But the very limited progress on getting the necessary global agreements to reduce greenhouse gas emissions over the last two decades suggests that even under the most optimistic assumptions there will be a considerable time lag between what is needed and what is achieved. There is also the time lag between when emissions are reduced and climate change impacts are reduced. This necessitates planning for adaptation now in order to limit the damaging consequences of climate change that international agreements fail to prevent. The longer it takes for the necessary global agreements to be reached and implemented, the greater the necessity to adapt. Well-planned, well-governed towns and cities are an important part both of mitigation and of adaptation. What this volume has sought to do is bring together chapters that suggest what form this action on adaptation should take.

Thus, adaptation plans must not slow progress towards mitigation. It would also be hypocritical of governments in high-income nations solely to contribute funding to adaptation costs in low- and middle-income nations instead of drastically reducing emissions – although perhaps this is also unavoidable given the political difficulties that they will face in getting the needed reductions in greenhouse gas emissions within their boundaries. It is also obvious that measures for mitigation must avoid disadvantaging the hundreds of millions of urban dwellers currently living in very poor-quality housing, in tenements, cheap boarding houses and illegal or informal settlements. These people include a large proportion of the population whose homes and livelihoods are most at risk from climate change. A technology-driven, market-led response to climate change does little for them. As Aromar Revi notes in Chapter 14:

> *A great risk in market-driven adaptation policy is the possibility of a slew of anti-poor interventions leading to a vicious cycle of displacement resettlement and increasing vulnerability in many cities. A number of successful programmes have demonstrated that the cost of* in situ *risk mitigation is often a fraction that of relocation, typically less than 10 per cent of the capital cost of new development.*

Thus, the key issue is how to build resilience to the many impacts of climate change in tens of thousands of urban centres in low- and middle-income nations. Such measures should:

*   support and work with risk reduction from other environmental hazards, including disasters (noting the strong complementarities between reducing risk from climate change, non-climate change-related disasters and most other environmental hazards);
*   be strongly pro-poor (most of those most at risk from climate change and from other environmental hazards have low incomes and very limited financial assets, which limits their autonomous adaptive capacity);
*   build on the knowledge acquired of reducing risk from disasters in urban areas;
*   be based on and build a strong local knowledge base of climate variabilities and of the likely local impacts from climate change scenarios;
*   address current risks and build for future risks: encourage and support actions that reduce risks (and vulnerabilities) now, while recognizing the importance of measures taken now to begin the long-term changes needed in urban form and the spatial distribution of urban populations to reduce vulnerability to risks that may become manifest only several decades in the future;
*   recognize that the core of the above lies in building the competence, capacity and accountability of city and sub-city levels of government and in changing their relationship with those living in informal settlements and working in the informal economy – and the importance within this of supporting civil society groups, especially representative organizations of the urban poor (this is also to avoid the danger of 'adaptation' providing opportunities for powerful groups to evict low-income residents from land that they want to develop);
*   recognize that government policies must encourage and support the contributions to adaptation of individuals, households, community organizations and enterprises;
*   recognize the key complementary roles required by higher levels of government and international agencies to support this (and that this requires

major changes in policy for most international agencies that have long ignored urban issues and major changes in how adaptation is funded);

- build resilience and adaptive capacity in rural areas – not only because of the very serious climate change-related risks for rural populations and economies, but also because of the dependence of urban centres upon rural production and ecological services, and the importance for many urban economies and enterprises of rural demand for (producer and consumer) goods and services; and

- build into the above a mitigation framework (if successful cities in low- and middle-income nations develop without this, global greenhouse gas emissions cannot be reduced).

Key areas for action for international funders

International aid agencies and development banks need to look for ways in which they can provide long-term support to the governments of cities or smaller urban centres that are at risk from climate change impacts in order to support locally determined, pro-poor actions. In effect, they should show what is possible, learn how best to support the necessary local processes and then increase capacity to support many more such initiatives. This also applies to any new funds or funding agencies set up to support adaptation.

There are at least five institutional challenges to international funders in doing so.[23] The first is in knowing what and whom to support in order to get the necessary action on the ground. Official development assistance agencies are only as effective as the local organizations that they fund since their staff do not themselves implement initiatives. Most of their staff also have a limited knowledge of the complex local political economies into which their funding is inserted, and this often includes powerful interests that oppose key adaptation measures – for instance, opposing support for infrastructure and service provision in informal settlements. There may be a mismatch between what needs funding and what the international agencies are allowed to fund – for example, controls on funding civil society groups or opposition by national governments to funding local governments. The local governments that international agencies have to work with may also have many limitations (e.g. in technical and financial capacity), and key local government staff or politicians may themselves oppose what is proposed. In any intended partnership between local government and local civil society groups, there are likely to be conflicts over who controls decisions and resources. This does not mean that locally driven pro-poor adaptation is impossible; but it does highlight constraints that development assistance agencies often ignore.

The second challenge is the difficulties that international funding agencies face in keeping external funding to a minimum, with external funding building local capacity and local resource mobilization. This is problematic for official development assistance agencies who rely on high-cost projects or large contributions to non-project (e.g. sector or programme) support to help keep down the proportion of their funding that goes to staff costs – all aid agencies and development banks are under pressure to do this. Obviously, the staff time needed to manage one US$200 million project is much less than that needed to manage 40 US$5 million initiatives, which, in turn, is far less than that needed to manage 4000 US$50,000 initiatives. But actually, US$50,000 available to representative community-based organizations can often achieve far more per dollar than much larger initiatives.[24] Bilateral aid agencies often have difficulty spending the money that they have been allocated so, again, high-cost initiatives are preferred. Multilateral development banks need to lend large sums to be able to cover their own overheads, including staff costs. The shift within development assistance agencies from project support to programme and sector support (including budget support) was, in large part, driven by this because it meant large loans or large grants with much lower staff costs per dollar provided. Arif Hasan has documented how, in Pakistan, initiatives funded by aid agencies and development banks often cost far more than initiatives that do not draw on external funding.[25] So, it is difficult for official development assistance agencies to address what might be considered good development practice – to support local initiatives that minimize reliance on external funding. There are also other associated difficulties, such as the timing of funding availability, which should be flexible in order to accommodate local possibilities and constraints; but external funders often have inflexible time frames. There are comparable problems for many disaster relief agencies, which are under pressure to spend the funding raised and get out – when longer-term, less expensive, far more participatory forms of support, working with those who were affected to rebuild their homes and livelihoods, would be more effective.

The third institutional challenge is how to provide the external support needed for a long-term partnership within any urban centre that engages and works with the groups most at risk, their own organizations and other civil society groups, as well as local governments. The staffing implications of supporting long-term, locally driven (often relatively low-cost) processes that maximize local resource mobilization and that work with the groups most at risk implies more international agency staff with the knowledge and capacity to work on the ground, to speak local languages and to support locally developed solutions. But this is difficult for the reasons noted above. In addition, if this succeeds in supporting effective local partnerships in which the groups most at risk are fully engaged, this will need new lines of accountability and transparency to these groups with regard to what funding is available and how it is used. Despite much talk about accountability, aid agencies and development banks have very little accountability to low-income groups concerning decisions on what is funded and how, even though the very basis for their operation is justified by these people's 'poverty'.

The fourth challenge is overcoming the likely reluctance of national governments for such support. No national government wants external funding agencies that make choices about which urban centres receive support within their national territory; indeed, political parties different than the national government may govern the more innovative urban governments with whom the external agency wants to work. External funding for civil society groups, perhaps most especially representative organizations of the urban poor groups, will always raise political complications.

The fifth challenge is the difficulty in getting the adaptation funding allocated to those cities or smaller urban centres that have been chosen because of the possibilities there of effective pro-poor partnerships. Obviously, it would make sense for an international funding agency to begin support for adaptation by choosing cities or smaller urban centres where local governments are committed to working with urban poor groups and are also supporting household and community-based adaptation. But these urban centres may be outside the 'focus countries' that the agency has chosen to concentrate on, or opposed by agency staff who manage the country programme because they have no expertise in urban development (or because they oppose urban development).

Much of the above might be seen as minor administrative issues that can be overcome if the funding is available; but many of the issues noted above have long limited the effectiveness of aid agencies and development banks in poverty reduction. They all actually imply changes in the way in which aid agencies and development banks operate and there is little evidence that they are being addressed. The above issues were hardly mentioned or not mentioned at all in the 2008 Accra Agenda for Action, endorsed by 'ministers of developing and donor countries responsible for promoting development, and heads of multilateral and bilateral development institutions'.[26] Incidentally, this document also fails to mention climate change impacts and the need for adaptation (climate change is just noted as a new global challenge).

The five institutional challenges also require changes in the understanding of the governments that supervise bilateral aid agencies and multilateral development banks of what makes for effective development assistance. For instance, none of the above can be achieved if the 'efficiency' of aid agencies and development banks is measured by how low staff costs are in relation to total funding. It may be that external funding agencies cannot address the issues above, so they will need to find intermediary institutions in the countries and urban centres where they want to work, through whom the funding and local support can be provided. For instance, many of the urban poor federations whose work was noted above have set up their own Urban Poor Funds to manage their savings and provide external funders with the accounting they require to ensure that their funding is well used. There are also many local NGOs working with low-income groups that have sought to set new standards of accountability for these groups, and allow them a central role in designing and implementing responses[27] – and also sought to support partnerships between these groups and local governments. But they often have difficulty obtaining external funding to support this. At the risk of stating the obvious, reducing vulnerability to climate change/climate variability (and, more generally, reducing poverty) requires local social and political changes that are not easily affected by external funding. Indeed, external funding may, in some circumstances, work against such changes.

It is also difficult to see the support needed for adaptation having to restrict itself to 'climate change'; what is needed is support for identifying and addressing all environmental health risks (including everyday, small disaster and large disaster risks) in ways that address the risks and vulnerabilities of low-income groups and high-risk groups and that include increased resilience to the likely impacts of climate change. So it is support for what many authors in this volume highlight as 'local development + adaptation'.

To complement the above, there is a need to build awareness and capacity in all city and municipal authorities, working with and through the international and national organizations and networks that work in this area. One important area for this would be the careful documentation of particular experiences with locally driven adaptation by local governments and by community-based organizations that demonstrate what is possible and that provide methodologies and precedents that other city or municipal governments can learn from. Chapter 11 provides a good first example of this for local governments.

International funding also needs to be available to support the engagement of low-income groups in addressing their vulnerabilities through community-based adaptation, but with a recognition of its limitations, as discussed earlier in this chapter. Support for community-based adaptation should also encourage possibilities for these 'communities' to develop better relations with local governments, including partnerships with them to address issues such as security of tenure for the land they live on and provision for infrastructure and services. In many urban centres, a high proportion of the people most at risk live in settlements on illegally occupied or subdivided land – and community-based adaptation depends upon them developing good relations with local governments. Again, it is difficult to separate out 'community-based adaptation to climate change' from adaptation to other environmental health risks. It would be odd, indeed, if there were a large increase in global funding available to urban poor communities to adapt to climate change, but not to adapt to risks of (say) earthquakes or tsunamis or monsoon rains that have long been causing floods. But the funding available for adaptation through the United Nations Framework Convention on Climate Change (UNFCCC) is explicitly targeted at climate change adaptation.

Many international funders are unable or unwilling to have working relationships with grassroots organizations and many national and local governments would oppose such working relationships. However, there are precedents on which to draw, as is the case with international funders who support national federations of slum and shack dwellers to address their housing, infrastructure and services needs (much of which is reducing risk from many climate change impacts) and to develop partnerships with local governments. As noted above, many of these federations have also developed their own Urban Poor Funds, through which external funding can be channelled.[28]

There is an obvious need to engage urban development specialists and disaster avoidance/preparedness specialists within NGOs, research groups, governments and international agencies in local development + adaptation. As noted in many chapters in this volume, not only has adaptation not received the attention it deserves; but within discussions of adaptation, too little attention has been given to urban adaptation. And within this, not much attention has been given to the political and institutional inadequacies within the very systems of government (and of the professionals, civil servants and politicians engaged in government) that are central to adaptation. This issue has particular importance for the future work of the Intergovernmental Panel on Climate Change, as it has produced the scientific basis to justify action on adaptation and must now help advance understanding on how to get appropriate action.

With regard to mitigation, obviously the form that urban expansion takes in terms of new buildings, new infrastructure and spatial layout has large implications for present and future energy use (including the use of fossil fuels) and, thus, for greenhouse gas emissions. While the key issue here is the demonstration by high-income nations of ways to delink high living standards from high greenhouse gas emissions, obviously there is a need for expanding urban centres in low- and middle-income nations to avoid buildings, infrastructure and spatial forms that imply high greenhouse gas emissions. As noted in Chapter 1, most of the world's population growth is now taking place in urban centres in low- and middle-income nations. Without distracting attention from the priority to local development + adaptation, this can be done with a 'mitigation lens', with knowledge of how to incorporate measures that contribute to lower greenhouse gas emissions. More generally, there is a need to identify constructive ways to engage cities – both urban authorities and local civil society organizations – in a variety of international activities that simultaneously address the concerns of mitigation, adaptation and adaptation financing. Table 16.1 compares and contrasts the characteristics of mitigation and adaptation. It highlights the point stressed already – that successful adaptation depends upon good local knowledge and local capacity.

Key areas for research[29]

Much of the necessary research agenda is to support the actions noted above. One important area is the means through which to build the information basis for action within any urban centre. This requires support for vulnerability mapping of environmental risks at a neighbourhood and city scale that utilizes local knowledge and awareness and fully involves the residents who are facing risks.

Table 16.1 *Characteristics of mitigation and adaptation*

	Mitigation	Adaptation
Benefited systems	All systems	Selected systems
Scale of efforts	Global	Local to regional
Lifetime	Centuries	Years to centuries
Lead time	Decades	Immediate to decades
Effectiveness	Certain in terms of emission reduction; less certain in terms of damage reduction	Generally less certain (especially where local knowledge of likely climate-related changes is weak)
Ancillary benefits	Sometimes	Mostly
Polluter pays	Typically yes	Not necessarily
Payer benefits	Only a little	Almost fully
Administrative scale/implementing bodies	(Mainly) national governments/international negotiations	(Mainly) local managers/authorities, households (**and community organizations**)
Sectors involved	Primarily energy and transport in high-income nations, forestry and energy in low-/middle-income nations	Potentially all
Monitoring	Relatively easy	More difficult (especially where this involves adaptation that stops damaging events happening)

Source: Bosello, F., Kuik, O., Tol, R. and Watiss, P. (2007) *Costs of Adaptation to Climate Change: A Review of Assessment Studies with a Focus on Methodologies Used*, Ecologic, Berlin, 112pp [emphasis added by the authors of this chapter]

These will have to cover the full range of risks as a basis for considering what additional and heightened risks that climate change is likely to bring. This needs to include careful, detailed local assessments of deaths, injuries and property losses from 'disasters' that drill down as far as possible to include 'very small' disasters and contribute to the risk vulnerability map for urban areas and their surrounds. This should contribute to a more nuanced understanding of patterns of vulnerability: geographically and socially specific (including a better understanding of how vulnerabilities vary by income group, age and gender). There are precedents that show how this can be done, which have been noted in earlier chapters – the city and national assessments of 'small disasters' using the DesInventar methodologies and the detailed household surveys and community mapping done by slum/shack dweller federations in informal settlements (often in settlements for which there are no official data).

There will be substantial variations in the quantity and quality of official data that can be brought into vulnerability assessments; in some nations, there are good census data available down to the 'street' level, whereas in others, no such data are available (in some nations no recent censuses have been taken). In some nations, useful data can be brought in from other official agencies – for instance, records kept by emergency response agencies. Thus, one important area for research is to develop the tools and methods that support locally driven risk and vulnerability mapping (and the engagement of those at risk with this) in different contexts – including those where there is good official data from different government agencies to draw on and combine, and where there is not. Geographic information systems offer some scope for merging different data sources so that local assessments can be layered over citywide assessments of vulnerability, capacity and hazard. This is useful for ground-truthing citywide assessments, which, in rapidly expanding cities, are difficult and costly to keep updated. A potential alternative and more process-oriented approach is to build local assessments into deliberative planning mechanisms such as community forums; here, the focus is as much on building democratic structures in local governance as it is about direct outcomes for risk reduction.

There is also the issue of the means by which the collection and combining of relevant data generates the basis for its incorporation within municipal planning, management and budgeting. In the previous discussion on action (point 6), the need for careful documentation of particular experiences with locally driven adaptation by local governments and by community-based organizations that demonstrate what is possible and that provide methodologies and precedents which other city or municipal governments can draw on was noted – and this has obvious research components.

There is also a need for risk assessments for climate change that are locally relevant. Politicians and civil servants within city governments are not going to give much attention (let alone funding) to risks and vulnerabilities identified at national or supra-national level (see, in particular, Chapters 11 and 14). They want evidence of vulnerability and risk within their city or within particular city districts. Thus, there is a need to make climate change modelling work better at a smaller geographic scale, and allow its combination with local contexts that have such a strong influence on how climate change will affect local populations, economies and ecosystems.

Building on the above, there is a need to develop precedents, tools and methods to support a far more location-specific, context-specific understanding of what adaptation requires. For extreme events, this needs to identify how to reduce the two components of risk – reducing hazards and reducing vulnerability – both in terms of protection (so the extreme event does not produce a disaster) and in terms of the three critical aspects of reducing the impact of disasters through pre-disaster damage limitation, immediate post-disaster response and rebuilding. Here, there is also a need to build on local knowledge and capacities, including those of individuals, households and community organizations.[30]

From the above, a research agenda should:

- Develop the tools and methods that encourage and support local governments and local research groups/NGOs to begin considering what adaptation is needed or will be needed, and possible complementarities between adaptation and local development.
- Consider what forms of financial and institutional support from higher levels of government and from international agencies would support the above. This includes avoiding the common tendency for many international agencies to fund preparatory studies – for adaptation or disaster preparedness – but with no capacity to fund the priority actions that these preparatory studies identify. It is worth recalling the comment by Debra Roberts (Chapter 11) about how external funding would be better spent capacitating people rather than implementing often *ad hoc* climate change-related projects.
- Develop a much more location-specific, context-specific understanding of what complementarities exist between adaptation and mitigation – and how mitigation can be incorporated within the expansion of urban areas and of their building stock, but without detracting from adaptation.
- Ensure that the identification of vulnerability and the preparation of adaptation strategies involve a participatory framework. The urgency of climate change may serve to justify many top-down approaches to research and planning. But responses worked out with low-income groups and their organizations that draw on local knowledge and activities are much more likely to serve the needs of the people whom they are meant to assist and, generally, have lower monetary costs.

Perhaps many readers will be surprised by the lack of attention in this concluding chapter to discussing the international frameworks and international funds to support adaptation and mitigation (drawing on Chapter 15). What we maintain is that unless there is a clear understanding of what is needed to support action within each urban centre that delivers local adaptation + development, which addresses the needs and priorities of low-income groups and other groups at high risk and which makes maximum use of local knowledge, resources and capacities, these international frameworks and funds will not be effective. It would be sad, indeed, if the international funding architecture for climate change reproduced the inadequacies of so much funding for development – the inability to structure the funding and other aspects of support to serve these kinds of context-specific, pro-poor local processes.

Notes

1. See, for instance, Co, R. and Christopher, J. (2009) *Community-Driven Disaster Intervention: The Experience of the Homeless Peoples Federation Philippines*, IIED/ACHR Working Paper, IIED, London.
2. Hasan, A. (2006) 'Orangi Pilot Project; the expansion of work beyond Orangi and the mapping of informal settlements and infrastructure', *Environment and Urbanization*, vol 18, no 2, October, pp451–480.
3. Mitlin, D. (2008) 'With and beyond the state; co-production as a route to political influence, power and transformation for grassroots organizations', *Environment and Urbanization*, vol 20, no 2, October, pp339–360; also D'Cruz, C. and Satterthwaite, D. (2005) *Building Homes, Changing Official Approaches: The Work of Urban Poor Federations and Their Contributions to Meeting the Millennium Development Goals in Urban Areas*, Human Settlements Poverty Reduction in Urban Areas Discussion Series 16, IIED, London, 80pp.
4. For an overview, see Hardoy, J. E., Mitlin, D. and Satterthwaite, D. (2001) *Environmental Problems in an Urbanizing World: Finding Solutions for Cities in Africa, Asia and Latin America*, Earthscan Publications, London, 448pp; also Budds, J. with Teixeira, P. and SEHAB (2005) 'Ensuring the right to the city: pro-poor housing, urban development and land tenure legalization in São Paulo, Brazil', *Environment and Urbanization*, vol 17, no 1, April, pp89–114.
5. Boonyabancha, S. (2005) 'Baan Mankong; going to scale with "slum" and squatter upgrading in Thailand', *Environment and Urbanization*, vol 17, no 1, April, pp21–46.
6. Stein, A. (2001) 'Participation and sustainability in social projects: the experience of the Local Development Programme (PRODEL) in Nicaragua, *Environment and Urbanization*, vol 13, no 1, April, pp11–35.
7. See the Slum/Shack Dwellers International website: http://www.sdinet.org/rituals/ritual2.htm.
8. Community Organization Resource Centre (2005) *Profiles of Informal Settlements within the Johannesburg Metropole*, Community Organization Resource Centre, Cape Town, 170pp; also Community Organization Urban Resource Centre (2006) *Profiles of the Informal Settlements within Cape Town Metropole*, Community Organization Resource Centre, Cape Town, 220pp.
9. Pamoja Trust (2006) *Social Economic Mapping in Kisumu*, Report prepared for UN-Habitat, Cities without Slums Kisumu Initiative, Pamoja Trust, Nairobi.
10. ACHR (Asian Coalition for Housing Rights) (2004) 'Negotiating the right to stay in the city', *Environment and Urbanization*, vol 16, no 1, April, pp9–26.
11. See reference 2.
12. Patel, S. and Mitlin, D. (2004) 'Grassroots-driven development: The Alliance of SPARC, the National Slum Dwellers Federation and Mahila Milan', in Mitlin, D. and Satterthwaite, D. (eds) *Empowering Squatter Citizen; Local Government, Civil Society and Urban Poverty Reduction*, Earthscan, London, pp216–241. For one particular example, see Bolnick, J. and Van Rensburg, G. (2005) 'The Methodist

Church's initiative to use its vacant land to support homeless people's housing and livelihoods in South Africa', *Environment and Urbanization*, vol 17, no 1, April, pp115–122.

13. Patel, S. (2004) 'Tools and methods for empowerment developed by slum and pavement dwellers' federations in India', *PLA Notes* 50, IIED, London.

14. Weru, J. (2004) 'Community federations and city upgrading: the work of Pamoja Trust and Muungano in Kenya', *Environment and Urbanization*, vol 16, no 1, April, pp47–62.

15. Glockner, H., Mkanga, M. and Ndezi, T. (2004) 'Local empowerment through community mapping for water and sanitation in Dar es Salaam', *Environment and Urbanization*, vol 16, no 1, April, pp185–198.

16. Patel, S., d'Cruz, C. and Burra, S. (2002) 'Beyond evictions in a global city; people-managed resettlement in Mumbai', *Environment and Urbanization*, vol 14, no 1, April, pp159–172.

17. This section draws on Huq, S., Kovats, S., Reid, H. and Satterthwaite, D. (2007) 'Editorial: reducing risks to cities from disasters and climate change', *Environment and Urbanization*, vol 19, no 1, April, pp3–15.

18. See UNFCCC (2005) *Sixth Compilation and Synthesis of Initial National Communications from Parties not Included in Annex I to the Convention* – Note by the Secretariat, United Nations Framework Convention on Climate Change, FCCC/SBI/2005/18/Add.2, 20pp.

19. This might be considered to understate the role of industry or particular sectors such as fossil fuel-powered electricity generation; but their production (and the climate change implications of their production) are underpinned by consumer demand, much of it from those with high-consumption lifestyles. It might also be considered to understate the contributions of middle-income groups in high-income nations – but these are among the wealthy, if the whole planet's population is considered.

20. See Satterthwaite, D. (2008) 'Cities' contribution to global warming; notes on the allocation of greenhouse gas emissions', *Environment and Urbanization*, vol 20, no 2, October, pp539–550.

21. Walker, G. and King, D. (2008) *The Hot Topic: How to Tackle Global Warming and Still Keep the Lights On*, Bloomsbury Publishers, London, pp199–200.

22. See Cruz, R. V., Harasawa, H., Lal, M., Wu, S., Anokhin, Y., Punsalmaa, B., Honda, Y., Jafari, M., Li, C. and Huu Ninh, N. (2007) 'Asia', and Magrin, G., Gay García, C., Cruz Choque, D., Giménez, J. C., Moreno, A. R., Nagy, G. J., Nobre, C. and Villamizar, A. (2007) 'Latin America', in Parry, M., Canziani, O. F., Palutikof, J. P., van der Linden, P. J. and Hanson, C. E. (eds) *Climate Change 2007: Impacts, Adaptation and Vulnerability*, Contribution of Working Group II to the Fourth Assessment Report of the Intergovernmental Panel on Climate Change, Cambridge University Press, Cambridge, pp469–506 and pp581–615, respectively.

23. This discussion on the institutional challenges for international funders being able to support local development draws heavily on the experiences of staff from local organizations with whom we have worked – especially the Orangi Pilot Project–Research and Training Institute and the Urban Resource Centres in Pakistan, the team at IIED-América Latina who works in San Fernando and Moreno

in Buenos Aires, the staff of SPARC in India, the Pamoja Trust in Kenya, the Community Organization Resource Centre in South Africa, and the Asian Coalition for Housing Rights in Thailand. It also draws on a series of profiles of local organizations that include discussions by these organizations' staff on the mismatch between available funding and what is needed on the ground. For an overview of these, see Satterthwaite, D. and Sauter, G. (2008) *Understanding and Supporting the Role of Local Organizations in Sustainable Development*, IIED Gatekeeper 137, IIED, London, 23pp.

24. Mitlin, D. and Satterthwaite, D. (2007) 'Strategies for grassroots control of international aid', *Environment and Urbanization*, vol 19, no 2, October, pp483–500.
25. Hasan, A. (1999) *Understanding Karachi: Planning and Reform for the Future*, City Press, Karachi, 171pp.
26. Accra High Level Forum (2008) *Accra Agenda for Action*, Statement from the 3rd High Level Forum on Aid Effectiveness, 7pp.
27. See, for instance, the work of local NGOs that support national federations of slum/shack dwellers: www.sdinet.co.za.
28. Mitlin, D. (2008) *Urban Poor Funds: Development by the People for the People*, Human Settlements Poverty Reduction in Urban Areas Discussion Series 18, IIED, London.
29. This section draws on Satterthwaite, D., Huq, S., Pelling, M., Reid, H. and Lankao Romero, P. (2007) *Adapting to Climate Change in Urban Areas: The Possibilities and Constraints in Low- and Middle-Income Nations*, Climate Change and Cities Discussion Series 1, IIED, London, 110pp; also Pelling, M. (2006) 'Measuring vulnerability to urban natural disaster risk: Benchmarks for sustainability', *Open House International*, Special Edition on managing urban disasters, vol 31, no 1, pp125–132
30. Moser, C. and Satterthwaite, D. (2008) *Towards Pro-Poor Adaptation to Climate Change in the Urban Centres of Low- and Middle-Income Countries*, Climate Change and Cities Discussion Series 3, IIED, London, 35pp.

Index